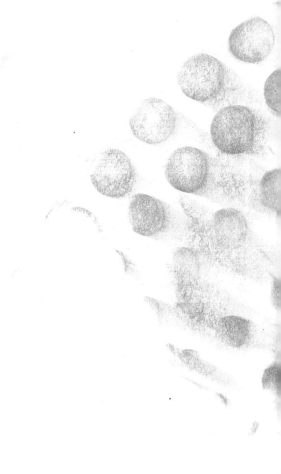

In Order to Live Untroubled

IN ORDER TO LIVE UNTROUBLED

INUIT OF THE CENTRAL ARCTIC, 1550-1940

RENÉE FOSSETT

THE UNIVERSITY OF MANITOBA PRESS

The University of Manitoba Press
Winnipeg, Manitoba R3T 2N2
www.umanitoba.ca/uofmpress

Printed in Canada.

Cover Design: Steven Rosenberg

Text Design: Karen Armstrong and Sharon Caseburg

Maps: Weldon Hiebert

Cover photograph: Inuit at Little Whale River, Quebec, c.1865 (National Archives of Canada).

Canadian Cataloguing-in-Publication Data
Fossett, Renée Evelyn.
   In order to live untroubled

   Includes bibliographical references and index.
   ISBN 0-88755-171-8 (bound)—ISBN 0-88755-647-7 (pbk.)

1. Inuit—Nunavut—History. 2. Inuit—Nunavut—Social conditions.
I. Title.
E99.E7F6117 2001   971.9'5   C2001-910330-1

The publisher would like to thank the Archives and Special Collections, the University of Manitoba Libraries, for permission to reproduce illustrations from the published accounts of George Back, Henry Ellis, Charles Francis Hall, William Gilder, George Lyon, Edward Parry, and John Ross.

The University of Manitoba Press gratefully acknowledges the financial support for its publication program provided by the Government of Canada through the Book Publishing Industry Development Program (BPIDP); the Canada Council for the Arts; the Manitoba Arts Council; and the Manitoba Department of Culture, Heritage and Tourism. This book has been published with the assistance of a grant from the Humanities and Social Sciences Federation of Canada, using funds provided by the Social Sciences and Humanities Research Council of Canada.

To William and Andrew

and
In Loving Memory of Ussak
who told me it was cold in the snowhouse

Contents

Maps and Illustrations

Preface: Evidence and Methods

In the 300 years between the mid-thirteenth and the late sixteenth centuries, encounters between the indigenous peoples of the North American arctic and explorers and fishermen from Europe were rare, brief, and often at a distance. Until 1576, few observers recorded what they saw. Between 1576 and 1620, a series of expeditions in search of an ocean passage from the Atlantic to the Pacific produced more than a dozen accounts of meetings with arctic dwellers, some of them in great detail. Because both parties expected hostility from the other, the meetings were at arm's length, and accounts of them were superficial and often speculative. After 1717, when the Hudson's Bay Company established its post at the mouth of the Churchill River, British fur traders began to keep more detailed records of meetings with Inuit. A few traders, such as James Isham and Andrew Graham, produced densely descriptive ethnographies of the Keewatin coast people. The British Admiralty mounted a new and intensive search in 1817 for a far northern sea route from the Atlantic to the Pacific, and more accounts of arctic peoples were added to the descriptive literature.

However, no systematic attempts to understand the social and political institutions or the history of the indigenous peoples took place until the 1880s, when both Germany and Denmark sent teams of investigators to study arctic societies as well as arctic climate, geography, and wildlife. Franz Boas, a recent doctoral graduate specializing in physics, mathematics, and geography, spent June 1883 to August 1884 as surveyor and cartographer with the German expedition to south Baffin Island. In the same years the ethnologist Gustav Holm, with the Danish Polar Expedition, conducted a comprehensive fieldwork study of the people of Ammassalik on Greenland's east coast.

Three more arctic expeditions with ethnographic goals took place between 1906 and 1918, on Canadian territory. The ethnologist and writer Vilhjalmur Stefansson was a major player in all three. In 1906-07 he was with the Anglo-American Polar Expedition on the arctic coast near the Alaska-Canada border, and in 1908 he was co-leader of the Stefansson-Anderson Expedition, with American zoologist Rudolph M. Anderson. In 1913 Stefansson and Anderson assumed joint leadership of an official Canadian Arctic Expedition (CAE). The Geological Survey of Canada was assigned responsibility for most of the necessary personnel, materiel, and support services, and in return the CAE was instructed to claim any previously unknown lands or islands for Canada.[1] Stefansson led the CAE's Northern Division, with geographical exploration of Banks Island, Victoria Island, and nearby territories as its major goal. Anderson led the Southern Division to Coronation Gulf to survey and map mineral and wildlife resources, and to collect specimens. Diamond Jenness, later Canada's Dominion Anthropologist, supervised archaeological investigation.

The sixth, and last, large-scale exploration was the Fifth Thule Expedition of 1921-24. The expedition was led by Danish-Greenlandic explorer and ethnographer Knud Rasmussen, and was financed by private subscription. Like earlier expeditions, the Fifth Thule Expedition focussed on uncovering the distant past through archaeological investigation, and on thick description of contemporary conditions. Unlike the earlier investigating parties, which concentrated on specific regions in Greenland, Baffin Island, and the western arctic, the Fifth Thule Expedition surveyed the entire arctic from Greenland to Alaska, and was the only one to meet and study the different Inuit groups of the central arctic.

Official interest in the Canadian arctic did not become immediate or intense until after the Second World War. The influx of American military personnel and money, the discovery of uranium deposits in the Northwest Territories, the decision to build the Alaska Highway and pipeline through Canadian territory, the presence of the United States Strategic Air Command, and the building of the Distant Early Warning and Mid-Canada lines brought increased contact between arctic aboriginal people and 'southerners' from Canada and the United States. The arctic and its people were in the news. At the same time, aboriginal peoples in the United States and southern Canada began to make claims to lands and resources that governments had regarded as publicly owned. Ottawa was alerted to the possibility of similar claims from its arctic peoples. The Canadian government, and Canadian intellectuals in large numbers, began to take a deeper interest in the still mysterious inhabitants of the far north.

New research fields in northern studies opened up in several academic disciplines: physical (or biological) anthropology, archaeology, and cultural (or social) anthropology. Physical anthropologists tackled problems of the distant past, which shed light on the origins of arctic peoples. Using biological and genetic evidence to create 'family trees' showing the ancestry and affinities of arctic peoples, they concluded that the first people to occupy the arctic permanently had entered the North American continent from Asia in the third millennium BCE (Before Common Era), and possibly as many as twenty thousand years after the ancestors of North American Indians. Studies in historical linguistics have supported these conclusions.

Arctic archaeologists produced dozens of studies under the sponsorship of the Geological Survey of Canada and the Archaeological Survey of Canada, and other public and private institutions in Canada, the United States, Britain, and Denmark.[2] As descriptive reports of sites in Alaska, Canada, and Greenland accumulated, the time sequences and relationships between arctic sociocultural complexes between 3000 BCE and 1700 CE (Common Era) were developed and refined. After considerable debate, most archaeologists agreed that the arctic peoples of North America and Greenland were descended from Asian immigrants who expanded into North America and occupied the lands north of the treeline following the retreat of the last ice sheets in the third millennium BCE.[3] Their conclusions fit with those of physical anthropologists and historical linguists.

Cultural anthropologists, for the most part, have concentrated on contemporary arctic societies, and have produced a vast body of mainly descriptive literature. With few exceptions, their studies are geographically, temporally, and topically limited, focussing on Inuit-white relations in specific places in the late nineteenth and early twentieth centuries. Some include brief chapters or sections of historical anthropology. Few have attempted to recover the history of Inuit as an autonomous people. Historians, for their part, have almost never included information about the Inuit past in their histories of Canada.[4]

Between the temporal focus of arctic paleostudies (that is, from genesis at the beginning of the third millennium BCE to the fifteenth century CE) and the contemporary period that anthropological fieldwork seeks to understand lies a 400-year interval, which remains largely undescribed and unexplained. *In Order to Live Untroubled* attempts to fill in at least some of the gaps through research based on the historical approach.

Histories of indigenous arctic peoples have not been attempted to date because most historians have assumed an absence of sufficient documentation. In spite of Raymond Fogelson's comment, made to a gathering of ethnohistorians, that "an understanding of non-Western histories requires ... an expanded conception of what constitutes documentation,"[5] and examples of aboriginal histories based on a wide range of evidence taken from many disciplines,[6] most historians, even in the 1990s, continued to believe that where written records do not exist (or are thought not to exist), there is no evidence for written history.

Until the mid-1970s, there was some reason to doubt the existence of adequate documentation for Inuit histories. Most eyewitness accounts of arctic events, held in specialized archives and rare book collections, were inaccessible to researchers. In the past twenty years, however, many out-of-print memoirs and narratives first published between 1550 and 1900 are again available in reprint or facsimile editions, or on microforms produced by the Canadian Institute for Historical Microreproductions. Others have been translated and published in English for the first time during the same period. There now exists a substantial body of literature describing events and processes in the years from the sixteenth to the twentieth centuries, produced by explorers, fur traders, and missionaries who were eyewitnesses to, or participants in, the events they described. The records of the Hudson's Bay Company have also become fully accessible since the early 1970s. The archives include censuses; birth, death, and health registers; Inuit dictionaries and vocabulary lists; wildlife, environmental, and meteorological records; and drawings and maps, many of them Inuit in origin.

Franz Boas's work with the German Polar Expedition resulted in two monographs, *The Central Eskimo* (1888), and *The Eskimos of Baffin Island* (1901), both based on his observations during fourteen months of fieldwork in 1883-84. Gustav Holm's observations were published in Danish in 1888, and in an English edition released under the title *Ethnological Sketch of the Angmagsalik Eskimo* in 1914. A generation later the principal members of the Canadian Arctic Expedition produced long, detailed reports of their investigations, and a number of them produced popular books as well, including Vilhjalmur Stefansson and Diamond Jenness. The Fifth Thule Expedition resulted in major collections of wildlife, fossils, mineral resources, artifacts, and folklore, and more than thirty volumes of botanical, geographical, zoological, meteorological, and ethnographic observations. Popular books by expedition members Knud Rasmussen, Kaj Birket-Smith, and Peter Freuchen were eagerly received by an adventure-hungry reading public in Britain, Denmark, Germany, Canada, and the United States. Whalemen from several countries, as well as missionaries, adventurers, and members of Canadian police forces, Canadian and American geological surveys, and the Archaeological Survey of Canada, added their observations in both official reports and popular works.

By 1930 it could no longer be claimed there was a shortage of written primary documents. Canadian historians, nevertheless, continued to see the Inuit past as "prehistory," dismissing the reports of the major arctic expeditions as secondary works of analysis and theory. The descriptions on which the interpretations are based, however, are eyewitness accounts of contemporary events, and can be used by historians just as the diaries, directives, and letters of other participant-observers are used. For such a purpose, the reports are primary evidence of Inuit activities.

Ideally, of course, no historical investigation should be limited to a search for evidence in written documents alone. In the area of Inuit studies, non-documentary evidence for arctic history has expanded significantly in recent years. Historians can now find evidence in oral sources, including folklore and language itself, in landscape, and in the collections of material culture from the distant past gathered by archaeologists, and those from the more recent past collected by the major expeditions, and by explorers, whalemen, and missionaries, such as Roald Amundsen, Captain George Comer, and the Reverend Donald Marsh.

Methods for interpreting non-documentary sources are also being developed; for example, the body of theory that attempts to explain social processes. Historians in general have avoided this approach, probably out of concern to avoid the pitfalls of unwarranted extrapolation across time and space, and suspicion of facile interpretations based on belief in universal laws of human nature. Nevertheless, general theories can be very useful in understanding past events and processes in specific situations. James Axtell, a leading American ethnohistorian, suggested that "when their sources on a particular group run dry, grow sparse, or become insolubly clogged with ethnocentric bias ... [ethnohistorians may] turn to ... abstract models of sociocultural change."[7]

Clues about human behaviour in specific situations may also be found in comparative studies, as early *annalistes* and ethnohistorians long ago discovered. Comparative studies are most sound when they compare a particular event or process with similar ones in an ancestral society, "on the assumption that major patterns of culture remain stable over long periods," or when they are drawn from "relative cultures in the same general culture area, preferably at the same period, which may be expected to share cultural traits."[8]

Drawing on general theory and comparing related societies as a means of breaking out of an impasse can yield useful insights, but both techniques do no more than suggest possible explanations. Neither confirms absolutely. The researcher must bear in mind ethnohistorian Eleanor Leacock's warning that "broad generalizations ... are hypotheses ... [that] yield clues."[9] They do not provide final answers.

Theories suggesting *why* and *how* societies change have been developed in several disciplines.[10] All must be used with caution. Arctic studies have been perceived as especially useful in arriving at broad generalizations about social and cultural change. Archaeologist Moreau S. Maxwell summed up the archaeological position. "Many of us feel that because of the nature of [the arctic's] environmental constraints and the necessarily limited scope of human biocultural adaptive response, much can be learned here [in the arctic] about general cultural processes and systems, at least among hunters, from data not available in more temperate regions."[11] The comment assumes that arctic human history has been played out on an environmental stage that narrows the number of options open to the players. It further suggests that for small human populations in harsh physical conditions, fewer variables complicate narrative and explanation than in the histories of peoples with greater numbers of individuals and a wider range of choices. There is some truth to these assumptions, but none to the idea that the responses of small societies to particular stimuli in one place or time are *necessarily* the same as those of small societies in other, albeit similar, places and times.

The responses of small societies to particular stimuli in one place may, however, cast light on the responses of their descendent societies who occupy the same geographical or ideological space. As Ernest S. Burch put it, "Studies of the North American arctic offer unusual opportunities for the study of long-term social and demographic change *because it is one of the few places in the world where prehistoric and historic populations can be linked with a high degree of reliability*. This linkage makes it possible to trace developments within a specific region or cultural tradition over comparatively long periods of time. This is true in particular of the Eskimo area east of Bering Strait, where the Thule people of a thousand years ago are known to have been the direct cultural and biological ancestors of all historic Eskimo populations" [emphasis added].[12]

The suggestion recognizes that catalysts for social change are not always or necessarily changes in physical and social environments. Social and economic changes can and do take place through individual and collective self-direction in so-called "traditional" societies. Identifying and explaining change over time in the Inuit past is a major focus of *In Order to Live Untroubled*.

By no means have all the problems facing the historian interested in the Inuit past disappeared, but perceptions of earlier generations of historians, that there was too little evidence and no methodology adequate for the task, are no longer valid.

Most of the primary evidence for events and processes in the central arctic between 3000 BCE and 1550 CE comes from archaeological studies. Summarized and synthesized, they form the basis of Chapter 1, which presents an overview of central arctic occupations before the sixteenth century. Succeeding chapters of *In Order to Live Untroubled* use evidence from all previously mentioned sources, including archaeology, to explain the patterns of the histories of central arctic communities from the mid-sixteenth to the mid-twentieth centuries. The explanations are historical; that is, they are specific to particular situations, rather than aspects of an overarching model with broad applicability to other situations. They locate past events in particular temporal, geographical, and sociocultural contexts, they search for and use evidence from a wide range of both documentary and non-documentary sources, and they include outsider and, wherever possible, insider explanations.

Along with the history of specific societies of the central arctic and explanations of particular events, *In Order to Live Untroubled* attempts to identify the aspects of society and culture that the peoples of the central arctic chose to change and those they chose to maintain, and to direct some light on *how* and *why* they rejected, adapted, or maintained particular sociocultural institutions. It focusses on specific arctic communities in periods when Inuit still retained their corporate autonomy. Societies in the central arctic are well suited to investigations of social change throughout the entire period of contact with Europeans, but particularly so in the period from 1700 to 1940. In the absence of a pervasive and permanent European presence, and attempts by outsiders to create neo-Europes in the arctic, Inuit social, demographic, and economic change was self-directed. At the same time, during their short visits to various arctic communities and from their more or less permanent establishments on the periphery of Inuit territory, Europeans produced a substantial body of eyewitness observations. From them can be derived a reasonably coherent narrative of Inuit activities in several places, and identification of broad patterns of change.

Questions about change and continuity are raised in the context of self-directed modification or perpetuation of particular sociocultural institutions. This book, therefore, does not deal with Inuit as a colonized or subordinate people, or with Inuit–white relations during periods of non-Inuit control. One by one, Inuit societies came under the control of non-Inuit institutions—missions, trading monopolies, and governments—and were no longer useful in an investigation of how Inuit managed their affairs before the era of pervasive outside interference. The dates at which various Inuit communities lost their ability to make decisions without reference to non-Inuit authority vary, and because loss of corporate autonomy is a process, not an event, the dates must necessarily be approximate, covering a range of years or decades. For instance, the freedom of Labrador Inuit to make both collective and individual decisions about place of residence, economic activity, family relationships, and religious practice was subject to constant and deliberate erosion after 1771, as a result of a government-guaranteed missionary monopoly on trade. The Inuit of Labrador are, therefore, considered in this study only until the beginning of the 1770s.

Other communities are treated for longer or shorter periods, and in more or less detail, because of the nature of the evidence. Human activities in Boothia Peninsula for the long period between the twelfth and nineteenth centuries can be known only through archaeological investigation. The people themselves were not observed or described, or even known to exist except by a few European traders and explorers who had heard stories about them, until the late 1820s. Even after that date, observation and description were intermittent and incomplete for nearly a century. Where there is little or no evidence for historical events and processes, little or no history can be written.

At the opposite extreme, there is considerable evidence for the history of the people of the Keewatin coast and its near hinterland over a 350-year period. Extensive archaeological work has produced an outline of human occupation, material culture, and economic activity in the area from about 1650. The observations of Hudson's Bay Company traders based in Churchill after 1717, of explorers, missionaries, and adventurers after 1820, and of whalemen between the 1860s and 1914, include detailed life stories of some Inuit individuals, and descriptions of Inuit subsistence activities, social organization, worldview, and technology. Members of the Fifth Thule Expedition of 1921-24 collected Inuit oral traditions, histories, and testimonies in the west Hudson Bay region, as well as conducting intensive linguistic work. With very few exceptions, in spite of regular and repeated, but not continuous, intrusive or coercive observation by outsiders, the societies of the Keewatin region retained control of their own affairs and made their own decisions without reference to outside authority until the Second World War.

In its study of central arctic peoples, *In Order to Live Untroubled* does not include histories of the Mackenzie River Inuvialuit, or the Copper Inuit of the western arctic coast and Victoria and Banks islands. Both these groups created social and cultural institutions more closely resembling (though not identical to) those of Alaskan peoples than those of the residents of the central barren lands and arctic islands. Their sociocultural institutions, for instance, were created to deal with larger, more sedentary populations, and their experience of contact with non-Eskimoan neighbours was longer and more intense, and introduced more innovations into their societies than was true in most central arctic communities.

The Inuvialuit were also latecomers to the Canadian arctic, relocating from Alaska in response to the presence of American whalers in the western arctic only in the closing years of the nineteenth century. They do not have a long central arctic history, and they do not consider themselves to be Inuit.

The Copper Inuit occupy the central arctic only in a geographical sense. Socially and ideologically, they are distinct from those groups identified in the scholarly literature as Central Eskimo and Central Inuit. As Marc G. Stevenson put it, "The Copper Inuit are so fundamentally different in social structure and ideology from other Central Inuit groups ... as to suggest that they represent an entirely different type of social formation.... In essence, Copper Inuit society constitutes a rejection of Central Inuit social structure and ideology. In fact, it would be difficult to conceive of a better antithesis."[13]

The focus of this book is the area that is now called Nunavut, but excluding the Copper Inuit territories of Victoria Island and the Coronation Gulf coast. Communities in Alaska, the far western arctic coast between the Beaufort Sea and the Mackenzie River delta, and Greenland have been occasionally and briefly discussed for purposes of comparison only. For example, in spite of the broad range of evidence now available for arctic studies, many aspects of central Inuit past activity remain hidden, including how they treated their assimilated and mixed-blood countrymen. The question has been more fully explored by historians of Greenland, primarily because there is more evidence available for such a study. Brief descriptions of Greenlandic material have, therefore, been used in this study in order to cast some light through comparison.

Similarly, archaeological, linguistic, and documentary evidence from the central arctic points to episodes of warfare between communities, but many details are lacking. The little that is known, however, parallels practices in the Eskimoan societies of Alaska and Siberia. Comparisons have been made between them and central arctic communities to point out obvious differences and apparent similarities.

In Order to Live Untroubled is intended as an *aboriginal* history. It focusses on central arctic Inuit and their Thule forebears before they lost control of their own decision-making processes. Communities disappear from the story at the point when they became subaltern groups assimilating with or resisting a dominant majority. Accounts of past events and processes in particular central arctic communities are, therefore, more or less detailed, and vary in length of treatment, depending on the periods in which they retained their corporate autonomy, and depending on the available evidence.

Because the passage of time is a constant of all history, the obvious default position for historical presentation is the chronological narrative. Narrative on its own, however, is not history, and has been rightly criticized when it has been presented as history. A recital of events may be an antiquarian chronicle worth mining as a source of primary data, or it may be a potentially useful reference list, but it is not history. The chronological narrative is a vehicle for telling history only when explanation is embedded within it, when the events and processes of the narrative are explained, and trends, tendencies, and patterns of behaviour are identified.

Beginning in the late 1960s, an entire generation of historians debated the desirability and means of making written history more scientific and, presumably, more reliable. As historians began to use computers and statistical analysis to identify patterns and relationships in their data, they tended to forget that method and presentation are different aspects of the historiographical exercise. It became fashionable to present conclusions arrived at through statistical analysis as scientific formulae or in mathematical language, out of context and unintelligible except to initiates. But history must be accessible outside the academic world as well as within it, and history is above all the story of human beings acting out of myriad emotions and motives. In his 1989 Presidential Address to the American Philosophical Association, Lionel Gossman may have gone too far when he said that it had become "the fad to sneer at narrative history,"[14] but the debate was good for the discipline in that it encouraged historians to become more rigorous in their methods. However, more rigorous, in the sense of more scientific, methods of finding and interpreting data does not mean that presentation must also follow the form in which the conclusions of scientific experiments are presented. Gossman's call for historians to return to a narrative style of presentation was a timely corrective to a growing habit of presenting material in obscure forms, and it should be applied to the *presentation* of conclusions, not necessarily to the *methods* used to arrive at those conclusions. Today's historians can choose the best of both sides of the debate: they can use more rigorous methods to find and examine evidence, and present their conclusions in accessible narrative prose.

Much work remains to be done before we can approach a comprehensive picture of the Inuit past. *In Order to Live Untroubled* is intended as one step toward that goal. It offers the first broad survey of a people who lived in communities separated by great distances, but who shared biological, social, and cultural ancestry, maintained much of it over long periods of time, and modified much of it in response to changing circumstances. It brings together evidence from the spoken and written observations of eye-witnesses and participants, from the mute traces of material culture, and from some of the many voices of Inuit intellectual culture. In positioning the events and processes of the Inuit past in a temporal and geographical framework, it was my intention to facilitate understanding by making the relations of events and processes through time and space more obvious than they have been in more limited studies. The chronological framework also provides a base for adding to and modifying evidence and interpretations as new studies are done.

Future studies using new research techniques may be expected to solve some of the dating problems associated with the distant past. New documentary and anthropological investigations will add to and correct the details in our current understanding of the more recent Inuit past. But perhaps the most fruitful area for new work will be the Inuit language itself and the oral memory embedded in it. The evidence for Inuit history, to date, is overwhelmingly etic, that is, witnessed, recorded, and interpreted by Others. Except for a very few snippets of oral history written down by outsiders, Inuit, as individuals and as communities, have had almost no opportunity to participate in the writing and interpretation of their history. However, a large body of central Inuit oral traditions and histories, gathered by the major ethnographic expeditions between 1883 and 1924, does exist. Most of it, so far, is not translated, edited, or analyzed. Opening up this neglected source of evidence for the Inuit past will allow at least some of the many voices of Inuit intellectual culture to be heard for the first time.

Acknowledgements

I am indebted to the faculty and staff of the history department of the University of Manitoba for assistance on a number of levels, which I gratefully acknowledge. Most especially I wish to thank Karen Morrow for unwavering encouragement, indispensable practical help, and most of all for valued friendship. Professors John Kendle and Tom Vadney supported the work through a Departmental Fellowship, which allowed me to use the inter-library loan services of Elizabeth Dafoe Library. Professor D.N. Sprague provided thoughtful and valuable comments on early drafts.

At the University of Winnipeg, Professor Jennifer S.H. Brown, besides making useful suggestions and giving encouragement, provided me with affiliate status at the university through The Centre for Rupert's Land Studies. She was also, as always, a friend. Professor Timothy F. Ball (Geography, retired) and Professor Christopher Meiklejohn (Anthropology) were generous in providing background materials in historical climatology and physical anthropology, as well as helpful criticism and friendly collegiality.

Barbara Bennell and Mary Ann McCuaig, of the document delivery desk at Elizabeth Dafoe Library (University of Manitoba), provided services of heroic proportions, finding obscure journal articles, out-of-print books, microreproductions, and government records beyond counting. They not only found the documents, they did it with smiles and cheery words, and not once did I see them wince as I approached their office. For all this I am very grateful.

Special thanks are due to the Hudson's Bay Company Archives (Provincial Archives of Manitoba). To attempt to function as an historian of early western and northern Canada without the splendid resources of the Hudson's Bay Company Archives is impossible. Keeper Judith Hudson Beatty and Research and Reference Head Anne Morton were always available to guide me through their unequalled collection, and to help solve sticky research problems. Debra Moore (Still Images Archivist) gave valuable assistance in locating illustrations. Thanks are also due to Katherine Pettipas, Ethnography Curator at the Manitoba Museum.

In addition to the Hudson's Bay Company Archives, other important sources of primary documents are The Canadian Institute for Historical Microreproductions, and publishers, presses, and societies that produce documentary volumes, reprints, and facsimile editions of archival and out-of-print works. Without them, many journals and memoirs would have been inaccessible.

I am grateful for many discussions with Sally Luttmer, a fluent Inuktitut speaker, who did her best to eliminate errors in my linguistic analysis, particularly in the matter of Champlain's comments on autonyms among seventeenth-century Grand Bay people. Scott MacNeil, friend and fellow historian, read the entire manuscript twice, and made useful suggestions. If I did not always heed their advice and have fallen into error as a result, the fault is mine alone. My gratitude also goes to several anonymous readers, one of whom deserves special thanks for alerting me to the existence of a 1997 publication by Marc G. Stevenson, which supported my intuitive realization that the Copper Inuit did not belong in the academic category of Central Inuit.

Patricia Sanders, Managing Editor at the University of Manitoba Press, worked on the manuscript with enthusiasm and enormous care, for which I am grateful. I also offer her my thanks for many private acts of kindness. Director David Carr not only saw me through the refereeing process with infinite patience, he used his considerable research skills to track down obscure illustrations in unlikely places. Their combined efforts have greatly enhanced both the usefulness and the readability of the book. They deserve more applause than words alone can convey.

My interest in the Inuit past began during the 1960s, the decade I spent in the Canadian arctic, as teacher, researcher, and fur trade company wife. My training in scholarly research methods was nurtured in the Ph.D. programme of the History Department at the University of Manitoba, and would not have been possible without the support of the Social Sciences and Humanities Research Council of Canada.

Finally, I want to thank my sons for the enthusiasm with which they encouraged me through the long process of research and writing, and my daughter-in-law, who kept my spirits up during the refereeing process. Andrew also gave invaluable help by preparing maps and illustrations; Will applied his analytical skills to identify unsupported assumptions and incomplete arguments; and Sharon helped me think through and identify the concepts underlying systems of justice and law in different societies, including that of the Inuit.

Therefore it is that our fathers have inherited from their fathers all the old rules of life which are based on the experience and wisdom of generations. We do not know how, we cannot say why, but we keep those rules in order that we may live untroubled.

– Aua, at Lyon Inlet

THE CENTRAL ARCTIC

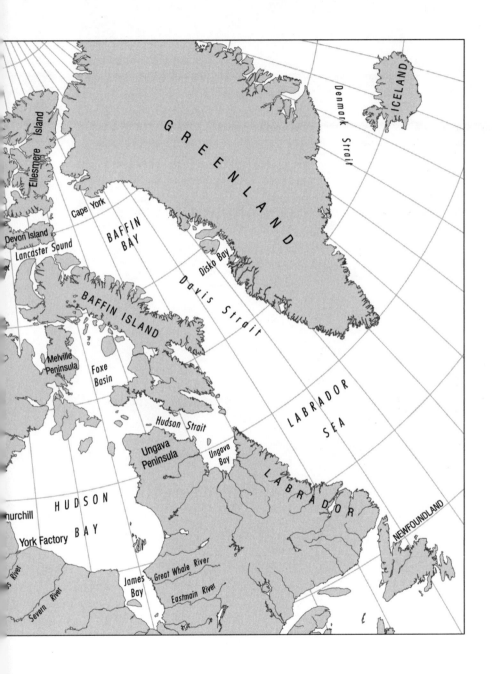

Introduction: Assumptions about the Other

In 1266 or 1267, on the west coast of a great, ice-capped island bounded by the North Atlantic Ocean and the Polar Sea, two parties of hunters—one moving from the north and the other from the south—met. The southerners were Norsemen, and they called the island Greenland. The northerners were Thule, and in later centuries their descendants called the island Kalaallit Nunaat, Land of the People.

Both groups were relative newcomers to the island. The Norse Greenlanders were descendants of Icelanders who arrived on the southwest coast some time in the two decades before the millennial year 1000 CE.[1] For the next two centuries, they expanded north along the fjords of western Greenland. By 1250 they were supplementing the poor harvests of their farms by hunting as far north as Disko Bay.

The Thule* were descendants of whale hunters who began to move across the North American arctic some time around the year 900 CE in a major expansion that took them from Alaska to Greenland in the course of two centuries. By 1250 they were harvesting the resources of their new home as far south as Disko Bay on Greenland's west coast.

Two sentences in *The Greenland Saga*, written in the early 1300s, recorded all that the Norsemen could say about the other arctic people at the time: "Toward the North, hunters have found some little people whom they call Skrellings; their situation is that when they are hurt by weapons their sores become white without bleeding, but when they are mortally wounded their blood will hardly stop running. They have no iron at all; they use missiles made of walrus tusks and sharp stones for knives."[2]

---

*See Appendix 1 for a discussion of ethnonyms and other naming practices among indigenous arctic peoples, and the literature concerning them.

Nothing of note was added to the European store of knowledge about the people the Norse called "Skraelings" until the second half of the sixteenth century, when the number of transoceanic voyages for exploration and harvesting of western Atlantic resources increased. Western European states and merchant corporations, motivated by a desire for information that would be strategically or commercially useful, began to show an intense interest in the indigenous peoples of North America.

The physical and cultural characteristics of arctic inhabitants were of particular concern. Proof that they were Asian would support the still current idea that America and Asia were one continent, and would sustain belief in the existence of a northwest passage that would give European commercial interests quick and easy access to the markets of the Orient. Access to what indigenous arctic peoples knew was as eagerly sought by the newcomers. After all, who but the inhabitants could be reliable sources of information on the geography of the country and the location of a possible northern sea route to the Orient? Who could better serve as potential allies in the exploitation of their country's mineral, and other, wealth?

A major obstacle to grasping the knowledge they needed was the lack of a mutually intelligible language. Captains and crews heading for the arctic were therefore instructed by their sovereigns and masters to make careful verbal and pictorial descriptions of indigenous people, and to bring representatives to Europe whenever possible. Mariners on a French vessel visiting the Labrador coast in 1566 obeyed their master's instructions and seized a woman and child. The following year, the captives were displayed at fairs in Augsburg, Nuremberg, and Frankfurt. A handbill advertising the exhibition in Augsburg summarized current popular beliefs about America's most northerly inhabitants: "This woman with her husband and little child were met by the French ... and the husband was shot through his body with an arrow.... He was struck and wounded in his throat so severely that he fell to the ground and died from this wound. This man was 12 feet tall and had in twelve days killed eleven people with his own hand, Frenchmen and Portuguese.... They took the woman with her child and brought her away; and none of the Frenchmen could understand a single word of hers or speak with her at all."[3]

Men, women, and children from Greenland, Labrador, and Baffin Island continued to be carried across the Atlantic by whalers, fishermen, and explorers in the following centuries. Frequently, they were kidnapped, but some were willing, even eager, visitors and were treated well by their hosts. A few sympathetic ship's captains presented their guests at court, taught them to read and write, showered them with gifts, and gave them safe passage back to their homes. Impresarios exhibited some at widely advertised fairs for the entertainment and education of the general populace. Scholars, as well as the merely curious, observed them closely and the European scientific community studied their clothing, customs, and language, and autopsied their bodies when they died, as many did.

Other European traders, explorers, and adventurers observed arctic peoples without taking them captive, and produced descriptions of their physical appearance, styles of clothing, weaponry, and housing, accounts of their economic and social lives, and dictionaries of their languages. Their reports, logs, and memoirs contained descriptions that were sometimes astonishingly accurate and insightful, and sometimes superficial and seriously mistaken.

As late as the mid-nineteenth century, the arctic peoples of North America were still generally believed to be coastal dwellers and hunters of marine mammals, highly skilled in the physical activities of paddling, harpooning, and stalking game, and, on the rare occasions when women's work was noticed, at sewing. They were frequently described by observers as being perennially cheerful, friendly folk, who made the best of their unhappy lot in life, satisfied to survive one day at a time. Their communities were understood to be thoroughly egalitarian, lacking both laws and leadership. Infanticide and gerontocide were believed to be characteristic of all Inuit societies in all periods. Temporally and geographically separated social units were perceived as a single, homogeneous society, which had existed essentially unchanged for millennia. Activities and behaviours noted at specific places in particular periods were assumed to be true for all arctic inhabitants, regardless of time and location. All these assumptions are incorrect, though each contains a grain of truth.

Inuit and their Thule ancestors were indeed masters of a coastal environment, but they were also fully familiar with terrestrial animal resources and inland venues, and used both when necessity dictated. Physical prowess and manual skills were certainly required in the course of making a living, but Inuit invested enormous intellectual effort into understanding their environment and shaping their societies, as well. Inuit were not always passive or friendly when their territories and resources were threatened, nor were they always cheerful when they planned long-term strategies for surviving in a hostile environment. Contrary to much popular belief, Inuit created highly complex, holistic systems of law, justice, and leadership, and an oral canon for teaching the generations the rules for correct living. The English words "infanticide" and "gerontocide" fail completely to describe the customs they are intended to describe. Neither killing nor dying is

implicit in these practices when they are seen in the context of Inuit cosmology. While the Inuit language, oral histories, and regulatory codes are
similar in most arctic communities from Alaska to Greenland, the communities are not carbon copies of one another, and the customs of one cannot
be assumed to prevail in another. The distinctions are, in fact, so sharp, and
so obvious to Inuit themselves, that scholarly observers were able to create
a taxonomy of bands and tribes, based on differences in dialect, subsistence
activities, clothing and architectural styles, tools, social organization, and
cosmology.

The mistaken assumptions are rooted in point of view. As a recent discussion of historical methodology pointed out, "Human beings are born
into a group which provides answers to the first and most basic questions
they pose about life. Few outlive the impress of that first organization of
consciousness. Hence, ethnocentrism is common to all folk."[4] The etic
position, that is, the outsider's point of view, is almost always different from
the emic position, or insider's view of things, at least initially.

Mistaken assumptions about The Other occur in all intercultural exchanges. Evidence from Inuit historians and oral sources has often fallen
victim to cross-cultural misunderstandings, seriously distorting information. Because of their pre-existing views of the world, some non-Inuit
observers of past events simply could not grasp the logic of what they were
told, or comprehend the practicality of what they saw. Similarly, Inuit informants sometimes misread the intentions and behaviours of the strangers
among them, with serious consequences. They also occasionally failed to
see that their explanations did not match reality. The emics of mental life,
that is, what insiders say they believe, do not always reflect what they actually do. Some degree of misunderstanding and distortion is inevitable because of bias on the part of both observer and informant, even in good-faith
exchanges between givers and receivers.

A second source of misunderstanding has been the lack of a mutually
intelligible system of communication. Inuktitut is an extremely complex
and sophisticated language, which differs in all fundamentals of grammar
and conceptual ordering from most European languages. Vilhjalmur
Stefansson, who became fluent enough to understand ordinary conversation only after five years of living where nothing but Inuktitut was spoken,
claimed that a European could more easily learn Latin, Greek, Russian, and
Hebrew than Inuktitut. While Stefansson may have overstated the case,
most non-Inuit explorers and ethnographers who left accounts of Inuit life
were linguistically incompetent, in spite of the claims some of them made
to the contrary. Hudson's Bay Company traders who spent years in the

arctic gained a surer knowledge of the language, but few reached levels of understanding at which they could discuss philosophy or worldviews. Inuit interpreters had an equally inadequate understanding of English, and some of them had trouble with unfamiliar Inuit dialects, as well.

A third reason for misunderstanding is that among Eskimo and Inuit, as among many other peoples, asking direct questions is, under certain conditions, considered an invasion of privacy. Many ethnographers have innocently recorded false information, deliberately given by informants. What the informants were doing was 'telling a whopper' in order to teach the questioner, through shaming, that nosiness is disrespectful and rude. When the ethnographer does not understand this, she or he may accept as true those explanations informants think are so obviously ridiculous that no one could possibly believe them. In short, many ethnographers, including amateurs like the arctic explorers as well as professional anthropologists, may not have understood that their informants were delivering a reprimand or attempting to teach the culture. As a result of such misunderstandings, fieldworkers have, on occasion, concluded that their informants either did not know what they were talking about, or were liars.

Anthropologist Ann Fienup-Riordan described her experience during fieldwork with the Yup'ik of western Alaska. "I had asked about naming procedures ... but with little solid response. I was made to feel acutely nosey. And, in fact, part of the message of this story is how little progress one can make in understanding the coastal Yup'ik people if one confines oneself to information acquired through a questionnaire approach. It certainly never worked for me, and in fact my best friends used to lie to me, in a good-natured way, to show me how foolish and misguided my occasional bouts of verbal curiosity were. Watching and listening, however, were different matters."[5]

My own experience was similar. During the 1960s, the decade in which I lived in Inuit communities, some of my acquaintances were willing to attempt my education by the methods to which I was accustomed. They simply answered my questions and corrected me when I got things wrong. Many, however, preferred to teach by putting me in situations where, they thought, I could see for myself. The assumption that "observers were always capable of understanding," made by many Inuit teachers and informants over the centuries, was charitable and flattering, but perhaps not always realistic or wise.

The difficulties of understanding and teaching were neatly summed up in the early 1920s by Ikinilik, a man from the Great Fish River. Having done his best to explain his views on how the physical and metaphysical realms worked, he concluded by recognizing that self-knowledge, like other kinds of knowledge, is clouded by subjectivity, and that all transmitted knowledge is inherently imperfect. "Of course it may be that all I have been telling you is wrong. For you cannot be certain about a thing you cannot see. And people say so much."[6]

1.

Empty Dishes and Days of Feasting: Human Habitation of Arctic North America to 1550

> *Hard times, dearth times plague us every one.*
> *Stomachs are shrunken, dishes are empty…*
> *Now is abundance with us once more.*
> *Days of feasting to hold us together.*
> — Tuglik's song, at Lyon Inlet in 1922[1]

The vast ice sheets that covered more than half of the North American arctic for 100,000 years during the last great ice age reached their greatest extent around 20,000 years ago. As the earth entered a long period of warming, they began to melt and shrink, and, except for a few remnants, they disappeared between 7000 and 6000 BCE. Some time during the next thousand years, human beings entered the barren lands east of Great Bear Lake for the first time.[2] They were a Paleo-Indian, caribou-hunting people who used the tundra on a seasonal basis, following the caribou herds north in the summer and retreating south to the forest for the winter. They continued to visit the barren lands for the next two or three thousand years, until the onset of a period of highly variable weather, beginning around 3000 BCE. Early in this period, identified by historical climatologists as the Sub-Boreal Climatic Episode, Paleo-Indians ceased to visit the treeless arctic plains.[3]

Some time after their withdrawal around 3000 BCE, but before 2200 BCE, another group of people, similar in many ways to the people of Siberia's Chukchi Peninsula, entered the North American arctic. By 1900 BCE they had established themselves along the mainland coasts of Coronation

Gulf and Foxe Basin, on most of the arctic islands, and in northern Green-land. By 1600 BCE, they occupied the Labrador coast as far south as Nain. Archaeologists, noting their exquisitely crafted microblade technology, which distinguishes them from earlier and later peoples, gave them the name Arc-tic Small Tool tradition (ASTt).[4]

From the time of their first venture into the arctic, human beings have depended for their survival there on certain minimum requirements: tai-lored clothing; shelter and transportation produced from available natural resources; techniques and tools for arctic hunting, fishing, and gathering; and food storage technology suited to available food resources. Acquiring the technologies necessary for successful adaptation to arctic conditions almost certainly took place in Siberia. Among Asiatic inventions previously unknown in North America were the bow and arrow, and tailored skin clothing. ASTt people were the first to occupy the barren grounds year-round, the first to possess the technological sophistication necessary to sur-vival in the arctic, and the first to depend entirely on tundra resources.[5]

The dozens of ASTt communities scattered across the North American arctic by 1600 BCE had some traits in common, particularly their use of distinctive microblades (blades cut from the innermost core of a stone) in their cutting tools, but as with all arctic occupations, there were also varia-tions in the way they organized their communities and made a living. At-tempts by archaeologists to classify ASTt communities created considerable confusion about who was who, obscuring biological and cultural affinities of some groups, and implying genetic and social relationships where none existed. The Joint Project of the National Museums of Canada and the School of American Research (1973) suggested the general term "Paleo-Eskimo" to describe all Canadian arctic occupations from the disappear-ance of Paleo-Indians after 3000 BCE to about 1000 CE.[6]

As with the withdrawal of the Paleo-Indians from the barren grounds, the emergence of Paleo-Eskimo groups, their continent-wide movements, and their disappearance during their 3000-year occupation of the North American arctic were temporally linked to climatic change. For a few cen-turies after about 2200 BCE, environmental conditions were favourable to a movement of people across the arctic: the climate generally was slightly warmer than in earlier periods, and Hudson Bay, Hudson Strait, and Lan-caster Sound were ice-free for part of each year.[7] During the same centu-ries, the evidence suggests, they worked out the principles of the domed structure and began to build snowhouses, making it possible for them to live on the sea ice and hunt ringed seals during the winter months. They had domesticated dogs, and used stone lamps that burned marine mammal blubber to warm and light their houses, instead of using open fires, which radiated little heat in the arctic cold. Most Paleo-Eskimo communities were adept at manufacturing and using the bow and arrow, and hunted marine mammals as well as caribou.

Populations were apparently very small in northern Greenland and the high arctic islands, and between 1800 and 1600 BCE, these communities disappeared during a brief period of rapid cooling. Farther south, in Melville Peninsula, Foxe Basin, and the north shore of Hudson Strait, larger populations flourished in areas where there were more food and other resources. Over the next 500 years, they expanded south along the coast of Hudson Bay to northern Manitoba, where their traces have been identified at Sea Horse Gully near Churchill and dated to about 900 BCE.[8]

By 1000 BCE a new warming trend within the Sub-Boreal Climatic Episode, probably lasting for about three centuries, made the central arctic coasts more attractive to the Paleo-Eskimo. However, milder climate, the re-establishment of the boreal forest at higher latitudes, and the increasingly northern range of the caribou herds also made the tundra more attractive to caribou-hunting Athapaskan people living in the transitional forest zone. As they moved north in search of caribou, Paleo-Eskimo groups withdrew to the mainland's northern peninsulas and the islands beyond. This ebb-and-flow pattern of people into and out of the tundra lands was repeated many times in the next two millennia.

The Dorset Period

Paleo-Eskimo people living on the arctic islands, and occupying the tundra mainland from time to time, remained essentially homogeneous for the first thousand years after they entered the central and eastern arctic. With the new warming trend between 1000 and 700 BCE, however, they began to make major changes. They developed styles of tools, weapons, utensils, and decoration so different from earlier ones that when these were first studied in the early 1920s, Diamond Jenness, Canada's Dominion Anthropologist, identified both the artifacts and their makers as belonging to a previously unrecognized cultural complex. Jenness called them the Dorset people, after Cape Dorset where their material remains were discovered.

The newly emerged Dorset societies occupied the regions around Foxe Basin and Hudson Strait for nearly 2000 years, until about 1000 CE. Characteristically, they lived in small settlements and occupied semi-subterranean houses, often with rectangular floor plans. The presence of snow knives in their tool kits indicates they were adept at working with snow and probably built snowhouses, as their Paleo-Eskimo ancestors had done. They did not have dogs, although they had small sleds, for which they made bone sled shoes. Their tools, weapons, and utensils tended to be made of antler or ivory, as were their delicately carved items of personal adornment. Many of them were exquisitely decorated with distinctive designs and motifs.[9]

After Jenness's identification of the Dorset as a new people, their origins became a major problem in arctic archaeology. Canadian and American archaeologists took the position that Dorset material culture was an ASTt variant that had developed in situ. Scandinavian archaeologists, on the other hand, suggested that Dorset material artifacts were so different from those of other Paleo-Eskimo groups that they could only have been introduced by immigration from elsewhere. The discovery on Baffin Island and Melville Peninsula of sites that had been occupied continuously for over 3000 years supported the in-situ theory. Arctic specialists now are in general agreement that Arctic Small Tool tradition and the Dorset culture complex exhibit "a parent-to-offspring relationship."[10]

A second problem in Dorset studies was the means and pattern of their expansion across the arctic. The occurrence, length of occupation, and distribution of Dorset sites indicate that the Foxe Basin-Hudson Strait area was the heartland, or core area, where the Dorset way of life was developed and maintained almost unchanged for nearly 2000 years, until nearly the end of the first millennium CE. Outside the core area, at different times, Dorset people occupied parts of the arctic islands, a few mainland sites at Dolphin and Union Strait, the west coast of Hudson Bay as far south as Churchill, and the Labrador-Newfoundland coasts.[11] The traditionalism and continuity characteristic of the core area are not found in the peripheries, where Dorset occupation seems to have appeared and disappeared over time. Robert McGhee's description of intermittent occupations in the arctic islands fits all the Dorset colonies. "The picture … begins to appear as one of sporadic migration by peoples from the [core area], followed by florescence and population expansion for a period of a few decades or a very few centuries, and then by extinction or abandonment of the area."[12]

Each of the short-lived outlier societies exhibited traits not found in the heartland. In some communities, tools and utensils had been adapted or created to suit local resources; in some, new kinds of housing material and construction methods appeared. To explain why Dorset outlier communities were sometimes so different from the parent society, anthropologists and archaeologists developed a "pulsation model" of expansion. In its first expression, prior to 1973, the theory suggested that migrants moved in successive waves out of the Dorset core area during 'good' economic times, and back to the heartland during 'bad' economic times. While they were separated from their parent community, the colonies developed or invented technologies and techniques suited to the different environmental conditions of the new homes. Dorset colonists in areas where food was less abundant than in the more ecologically secure heartland became more flexible and innovative.

The problem with the pulsation model was that while traits existing in the core area could be clearly seen in artifacts from outlying communities, no evidence demonstrated the introduction of technology and techniques from the periphery back to the heartland. In a working seminar in 1973, the Joint Project of the National Museum of Man (Canada) and the School of American Research rejected the old pulsation interpretation, and suggested a new explanatory model that fit with all the known evidence. The new model theorized that while there were successive waves of emigration out of the core area under favourable environmental circumstances, the outlying communities did not return to the heartland during periods of environmental stress. The editor of the Joint Project proceedings, Moreau S. Maxwell, summarized its conclusions. "Periods of occupation in peripheral regions appear to cease abruptly. Within their time span they ... developed regional trait specialties. These, however, appear not to have been transmitted back to the core area. Combining these points they can best be interpreted as reflecting expansion followed by catastrophic decline in ecologically marginal regions, rather than the ebb and flow of people from centers of high food resource reliability."[13]

The literature of arctic archaeology identifies the fundamental catalyst for change as environmental. The explanation suggests that climatic fluctuations, which affect the size, availability, and density of animal populations, necessarily affect the human economies that depend on them, and force adaptations of human subsistence activities, social organization, and demography.

After five centuries of living with relatively mild and stable climatic conditions, Dorset social units began to experience environmental stress with the onset of a new cooling trend, the Sub-Atlantic Climatic Episode, which began about 550 BCE and lasted until about 400 CE.[14] During the cooling period, Dorset outlier communities disappeared, one after the other. All Ellesmere Island and northern Greenland sites were abandoned, and there is no evidence that people moved in large numbers to other areas, or joined other communities.

In reduced numbers, people continued to occupy the coasts of Banks and Victoria islands, Boothia Peninsula, Baffin Island, the arctic islands of Lancaster Sound, northwest Hudson Bay, Foxe Basin, and Hudson Strait, the Labrador coast, northern Newfoundland, and the southwest coast of Greenland. Extinction seems to have occurred only in the most northerly regions at first, but by the final years of the Sub-Atlantic Climatic Episode, most of the peripheral areas had been abandoned. No evidence exists to suggest that the inhabitants withdrew to the Foxe Basin core area. The most likely explanation is that populations diminished beyond the point from which they could recover, and one by one the communities died out.

During the same years that Dorset communities were disappearing from the Keewatin barren lands, through extinction or voluntary withdrawal, Athapaskan people were once more following the caribou herds north, leaving traces of their seasonal occupations at the mouth of the Coppermine River and at Aberdeen Lake in the central Keewatin.[15]

The Sub-Atlantic Climatic Episode, characterized by global cooling and, in the arctic, by increased precipitation, gave way to the still relatively cool, but much drier, Scandic Climatic Episode beginning around 400 CE. It lasted for nearly 600 years and had a significant effect on arctic occupations. During that time, most Dorset peoples enjoyed a predictable environment and economic security. Their lives were apparently affluent and comfortable, and growing populations expanded once more to the west, north, and south, reoccupying Boothia Peninsula, King William Island, Victoria Island, and some parts of the mainland coast around Coronation Gulf. They developed new art forms, becoming masters in the creation of small carvings. The evidence of their artwork and finely decorated tools suggests they experienced a rich spiritual life as well as economic security. In the words of Robert McGhee:

> There was a great explosion of artistic production ... [which coincided] with a major expansion of Dorset occupation to many parts of the Arctic Archipelago which appear to have been abandoned, or very sparsely populated, during the preceding centuries. For a few generations, Dorset people lived from Labrador to northwestern Greenland, and across the Arctic Islands to the shores of Amundsen Gulf. It is these people who produced most of the carvings that make up our collections of Dorset art. It was an artistic tradition rooted in the Paleo-Eskimo past, but which flourished for only a few generations, and was remarkably standardized across the Arctic, apparently through widespread communication networks, and perhaps even through trade in carvings themselves.[16]

It was the final florescence of Dorset societies. The same beneficent climatic conditions that had provided ample resources as a necessary condition for the economic, artistic, and spiritual flowering of Dorset peoples also created opportunities for the emergence of the people who would ultimately destroy them.

The Thule Expansion

In the final hundred years of the Scandic Climatic Episode, temperatures throughout the northern hemisphere began to rise more rapidly and more consistently than in earlier periods. On the west coast of Alaska, far from the Dorset-inhabited lands, other northern peoples had already perfected techniques and technology for the efficient harvesting of coastal areas where seal and walrus were abundant, and were beginning to develop the skills necessary for whale hunting.[17] In the new, warmer conditions, they moved into the coastal tundra areas north of the Brooks Range, where they hunted seal and walrus along the coast and at the edges of the fast ice, and captured whale in the open water of ice-leads. By the end of the Scandic Climatic Episode, they had developed a marine technology suited to open-sea whaling.

The Scandic Climatic Episode was only the beginning of the warming trend. More pronounced and even more rapid warming occurred during the climatic period known as the Neo-Atlantic (900 to 1200 CE), sometimes called the Little Optimum. The entire northern hemisphere was affected: the North American arctic and Greenland experienced average air temperatures from two to four degrees Celsius higher than today's, and in Europe the mean summer temperature rose about two degrees Celsius.[18]

In Europe's Scandinavian peninsulas, an increase in agriculturally viable land provided abundant cereal crops such as barley and rye, while warmer ocean temperatures resulted in greater yields in the Baltic and North seas of cod, herring, and other marine resources. Surplus food, a growing population, and a new measure of affluence encouraged the Norse to search for new territory and new trading contacts. In a burst of expansion, they sailed and rowed their longships up the Russian rivers to the edges of the Byzantine Empire, and their ocean-going *hafskip* along the northern and western shores of Europe to the Mediterranean, and across the Atlantic to Iceland, Greenland, and Labrador. By the 880s they had established a colony in Iceland, and by 995 two communities of Icelanders on the west coast of Greenland were adapting Norse farming and fishing techniques to the arctic environment.[19]

Far to the west, in Bering Strait and along the northern coast of Alaska, the polar ice pack shifted northward and became thinner. The consequences for animal habitats were significant. Both seal and walrus are seriously affected by changes in ice-pack conditions: thick ice is unsuitable as a seal denning area and results in smaller populations of ringed seals, while walrus herds are forced away from the shallow coastal waters where they have access to the bottom-feeding invertebrates that are their preferred food. In deeper water, they turn to preying on seals, which further reduces already threatened seal populations.[20] The increased difficulties of hunting both species at greater distances would certainly bring about hard times for people who depend on them for food and as material for tools, utensils, clothing, tents, and boat covers.

On the north coast of Alaska, however, the same climatic circumstances that removed major food resources created conditions that encouraged an increase in another important resource. Longer periods of open water resulted in changes to the migration habits of Pacific Ocean baleen whales. Instead of returning to the Pacific Ocean via Bering Strait in late summer, whales began to winter in the Bering Sea, and then in the Beaufort Sea. Decade by decade, as the southern edge of the ice pack moved farther and farther north, migrating whales moved eastward into the arctic.[21]

Some north-coast Alaskan communities were well prepared to take advantage of the increasing numbers of whales entering local waters. They already had the boats and other technology necessary for open-sea whaling, and they were competent whale hunters. They followed their prey eastward across the arctic, perfecting their whaling technology and adapting to local conditions as they went. By the twelfth century, they occupied the arctic coasts and islands from Alaska to Greenland, and had developed new economic and social organizations, as well as new technologies to suit new ecological conditions. They had highly efficient transportation, using dog traction on land, and sea-going kayaks and multi-passenger umiaks on water.*

Their hunting equipment included whale harpoons, seal scratchers, and seal-breath indicators,☆ and they had perfected a complex and highly efficient system of caches for food storage and preservation. They used toggles of wood, ivory, bone, or stone on clothing, tent covers, and dog harnesses. They were expert at the tanning and working of hides, and their wardrobes consisted of finely tailored parkas, pants, leggings, stockings, boots,

---

*Like the one-person kayak, an umiak is a skin boat, but unlike the kayak it is not enclosed. It resembles a large rowboat, can hold as many as thirty people (some eighteenth-century observers noted umiaks holding fifty people), and may be equipped with as many as twenty oars.

☆A seal scratcher was made of bone, antler, or driftwood, often in the shape of a seal claw, and was used to scratch the ice surface to make the seal below believe it was safe to surface. This was only for late-spring or summer sealing when seals came up onto the ice to lie in the sun. A breath indicator was a feather or tiny piece of swan's down or eiderdown placed over a small hole the hunter made in the ice covering the breathing hole. When a seal entered the breathing hole, the change in air current made the down move, the hunter would know a seal was in the hole, and would strike.

and double-thumbed mitts, as well as snow goggles for eye protection. They built permanent villages of warm, comfortable dwellings with cold-trap entrances. In the first few centuries of their occupation, villages sometimes held as many as thirty households.

They were able to establish and maintain permanent, year-round villages with large (in arctic terms) populations because whales were abundant. It has been estimated that "a single 40-ton bowhead whale" was sufficient to feed a community of five families, between twenty-five and fifty individuals, for a year. Every person in the village could count on"between 2 and 4 kg of meat a day (and quantities of flammable blubber)."[22] The flammable blubber was the fuel that provided both heat and light during the dark arctic winters. In addition, bones and baleen could be made into needles, toggles, buttons, spoons, serving dishes, scrapers, and a great variety of other useful tools and utensils. How these people identified themselves is unknown. Therkel Mathiassen, the senior archaeologist of the Fifth Thule Expedition of 1921-24, called them Thule, after the site in northern Greenland where he first uncovered their remains.

The spread of whale-hunting people from the Beaufort to the Greenland Sea in the tenth and eleventh centuries was not a simple relocation of people from one place to another along a passage through intervening territory. The move involved expansion, invasion, and occupation of territories between the two ends of the journey. The Little Climatic Optimum, which created conditions favourable to the Thule eastward migration, did not offer similar opportunities for economic expansion to the Dorset who already occupied the territory. On the contrary, pronounced climatic warming presented them with serious subsistence problems. Their societies were based on the harvesting of multiple resources at different times of the year: seal hunting on the ice in late winter and early spring, and caribou hunting and fishing from late spring to late fall. Waterfowl, muskox, walrus, and small land animals such as hare and fox were taken when available. Resources and the rhythm of harvesting varied with location and short-term climatic conditions.

For practitioners of a Dorset-type subsistence pattern,[23] the Little Optimum posed a serious threat. Shorter, milder winters and the attendant general decrease in sea ice reduced access to seal herds. Simultaneously, caribou herds were more widely dispersed and their migration routes were longer. The seasons when food resources were available changed. A people who had enjoyed a reasonably stable and predictable economy for 2000 years, and had developed a certain conservatism, may have been unprepared for the suddenness of the changes.

For people already hard-pressed by environmental and ecological changes, the appearance of Thule immigrants was a catastrophe. The Thule invasion resulted, as Robert McGhee has so precisely phrased it, in "the archaeological disappearance of the Dorset people."[24] To date, archaeological research has not been able to explain what happened to them during and after the Thule expansion into their territory, except that their remains became extremely rare in the archaeological record after 1300. Guesses can and have been made: they may have been destroyed during violent encounters with the newcomers; they may have been assimilated into Thule society, forcibly or willingly, quickly or gradually; or survivors may have withdrawn out of range of the invaders, and maintained their sociocultural distinctiveness in isolation for varying periods of time.

While archaeology cannot describe the precise events of contact, central and eastern Inuit histories describe hostilities between invading Thule and indigenous Dorset, called Tunit by today's Inuit, ending with the expulsion of the Dorset from their lands. Most tales of violence come from the Igloolik area,[25] the heartland of the Dorset people, where occupation was continuous over 2000 years and where Dorset populations were greatest. Stories from south Baffin Island on the eastern periphery of the Dorset core area, collected by Franz Boas,[26] also tell of feuds and violence between Tunit and Thule, ending in the expulsion of the Tunit and permanent occupation by the Thule. West of the Dorset heartland, in the Boothia Peninsula region, Netsilik histories less often describe violent encounters, but they agree that "when their [Thule] forefathers came to their present hunting grounds the lands were already populated with Tunrit," who were chased away by the newcomers. They also recount how they and the Tunit "hunted in company and were good friends" for some time after the arrival of the first Thule.[27] Whatever the relations of the last Paleo-Eskimo societies (Tunit/Dorset) and the first Neo-Eskimo societies (Thule and Inuit) may have been in different places across the arctic, there is at least a possibility they exchanged ideas and technologies. The use and construction of snowhouses and soapstone lamps, which have not shown up in the Alaskan record, may have been learned by Thule during periods of coexistence with the Dorset.

A few Dorset groups may have survived the Thule invasion in isolated pockets. As late as the nineteenth century, some communities existed that did not fit the typical late Thule description: the Sallirmiut* at Southampton Island in northwestern Hudson Bay; the Maniktunik on the Belcher Islands in southeastern Hudson Bay; and the Ammassalik on the east coast

---

*The Inuktitut suffix -*miut* means "people of." The suffix -*mio*, as in Sallirmio, is the singular form, "person of."

of Greenland. Some archaeologists have suggested they may have been Thule-acculturated Dorset remnants.[28]

Physical Environment as Catalyst for Change

To some degree, all interpretations of the arctic human past have identified the physical environment as the chief forcing factor in demographic, economic, social, and cultural change. The conclusion is reasonable enough, given the obvious temporal links between the two areas of change, and the limited evidence from paleostudies. However, the identification of physical environment as a major influence in human history is an uncomfortable idea for many contemporary historians.

Fear of geographical determinism as an historical explanation springs from semantic confusion and is reinforced by instances of misuse of the concept by historians. The Latin verb *terminare* means "to set limits." English derivatives such as "term" (a limited period of time), "terminals" (end limits), and "terminate" (reach the limit) retain the meaning of a range bound by its two extremes. "To determine," meaning "to set limits," was common English usage until the middle of the nineteenth century, when theories that noted a cause-and-effect relationship between pairs of sequential events or actions were labelled "determining," and the idea of causation was attached to the word. Historians and other social and political theorists too often have used (or misused) both phrase and concept to mean that certain circumstances or phenomena inevitably cause or result in specific other occurrences. Geographers and anthropologists, for the most part, have used the concept of geographical or ecological "determinism" to refer to limits or sets of restraints on human activities, within which there is a range of possibilities, and outside of which some responses are not possible. Few, if any, have even come close to "rigorous environmental determinism."[29]

By denying human free will and the possibility of both individual and group choice, mechanistic explanations of cause and effect fly in the face of empirical evidence that human beings do indeed have choices, and historically have reacted in different ways to similar stimuli. When "determinism" is used to mean only that there are limits to the kinds of human responses that will be possible or effective in particular physical and social environments, it is an explanation that can scarcely be avoided. Climate and weather most certainly do "affect food production, energy use, land use, water resources, and other factors vital to national security and human welfare," as geographer Robert Claxton has pointed out.[30] Population size, contact with outsiders, the aspirations and attitudes of neighbouring polities, and other factors in the social environment are equally constraining. At the same time, both physical and social environments may create opportunities.

Physical and social environments set limits on what *can* happen, but neither ensures what *will* happen. The "possibilist approach" recognizes that climate may dictate that, under present climatic and technological conditions, wheat farming is not a viable choice in Greenland, for example, or that the military mindset of a neighbouring nation may preclude peaceful coexistence, but only the impossible is ruled out. An array of options remains, and nothing is inevitable.

Environments can also be understood as *eventual,* to use Lucien Febvre's word.[31] Some events provoke human responses. A river rising out of its bed and pouring across the flood plain has implications for human societies in its vicinity, and may invoke a response from them, but it does not dictate, or even suggest, a particular response. People might attempt to escape the flood by deserting their village, either temporarily or permanently; they might try to control the rising water by technological means, such as dams, dikes, and spillways; they might ask supernatural powers for protection and preservation, or attempt to appease transcendental forces; or they might remain in their homes and live or die as chance allows. There are, of course, other possibilities, but no necessities. Even when the forcing factors for response appear to be the same, societies are free to make different choices appropriate to the physical circumstances, suited to their ideological systems, and logical in the light of their past experiences.

In his denunciation of geography, that is, physical environment, as causative, Lucien Febvre insisted that the idea of causality implied similar and predictable results consequent to similar conditions, an outcome not consistent with the unique and particular events of the human past. The problem with all determinisms as historical explanation is that human activity is contingent on too many variables for the precise relationships among them to be understood. The variables can be identified as economic factors, social relations, technology, worldview, power relations, government activity, individual action, and historical experience, as well as many others. Different historians and schools of thought tend to choose one or another of the factors as "the controlling variable of a societal system," as geographer Joseph Petulla has pointed out. He suggested that instead of one controlling factor in any set of circumstances, "each geographic location of a societal/cultural system at a particular time is characterized by a unique mix of the above-mentioned historical factors, perhaps controlled by one or more of them for a short time, but no one of them operating independently from the rest."[32]

The exact mix of relevant variables is always unknown. The causes of past human activities can never be known with certainty, nor can future human actions and reactions be predicted. Any determinant cause, if such a thing is even conceptually possible, is a combination of interdependent and mutually influential elements, and, as Petulla suggested, historical explanation is to be found only in the "unique relationship among the variables."[33]

Human activities in harsh environments such as the arctic are generally assumed to be more constrained by the physical environment than in other societies. However, the limitations are not intractable; they can be compensated for by the development of technologies that mitigate the effects of physical environment. The higher the degree of technological insulation from environment, the less limiting an environment is; or, to put it another way, techniques and tools can broaden the range of possibilities of human action. Of course, the higher the degree of technological insulation from the physical environment, the greater will be a society's vulnerability to failures of the technological environment: electrical failure in a city of a million people during a period of minus-thirty-degree temperatures will be devastatingly costly in terms of human life and the ability of the city to continue functioning.

However, the inability to control physical environment through technology does not necessarily make society unviable under conditions of extreme physical or social constraints. Where technological insulation is not possible, or has reached the limits of its effectiveness, societies can make cultural adaptations that enable them to satisfy their needs within specific environments. Population control through social proscription and prescription is an example of cultural adaptation that enables social groups to survive even in the face of seemingly unyielding constraints.

Because attempts have been made to use environmental explanations of human conduct as justification for racist behaviour, historians have tended to avoid them. However, the conflict between geographical determinism, as perceived and feared by many historians, and human free will can be disposed of in the light of the foregoing discussion, and summed up in David Hackett Fischer's comment: "Important linkages may appear in the relationship between climate and culture [i.e. society]—not in the form of mindless, monistic determinism, but rather in the form of an intricate interaction of challenge and choice."[34]

The general pattern of arctic human history to 1200 is one of small societies emerging during periods of climatic stability, and disappearing during periods of increased variability. There is evidence that in some periods, separated communities stayed in touch and exchanged ideas and trade

goods over great distances, and, in other periods, experienced loss of communication and increasing cultural diversity. Changes in subsistence economies occurred in response to changes in local conditions as often as they
did in reaction to widespread modifications of the environment.

On the basis of its material remains, Dorset society can be described as
one in which a core area was continuously occupied over 2000 years and
for which there is little or no evidence of demographic or cultural change.
Repeated expansions were apparently successful only in the short term,
during periods of climatic amelioration. Conservatism was more characteristic of the heartland than of the colonies, where adaptability and change
were frequent, or may simply have left more obvious traces in the archaeological record. Perhaps conservatism was a survival strategy that worked in
the resource-rich, predictable ecozone of the core area, and was therefore
highly valued. In the more marginal ecological areas, where traditional
solutions were inadequate, greater flexibility was practised. The waxing and
waning of social groups in the expansion zones suggests that neither conservatism nor adaptability was successful in the long run.

The pattern of Thule history was similar. During periods of environmental stability, such as the Little Optimum, and in areas where resources
and access to resources were reliable and predictable over long periods,
Thule subsistence strategies and technologies remained relatively constant.
Archaeological evidence suggests that thirteenth- and fourteenth-century
Thule societies, from the Alaskan north coast across the Canadian arctic
coasts and islands to Greenland, were similar in their material culture, residential patterns, technology, and subsistence activities. In the centuries that
followed the Little Climatic Optimum, however, communities became increasingly hard-pressed.

Where resource availability and accessibility were problematic, some Thule
communities disappeared, through extinction or dispersion, as Dorset outlier
communities had disappeared before them. In less difficult but still marginal and uncertain environments, other communities made changes that
improved their chances of survival. Thule societies, economies, and culture
underwent major changes, and a new people, or peoples, the Historic Inuit,
emerged from Thule roots.

The Thule-Historic Inuit Transition

The process that transformed classic Thule societies to Historic Inuit began
as early as the twelfth century in the Coronation Gulf area. The first Thule
immigrants quickly discovered that whales and walrus, which had been the
basis of their economy in Alaska, did not thrive in the shallow straits and

channels of the central arctic coast. To wrest a living from the new environment, the newcomers created techniques and technologies for efficient hunting of local caribou, fish, and ringed seal, which became the bases of their livelihood.

At Coronation Gulf, the Thule found surficial copper deposits in abundance and began to manufacture copper-tipped and sheathed tools, which also became items of trade with groups farther west. As they moved east, they found that local clays were not well suited to the manufacture of pottery such as they had known in Alaska. They substituted new, available materials, learning to use soapstone from local quarries for carved lamps and pots. Most were for their own use, but some were traded to their compatriots in northern Alaska, from whom they were able to get clay vessels in exchange.[35]

Just east of Coronation Gulf, on King William Island, Adelaide and Boothia peninsulas, and Somerset Island, the newcomers found that bowhead whale were infrequent visitors. They had to make immediate and sometimes drastic changes in residential patterns, hunting techniques and technologies, and diet. They switched successfully to winter sealing, and summer fishing and caribou hunting. They became highly mobile in order to make efficient use of widely scattered summer food resources. Permanent summer villages of the classic Thule type, consisting of between fifteen and thirty stone-sod-whalebone structures, were replaced by communities of one to five nuclear families living in widely separated locations. Portable skin tents were constructed for summer occupation, and snowhouses began to be used for winter sealing on the sea ice.[36]

Maintaining communities on Boothia Peninsula was even more problematic than in other central arctic areas; whale seldom entered the shallow, enclosed waterways of the peninsula and its islands, and caribou were scarce and unpredictable. Caribou moving from the Adelaide Peninsula to King William Island followed either of two major routes year after year, and people knew exactly where to find the herds at the proper season. In Boothia Peninsula, however, there were a dozen and a half possible crossings,[37] making it difficult to predict where the greatest number of animals would be during seasonal migrations, and adding more uncertainty to an already uncertain situation. Out of necessity, communities on Boothia Peninsula had to become highly diversified from the time the first Thule immigrants arrived.

Initially, on the north coast of Somerset Island, the newcomers were able to continue an almost classic Thule way of life, based on the hunting and use of bowhead whale, which were easily accessible during their migrations through Parry Channel. Conditions began to change, however, around 1200 as a new climatic regime, the Pacific Episode, began. By about 1350 ocean temperatures had fallen, the season of heavy sea ice was longer, and whales were more scarce. The human response was diversification. Communities began to depend more on other food resources, such as fish, seal, and caribou. The strategy was only moderately successful, largely because of an inadequate and highly unpredictable caribou presence. By the mid-1400s populations were decreasing, and around 1500 Somerset Island was effectively abandoned.[38]

Thule descendants established around Amundsen Gulf did not begin to experience severe shortages of food resources until the fifteenth century. But the new century was colder than any period had been during the preceding millennium,[39] and by mid-century, many animal habitats had become unviable. Within a few generations, the people living just east of Franklin Bay had disappeared, as had been the case on Somerset Island. Precise dating of the abandonment has proved difficult, and different studies have suggested dates ranging from the early 1400s to the mid-1500s.[40]

Abandonment of territory was also the choice of at least some of the Thule peoples of south Baffin Island. Because of the island's alpine topography and proximity to a large body of open water to the east, it is particularly vulnerable to climate change.[41] Shortfalls in subsistence resources occurred as early as about 1300, when there was a minor but sudden shift to colder weather. At least some of the inhabitants of southern Baffin Island opted for the remedy of immediate migration. In the years between 1300 and 1330, they began moving across Hudson Strait to the Ungava and Labrador peninsulas via Resolution Island and the Button Islands.[42] Climatic cooling in the early decades of the century, with consequent decreases in both marine and terrestrial food animals, was the most likely 'push' factor behind the southward move. The reappearance of Greenland right whales on the north Labrador coast at precisely that time[43] may have served as a 'pull' factor in determining the destination.

Labrador Inuit histories speak of what happened when the indigenous Dorset of north Labrador realized that their control of resources was being challenged by newcomers. They tell of wars, exterminations, and dispersions of Tunit (Dorset) communities.[44] The archaeological record is less clear. Some Dorset may have fled to the interior of Ungava Peninsula, while others may have attempted to move south, to be met and stopped by other aboriginal groups determined to hold their territory. On the east coast of Ungava Bay, a number of fourteenth- and fifteenth-century sites contain both Dorset and Thule ruins and artifacts, suggesting some kind of coexistence for a time before the disappearance of Dorset people as a group, perhaps by assimilation into Thule society. A few sites are identifiably Dorset, showing no signs of a Thule presence. The west coast of Ungava Bay was almost entirely unoccupied at the time of the Thule arrival, and subsequent Thule communities there show no signs of Dorset co-occupation or cultural influence. Nowhere in Ungava Bay did Thule and their Historic Inuit descendants build on the ruins of older Dorset sites,[45] suggesting that the two groups had different ideas of what constituted a good residential site.

Along Hudson Strait west of Ungava Bay, a few sites were occupied simultaneously by both Dorset and Thule, as happened on the east coast of Ungava Bay, which again indicates coexistence in mixed Dorset-Thule communities. Some Thule villages here were built on the ruins of old Dorset ones, suggesting that both groups valued the same sites. It is not clear if Thule newcomers took over sites from which they had driven the former occupants, or whether they built their homes on sites that had already been abandoned. Still farther to the west along Hudson Strait and south along the east coast of Hudson Bay, Dorset communities existed as late as 1600, physically separated from, but contemporaneous with, Thule winter villages.[46]

While some communities became extinct, and others managed to survive through diversification or migration, there was also a general movement southward to areas where the seasonal balance between frozen and open oceans offered a more equitable distribution of food resources. The efforts of communities to adjust to local conditions, and their increasing separation and isolation from each other, fostered the emergence of territorial distinctiveness.[47]

Increasing diversity, however, did not mean that ancient trade and communications routes and networks were abandoned. In every village, anomalous objects and resources have been unearthed, confirming the movement of both raw materials and manufactured goods over long distances. For instance, one item in an indigenous trade, which predates both Dorset and Thule occupations, was Ramah chert* from the Saglek Bay region in extreme northeastern Labrador. It was traded at least as early as 2500 BCE, as far south as Maine.[48] It continued to be an item in Inuit trade well into the nineteenth century.

---

*Ramah chert, also known as hornstone, is a flint-like quartz occurring in layers, and therefore easily split or flaked. Because it has a high silicon content, it can be honed into particularly sharp edges.

Because many metals are site-specific, it has been possible to trace copper and iron items found in archaeological sites in the Canadian arctic back to their points of origin. From Dorset times to the twentieth century, native copper from the Coppermine River-Coronation Gulf region was traded east to Boothia Peninsula and Hudson Bay, northeast to Cornwallis Island, Somerset and Ellesmere islands, north across the gulf to Victoria Island, and west to the Mackenzie River delta. Some meteoritic iron artifacts found in arctic sites can only have come from the Melville Bay-Cape York region of northern Greenland, where an ancient meteor shower had deposited some fifty-eight tonnes of iron over an area of about 130 square kilometres. Cape York iron discovered near Chesterfield Inlet was probably moved through an ancient trade route that connected northern Greenland with the west coast of Hudson Bay, via Ellesmere Island, north Baffin Island, and Melville Peninsula.[49]

Many arctic artifacts were also created from European and Siberian metals. The most obvious source of European metal after 1200 was Greenland, where Thule people obtained metals through trade with the Norse colonies, or took it from abandoned Norse sites. A Norse copper pendant found in a Dorset site on the east coast of Hudson Bay may have arrived there with Norse visitors to the area, but it is more likely the amulet was moved between its points of origin and destination through an ancient trade route leading from the Norse landfalls on the Labrador coast, across or around Ungava Peninsula. After 1500, Greenlanders began to acquire metal articles from the more frequent visits of Basque, Danish, Dutch, French, Portuguese, and Spanish whalers. Some vessels, particularly the Portuguese, explored Hudson Strait and may actually have entered Hudson Bay.[50]

Both meteoritic and European iron from Greenland were traded from Ellesmere Island to Somerset Island and Boothia Peninsula, and from there east to Hudson Bay and west to the Coppermine River. Iron was also moved from Ellesmere Island to north Baffin Island and the Melville Peninsula, and from there southward along the west coast of Hudson Bay.[51]

Other iron items were of Siberian origin, carried across Bering Strait to North America at least a thousand years before the Thule replaced their Dorset predecessors. Siberian iron has been traced from the Amur River-Okhotsk Sea region to the west and north coasts of Alaska, and from there to the western edge of the Mackenzie River mouth, and to Banks and Victoria islands.[52] Iron goods manufactured in Siberia, along with raw materials, continued to be important trade items until the Soviet government put a stop to trans-Bering travel in the 1930s.

The presence of iron bars and dart heads, metal needles, and copper brow ornaments among the people of south Baffin Island in the late sixteenth century indicates trading activities between regions. George Best, who sailed into Frobisher Bay with Martin Frobisher in 1576, gathered some information about trade in southeastern Baffin Island: "They trade with some other people for such things as their miserable country does not provide....They also told us that they had seen gold and bright metal plates which were used as ornaments among some people with whom they trade."[53]

Travel and exchange of goods within each of the two major trade networks, Siberia-Alaska-central arctic and Greenland-central arctic, continued into the seventeenth century, when goods were being exchanged where the trade networks intersected along the shores of Coronation Gulf. As the seal-hunting communities of the gulf became extinct or migrated to more favourable areas in the late seventeenth century, the connections between Alaskan villages and the people of the central arctic collapsed.[54] However, within each of the two trading spheres, which together encompassed roughly half the circumpolar world, many smaller trade networks continued to operate at regional and local levels. While social and cultural change was always present within the Thule region, the persistence of trading relations between regions helped to maintain the similarities and continuities evident within indigenous arctic societies over long periods.

Just as the descendants of Arctic Small Tool tradition people created the new culture we call Dorset, the direct descendants of Thule people created new ways of earning a living and organizing communities, suited to the environmental conditions of the Little Ice Age. By the beginning of the sixteenth century, they had become the Historic Inuit. Centuries of adaptation to local conditions had resulted in groups of people who were socially and culturally different from their biological ancestors and, in varying degrees, from each other. Because whale were less abundant, and available only in some seasons, Thule people in Coronation Gulf, Boothia and Melville peninsulas, and northern Baffin Island made major changes in their subsistence economies soon after their first arrival in the areas.[55] They created new techniques and equipment appropriate to fishing and terrestrial hunting in the new lands, and, in some areas, learned and adapted Dorset technologies. Communities that could no longer depend on deep-water whaling ceased to build sea-going kayaks and umiaks, and replaced them with smaller coast and river kayaks. In places where hunters needed to be highly mobile in order to find food resources, people less often built permanent winter houses of sod, stone, and baleen, replacing them with summer skin tents and winter snowhouses.[56]

Southeastern Baffin Island, which had been wholly or partly abandoned during the sudden cooling of the 1300s,[57] was well populated again by 1550. People lived much as their Thule ancestors had done, depending mainly on whale for subsistence, and duplicating many of the technological and social features of their Thule forefathers.[58] They maintained permanent year-round villages, moving to other sites only briefly to harvest resources needed for clothing and tool manufacture, or to find food resources to add variety to their diet. In the early sixteenth century, the people of southeastern Baffin Island were competent caribou hunters as well as skilled whalers. Because of their efficient use of two major food resources, they were able to maintain some of the largest populations in the eastern arctic.[59]

Village sites were selected on the basis of particular local conditions. Archaeological examinations on Cumberland Peninsula have found that nearly all late-Thule villages were located on beaches sheltered from sea winds by islands or opposite shores. Most were nestled under the sheltered side of a hill where heat loss is significantly less than on the windward side. Over eighty percent faced either south or west.[60]

Observing conditions in 1576 and 1577, British mariner George Best understood the rationality of Inuit preference for south-facing villages 500 years before it was noted in the literature of scientific archaeology. Describing Frobisher Bay and south Baffin Island, he wrote: "The north side of the strait is less mountainous and snow-covered than the south and is more richly clothed with grass. This may be caused by the fact that the south side receives all the snow that the cold winds and piercing airs bring out of the north, while the northern shore receives warm blasts of milder air from the south. This may also be the reason that the natives are more plentiful along the north shore than along the south, as was suggested by our experience."[61]

The same conditions dictated the route sailing ships took through Hudson Strait from the first decade of the 1700s to the 1900s; the "warm blasts of milder air from the south" hastened the melting of winter ice on the north side of the strait, opening a passage through which ships could more quickly and safely reach Hudson Bay. The London headquarters of the Hudson's Bay Company cautioned its sailing captains, year after year for at least two centuries, to cling to the north side of the strait, out of the way of the fast ice and floes that choked the southern side.

Ice conditions were also a critical factor in the selection of Thule and Inuit village sites because of their role in resource availability. Expanses of smooth, thick ice that form along more or less straight coastlines provide easy winter travel conditions, but their very thickness and the absence of patches of open water make them unsuitable as living and denning areas for seal and walrus. Preferred village sites were along the deeply indented coasts where there were more food animals.

The communities of Cumberland Peninsula on the east coast of Baffin Island were clustered within three or four regions, each region centring on a bay, fjord, or inlet, and separated from other regions by mountains, headlands, and straight coasts. Each cluster consisted of two or three villages at any one time. With increasing latitude, villages were fewer, farther apart, and had smaller populations.[62]

Once again, George Best noted the preference of Baffin Islanders for the more southerly regions, and related it to the presence of more abundant food resources in the south. "This whole stretch of coast," he wrote, "seemed to be more fruitful and populous than any area we had yet explored, with better pasture and more deer, and more wild fowl.... There also [we] saw some of the larger boats of the country with twenty people in each."[63]

Excavated middens indicate that, until the second half of the sixteenth century, food supplies were adequate for the numbers of people.[64] Archaeologically speaking, food supplies are considered to have been adequate when middens contain animal parts that might have been used as food if there had been a shortage. In addition, the Baffin Island middens for the period contained game animal parts and bones that had been eaten by dogs, rather than by humans, suggesting that people were not suffering shortages, and there were no signs that the dogs were underfed or being used as food for people.

Mid-century, however, saw rapid and steady climatic deterioration as the already cold Pacific Climatic Episode of 1200 to 1550 gave way to the even colder Neo-Boreal Episode, popularly known as the Little Ice Age. It was a 300-year period (roughly 1550 to 1850) of general cooling throughout the northern hemisphere, as severe as any period since the end of the last great ice age. Within it were shorter periods of extremely cold winters, and summers that were warmer than usual in some times and places, and in others, unprecedentedly cold.

Overall cooling of arctic waters began about 1550, and the advancing polar ice pack forced the North Atlantic Current towards the south. In some parts of the northern oceans, temperatures fell after 1550 and average air temperatures were colder by as much as three degrees Celsius from their previous levels.[65] There were years when the polar pack ice around the islands north of Lancaster Sound did not break up. Glaciers expanded in Greenland, Baffin Island, and the high arctic islands. Glacial advance on Baffin Island was also significant.[66] The island's alpine topography and the large body of polar water to the east combined to produce greater precipitation, lower temperatures, and higher winds than were experienced in other parts of the arctic.[67] Permanent ice spread over major portions of the island, destroying lichens and grasses, and, as grazing lands disappeared, the size of caribou herds declined.

Like the Little Optimum, the Little Ice Age was global. Glaciers advanced in the European alps, in Scandinavia, and on the islands of the North Atlantic. By 1600 barley could no longer be grown in Iceland, and northern European grape harvests were the latest in either living or recorded memory. A general rise in wheat prices indicates to today's historians that harvests were reduced and cereal grains in short supply.[68] By the late 1600s polar water had spread across the Norwegian Sea and as far south as the Faeroe Islands, where, according to H.H. Lamb, "water temperatures prevailing about the Faeroe Islands presumably were on overall average 4° to 5° Celsius below the average of the last hundred years."[69]

In North America the resulting changes in the extent and thickness of pack ice throughout the arctic had major effects on wildlife resources necessary for human subsistence. Seal and walrus habitats shifted away from the coasts, whale migration routes were drastically changed, and in many places whales disappeared altogether,[70] leaving whale-hunting peoples with greatly reduced access to food, and technologies that were suddenly obsolete. During the 1600s whale refuse in many Baffin Island middens decreased steadily,[71] and many coastal winter villages were abandoned, suggesting lower human populations and possible extinctions of small societies in marginal areas.[72]

Communities transformed their social organizations, as well as their subsistence economies, to meet their changing situations, replacing social institutions that were no longer appropriate with systems that increased their chances of survival. The permanent, coastal, winter settlements characteristic of the Thule began to disappear as people became more mobile, harvesting larger territories in smaller groups. House ruins suggest that snowhouses were used more often, possibly by large groups spending the winters seal hunting on the ice. Increasing cultural variation is highly evident in the archaeological records of the Little Ice Age, suggesting that communications among groups were becoming more difficult.

All natural environments, to some extent, constrain the behaviour of the groups within them, creating problems of uncertainty and scarcity. Because of their dependence on the seasonal movements of whale, caribou, fish, seal, and walrus, arctic communities have always experienced periods of short-term scarcity and coped with it in various ways: by moving season-ally between resource areas; by division and dispersion of communities during certain periods of the year; by storing food supplies in different parts of their territory for use during times of game scarcity; and by con-trolling human population numbers. The Little Ice Age, however, brought conditions that could not be met adequately by existing strategies.

Unlike periods of short-term scarcity, which arctic peoples were well able to handle, the Little Ice Age was a time when resources were scarce over the long term. Environmental conditions seriously jeopardized the continued existence of many communities. Societies faced with long-term shortages of resources such that members cannot maintain acceptable stand-ards of living, or such that life itself is threatened, must take action to in-crease their access to needed supplies, or die.

Perhaps the most immediate response to scarcity is to increase produc-tion within the home territory through intensified effort.[73] However, there are limits both to the amount of effort an individual or group can make, and to the extent of the available resources. When either of those limits is reached, other alternatives have to be considered. Intensification of effort is essentially a short-term strategy, which will not solve problems posed by long-term disappearance of resources.

Another strategy that might be used by a community is to lay claim to the resources of other areas. Trade, expansion, migration, and war are all potentially effective strategies toward that end, and each has costs and limi-tations. Trade is a successful solution to scarcity of some resources only when each party to the trade has sufficient surplus resources of the type needed or desired by the other party. When both parties have the same resources and neither party has a surplus, trade ceases to be an effective solution.

Expansion of territory has different costs and consequences, depending on whether neighbouring lands are unoccupied or are already being used by other human groups. Assuming that neighbouring territory is unoccu-pied and has resources worth harvesting, intensification of effort is only the first of the costs that must be considered in expanding into new territory. The investment of additional time, energy, and equipment necessary for the travel and transportation required to harvest larger territories and dis-tribute its products may prove prohibitive. When scarcity is long-term, sepa-ration and dispersion of a fragment from the parent group may become permanent.[74] In such an event, the costs in terms of cultural loss may be high. Even more expensive complications appear when the new territory is already occupied, particularly if the inhabitants are also facing environmentally imposed pressures.

Yet another option is abandonment of a resource-poor territory and relocation to one that offers increased ability to satisfy subsistence needs. But, like the expansion alternative, migration is an effective solution only if the new territory has adequate supplies of the needed resources and is unoccupied, or relatively empty.

War is a particularly expensive alternative as a means of gaining needed resources or access to them, whether of the one-time raid or long-term sustained variety. It requires capital investment in material; it involves major expenditures of time and energy taken away from hunting and production; it jeopardizes future trade alliances and transit agreements; it can lead to blood feuds and revenge situations that put future generations at risk; and it carries heavy emotional costs, particularly when small neighbouring societies are involved, because it may require the killing of kin and other known individuals. The costs of war also include the loss of warriors who are hunters, of the elderly on whose wisdom and experience the group's success depends, and of craftswomen who process the raw products of animals into usable items. Finally, war may imperil the very existence of the group if losses are great enough to reduce the fertile adult population below the levels needed for effective reproduction, as can easily happen in societies of fewer than twenty adults.

All these strategies—intensification of labour, trade, long-distance harvesting, extension of territory, relocation, and pre-emption of lands and resources through war—may be the means by which communities can gain access to new resources. War is also a means of protecting scarce resources from outsiders.

2.

Strangers Are Necessarily Hostile: War and the Protection of Resources, 1550–1670

Nothing is more ingrained in the real Eskimo and nothing pervades more thoroughly his traditions and folklore than the idea that strangers are necessarily hostile and treacherous.[1]

Southeast Baffin Island

Around 1550, communities at Frobisher Bay began to make changes in their subsistence economies, diet, demographic distribution, and architecture. Like other Thule whale-hunting peoples across the arctic, they had until then lived in mainly sedentary villages.[2] As the Little Ice Age settled in and whale resources declined, they became more mobile, harvesting a greater variety of resources at different places. Increasingly, they spent their summers in portable skin houses more suited to frequent moves than were the stone-sod-whalebone houses typical of whale-hunting people.

In the 1570s several communities occupied the shores of Frobisher Bay. One, at Hall Island, had a population of about fifty people in 1576. Another village, in which there were at least eighteen adult males[3] and possibly a total population of fifty souls, was on the south side of the bay. For at least a generation, they had been pressed by climatic deterioration and decreasing food resources.

During the third week of July 1576, members of the community on Hall Island encountered Europeans, probably for the first time. The strangers were the crew of the English vessel *Gabriel*, commanded by Martin

Frobisher, seeking a northwest passage from the Atlantic Ocean to Asia. The local people watched as nine of the strangers rowed ashore and climbed to the highest point on the island. Some of the watchers, keeping their bodies low and hidden, moved closer, but they had left seven of their skin boats on the beach, and Frobisher's people saw them from their vantage point at the top of the hill.

The cautious approach was interpreted by Lieutenant George Best, Frobisher's second in command, as an attempt at ambush. The villagers, he wrote, "sneaked through the rocks ... [and] ... almost cut him [Frobisher] off from his boat."[4] Communicating with gestures, the local people and the visitors arranged to meet on the beach, where Frobisher ceremoniously presented each person with a metal needle. Again through gestures, the two groups agreed (or so the Englishmen thought) that one of the Inuit would board *Gabriel*, provided two sailors were left on shore to guarantee his safe return. When the man was escorted safely back to the beach after his visit to the ship, his compatriots became more trusting, and nineteen individuals went on board.[5] They "exchanged coats of seal skins and bear skins and similar objects, for bells, looking-glasses and other toys."[6]*

The next day, probably July 20, a Hall Islander was again a guest on *Gabriel*, where Frobisher gave him gifts of a bell and a knife.[7] Five crewmen volunteered to carry the guest back to shore in the ship's boat. Still somewhat wary, Frobisher ordered his men to avoid the village, where they would be greatly outnumbered, and to deliver their passenger to an empty beach within sight of *Gabriel*. The excited sailors ignored the order, rowed around a point of land in the direction of the village, and disappeared from the ship's view. They did not return, that day, during the light hours of night, or the next morning.

On July 21 Frobisher began to search for them, and in the following days tried to negotiate for their return. The local people avoided the searchers, refusing all communication. By offering a variety of gifts, Frobisher enticed one man in his kayak within reach of *Gabriel*, where one of the sailors was able to "pluck him out of the sea by main force, boat and all, and into the ship."[8] An attempt to get the missing sailors back through an exchange

---

*In seventeenth-century English usage, a "toy" was a small item without much practical use, a luxury item valued for recreation, ornamentation, and other frivolous pursuits. Toys, not being intended for serious purposes, were "thynges unseemly for menne to use," but were considered suitable as gifts for women and children. Such classification is, of course, culture-specific. What an Englishman might classify as a "toy" might have been recognized by Inuit as a useful and desirable object that could ease labour, enhance productivity, and increase the chances of survival.

of hostages failed; the Inuit refused to respond to all further overtures. With his crew reduced by five, the expedition's only boat gone, ice closing in around them, and the weather daily becoming colder and windier, Frobisher decided to return to England without having learned the fate of the missing men.

Nearly 300 years after George Best wrote his account, the Inuit of Cornelius Grinnell Bay told a story that may be the sequel to Best's account. "Five white men were captured by Innuit people at the time of the appearance of the ships a great many years ago … [they] wintered on shore … they lived among the Innuits ... they afterward built an oomien (large boat) … they succeeded in getting into open water, and away they went, which was the last seen or heard of them."[9]

Frobisher's captive, a "strange infidel, whose like was never seen, read, nor heard of before, and whose language was neither known nor understood of any,"[10] survived the journey to England, but fell ill soon after arriving in London. Frobisher's backers, the Cathay Company, spent £1/10/6 for his food, lodgings, and medical care. In spite of the ministrations of the "apothecary … and folk hired to tend him," the man died. A further £5 was paid to the surgeon who performed an autopsy and embalmed the corpse, and 11 shillings, 4 pence was spent on a coffin and a grave in Saint Olave's churchyard in London's Hart Street.[11]

A year later, on July 19, 1577, the Hall Island community witnessed the arrival of a second Frobisher expedition, this time consisting of three sailing ships—the 200-tonne *Aid*, and two thirty-tonne barks, *Gabriel* and *Michael*. The purpose of the new expedition was to fill the ships' holds with the 'gold' that Frobisher believed lay on the surface of an island he named Countess of Warwick's Island. The three ships together carried close to 150 men of all ranks, including mariners to sail the ships, miners to dig the gold, and soldiers to protect them. The watchers made no attempt to come upon the strangers unawares, as they had done the year before. Instead, after watching the newcomers erect a cairn on Mount Warwick, the highest point of the island, and kneel briefly around a flag before marching to their boats drawn up on the beach, the islanders hurried to the top of the hill and, with loud cries and waving of flags, attracted the attention of the marchers. Communicating with gestures, the parties arranged for two unarmed emissaries from each group to meet and exchange gifts. The two Inuit brought a bow case for each English ambassador, along with some other "lesser things," and the Englishmen brought pins and needles and other small items. All efforts on the part of Frobisher and his men to get information about the five lost sailors of the previous year failed. Each side invited the other to join the larger group, but as George Best, Frobisher's lieutenant, put it, "Neither party trusted the other enough to visit them in their own territory."[12]

However, one of the Inuit, whose name has been recorded sometimes as Kalicho and other times as Calicough, was soon to be an unwilling visitor in the others' 'territory'. Kalicho and one companion, using gestures, requested a meeting with two of the Englishmen. Frobisher and Christopher Hall, master of *Aid*, responded and, during the meeting, tried to seize the other two, who fought back "with great fury and desperation." In response to Frobisher's cries for assistance, one of the English mariners managed to grab Kalicho and pull him on board *Aid*.[13]

Kalicho gave every appearance of cooperation. During explorations of nearby islands, he demonstrated the methods by which his people harnessed and trained dogs, and explained the use of "some sleds, bridles, fish-skin kettles, bone knives, and other things belonging to the people of the country."[14] When shown a drawing of the Inuit hostage taken the year before, he apparently tried to give information about the five sailors who had been captured, but the expedition members could not understand his efforts.

While Kalicho was becoming acquainted with the crew of *Aid*, residents of a village at Jackman's Sound on the other side of the bay were alarmed by the appearance of *Michael* and *Gabriel* on their shore. They hastily abandoned their tents to withdraw a short distance inland. In one of the tents they left "a doublet of canvas that was made in the English fashion, a shirt, a girdle, and three shoes for contrary feet and of different sizes." The doublet was "full of holes that had been made with their arrows or darts." Sailors from the two ships found the items and identified them as the property of the five sailors captured a year earlier. Thirty or forty officers and soldiers formed a plan to approach the village in two parties, one from the land and one from the sea, and to "entrap or entice the people" into giving information on the fate of the missing Englishmen.[15]

While the Englishmen were regrouping, the owners of the tents returned and began moving their belongings inland. The English land party came upon them unexpectedly, and the entire population of between sixteen and eighteen villagers raced for the coast, where they put to sea in two skin boats. If it had been their intention to escape from the English explorers, their plan failed. The seaward end of the channel was blocked by the English sea party, and the Jackman Sound people were forced back to the point of land. They pulled their boats up onto the beach, then turned to their pursuers and tried to hold them off with a rain of arrows. "That point has since been named Bloody Point because of the slaughter that occurred there that day," wrote George Best.[16]

The residents of the country fought to the death, shooting their own arrows, and also snatching up those fired at them and sending them back against the English sailors. Some of the wounded ended their own lives by leaping into the sea. Altogether, five or six of them died; the rest escaped, except for a woman who could not outrun her pursuers because of the child she carried on her back. The woman was taken with her baby, a boy estimated to be about a year old, across the bay to the site of the mining operation, called Kodlurnan Island by the local people and Countess of Warwick's Island by Frobisher. Expedition members thought the mother's name was Ignorth, also spelled Egnock in some contemporary documents. Either could be a phonetic rendering of the Inuktitut word *arna*, which means "woman." Similarly, the two versions of the child's name that appear in contemporary documents, Nutaaq and Nutioc, could be renderings of *nutaraq*, the Inuit word for "baby." On the other hand, both Arna and Nutaraq are also common Inuit personal names.

When Ignorth was presented to Kalicho, the two behaved in a manner that the English thought indicated they had not previously known one another, which suggests they were members of different communities that did not meet at social gatherings during the year. They did, however, live amicably and chastely together on the ship, comforting and caring for each other.

Their people did not let them go easily. On August 6 a number of Inuit, identified by the mariners as those who had been involved in the recent battle on the south coast of the bay, appeared at the mining site on Kodlurnan Island. Their gestures were interpreted as requests for the return of Ignorth and Nutaaq. Kalicho was the interpreter in the parley that followed. The English asked for the return of their five missing sailors, or for some information concerning their fate, and offered in return the freedom of Kalicho, Ignorth, and Nutaaq, along with handsome gifts and treaties of friendship for all their people. No memoirs exist to tell what Kalicho and Ignorth might have made of the proceedings, or what information Kalicho intended to convey to Frobisher. George Best believed that the Inuit promised to return in three days, either with the captured sailors or with news of them.[17]

Over the next few days, Kalicho's signs and gestures convinced Frobisher that a great chieftain named Catchoe (or, perhaps, Kajjuk, a common name among Inuit, which means "projectile") would soon arrive, prepared for war. Frobisher believed "these strange people to be of countenance and conversation proceeding of a nature given to fierceness and rapine [i.e., theft]."[18] He took the precautions he thought necessary to protect his men and property, ordering the construction of fortifications around the camp and setting additional watchmen.[19]

Between August 11 and 14, increasing numbers of Inuit gathered around the English camp, for the most part hiding among the rocks. Occasionally they showed themselves. On August 11, twenty "lined up in plain sight on the top of a hill, holding their hands over their heads and dancing and singing with great gusto." On August 14 they appeared again, and "made a great noise and waved a white flag made of bladders sewn together." Catchoe finally arrived and with him a "great multitude of them creeping among the rocks."[20]

George Best described the events that followed. For a week, or perhaps longer, Frobisher's men had not hunted or fished for fear of the watching natives. Nor had the watchers been willing to trade food in exchange for the knives, nails, and other items they had previously been anxious to obtain. Catchoe's first tactic was to invite the tired and hungry Englishmen to come to his camp for food and sleep. When they refused, he called one of his men out from a hiding place among the rocks. The man, who appeared to be lame, limped across the beach for some distance, and was then lifted up by Catchoe and carried to the water's edge. It was only with difficulty that Frobisher prevented his men from going ashore, but he did give permission for one of his archers to shoot at the 'lame' individual, who immediately leaped to his feet and, with no trace of his former limp, "darted behind a rock."[21] "Then his companions, who had been hidden among the rocks, suddenly came forward to continue the skirmish with their slings, bows, and arrows, dashing fiercely to the very edge of the water. They followed us along the coast in complete desperation, and totally without fear of our arrows or anything else.... These natives had been lying in wait for us all along the coast and, being spread out like that, were not easy to count, but we could see over 100 of them, and had reason to suspect that a greater number were present."[22]

For another week, the Englishmen remained on the island, winding up the mining operations and loading their ships. All the while they maintained careful watch, remaining close to their fortifications and within reach of armed soldiers. On August 21 the miners finished their work and two days later the ships sailed for home.

Kalicho and Ignorth, having made several attempts to escape while the expedition's ships were near the coasts of their own country, were carefully guarded and they, along with the child Nutaaq, were carried to Bristol aboard *Aid*. Both adults died during the first week of November and were buried at Saint Stephen's Church, Bristol. The baby Nutaaq, in the care of a nurse, was sent to London, where he was to be taken under the queen's protection. However, he fell ill along the way and died before reaching the court. He was buried at Saint Olave's Church in Hart Street,[23] in the same graveyard that held the body of his countryman, captured and taken to England the previous year.

In the summer of 1578, for the third year in a row, the people of Frobisher Bay saw the arrival of foreign sailing ships, fifteen of them this time. They kept their distance, watching the activities of the strangers, but avoiding contact. George Best noted that from time to time "a company of seven or eight boats ... [was seen] acting as though it intended to attack," but the people never came near, nor did they call to the strangers or ask for a meeting, as they had done in the previous two years. The visitors, still interested in a meeting, had few opportunities to suggest one. On August 15 Edward Fenton, captain of *Gabriel* in 1577 and of *Judith* in 1578, spotted two men in kayaks. Hoping to open negotiations with them, he ordered his men "not to make any shouts or cries at them" for fear of scaring them away and, with Captain Yorke of *Thomas Allen*, went a mile up the beach, where they showed themselves and "offered them trafique and showe of all the courtesie we could devise." The natives responded by "rowinge verie swiftlie" away.[24]

On August 23, four or five umiaks appeared in Beare Sound, where *Salmon* and *Thomas of Ipswich* had been loading ore. When Captain Randel of *Salmon* went to report the sighting, Frobisher censured him for having left the two ships unguarded.[25] The two men in kayaks seen earlier by captains Fenton and Yorke had not frightened the Englishmen, but the presence of four or five umiaks with a possible sixty or more people on board created considerable anxiety.

Two themes stand out in the stories of meetings between the people of Frobisher Bay and intruders in the 1570s: mistrust of strangers on the part of the islanders and willingness to fight. The responses of the Hall Island people to the appearance of strangers in 1576 were, first, cautious observation, then careful approach, which may or may not have been a failed attempt at ambush, as the English observers believed, then an exchange of hostages, a willingness to meet, accept gifts, and trade, followed by the taking of five prisoners and a boat in what the visitors regarded as an unprovoked act of ill will.

During the 1577 encounter, the sequence of events was initially the same: Inuit first watched from behind a shield of rocks and hills, then opened negotiations by hailing the visitors, and, finally, suggested a meeting of emissaries, during which gifts were exchanged. Whatever they had planned as their next move was pre-empted by the capture of Kalicho. After the discovery of clothing that apparently had belonged to the sailors captured the year before, the Inuit seized the offensive. Five or six of them died, and two more of their number, Ignorth and Nutaaq, were taken prisoner. Their response was to muster their ranks under the leader Catchoe, refusing all overtures to trade and denying the visitors opportunities to go ashore for food and water. When more than a hundred Inuit had assembled, they opened fire with a rain of arrows.

In the third year, 1578, residents and strangers alike showed extreme wariness. Although they watched from a distance, the Inuit avoided face-to-face meetings. George Best thought a fighting force was gathering, but violence did not erupt and the expedition's ships sailed for home with a full complement of men.

The next meeting between east-coast Baffinlanders and Englishmen for which there are written records took place seven years later. On July 29, 1585, the inhabitants of a village in Cumberland Sound, north of Frobisher Bay, watched two ships, the barks *Sunneshine* and *Mooneshine* under the command of John Davis, drop anchor in their harbour. The residents hurried to greet the visitors. When Davis ordered his musicians to play, "they [the Inuit] tooke great delight, and fals a dauncing."[26] The next morning, thirty men in kayaks paddled out to the ships for some brisk trading. The local people showed marked preference for trade items of wood and metal. After a week of amicable relations, during which the English party explored the nearby shores and islands, they left to continue explorations to the north.

Between August 11 and August 26, *Sunneshine* and *Mooneshine* were back in Cumberland Sound, but the people of the sound were occupied elsewhere. Davis and his party examined a number of villages and camps but saw no people. In the villages they found the heads of three recently killed "beasts," a number of tame dogs with collars, and some sleds, one made of "furre, spruce, and oaken boards," the other of baleen.[27] The boards could have come from one of the Basque, Portuguese, or Dutch vessels beginning to frequent Davis Strait,[28] or they could have been of English origin, having been left in Frobisher Bay by the expeditions of 1576 to 1578.

At the same place the next year, eighteen people were on the beach when Davis arrived for his second visit, this time with only one ship, *Mooneshine*. They greeted the Englishmen "with great joy ... dauncing and leaping; and [making] signes [that] they knew all those that had beene there the year before." Davis presented each man with a knife, refusing their offer of skins in exchange. On the second day of the reunion, trade between the two groups was lively, and fifty people joined a party from the ships in games of jumping and wrestling on the beach.[29]

Some of the local inhabitants acted as guides while Davis examined their tent villages, discovering both black and red copper, evidence that they conducted trade with other communities. It was during this period of close and friendly companionship that Davis noticed and commented on the number and nature of the wounds and scars visible on some of the local men, and suggested they must be at "warre with some other Nation or Inland people for many of them are wounded."[30]

Relations between the natives and the explorers soon soured as the people began to take iron and wooden objects from the ship, including oars, a spear, and a sword, even cutting pieces from the ship's cables and liberating a boat from the stern. In spite of Davis's protests, and what he thought were their promises to reform, they seized an anchor and began pitching stones into the ship with slings. After another round of protests, presents, and promises, they mounted a new attack against the ship, striking *Mooneshine*'s bosun with stones from their slings and knocking him to the deck. At the next truce talk, Davis took a hostage to ensure their good behaviour. When the wind rose and the ship had to move quickly into deeper waters, the hostage became a captive.[31]

After leaving Cumberland Sound, Davis took *Mooneshine* south and on August 20 made a landfall at Cape Chidley on the mainland promontory at the entrance to Hudson Strait and Ungava Bay. Five of *Mooneshine*'s sailors went ashore to dry fish, unaware that "the Countrey people lay lurking in the wood." The local people offered a decidedly unfriendly greeting. John Janes, keeping the ship's diary for Davis, wrote that they "on a sudden assaulted them. They slew 2, and greatly wounded other 2; one escaped by swimming, with an arrow shot through his arme."[32]

In 1587, when Davis arrived for the third time in Cumberland Sound, this time on board *Ellen*, the local people were anxious to trade and had firm ideas about what they wanted. One man refused all items of trade "until he saw a knife, and then he truckt [bartered]." Others were willing to trade anything they had for "a Knife, a Naile or a Bracelet"; in short, for metal. On one of their visits to the ship, the local people destroyed a little prefabricated pinnace, which the sailors were putting together for use as an inshore exploration boat. Davis was convinced the attack on the little vessel was motivated by desire for the iron in its construction, rather than by any desire to harm the visitors.[33]

Neither Davis nor Janes took any kind of census. They did mention numbers of Inuit watercraft, but like many later visitors they did not distinguish between kayaks with their one male occupant, and umiaks, which could hold twenty individuals or more and were usually rowed by women. In 1585, on Davis's second day at anchor, thirty "canoes" surrounded his ships; in 1586, there were fifty "canoes."[34] If by "canoes," Davis and Janes meant kayaks only, then the total population of the area in either year could have been anywhere from 100 to 200. Davis's (or Janes's) canoe-counts, on their own, are not very useful for estimating populations. They do, however, fit well with other observations. Archaeological investigations in Baffin Island, and particularly in the Cumberland Peninsula region, have suggested two things about the size and placement of Thule villages: one, that each was probably occupied by about fifty people; and two, that they occurred in clusters of three or four villages, separated from other clusters by topographical barriers. Davis's (or Janes's) canoe counts indicate that in the 1585 and 1586 visits they met with beween 100 and 200 people from two, three, or four villages within one region.

Labrador and Hudson Strait

During the two decades after Davis's visits, increasing numbers of French, Portuguese, Dutch, and Danish vessels fished and hunted in the waters east of Baffin Island and in Hudson Strait. Their interest was in harvesting the resources of the ocean, particularly cod, and if they went ashore at all, their visits were infrequent and brief. The climatic conditions of the period, which pushed the large whales out of reach of Inuit hunters, also forced European whalers to hunt in the open sea.[35] It is unlikely they introduced European goods into Inuit societies, and archaeological investigations in the Cumberland Sound region have not found evidence of pre-nineteenth-century contact between local inhabitants and whaling ships.

In 1606 Inuit at Cape Grimington, on the Labrador coast between Cape Chidley and Saglek Bay, carried out the kind of ambush George Best had feared at Frobisher Bay in 1576. That year, Captain John Knight in *Hopewell*, in a search for the elusive northwest passage, missed the entrance to Hudson Strait and made landfall at Cape Grimington.[36] Not having seen any evidence of villages or inhabitants along the coast, Knight and five others went ashore about mid-morning on June 26. As soon as they were out of sight of the ship, they realized they were not alone. The Inuit response to Knight's incursion into their territory was immediate and violent. As Frobisher's five sailors had disappeared, so also did Knight and his men. After keeping watch through the day and night, Knight's next in command, Oliver Brownel (or Brunel), sent out a series of search parties. They found no traces of Knight and the others, and had to cease their efforts when "they were assaulted by the salvages."[37] On his return to England, Brownel described the final encounter. "On Saturday, the 28th [of June 1606], while the crew were pumping out and repairing the ship, a crowd of natives came over the hill and seized the boat. [The English] were but eight men and a great dog; but when the natives saw them resolutely against them, the dog being foremost, they ran away. They numbered about fifty men."[38]

Five years later, an incident in northeastern Hudson Bay had several of the elements that characterized earlier encounters between arctic people and European visitors. On July 28, 1611, the inhabitants of Digges Island made friendly overtures to a ship that sailed into their harbour. It was Henry Hudson's *Discovery*, in the hands of mutineers who had set their captain adrift in the bay that bears his name. The Digges Island people, after arranging for an exchange of hostages, accompanied the strangers on a bird-hunting expedition. When the parties came together again, the inhabitants "made great joy, with dancing, leaping, and striking of their breasts, they offered divers things."[39] There followed some mild trade, and the parties separated.

The next day, they met again on the beach. "The people were on the hills dancing and leaping ... and every one had something in his hand to barter."[40] Five of the sailors went ashore, unarmed and unwary, carrying looking-glasses, harps, bells, and bottles to trade. The sixth sailor, Abacuck Prickett, having a lame leg, stayed in the boat, where he was suddenly attacked. Writing of himself in the third person, Prickett described what followed.

> Suddenly hee [that is, Prickett] sawe the leggs and feete of a man by him ... with his knife in his hand, who stroke at his Brest over his head; hee casting up his arme to save his brest, the Savage wounded his arme, and stroke him into the body under his right Pape; the Salvage stroke a second blow ... and then stroke him into the right thigh, and had like to have cut off his little finger of his left hand.... Whilst he was thus assaulted in the Boat, their men were set upon on the shore. John Thomas and William Wilson had their bowells cut; and Michael Pierce and Henry Greene, being mortally wounded, came tumbling in to the Boat together. When Andrew Moter saw this medley, hee came running down the Rock and leaped into the Sea, and so swam to the Boat, and hung at her sterne.... The Salvages betake them to their Bowes and Arrowes, which they sent

so amongst them that Henry Greene was slain outright, and Michael Pierce received many wounds, and so did the rest.... Pricket received a cruel wound on his back with an Arrow.... That day dyed Wilson.... Michael Pierce lived two dayes and then dyed.[41]

A year later, in 1612, the people of Digges Island reacted in almost identical fashion when two ships commanded by Thomas Button appeared, and a party of sailors rowed ashore to hunt birds. One of the ships was *Discovery* and two of its crew members, Abacuck Prickett and Robert Bylot, had been aboard during its first visit to the island a year earlier. The new encounter was as sudden and as bloody as the attack of the previous year. Between seventy and eighty of the local people attacked the bird hunters from hiding places on the rocky beach. The shore party escaped to the boat and safety. Some failure of observation and understanding led them to make an ill-advised second sortie to the island in search of fresh water. The Inuit, again watching from the shelter of rocks, attacked and killed five of the strangers before they were able to reach the security of their vessels.[42]

An entirely different strategy for dealing with strangers was used by the people of the Lower Savage Islands in 1615 and 1619. In 1615 the forty or so inhabitants of one village withdrew to some place of safety when they saw *Discovery*, now commanded by Robert Bylot, anchor in their harbour. They left behind and unprotected five tents, several canoes, and about three dozen dogs, probably representing the greater part of their total wealth. Fourteen of the men took up a station in a large boat, a short distance from shore and out of sight of the foreign ship, but allowed themselves to be seen by Bylot and his shore party of seven. They responded with "signes of friendship" when Bylot called out to them using a few words in the Greenlandic dialect, but did not come any closer.[43] Bylot's use of some Greenlandic words may have been significant in the brief encounter.

In 1619 inhabitants of the Lower Savage Islands, possibly but not necessarily the same as those who had seen Bylot's ship four years earlier, responded in similar fashion to the appearance of two sailing ships. Their village was empty when Danish explorer Jens Munk examined it, but the people were not far away. Some of them let themselves be seen on the opposite side of the harbour, and watched as Munk and his oarsmen drew near. In full view of the approaching strangers, the Inuit laid down their weapons and stood back from them. Munk inspected the weapons, left them lying on the ground, and laid out knives "and all sorts of other iron goods," which the Inuit took, leaving fowl and seal meat in their place.[44]

Patterns of behaviour are discernible in the encounters between Inuit and strangers described above. Local inhabitants watched from the cover of rocks and hills for varying periods of time. About half the groups opened negotiations by letting themselves be seen or by hailing the newcomers, always from a safe distance. The first meeting was between emissaries of each group, and usually included formal greetings and exchanges of gifts, followed by trading and, to use Captain John Davis's word, "merrymaking." On at least two occasions, at Hall Island in 1575 and at Digges Island in 1611, initial encounters involved an exchange of hostages between the parties.

At every meeting the Inuit took possession of desirable goods, in trade, as gifts, or through pilferage. Of the ten violent encounters, at least six—the taking of five captives from Frobisher's party in 1576, the attack on Davis's ship in Cumberland Sound in 1586, the sudden assault on Davis's shore party near Ungava Bay in 1586, the kidnapping and probable killing of John Knight and his men at Cape Grimington, and the two assaults at Digges Island in 1611 and 1612—were apparently unprovoked attacks of local people against strangers. In each case the attackers gained metal or wooden items. The fight at Jackman Sound in 1577 appears to have been an accident, unplanned by either side, and sparked by the nervous tensions of two groups, each desperately afraid of the other. Following the discovery of the cast-off clothing of the missing sailors, the crews of *Michael* and *Gabriel* were on edge, experiencing anger and possibly a desire to avenge their kidnapped colleagues, and fear of the local people they believed capable of murder. Equally, the Inuit may well have been apprehensive that a revenge strike might be launched against them. The destruction of Davis's tiny coastal boat at Cumberland Sound a decade later may have been, as Davis himself explained, motivated by "love of the Iron" rather than by any desire to harm the visitors.[45] In each of the violent encounters, the Inuit outnumbered the visitors.

Only three encounters were without violence or threats of violence: the first meeting with Davis in 1585 in Cumberland Sound; and the two encounters at the Lower Savage Islands, with Bylot in 1615, and with Munk in 1619. In each of these incidents, the Inuit were greatly outnumbered.

The Purposes and Conditions of Arctic Warfare

Except for the European explorers' accounts of hostile encounters with Inuit in the far eastern arctic, there are no descriptions, and very little non-documentary evidence, of the frequency, nature, or causes of hostilities between Inuit communities, or between them and their non-Inuit neighbours prior to 1620. The quick resort to violence against outsiders, apparent in events in Baffin Island and the north Labrador coast between 1576 and 1612, was, however, a feature of Eskimo* life in Alaska and Bering Strait during the same period. A brief description of war activities among Alaskans may cast some light on the purposes and conditions of violent hostilities in central and eastern arctic communities of the time.

During the seventeenth century, western arctic societies met more frequently in war than in trade.[46] Raids for the purpose of taking captives occurred between groups from both sides of Bering Strait, and almost continuous warfare existed between Eskimo nations and neighbouring Athapaskans in North America. A long series of bitter hostilities accompanied the expansion of the Tlingit (Pacific northwest coastal people, living in the southeastern Alaska panhandle) to the north and west, during which the Eskimo were displaced from their former territories.[47] According to Eskimo accounts, "material gain and territorial expansion were motives in addition to prestige and plain hatred."[48]

Enmity also existed between compatriot groups in Alaska. Long-standing hostile relations among the Yup'ik of southwestern Alaska in the late sixteenth and early seventeenth centuries have been well documented. The eleven Yup'ik bands known by name during the period were split into two factions. The members of each faction maintained military alliances in order to mount offensives against other factions, and to provide each other with mutual defense when attacked.[49]

Descriptions of warfare between Yup'ik and Inupiat (northern Alaska Eskimo) contain all the elements noted by George Best, Oliver Brownel, Abacuck Prickett, and other eyewitnesses in the eastern arctic: the surprise raid as a first strategy; the firefight, or "rain of arrows," in open battle; and the use of bludgeoning and cutting weapons in one-on-one combat to the death.[50] Battle tactics were similar on both sides of Bering Strait. Attackers relied on the element of surprise to destroy their enemies, entering a village or camp when everyone was asleep or gathered together in the community house, sealing the doors, and then shooting arrows through the smoke holes until all were dead.[51] Descriptions of the eastern arctic encounters from 1576 to 1612 do not include any incidents of precisely this kind, but, according to George Best, the Baffin Islanders several times attempted to approach the strangers from behind and in secret.

---

*Alaskan indigenous peoples use the terms "Eskimo" and "Eskimoan," and specifically reject the use of "Inuit" as an ethnic identifier. See Appendix 1 on indigenous ethnic identifiers.

The rain of arrows was a widespread military tactic among Alaskan Eskimo,[52] although it was seldom seen among North America's non-Eskimoan indigenous peoples. The people of Frobisher Bay used the strategy against Frobisher's men twice in 1577: at Jackman Sound in the Bloody Point battle; and at Kodlurnan Island when a large force under Catchoe appeared on the beach. Because they understood the principle of firing by volleys, the winners tended to be those who had the most archers and the most arrows.

When the rain of arrows did not destroy the opposing force, attackers resorted to teasing the enemy, calling out insults, laughing at them, and offering some of their force as easy targets, in the hope the enemy would waste its arrows. The tactic was known among the Alaskans as *qarzuigutsaq*.[53] A similar goading tactic was part of the incident of the pretended lame man during the final confrontation between Baffin Islanders, under the leadership of Catchoe, and Frobisher's people in 1577.

The immediate objective of Alaskan Eskimo warfare was complete destruction of the enemy, including all men, women, and children. Sometimes one person might be left alive to inform other groups of the attack and its outcome, thereby spreading terror among other potential enemies. Alaskan Eskimo seldom took prisoners. On the few occasions when captives were taken, they were kept alive in order to carry booty, or, in the case of female prisoners, to cook and sew on the journey home. They were put to death when their usefulness was over. It was not uncommon for captured women to be tortured before being killed. "Among the Yup'ik, mutilation of enemy bodies was common, although not inevitable. [Severing] the heads and genitals of the corpses … might have been related to the Yup'ik belief that to finally kill an opponent, especially one believed to have supernatural powers, the victor must sever the body of the vanquished at the joints."[54] Asian Eskimo tended to take more prisoners, nearly always women who were later sold as slaves.[55]

The Yup'ik publicized their victories by tattooing their bodies; a man with many tattooed lines across his forehead was easily identifiable as a great warrior who had killed many enemies. The practice also occurred among Canadian Inuit until less than a century ago. In Hudson Strait communities in the late nineteenth and early twentieth centuries, Inuit men known to have committed murders kept track of the number of their victims by tattooing lines on their foreheads.[56]

For the vanquished, surrender was not an option, because of the practice of not taking prisoners. The apparent determination of the Baffin Islanders at Bloody Point in 1577 to fight to the death, and their suicidal leaps into the sea when the battle turned against them, may have been the result of belief that capture would inevitably lead to an even more painful death.

In the eastern arctic incidents between 1575 and 1612, Inuit did not attack the four parties of strangers that had superior numbers. Alaskan Eskimo are also known to have attacked only when they held the numerical advantage. When they were outnumbered, their usual response was to flee.[57] Withdrawal of forces in the face of superior numbers, however, did not mean that a planned attack was permanently aborted. In such situations, the usual practice was to send out a call for more men so as to outnumber the enemy. Alliances with other groups, often arranged well in advance of a planned attack, gave a community intent on war the ability to recruit the necessary manpower.[58] Parallels from Frobisher Bay are the mustering of forces under Catchoe's leadership in 1577 and the steady build-up of armed Inuit in 1578.

While violence in interpersonal relations within discrete Eskimo societies has long been recognized, the common and widespread perception is that Eskimo and Historic Inuit were a peaceable people, among whom war was unknown.[59] The perception is part of a larger view that non-state societies were and are always peaceful societies, a bias especially dear to social theorists in state societies. Lawrence H. Keeley has pointed out that, in the view of some social scientists, "real war is motived by economic and political goals, whereas primitive conflict is directed only toward fulfilling the personal and psychological aims of individual warriors (such as revenge or prestige)."[60] Others have noted that war has been defined in ways that stipulate the existence of sovereign states, professional armies, training and mobilization of forces, and long-term planning of strategies and logistics, in varying degrees.[61] The bias of many (perhaps even most) Euro-American ethnologists that 'real war' does not occur between extended-family, face-to-face societies is reflected in their choice of terms. By defining war as an activity of state societies, and rejecting the words "war" and "warfare" in connection with small, non-state societies, they have no choice but to assign the extra-communal violence of non-state societies to the categories of blood feud or murder. Keeley made much the same point when he recognized that "armed conflict between social units does not necessarily disappear at the lowest levels of social integration; often it is *just terminologically disguised* as feuding or homicide" [emphasis added].[62]

The assumption of many social theorists that certain conditions—a state society, professional armies, training, and long-term planning—are necessary to true warfare implies that small societies, which are perceived as more or less consensual and without government and political leadership, engage in blood feuds and seek revenge, but do not and cannot engage in war. The assumption is wrong. The societies of Frobisher Bay in the 1570s were not state societies as generally defined, but they did have a well-trained militia, a designated military leader, a method for mustering and mobilizing forces, and strategies and tactics agreed upon in advance of the emergency they faced. The definition of true war as an activity of state societies fails: it does not look closely at the hard evidence from archaeology and ethnography, in part because it depends on (false) assumptions about leadership, government, access to resources, and national boundaries in non-state societies; it arises out of circular reasoning; and it overlooks the question of societal sanction.

Blood feuds and revenge killings undertaken by individuals or groups for personal, family, or clan reasons, both within a community or against another community, may be accepted to some degree by the rest of the society. Inuit communities sometimes ignored feuds at the personal level unless or until they threatened to endanger the group as a whole. At that point, the community took steps to end disharmony by separating the participants from each other or from the social unit, or, in cases of extreme disruption in community life, by executing the perpetrators. As long as blood feuds and revenge killings are perceived as sub-cultural, that is, as private and personal acts that do not have whole-community sanction, they cannot be considered war.

On the other hand, violent acts against outsiders with the explicit or implicit approval of the social unit are war, regardless of the size of the social unit or its form of government. A definition of war suggested by R. Brian Ferguson allows for the occurrence of warring conditions in small societies. "[War is] organized, purposeful group action, directed against another group that may or may not be organized for similar action, involving the actual or potential application of lethal force."[63]

"Purposeful group action" implies that acts of war are sanctioned by the group as a whole, even if the group is small by Asian and European standards, and even if there is a dissenting minority. When blood feuds and revenge killings against outsiders are part of hostile relations approved by the social group in general, they are war.

As arctic studies in the last twenty years have shown, there are no grounds for denying the existence of Eskimo, Thule, and Historic Inuit warfare.[64] Five hundred years before the events of 1576, war was an element, along with assimilation and expulsion, in the Thule takeover of the arctic coasts and islands from Alaska to Greenland. The outcome of that invasion was the virtual disappearance of the Dorset (Tunit) people. In western and northern Alaska, Eskimo wars were an integral part of relations among communities, and declined only gradually in the century that followed the first Russian arrivals in the 1750s. A long list of Alaskan Eskimo material and linguistic artifacts testifies to planned, persistent, violent confrontation: battle armour made of bone and ivory plates; a battlefield littered with hundreds of skeletons;[65] the custom of referring to people from neighbouring villages as "attackers," which antedates the arrival of Russian traders in the 1750s and continues to the present; battle arrowheads deliberately fractured during production in order to cause more damage to the enemy's body than would ordinary hunting arrowheads; and the existence of a special vocabulary for weapons intended for use against human beings, not animals.[66] A carved ivory bow drill found in northern Baffin Island depicts a battle scene in which confronting groups of men are exchanging arrow fire,[67] and suggests that Inuit archers in battle formation were not unknown among Baffin Islanders. Finally, Inuit histories and European observers have identified many specific occasions of war.

Theories about the nature, causes, and conditions of war are even more numerous and various than the definitions of war. General theories of causation have been summarized by Marvin Harris and R. Brian Ferguson: war diverts humanity's innate killer instincts away from the social unit onto foreigners; war creates group identity; war preserves the group's biological integrity by eliminating reproductive rivals; war affirms personal and group superiority, and satisfies the human desire for prestige and admiration; war is a means of expanding territory and expropriating resources; war is a means of regulating population size; war satisfies personal and group honour by avenging past wrongs.[68] At some time or another, social theorists have advanced almost every imaginable psychological, sexual, biological, social, political, and ideological reason to explain why war exists.

Most of the above have been suggested as reasons for particular arctic wars in the few recent studies that recognize the existence of Eskimo and Inuit warfare. The fear of strangers has been suggested as an additional reason. Just as the myth of the peaceable Eskimo and Inuit has become solidly entrenched in the popular imaginations of both Inuit and non-Inuit today, so has the myth of the ever-friendly Inuit welcoming all and sundry to his house. The evidence suggests otherwise. All Eskimo and Inuit societies have shown intense fear of strangers, who were always assumed to be enemies.[69] In the words of Vilhjalmur Stefansson, "nothing is more ingrained in the real Eskimo and nothing pervades more thoroughly his traditions and folklore than the idea that strangers are necessarily hostile and treacherous. Every Eskimo group always believes that wicked Eskimos are to be found on the other side of the mountains or down the coast at a distance."[70]

An analysis of Franz Boas's collection of folktales "shows that over 70% of encounters with strangers involve murder, evil spirits, monstrous people or some other fearful event."[71] In Inuit folklore from all parts of the arctic, strangers nearly always have evil intentions. An attitude of deep and fearful suspicion towards strangers was deliberately inculcated in all individuals through education and reinforced by experience.

Inuit may have been hostile toward Europeans in the late sixteenth and early seventeenth centuries because of their preconceived assumptions that all strangers had evil intentions, or from experiences with murderers and kidnappers. They may have interpreted some innocent actions and attributes as threats. The relatively large numbers of people on board foreign vessels, for example, may have been seen as menacing. Eskimo and Inuit attitudes about women's roles in war may also have played a part in their responses to foreigners. The absence of women on the European ships may have been interpreted as evidence that the newcomers were not on a peaceful mission. While Netsilik and Keewatin coast women acted as first contacts, decoys, information gatherers, and sometimes as fighters,[72] there is no evidence they were active participants in the hostilities faced by Frobisher, Davis, Prickett, and others in the eastern arctic. Among Alaskan Eskimo, women were never belligerents, at least in theory,[73] although, considering their fate as slaves and sacrificial victims if captured, they surely had a stake in helping their communities to resist attackers.

In other instances, the actions of strangers were obviously provocative. The crews of many European whalers and fishing vessels behaved toward aboriginal peoples in ways that could only arouse fear, hatred, and desire for revenge on the part of their victims. European governments, for the most part, judged the kidnappings to be criminal and immoral. In 1720 the States General of the United Provinces of The Netherlands adopted a resolution banning the kidnapping and transporting of Greenlanders to Europe. In 1732 Denmark followed the Dutch lead with a Royal Proclamation against bringing any Greenlanders, either hostages or willing travellers, to Denmark.[74]

Greenlandic oral histories recorded by missionaries in the 1740s and 1750s include stories of attacks by ships, probably Basque, against both Norse and indigenous communities in the fifteenth to seventeenth centuries. One of them, preserved in the legislative records of The Netherlands, gives details of the 1654 kidnapping of three women. When the Greenlandic histories became known in Europe, governments whose whaling fleets frequented Davis Strait made new attempts to control the behaviour of mariners overseas. In Denmark the 1732 Proclamation was reissued in 1758 and 1776, and, before the end of the 1760s, The Netherlands States General had issued a new decree prohibiting attacks on, and ill treatment of, Greenlanders.[75] For Greenlanders and other North American aboriginal peoples, however, the unenforceable prohibitions of European states were no protection and no comfort when individual captains and crews flouted the instructions of distant governments.

The explanation that war affirms personal and group superiority, and satisfies the human desire for prestige and admiration, is unsatisfactory in an Inuit context. In the small, relatively egalitarian societies of the eastern arctic in the sixteenth and seventeenth centuries, the war hero could not have expected to satisfy his material or psychological needs any better than other members of the society, although the best procurer of resources could. Among Inuit, male prestige depended on how effectively a man brought home needed resources, not on how many enemies he destroyed. Most of the time, procurement could be achieved more easily, safely, and cheaply through successful hunting, stealing, or scavenging, than by war. In cases where resources could be obtained only through war, the successful warrior would still be acclaimed for his ability to gain access to necessary resources, rather than for his prowess at killing the enemy. In situations where the goal was to protect resources from direct threats by outsiders, the individual who killed the most enemies or planned a successful strategy would be highly valued by his community, but adulation would last only as long as he continued to defend communal resources. A war leader could not expect to benefit materially by getting better access to, or a greater share of, communal stores. His value to the community, and therefore the prestige accorded him, would still depend on his skills of procurement.

The explanation that wars are fought in order to affirm group superiority does not fit arctic circumstances. All available evidence supports the conclusion that the goal of Eskimo and Historic Inuit warfare was complete annihilation of the enemy.[76] Since nobody would be left to recognize the pre-eminence of the victorious group, it is difficult to see how violence against neighbours could have enhanced either individual or group longings for prestige in an Inuit context.

War as a means of regulating population size also fails as an explanation upon examination of its consequences. If women were the main casualties in war, the argument would make sense, because it is women's reproductive limits that determine population size, not men's. The loss of male warriors will not affect population growth as long as one male is left alive, potent, and fertile. On the contrary, among Eskimo and Inuit, it is in the group's interest to prevent the best warriors from going to war whenever possible because their loss as hunters would seriously undermine the group's chances of survival. In the context of the hostilities in Frobisher Bay between 1576 and 1578, any problems of overpopulation would not have had to await an unpredictable chance meeting with Europeans to find a solution.

The theory that wars are fought for the purpose of preserving the group's biological integrity by eliminating reproductive rivals has put the cart before the horse. Given the annihilative character of Eskimo and Inuit warfare, biological integrity of the victors could well be the result of war, but it is not likely to be the cause. Also, given the flexibility of Inuit group membership and the ease with which individuals adopted, and adapted to, new community affiliations, ethnic purity does not seem to have been an Inuit ideological imperative. Insistence on complete destruction of opponents is more logically understood as the means of avoiding hereditary bad relations, which have to be paid for in the next generation.

War to provide an outlet for innate aggressive instincts is also a questionable theory when the costs and benefits are weighed. As Marvin Harris has pointed out,[77] in conditions of stress from overpopulation and decreasing resources, war may help to divert anger and aggression away from the group, but the theory does not explain why the costs of war would be lower than the costs of minimal group solidarity or even contained violence within the group.

The same reasoning undermines the notion that war creates group identity. A sense of belonging, and the ability to recognize and distinguish between insiders and outsiders, can be inculcated in group members at much less cost through enculturative and educational means than through warfare. War is not an effective means of creating group identity; it is more likely to be the other way around—a pre-existing sense of group identity may result in the establishment and maintenance of boundaries, and the protection of boundaries may lead to war.[78] In any case, as already noted, Historic Inuit did not define their group identity through biology; group membership was a matter of residence and choice, rather than genetics.

Boundaries exist in order to include group members and exclude strangers, and this, in turn, implies that it is in the group's best interests to exclude outsiders. The question that arises is: What interests are protected by the creation and maintenance of boundaries that identify insiders and outsiders? One such interest would be the ideological one of preserving specific and unique cultural traits; another is the protection of resources.

Raids and warring activities in Baffin Island between 1576 and 1612 were unlikely to have been undertaken for ideological reasons. At that time, Baffin Islanders could have had no reason to fear that contact with others, either their indigenous neighbours or the visitors who suddenly appeared on their coasts, would undermine their cultural or ethnic traditions. They did know that an increase in the number of people dependent on the land's material resources, or a decrease in the quantities of those resources, would have serious negative effects on their ability to survive. The available evidence suggests they were determined to protect their resources against expropriation by newcomers, to get new resources, and to gain access to new resources. Examination of other seventeenth-century incidents when Inuit used violence against strangers and outsiders confirms that in the majority of cases they acted in order to gain material benefits or to protect their resources.

Confrontations between Athapaskans and Inuit were common all along their shared frontier, the central Canadian transitional forest that separates the barren grounds from the wooded lands to the south. It is impossible to estimate the time-depth of the hostilities. At the western edge of the barren grounds, the Coppermine River Inuit were involved in uneasy trading and warring relations with Chipewyan peoples living to the south of them at least as early as the seventeenth century.

While the Chipewyan often explained the hostilities as resistance to the Inuit use of witchcraft to bring down disease and death on their communities, Inuit motives were more clearly rooted in economics. Hostilities were common at resource sites such as the lower Coppermine River, where outcroppings of surficial copper attracted both peoples, and the stone quarry near Peel River, where battles were fought as both Inuit and Athapaskan tried to secure their own rights of access and to prevent its use by other groups. Trading relations between Inuit and Gwich'in (formerly called Kutchin, an Athapaskan group whose easternmost territory was just south of the Mackenzie River delta, where they competed with arctic coast Inuit for resources) were another frequent locus for conflict.[79] In all situations, Inuit stood to gain access to resources if they were victorious.

Almost nothing is known about the relations of Inuit communities with one another in the eastern arctic in the sixteenth and seventeenth centuries. Only one contemporary observer, John Davis, suggested that hostility existed between groups when he concluded that they were at "warre with some other Nation or Inland people for many of them are wounded."[80] While Davis's comment and the known actions of natives in southeast Baffin Island and Hudson Bay suggest they may have been involved in warfare in defense of existing resources and in attempts to gain access to new resources, there is no other evidence to support or deny an assumption of war between indigenous groups in that area. Intramural warfare in protection of resources did, however, take place elsewhere, most notably in Alaska, where Yup'ik and other Eskimo nations were at war for over a century in protection of their territories and resources.[81]

The hostility of eastern arctic Inuit communities to strangers in the late sixteenth and early seventeenth centuries may have had roots in their historical experiences or have been related to their views of the world, as general theories of the causes of war suggest. However, the explanation which best fits eastern arctic conditions in the period from 1576 to 1670, borne out by descriptions left by observers, is that people with serious concerns about diminishing food supplies were prepared to use force against newcomers for two reasons: the newcomers might turn out to be competitors for already scarce resources and any intended takeover on their part had to be discouraged; and the newcomers apparently had an abundance of the precious materials that would increase hunting efficiency, such as knives, other metals, and wood.

Most of the known incidents of Inuit attacks between 1576 and 1670 were against Europeans who were hunting or fishing in Inuit lands, and may be construed as pre-emptive strikes against competitors for resources. In all the incidents, the Inuit, if victorious, could reasonably have expected material gains, either directly through expropriation, as in the cases of Frobisher's lifeboat and Davis's pinnace, or indirectly by eliminating potential competition for scarce resources during a period of increasing shortages. Compared to the costs and rewards of migration or of raiding neighbouring communities, raids on unknown visitors were an inexpensive means of accomplishing economic goals, at least initially. They involved no significant investments of time and energy, and carried none of the emotional costs related to killing known individuals, or even distant compatriots.

There were also few social costs. From the local point of view, the foreigners were one-time visitors; attacking them would not lead to feuds and revenge wars lasting for generations. As far as the Inuit were concerned, Europeans were not in a position to deny them passage across territory to resource sites, or rights of access to shared resource sites, as a neighbouring community could do. Attacks on them did not involve breaking alliances and the subsequent destruction of partnerships, alienation of trade, and reduced access to spouses and adopted children. Not only were the costs of raiding Europeans considerably lower than the costs of attacking neighbouring communities, the rewards—metal and wood—were significantly higher.

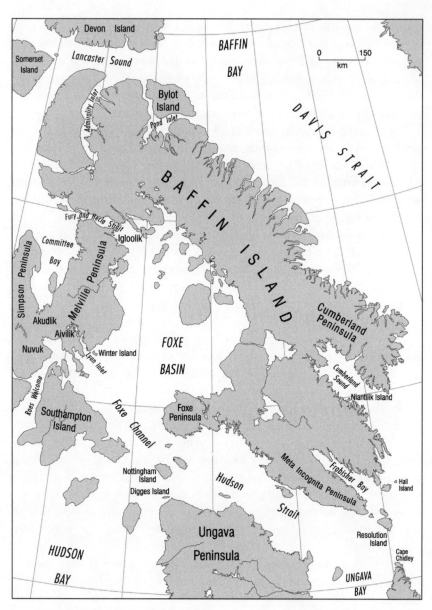

BAFFIN ISLAND AND FOXE BASIN

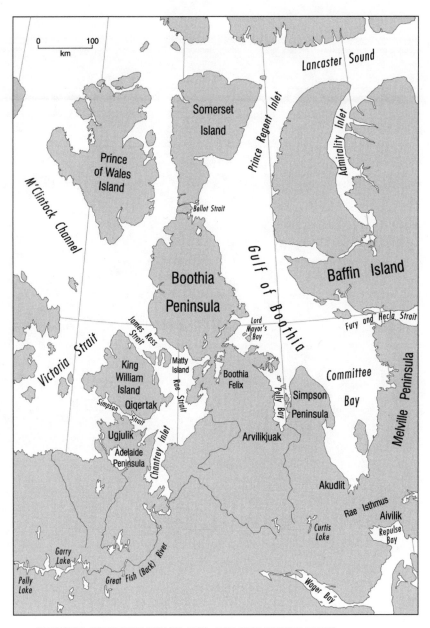

BOOTHIA, KING WILLIAM ISLAND, AND GREAT FISH RIVER

WEST HUDSON BAY

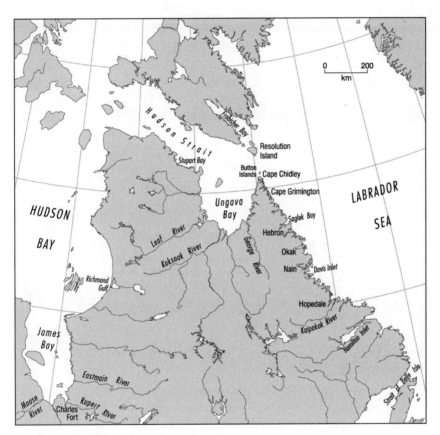

UNGAVA PENINSULA AND LABRADOR

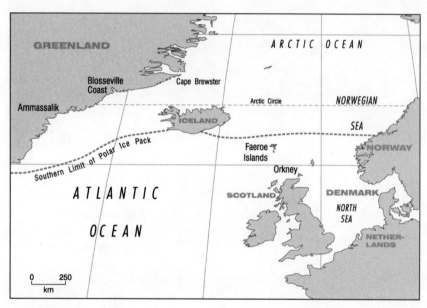

NORTH ATLANTIC

HUDSON STRAIT AND FROBISHER BAY

3.

Fear when Winter Comes: Migration and the Search for Resources, 1670-1700

There is fear when winter comes to the great world, And the great moon—now full moon, now new moon—follows its footprints in the winter night.

- Ulipshialuk's wife[1]

People in the lands around Frobisher Bay and Cumberland Sound in the first century or so of the Little Ice Age engaged in aggressive attacks and organized warfare against foreigners to gain or defend important, scarce resources. The costs of war were manageable because they were short-term; strangers who might turn out to be threats to local control of resources or who might be a source for new resources appeared only infrequently. In other places, however, the threats and the opportunities were more frequent, and repeated mobilization and active fighting were too costly to be resorted to on a continuous basis. Other, less costly, strategies were necessary to protect existing resources and to gain new ones.

The Labrador Inuit: Raids and Relocations

In the same years that Frobisher and Davis were leading the first British probes into the arctic, Inuit descendants of Thule who had left Baffin Island 250 years earlier were established in villages as far south as Hebron and Okak on the northern Labrador coast.[2] The same climatic cooling that had prompted the southward migration from Baffin Island had intensified by 1550, leaving the cod-fishing grounds of the eastern Atlantic seriously depleted. European fishing vessels were forced to venture farther and farther from their own coastal waters in search of needed food resources. By the mid-1500s about 350 European vessels,[3] mostly Basque, Portuguese, and French, were fishing the coasts of Newfoundland and Labrador every year. More and more frequently, Labrador Inuit saw strangers fishing off their coasts and drying fish at shore stations. They were well aware that increasing competition for resources could have dangerous consequences for them, but at the same time they recognized new opportunities to obtain scarce resources.

Initially, the people of the northern Labrador coast responded to the appearance of strangers with tactics similar to those of Baffin Islanders and Digges Islanders at about the same time. The attacks on the shore parties of John Davis at Cape Chidley in 1586 and of John Knight at Cape Grimington in 1606 are examples, as is the 1657 raid at Kaipokok River, when Inuit ambushed and killed the Huron soldiers guarding a French expedition heading for Hudson Bay under the command of Jean Bourdon.[4]

The attacks, like those in Frobisher Bay and Cumberland Sound, were ad hoc responses to the unexpected appearance of strangers, whether they were motivated by a perceived need to protect resources or to obtain them. Resources acquired from chance encounters were unpredictable, unrepeatable windfalls, which did not provide long-term solutions to long-term problems. Raids on European shore stations and depots were a more reliable means of obtaining scarce goods, and orderly and friendly trade was more reliable still, besides being much less dangerous.

It was probably no coincidence that small groups of northern Labrador people began to appear on the coast as far south as Hamilton Inlet shortly after 1550, immediately after the establishment of Basque whale fisheries there. By moving southward, Inuit traders and raiders put themselves into positions from which they could obtain much-desired European goods, the most popular items being wooden boats and all kinds of metals. Preferred targets were the deserted shore stations of seasonal European fishing and whaling concerns, and the preferred tactics were looting and destruction. Occupied fish-drying stages and onshore camps, as well as travelling parties, were sometimes attacked, but only when Inuit held the numerical advantage.

Southward movement continued during the next half-century or more.[5] At first it was intrusive, rather than expansive. Contemporary observers noted that Inuit were seen in larger numbers on the northern coast than in the south. John Knight's shore party at Cape Grimington in 1606, for instance, was attacked by an estimated fifty men, suggesting that a summer village of about 200 people was nearby. In more southerly locations only small groups of travellers were seen, such as the party of three—man, woman, and infant—that was killed or captured by a French crew in 1566.[6] None of the known accounts of meetings between Europeans and indigenous people reports the existence of permanent villages or of large numbers of people south of Okak.*

By about 1600, however, Inuit had established a permanent village at Eskimo Island in Hamilton Inlet, and between 1600 and 1630, they were making forays as far south as the Strait of Belle Isle, where French trading posts and settlements had begun to appear.[7] Samuel de Champlain described them as "impossible to make peace with ... as they go prowling about and making war." Their hostility toward French fishermen is not surprising in the light of Champlain's next comment. "They have killed a number of St. Malo men, who had previously often paid them back in double measure. The origin of this war was the killing—accidentally or otherwise—of the wife of a chief of that nation by one of the St. Malo sailors."[8]

Other Inuit at Belle Isle were peaceful family groups. A few may have been year-round residents, although there can never have been more than a few hundred individuals living permanently in the extreme south.[9] Most were itinerant families, travelling north or south along the coast. One such group was described by the priest, Antoine Silvy, who met travellers on the Belle Isle north coast in 1684, and recognized some whom he had met a year earlier at Nain. "We saw some Eskimos in canoes and with blunderbusses.... Among them were some of those whom we had seen the other year, one hundred and fifty leagues from there, on the coast of Labrador. This makes me think there are only a handful of people who extend along these fearful coasts."[10]

Summer trading with European crews and winter raiding of their empty shore stations were profitable activities for Labrador Inuit. By 1650 the people of Hamilton Inlet had European goods in such quantities and duplication that it is almost impossible to avoid the conclusion that some of them were middlemen who maintained depots of surplus goods for trading farther north. Inuit far distant from Hamilton Inlet were acquiring astonishing amounts of European goods. In 1683, near Nain, Chouart des

---

*Absence of evidence is not necessarily evidence of absence. Until a systematic search for Portuguese and French logs, diaries, and other accounts of the period has been made in European archives, it is impossible to say with certainty that no villages existed. The discovery of previously unknown documents and sites could alter the current understanding of Inuit activities on the Labrador coast.

Groseilliers and Pierre Radisson engaged in amicable trade with local people, a meeting profoundly different from the hostile one at Cape Grimington in 1606, which had resulted in the disappearance of John Knight and his men. Communities such as the one near Nain apparently recognized they stood to benefit more from peaceful relations and friendly trade with most Europeans than they did from violence and looting. In 1694 Louis Jolliet, exploring the coast as far north as Nain, noted European trade goods in all the villages along the way. The Inuit had "many articles of European manufacture, including wooden boats with sails and grapnels, barrels, sea chests, screws and nails, knives, cloth and various items of European clothing.... Some of it of Spanish origin."[11]

By 1700 the Labrador Inuit population had increased to six times what it had been two centuries earlier. Other demographic changes had also taken place during the intervening two centuries. Outer-island villages typical of the early period of Thule occupation had largely been abandoned in favour of settlements on the inner islands. The refuse dumps of the inner-island settlements show that caribou and freshwater fish were increasingly common supplements to the usual diet of seal and whale meat.[12] Increased harvesting of inland food resources opened the way to a wide range of material and intellectual changes: new hunting and fishing technology and techniques; new forms of transport appropriate to new terrains; increased access to and use of other inland resources, such as wood; the acquisition of new geographical, ethnological, and botanical information; the invention or adoption of vocabulary to identify previously unknown materials and landforms; changes in social organization appropriate to the occupation and use of larger, more diversified territories; and the incorporation of new spirits and deities into the existing worldview.

Movement inland and use of inland resources also increased the possibilities for confrontation with long-established inland groups. Unlike the communities of Baffin Island, the people of the Labrador coast and Ungava Peninsula shared frontiers with non-Eskimoan peoples, apparently not always peacefully. In the 1620s Samuel de Champlain noted "an Indian tribe inhabiting this territory, who call themselves Eskimos, and against whom the Tadoussac Indians go to war."[13] Jesuit accounts throughout the seventeenth century and Montagnais oral histories also describe unfriendly relations between Indian and Inuit. On the basis of observations and oral sources, Lucien Turner concluded "the prime cause of hostility was trespassing upon the hunting-grounds of each other, the Innuit asserting priority of right and endeavoring to repress the encroachment of the Naskopies. The usual mode of attack was from ambush, and by the attempted annihilation of the other party."[14]

While this accurately describes relations in the nineteenth century when Turner was in northern Labrador, it is impossible to say with certainty that it was true of the seventeenth century. However, it is reasonable to assume that competition for game resources in the barren grounds could have brought Inuit into conflict with their non–Eskimoan neighbours in the northern interior of Labrador-Quebec.

East Hudson Bay

Competition for resources may also have been the underlying reason for the violent encounters and lingering hostility between the Inuit of east Hudson Bay and their Lowland Cree neighbours in the seventeenth and eighteenth centuries. Cree oral histories recorded between 1670 and 1750 relate that in earlier times Inuit had occupied territories as far south as the Eastmain River at the bottom of James Bay, from which they had been driven north in a series of territorial wars with the Cree. The accounts suggest that Inuit and Cree met more frequently in hostile confrontations than in peaceful encounters.[15] No evidence indicates the time-depth of the Inuit occupation, or the period and length of Inuit-Cree conflict, but it was over by 1670. The first European eyewitnesses reported that the Inuit had been pushed north of Richmond Gulf, "so that a tract of land of more than three hundred miles extent from north to south, lies almost waste, without trade and without inhabitants."[16]

Inuit excursions against the Cree usurpers continued for a short time after the establishment of the first trading posts. An observer in the 1670s noted that the Inuit who lived "on the Borders of Hudson's Streights ... sometimes in slight Parties make Incursion on the other Indians, and, having knock'd 8 or 10 on the Head, return in Triumph."[17]

During the winter of 1673-74, they attacked the "Onanchanoes [near Moose River], most of that Nation being destroyed," and threatened a springtime attack against the "Cuscididah" Indians and the Hudson's Bay Company trading post at Rupert River. The traders "prepar'd every thing necessary in the Fort for Defence." The expected party of Inuit arrived in June and camped about a quarter of a mile from Charles Fort, but withdrew without attacking,[18] possibly because they were badly outnumbered by the combined forces of the well-fortified English and their Indian allies.

By the end of the century, Inuit had ceased to attack their Cree neighbours along the eastern Hudson Bay coast, and their threats against European traders and military personnel in Hudson Bay were ineffective. They had, however, gained a reputation as a "people [who] are so utterly savage and cruel that it is impossible to trade with them."[19] Their reputation for violence and fierce fighting also lived on in the memories of the Lowland Cree, whose raids against them continued for another hundred years. At Charles Fort in 1686, for instance, the Chevalier de Troyes met four James Bay Indians who were travelling north to make war on the Inuit.[20] Hudson's Bay Company journals for more than a century after 1670 contain frequent references to Indian war parties going north to attack Inuit.

West Hudson Bay Inuit and the Little Ice Age

On the west coast of the bay, Cree and Chipewyan had a long history of hostile relations, and both were also ancient enemies of the Inuit living north of them. Cree and Chipewyan histories recalled a time when Inuit had occupied the west coast of the bay as far south as Churchill, or even farther, and had been forced north only after a series of bitter wars.[21] Like the Lowland Cree histories from the east coast of the bay, the narratives did not suggest dates for the occupation, the wars, or the retreat, or elaborate on the causes of the conflict. Nevertheless, eighteenth-century European observers came to certain conclusions about the human history of Churchill River.

James Knight of the Hudson's Bay Company reported to his superiors in London in 1717 that "Eskimos" in large numbers frequented the Churchill River.[22] His claim was based solely on the existence of a large, and possibly old, tent village site, which is still visible, and which was Cree or Chipewyan, not Thule or Historic Inuit.

James Isham, writing his *Observations* in 1743 after nine years' residence in Hudson Bay, believed that "the Ehuskemay's, who before the English Setled here us'd frequently to come to Churchill River or Ehuskemay Point so Call'd, from their g'raves and mark's of the Dwellings, some of which are still Remaining."[23] Like James Knight, Isham cited the presence of old village sites at the Churchill River as the basis for his belief in a former Inuit occupation. Unlike Knight, he did not speculate as to the date of the occupation or the reasons for the withdrawal to the north, matters for which he had no evidence.

Joseph Robson, who worked at York Fort and Churchill River from 1733 to 1736 and 1744 to 1747, wrote a history that assumed a chronology and included an interpretation of events. "Churchill-river was much frequented by the Eskimaux before we settled there, the point on which the fort is built being called Eskimaux-point....They were at length forced to go farther northward, to Cape-Eskimaux and Whale-cove; and are now totally dispossessed of this retreat, by our making a settlement here, and drawing down the northern upland Indians to trade, whom also we have supplied with arms."[24]

Andrew Graham, a resident of Rupert's Land between 1749 and 1775, echoed Robson."Many of them [Eskimos] formerly resided upon Churchill River, but on the Company's building a Fort there, in the beginning of this present century, and the Indians resorting thither to trade, the Esquimaux retired farther to the north."[25]

Isham, Robson, and Graham did not state the sources of their information, who could have been Cree or Chipewyan, or Hudson's Bay Company personnel who had been told by local informants of the former Inuit occupation. While the fact of an earlier occupation is certainly accurate, the phrases "before the English Setled here," "before we settled there," and "formerly resided upon Churchill River" offer no clues as to the date of the earlier Inuit occupation. Europeans in Hudson Bay after 1670 believed that Inuit had lived in the vicinity of Churchill River within a generation, but that belief is not supported by Indian or Inuit oral histories, by archaeological evidence, or by any eyewitness testimony from the seventeenth century.

In giving a recent date to the former Inuit occupation, Knight, Robson, and Graham ignored the (arguably negative) evidence of a dozen European exploration parties, which had visited the west coast of the bay between 1612 and 1718 without seeing either inhabitants or signs of recent habitation. They also took no notice of evidence from Henry Kelsey and his Chipewyan companion in 1689, who, on their journey more than 450 kilometres north of Churchill, saw no Inuit and no signs of Inuit. On the contrary, the few items they found, including a canoe, were unquestionably of Chipewyan manufacture. Perhaps the most telling evidence for the absence of Inuit along the coast before 1717 came from knowledgeable Chipewyan hunters and travellers who used the region seasonally and knew it well. James Knight himself sketched a map of the coast from Churchill to Coppermine, according to their specifications. Along the coast appear the words "At this river the Usquemays begen." The "river" to which they refer, and which marks the southern limit of Inuit occupation, could be either Chesterfield Inlet or Wager Inlet. In either case, it is clear that Inuit did not inhabit Churchill's near north in 1717.[26]

Archaeological investigation supports Chipewyan memory with evidence of a Thule occupation as far south as the Churchill River, and puts the date between 1200 and 1450, with the Inuit withdrawal occurring between 1450 and 1500.[27] The southern occupation followed the climatic optimum during which Thule peoples expanded from Alaska to Greenland. The northward withdrawal took place at the end of the long period of climatic deterioration that culminated in the Little Ice Age.

In the two centuries or so after their retreat, that is, between about 1500 and 1700, Inuit were essentially absent from the coast south of Chesterfield Inlet. Their settlements in Keewatin were restricted to the Chesterfield Inlet-lower Thelon River axis.[28] Estimates of their numbers before about 1700 are highly speculative. Most living sites contain between one and three house ruins or tent rings, so it is probable that most communities consisted of no more than three or four nuclear families. It is impossible to know how many communities might have existed at any one time, how they were distributed, how often any one site was occupied, and whether seasonally or for longer periods. Given the steady drop in temperature, changes in wind patterns, the increased ice cover that affected the entire northern hemisphere, the inherent instability of the Keewatin climate, and the widespread famines described by early observers, there is a strong possibility that late Thule populations on the west bay coast were seriously reduced by starvation. The total population in the mid- to late 1600s probably did not exceed 100 individuals.[29]

Yet, after 1718, Inuit were present on the coast every summer as far south as Knapp's Bay. During most of the present century, their origins were one of the major problems of Inuit historiography, and a matter of considerable debate among arctic ethnologists and archaeologists. In two important studies, Ernest S. Burch[30] suggested that the sudden repeopling of the bay coast was connected to another problem of arctic historiography: the abrupt disappearance of a community or communities from Coronation Gulf. Burch's reconstruction of events, which links the abandonment of the Coronation Gulf south shore with the repeopling of west Hudson Bay, is speculative in some of its details, but overall it accounts for, and fits with, the known evidence from archaeological, documentary, linguistic, and environmental studies.

The Little Ice Age and the First Maunder Minimum

Much of the historical movement was affected by geographical conditions. A thousand or more years of gradual global warming, which had culminated in the Little Optimum, roughly 900 to 1250, began to reverse during the long, slow, sporadic cooling of the Pacific Climatic Episode (1250 to 1550). It was followed by the Neo-Boreal Climatic Episode. The Neo-Boreal, also known as the Little Ice Age, was a period of rapid and consistent cooling on a global scale. Environment-related famines and epidemics, and their demographic consequences, were facts of life and death in six-teenth- and seventeenth-century Europe as well as in North America.[31] At the onset of the Little Ice Age around 1550, the extending polar ice pack had already forced the North Atlantic Drift farther south than it had been since before 900, and its track had shifted from northeasterly to almost due easterly.[32] The storms that Martin Frobisher's expeditions encountered in southern Baffin Island and Hudson Strait in the 1570s were characteristic of deteriorating weather conditions. Decade by decade, the ice pack ex-tended southward, until by the 1580s, when John Davis visited Baffin Is-land and Labrador, Denmark Strait was filled with pack ice that cleared only occasionally.[33] In 1592 Pope Alexander VI noted that "at the ends of the Earth in Greenland ... extensive freezing of the water" made attempts to reach Greenland impossible.[34]

During the same half-century, changes in atmospheric circulation car-ried polar air masses to the south, replacing the prevailing westerlies with north winds. The effects were felt throughout the northern hemisphere, on both sides of the Atlantic, with disastrous results. In the winter of 1603-04, close to 9000 people died in Iceland from climate-related causes. In eastern North America during the hard winter of 1607-08, many deaths of both native Americans and Europeans were reported in the St Lawrence valley and parts of New England and the Maritimes.[35]

In Baffin Island's mountainous Cumberland Peninsula, extreme glacia-tion occurred after 1610, more severe than at any other time in the previ-ous millennium.[36] Jens Munk's passages through Hudson Strait and Hudson Bay to the Churchill River in 1619-20 took place during a period of brief, slightly milder summers, and probably would have been impossible a dec-ade earlier or later.

The slow and steady global cooling intensified between 1645 and 1715, during a period of reduced solar radiation known as the First Maunder Minimum.[37] Even colder episodes occurred within the Minimum because of a further reduction in solar radiation due to increased atmospheric dust following major volcanic eruptions in 1673 and 1693.[38] At New Severn River in 1674, John Oldmixon of the Hudson's Bay Company described the effects of the extreme cold on one local community, which caused "great Mortality among them, and several were starv'd to Death for want of food; this country being such a miserable Wilderness, that it affords not Sufficient Sustenance for the wretched Inhabitants."[39]

The suffering was not restricted to the North American arctic and subarctic; this climatic pessimum was global. In Europe, the summers of the 1680s and early 1690s were wet and cold, the 1690s being one of the coldest decades ever reported there. European statistics for the terrible winter of 1695 appeared in a German newspaper in 1702, with reports of severe famines in Scotland and Norway after massive crop failures. Figures for Estonia indicate that twenty percent of the population died during that one winter of starvation and famine-related disease. In Finland human losses amounted to over thirty percent of the population.[40] In the first decade of the next century, the cold destroyed the entire poultry population of northern France, and by 1709 the French people were suffering massive mortality from starvation and exposure.[41]

In the 1680s and 1690s, Iceland was almost continuously surrounded by heavy ice. By 1695 the influx of polar water had lowered the temperatures of the Norwegian and Iceland seas "an overall average 4° or 5° Celsius below the average of the [previous] hundred years."[42] The diary of Magnus Magnusson, an Icelandic farmer, confirms modern interpretations of ice conditions in the North Atlantic between 1673 and 1703. He noted that in 1695, ice along the west coast of Iceland lasted months longer than usual. "No one could remember such ice cover, nor had anyone heard of such ice from older people ... [people] also told of such a girth of ice in the sea round this country that ships could hardly reach the shore except in a small area in the south."[43]

Temperatures in the 1690s were even lower in North America. The Hudson Bay region experienced the coldest weather and greatest extent of sea ice of the entire century. By 1700 Baffin Island was seventy percent covered with snow and ice that did not melt during the summers, compared to permanent coverage of between two and three percent in the twentieth century.[44]

Increased precipitation, lower temperatures, thicker ice, greater snow cover, and the disappearance of some food resources are not necessarily threats to human existence. Human communities have always found ways to survive, even in apparently inhospitable environments. Change and changing conditions do not have to be life-threatening, if people can prepare for them. Unforeseen and unpredictable situations, on the other hand, pose major threats to human life.

Unstable physical environments carry high risks for most wildlife. In the North American arctic, caribou herds, migratory birds, and marine mammals are highly vulnerable to climatic fluctuations, even short-lived, apparently minor ones. One particularly cold or wet summer can cause high mortality among caribou calves, seriously depleting a herd; ice a mere two inches thicker than usual in one winter can depopulate a seal denning area for years; birds fighting unfavourable winds may not reach their accustomed nesting sites. Food resources become highly erratic in unstable environments, and the unpredictability of fluctuating environmental conditions increases the difficulties human beings face in planning for their subsistence needs.

Coronation Gulf Inuit: Relocation

Like societies almost everywhere in the northern hemisphere during the First Maunder Minimum, a community or communities in Coronation Gulf on the arctic coast faced a potentially life-threatening environmental crisis as the caribou herds and seal populations, which were their major food resources, became increasingly inaccessible.

Coronation Gulf was one of the least welcoming of the new environments into which the first Thule moved during their eastward expansion out of Alaska between the eleventh and thirteenth centuries. They found local conditions very different from those on the Alaskan shore of the Beaufort Sea. Whale and walrus did not flourish in the shallow, enclosed waters of the central arctic. The first Thule immigrants had to adapt old technologies and techniques, or develop new ones, to take best advantage of local resources. Limited resources harvested during the short summer season had to be stored in sufficient quantities to carry the communities through the long winter, and required the development of highly efficient storage technologies.[45]

Around the middle of the seventeenth century, the already precarious existence of Coronation Gulf communities was severely threatened by the climatic changes of the First Maunder Minimum. Shorter, cooler summers, longer, colder winters, and increasingly thicker and longer-lasting ice further reduced the already scarce resources. The rare beluga whales disappeared, the caribou herds of Victoria and Banks islands and the mainland coast dwindled, and the ringed seals extended their winter range, making them more difficult to find and kill.[46]

Environmental constraints of the magnitude posed by the onset of the Neo-Boreal Climatic Episode around 1550 and the First Maunder Minimum after 1645 are forcing factors for economic and social change, and set limits to what human beings can do, although they do not compel particular human responses. People who are faced with the disappearance of major subsistence resources can choose from a number of possible responses: they may attempt to increase food-gathering efficiency through greater effort, through increased mobility, through development of new technologies, or through increased use of alternative food resources; they may attempt to exploit larger territories through expansion or by import strategies such as trade and long-distance harvesting; they may attempt to claim the resources of other groups through war, trade, alliance, or changes in group membership; they may migrate to richer resource areas; they may accept a reduction of the population to the minimum level at which the social unit can be maintained, or to a level at which the social unit is extinguished and the survivors seek refuge with more affluent neighbouring groups; or any combination of the above, or other, strategies.[47]

Most of the options were not available to the people of Coronation Gulf in 1650. Increased hunting efficiency through intensification of effort or new technologies may have been tried, but it could have had only short-term and limited success in a situation where the fundamental problem was long-term disappearance of major resources. Increased use of alternative food resources was not a possibility because all food resources were threatened or increasingly inaccessible. Importation of resources by trade requires surpluses in the hands of both trading partners, which was not the case on the arctic coast. Acquisition through long-distance harvesting is a highly expensive alternative, costly in terms of travel time and of time taken away from subsistence hunting. It also carries with it the possibility of conflict with neighbouring groups who are themselves experiencing long-term shortages. For a community of 100 or 200 individuals, the time and energy costs of long-distance harvesting or procurement of necessary resources through raiding can prove prohibitive.

Nothing indicates that Coronation Gulf communities experienced widespread extinctions, or annihilative warfare, or that they dispersed and joined neighbouring communities. Archaeological evidence suggests instead that a period of severe food shortages, lowered populations, and high mobility was followed by the disappearance of all, or nearly all, the population of Coronation Gulf some time in the second half of the seventeenth century. Because of an almost complete absence of tool artifacts and food remains, and the evidence of declining populations during the period, archaeologists have called it the "Intermediate Interval."[48]

The material evidence of the Intermediate Interval is consistent with a theory of a planned mass migration from the area. The theory accounts for two peculiar features of Coronation Gulf sites from the interval: the absence of tools and utensils, and the absence of interior construction in the semi-subterranean houses of the period.[49] People planning a permanent or long-term move would tend to take serviceable tools, utensils, furniture, and scarce materials such as wooden or whalebone house supports to their new homes, rather than leave them in abandoned structures to which they did not intend to return.

If, as the archaeology of the Intermediate Interval suggests, one or more Coronation Gulf communities chose to solve problems of serious long-term shortages by migrating to territory where resources were more abundant, where did they go? They could not have expected to find adequate resources to the north, where environmental pressures were also increasing, or to the west and southwest, where the presence of well-established communities effectively barred the way. The only direction in which they might have hoped to find uninhabited territory richer in resources than their own was to the southeast.

The forested areas around the middle and upper Thelon River, southeast of Coronation Gulf, were already known to them as sources of wood. They were also aware that the area had recently been abandoned by Athapaskans, whose own response to deteriorating climatic conditions was withdrawal to more southerly, forested regions. They may also have known that the lower Thelon and Chesterfield Inlet areas were only sparsely populated. It is possible, but less likely, that they believed the coast south of Chesterfield Inlet was not occupied at all.

The hypothesis that Coronation Gulf people moved across the barren grounds and along the Thelon-Chesterfield Inlet to the bay coast raises the question of evidence to support a migration-from-the west theory. A number of otherwise inexplicable changes in the material and intellectual cultures of the people of west Hudson Bay in the late seventeenth century make sense within the migration hypothesis suggested by Ernest S. Burch.[50] For example, there was a sudden change in the style of winter houses on the Keewatin coast in the mid- to late 1600s. Before 1684 the usual bay coast winter house was the classic Thule semi-subterranean stone and sod construction. By the mid-1740s surface dwellings were the norm.[51] Why did the Keewatin coast people switch from the warm, comfortable, semi-subterranean dwelling to one with apparently much less to recommend it? Burch has suggested it is extremely unlikely that people would make such a change on their own, but that newcomers with a long tradition of building surface dwellings would, in all likelihood, continue to build houses in the style they knew best. As it happens, exactly similar surface dwellings had been used since about 1500 in the Coppermine River area of Coronation Gulf.[52]

A second problem that had long puzzled arctic researchers was a dialect anomaly. Communities speaking variants of the same language tend to develop dialects similar to those of their near neighbours, and to diverge from those of more distant co-linguists. For example, the dialects spoken by the Iglulik people of Melville Peninsula are closely related to those of their

neighbours in Baffin Island, which in turn are closely related to the Labrador and Quebec dialects. Logically enough, the Iglulik variants are less like
the Labrador–Quebec dialects than Baffin Island speech is to either of them.
If the Keewatin Historic Inuit had developed in situ, their dialects should
be more similar to those of their nearest neighbours, the Iglulik, than to
more distant groups. But this is not the case; they are phonologically more
similar to the dialects of the Netsilik.[53] Copper (on Coronation Gulf),
Netsilik (on Boothia Peninsula), and Keewatin dialects are similar enough
to be considered a dialect group, and the greatest similarities are between
the Copper and southern Keewatin people. The language anomaly cannot
be accounted for outside of the migration theory.[54] Other similarities of
intellectual and material culture—for example, trading practices, mythology, and clothing styles—also suggest a closer link between the Keewatin
coast and Coronation Gulf societies than between Keewatin coast people
and the Iglulik people of Melville Peninsula and north Baffin Island.

Inuit oral histories, an often-overlooked source of evidence for past events,
support the migration hypothesis. On the question of a possible migration
from Coronation Gulf, the oral sources are sparse, and limited to bare statements concerning an ancestral home and a journey across the great land.
The ancient home they point to is in the northwest.[55] Keewatin Inuit
histories do not offer a reason for the move, or suggest when it took place.
However, the oral sources, as far as they go, support the conclusion that a
migration from Coronation Gulf to Chesterfield Inlet took place at some
period before, possibly just before, the establishment of the first trading
post at Churchill.

The available evidence suggests Coronation Gulf people made a decision to move en masse in a southeasterly direction. They may have entered
unoccupied territory, or perhaps met inhabitants also suffering from deteriorating climatic conditions, whose total population was less than their
own. Whatever the case, the Coronation Gulf people "were able to over-
whelm them in their scattered small camps. Some of the local people were
killed, while others fled to the north. The remainder was simply assimilated
by the immigrants. Confronted by more heavily populated territory toward
the north, and presented with a virtually uninhabited area toward the south,
the newcomers quickly established themselves around Rankin Inlet."[56]

Ernest S. Burch and W.E. Taylor have suggested the move took place
some time after 1650 and, in light of the change in house styles, probably
no earlier than the 1680s.[57] A more recent interpretation by Marc G.
Stevenson[58] postulates a two-step relocation: an earlier one to the Thelon
Woods and Beverly Lake during the first severe cooling of the Pacific

Climatic Episode in the mid-fifteenth century; and a second shift down the Thelon River to Chesterfield Inlet and the Hudson Bay coast in the mid- to late eighteenth century.

Whichever was the case, within a generation after their arrival on the coast, the immigrants had established small communities on the offshore islands and isolated peninsulas as far south as Whale Cove, and occasionally as far south as Knapp's Bay.[59] Here they met Europeans for the first time in 1718.

Mobility, Migration, and Relocation

In the generally unstable and often unpredictable environments of the arctic, mobility has always been a necessary, common, and effective solution to problems of resource scarcity. It is the basis of the seasonal round that enables people to harvest the resources of more than one region within their territory, it is implicit in occasional long-distance harvesting of resources, and it is an inevitable component of trade. Societies that practise routine mobility recognize the fact of temporary and recurring periods of short-term scarcity, plan for them, and survive them without disrupting their accustomed demographic and social organization.

Mobility as a solution to unpredicted, but life-threatening, situations requires a level of response beyond the routine of seasonal round, possibly to the point of abandoning territory and relocating elsewhere. Warfare, climatic degradation, social upheaval, epidemic disease, and geologic disaster are among the forcing factors. Abandonment may be an unplanned and unorganized response to unpredicted catastrophic events, or it may be a planned movement when impending disaster is identified in advance.[60] In either case, eventual return may or may not be anticipated.

The unplanned flight from immediate danger such as geologic disaster or epidemic disease, identified by migration theorists as the "fragmentation model," is characterized by the sudden abandonment of homes and workplaces as unprepared refugees flee in all directions in search of immediate safety.[61] Planned moves of entire social units or mass migration of significant portions of a population are responses when societies have clear warning of impending catastrophe and time to prepare for it. In the arctic, planned mass migrations have occurred only when neighbouring regions were either completely unoccupied or occupied very thinly by populations significantly smaller than the migrating group.

Traces of permanent abandonment of territory, particularly fragmentation-type moves, are difficult to recognize in the archaeological record because abandoned regions tend to be reoccupied when local conditions change.[62] In the arctic, the scarcity of many building materials guarantees that later residents will use materials from previous occupations whenever possible, resulting in the destruction of older sites. However, some migrations have been on a scale large enough to leave visible traces. Examples are the Thule expansion of the eleventh to the thirteenth centuries, the southward movement along the west coast of Hudson Bay to Churchill between 1200 and 1300, the intrusion of south Baffin Islanders into Ungava and Labrador around 1300 to 1330, the abandonments of Somerset Island and Amundsen Gulf, and the forced retreat from Churchill to Chesterfield Inlet in the period from 1450 to 1500.

The movement of Thule out of Alaska, across arctic North America, to Greenland in 900 to 1100 is perhaps the best-known example of an arctic mass movement of people. However, it differs from other movements of arctic people in a number of ways. It was not so much a migration as it was an expansion; the Thule did not leave empty territory behind them. The impetus for the move was not a catastrophic event or life-threatening circumstance. It occurred during a climatic optimum when all resources were adequate and at least some were abundant. It was provoked by the appearance of new opportunities, rather than forced by catastrophe. While not necessarily a planned movement, it was not a panic reaction leading to a fragmentation kind of dispersal.

The movement of people from southern Baffin Island to the Labrador and Ungava peninsulas between 1300 and 1330, a mass migration in terms of arctic populations, may not have been a total abandonment of territory. A small population may have remained,[63] and may have been ancestral to the people who met the Frobisher and Davis expeditions in the 1570s and 1580s. The movement was probably motivated by the 'push' factors of extreme climatic cooling and serious shortfalls in both marine and terrestrial food animals, and the destination was probably chosen because of the presence across Hudson Strait of increasing numbers of Greenland whales. It appears to have been a planned move.

The population crash on Somerset Island between 1450 and 1500 may have involved mass migration, albeit of a much reduced population following a period of resource loss and famine. It is also possible the abandonment was not due to migration at all: the communities may have become extinct. If there were survivors, they may have joined other communities as refugees or immigrants in numbers so small that their assimilation left no archaeological or linguistic traces. Because of historiographical problems, mainly the absence of linguistic and artifactual evidence, exactly what took place in Somerset Island in the late fifteenth century may never be clearly understood.

The disappearance of the peoples of Amundsen Gulf, also in the years between 1450 and 1500, seems to be another case of abandonment, or near abandonment, of territory. However, like the example from Somerset Island and unlike that of south Baffin Island, the ultimate destination or destinations of the inhabitants and their subsequent history are unknown.

The southward expansion along the west coast of Hudson Bay in the thirteenth and fourteenth centuries was part of the general movement of Thule peoples across the arctic. Their subsequent abandonment of the area was forced on them by neighbouring people, the Cree and Chipewyan, whose coercive power was strong enough to compel their withdrawal from the Churchill River to Chesterfield Inlet some time in the fifteenth or early sixteenth centuries.

Abandonment of territory and subsequent relocation of whole social units are powerful catalysts for social and economic change. When a migrating population enters unoccupied territory, it may have to adjust its subsistence economy and social organization to make the best use of the resources of the new environment, but it can safely maintain old traits that do not jeopardize the social unit. This was the experience of the original Thule people who arrived in Coronation Gulf in the twelfth and thirteenth centuries, and of the Baffin Island Thule who moved across Hudson Strait in the early fourteenth century. They adjusted their subsistence economies and social structures enough to ensure survival in the new territory, while at the same time remaining identifiably Thule.

When immigrants intrude into already populated territories, the maintenance of former identities is less certain. Their numbers, relative to the numbers of indigenous people, influence the kinds of adjustments they make. In theory, if the incoming group is smaller than the already established society, and socially passive, its members will be assimilated into the majority society; if the incoming group is big enough, and socially aggressive, it may drive out the local population or absorb it.[64] The withdrawal of some Tunit (Dorset) groups from their territories in the face of Thule expansions, as told in Inuit histories, is an example of local populations being driven away by relatively massive influxes of newcomers. In most places colonized by Thule, Dorset people were unable to survive as separate and identifiable social units.

The adoption by Thule of Dorset snowhouse technology is an example of majority society maintenance of minority society traits that prove particularly useful under local conditions. The social, cultural, and economic changes made by Coronation Gulf immigrants on the west coast of Hudson Bay shortly before 1700 also followed this pattern. The new inhabitants adopted some of the traits of the indigenous population they replaced or absorbed, retained some of the characteristics of their earlier way of life, and made changes appropriate to their new environment.

In fragmentation dispersals, refugees joining already established communities may bring their own kinship networks and alliances with them,[65] with varying degrees of benefit or harm to the enlarged community. The ideas they import may result in technological innovations, and the creation of new, syncretic worldviews. At the same time, they may bring a legacy of bad blood and ill will, and involve their new community in old, non-indigenous feuds.

The exodus from Coronation Gulf was apparently the movement of an entire community of at least a hundred individuals. The migration was a response to increasingly severe environmental pressures and a potentially life-threatening environmental crisis. The keywords are "increasingly" and "potentially." The basic problem was not climatic instability and sudden, disastrous depletion of resources; it was inexorable intensification of cold, and the consequent slow but steady reduction of seal, whale, fish, and caribou. The declines may have been almost imperceptible from year to year, but would certainly have been obvious over the lifetime of a generation. People had prior notice of impending hard times, and time to make plans. In their former territory, house ruins exist that lack all interior constructions, suggesting they had removed the rare and valuable house supports and other fittings for use in their new homes. The curious absence of artifacts for the Intermediate Interval is also suggestive of a planned, permanent relocation. A community that has decided to abandon its homes and homeland permanently, and to establish itself in a distant and little-known place, might be expected to take as many of its usable tools and utensils as possible. The process of removing useful items from one residential site for use in another is known as "curate behaviour." A high level of curation is assumed to indicate that abandonment is permanent, and also implies that the need for abandonment was foreseen and the relocation was planned. An absence of evidence for curation behaviour suggests that abandonment was sudden, unplanned, and probably took place in response to an unforeseen and unpredictable emergency. 'Mining' abandoned structures or settlements for resources that may be useful at another location is considered a form of curation behaviour.[66]

All the evidence of the Intermediate Interval at Coronation Gulf points to a planned move, not a panic-driven flight of refugees fleeing in all directions from an unanticipated threat to existence. People moved into territory not entirely unknown to them: they knew it offered the possibility of adequate resources, and were probably aware that it was too thinly populated for there to be an effective resistance to their intrusion.

Extinctions and abandonment of territory are obvious in the archaeological record; relocations leave fewer traces. Evidence of a planned relocation such as the Coronation Gulf exodus is also missing from the documents of European observers, for obvious reasons. Inuit histories have more to say about great migrations and relocations of societies to new territories. All arctic communities have traditions and histories that tell of long journeys to both known and unknown destinations, usually in search of resources needed by communities under stress. The histories, however, almost never say *when* the journeys were made, or what the terminal points of the journey were. Some identify Akilineq as the goal of the journeys, but the place name is little help in identifying locations. One or two actual places are, or have been, known by the name; one such is the Akilineq Hills near where the Thelon River flows into Lake Beverley in the Northwest Territories.[67] However, most references to Akilineq, which means "the place across," are to unknown lands, which heroes of the past often sought, sometimes found, and from which they usually returned.

The Ammassalik people of East Greenland have an especially extensive and detailed collection of histories that suggest that their ancestors, like the Coronation Gulf people, may have responded to problems of diminishing resources in the late sixteenth and early seventeenth centuries by attempting to reach unknown lands across the sea to the east.

From Greenland to the East

In the 1850s the Danish government commissioned naturalist Hinrich Rink to investigate the state of trade and government in its Greenland colony and, after receiving his report, appointed him Director of the Royal Greenland Trade. In 1861 he began publishing *Atuagagdliutit*, the first Greenlandic-language newspaper. One of his purposes was to provide a vehicle for Greenlanders to record their oral traditions and histories.[68] In 1875 he published a selection of the stories, with comments about the nature and regulation of Greenlandic storytelling.

Greenlandic storytellers of the time made a clear distinction between two kinds of stories. *Oqalugtuat* (plural; singular is *oqalugtuaq*) were very old stories known almost everywhere from western Alaska to eastern Greenland, many of which have their counterparts in Siberia. The *oqalugtuat* often incorporated supernatural occurrences, and were intended to give instructions for proper living, rather than to relate facts about past events. *Oqalualat* (plural; singular is *oqalualarut*) were accounts of actual events, often within living memory, but never more than 100 to 150 years old; that is, within five or six generations of their telling, and known only locally. One of the characteristics of western Greenlandic storytelling noted by Rink was that each story was prefaced by a clear statement of the category to which it belonged.[69] Both kinds of stories made references to Akilineq, but not as just a distant and well-endowed place, as it is in the stories from other parts of the arctic. In the east Greenlandic oral tradition, in addition to being distant and rich in resources, it was also always a "country beyond the seas."[70]

In 1883 to 1885, Gustav Holm, ethnographer and leader of the Danish Polar Expedition to Ammassalik in east Greenland, collected a number of puzzling stories about visits the Ammassalik people of east Greenland had made to Akilineq. The references were even more specific than in the west Greenland histories. The people of Ammassalik consistently placed Akilineq "far out at sea *towards the east*" [emphasis added]. The animals there were said to be very big and the inhabitants not quite human. Because he was repeatedly told the clouds over Akilineq were distinctly visible from the Blosseville Mountains north of Ammassalik on a clear day, Holm concluded that the people were referring to Iceland.[71]

Akilineq is the scene of the action in the well-known story of Kamikinak, an Ammassalik boy of notably small stature. One day, after his mother had called him "a puny good-for-nothing," he took his kayak out to sea. Eventually he arrived at an island where he met a very large man with strength enough to pluck both Kamikinak and his kayak out of the sea. The man became Kamikinak's foster father and took him to his home in Akilineq, where all the men were tall. In time, Kamikinak grew to similar size and then returned to his own country.[72]

Another story, apparently (and perhaps significantly) known only in Ammassalik, concerns five brothers. The first brother went out to sea and did not return; the second went in search of him and also did not return. A third brother disappeared on the same errand. The fourth brother took up the search and also went eastward out to sea. While he was resting on the beach of an uninhabited island, he was discovered by one of his missing brothers. Together they went even farther out to sea until they lost sight of the island where they had met, and came to yet another island, the second in the series of islands in the story. The brother who had been missing did not live on this island, but he had left his sled and a dog team there. After travelling a great distance on the ice, and losing sight of the land where the sled had been, they came at last to Akilineq, the third island in the series. In a house surrounded by clouds, the brothers joined several other people feasting on whale meat and ringed seal. None of the company felt satisfied by the meal. Shortly after, they were all sick. The fourth brother then returned to his own home, where the fifth brother had remained, and reported that all three of their missing brothers lived in Akilineq.[73]

Holm also recorded stories of giants, the not-quite-human persons who appear in all Eskimo and Inuit oral literatures from Alaska to Greenland. One tale told to Holm at Ammassalik in the 1880s described houses with chimneys,[74] an architectural detail unknown among Eskimo and Inuit except in Alaska and the Mackenzie River valley, but common in Iceland.

Scholarly research into the meanings of folkloric materials such as the Ammassalik stories is only just beginning at places like the Alaska Center for the Study of Native Languages. We still have very little understanding of how historical fact, prescriptive parable, and fictional embellishment are combined in oral traditions and histories, and almost no understanding of how to separate the various elements. Given our present state of understanding, we cannot identify historical material in the Ammassalik stories with any kind of certainty. What is clear is that stories about journeys eastward from Ammassalik into or across Denmark Strait were not especially rare. Some details in the stories suggest a degree of historical accuracy: the description of dwellings with chimneys; comments on the visibility of Akilineq from the Blosseville Mountains; the account of an ice crossing from one island to the next in the story of the lost brothers; and the account of a house surrounded by clouds, which could be a description of island fog. The Ammassalik stories fall into the category of *oqalualarutit* (in West Greenlandic, *oqalualarut*), which means they were intended as true histories of actual events that took place no more than five or six generations earlier; that is, within the past 100 to 150 years.[75] Therefore, the actual events would date to a generation living around 1700.

One of the coldest periods of the Little Ice Age, the First Maunder Minimum, occurred between 1645 and 1715. The polar ice pack during this period was farther south than at any other period for which there are documentary records. In the story of the five brothers, the description of a journey across the ice from one island to another fits precisely into this time frame.

Given the place and period, and the present state of folklore studies, the search for evidence in support of the Ammassalik histories might seem futile. However, there are hints in contemporary oral testimonies of people in Orkney and northern Scotland that suggest east Greenlanders may indeed have crossed, or attempted to cross, Denmark Strait and the north Atlantic Ocean on a few occasions.

Between 1682 and 1701, in the last desperate decades of the First Maunder Minimum, several local historians in the Orkneys and northern Scotland commented on the appearance of mysterious strangers in skin boats along the coasts. An early incident was recorded by the Reverend James Wallace of Kirkwall, Orkney. "Sometimes about this Country are seen these Men which are called *Finn-men*. In the year 1682 one was seen sometime sailing, sometime Rowing up and down in his little Boat at the south end of the Isle of *Eda*, most of the people of the Ile flock'd to see him, and when they adventur'd to put out a Boat with Men to see if they could apprehend him, he presently fled away most swiftly."[76]

Two years later, in 1684, another was seen off the coast of the Isle of Westray. The Reverend Wallace was firm in his identification of the strangers. "And in the year 1684, another was seen from *Westra*, and for a while after they got few or no Fishes for they have this Remark here, that the *Finnmen* drive away the fishes from the place to which they come. These *Finnmen* seem to be some of those people that dwell about the *Stretum Davis*."[77]

In 1700 Reverend Wallace's son, Doctor James Wallace, commented in a second edition of his father's popular book that "Be the Seas never so boisterous their Boat being made of Fish Skins, are so contrived that he can never sink, but is like a Sea-gull swimming on the top of the Water. His shirt he has is so fastned to the Boat, that no Water can come into his Boat to do him damage, except when he pleases to unty it, which he never does but to ease nature, or when he comes ashore."[78]

In 1701 the Reverend John Brand noted frequent appearances of strangers in skin boats off the coasts of the Isles of Orkney, in particular a sighting near Stronsay in 1699 and one near Westray in 1700. Brand's description of the unknown visitors agreed in most particulars with that of Wallace. "There are frequently *Fin-men* seen here upon the Coasts, as one about a year ago [1699] on *Stronsa*, and another within these few Months on *Westra*, a Gentleman with many others in the Isle looking on him nigh to the shore, but when any endeavour to apprehend them, they flee away most swiftly.... His boat is made up of Seal skins, or some kind of leather, he also hath a Coat of Leather upon him, and he sitteth in the middle of his Boat, with a little Oar in his hand, Fishing with his Lines."[79]

Yet another clergyman, the Reverend Francis Gastrell, described a kayak he saw in the museum of King's College Chapel, Aberdeen, in 1760. The canoe, he wrote, "was driven into the Don with a man in it who was all over hairy, and spoke a language which no person there could interpret. He lived but three days." Gastrell placed the incident "about thirty-two years since"; that is, around 1728.[80]

Uncertainty as to the identity and origin of the leather-clad strangers in skin boats continued long after Wallace and Brand presented their different opinions. A popular explanation among people other than the educated clergymen was that the mysterious visitors were Selkies. In the folklore and folksong of Orkney, Shetland, northern Ireland, and northern Scotland, Selkies are seal-people, creatures who have seal bodies while they are in the sea, and become human when they remove their seal skins on land. Their homeland was thought to be an island far to the west. Many stories tell of lonely maids and unsatisfied wives who took Selkie lovers and gave birth to dark-skinned, dark-eyed infants. Others relate how Scottish fishermen captured and married Selkie women. Human husbands and wives kept their Selkie spouses on land by hiding their shape-shifting outer skins. Much Selkie folklore centred around the quest of homesick seal-people for their skins, which they needed in order to return to the sea.[81]

Selkies were never confused with common seals, which were considered to be fish and were treated with no more fear or respect than a North Sea herring. There was, however, a suspicion among the local inhabitants that the large and relatively rare Greenland and grey seals were Selkies, and their appearance on Scottish coasts caused concern and extra caution among the fishing villages. Seal-people were associated with strong tides, heavy seas, and fierce storms. Whether they appeared as a result of unusually strong westerly winds and currents, or were the cause of extreme weather conditions, is not clear in the folklore, but the tales caution against wounding or killing a Selkie because of the bad luck and hazardous weather conditions associated with them.[82]

In the context of seventeenth-century European cosmography, an observer who failed to recognize the true nature of a sealskin-clad Inuit in a body-hugging sealskin boat cannot be charged with being particularly naïve. Inuit hunters were extraordinarily good at imitating the creatures of the sea. Lieutenant George Best noted, after observing the activities of the Frobisher Bay people in the 1570s, that "they are good fishermen, and in their small boats, and disguised with their sealskin coats, they deceive the fish, who take them for fellow seals rather than deceiving men."[83]

Some commentators, such as Wallace, Brand, and historians of the next two centuries, put forward more mundane explanations. The strangers were either of Scandinavian origin, as Brand believed, or inhabitants of North America, as Wallace claimed. All attempts to show a northern European provenance for the strangers, which would prove Brand's theory, have been unsuccessful. Scandinavian peoples had, in fact, experienced visits from the seal people at least as early as the thirteenth century, and were as puzzled as the Orcadians. In the 1420s the Danish cartographer Clavus Swart noted he had seen "the little pygmies ... after they had been caught at sea in a skin boat which now hangs in [the] Cathedral [at Trondheim]. In the cathedral there is also a long boat of skin which was taken with the same kind of pygmies in it."[84] On his maps, Swart placed a large island halfway between Norway and Greenland, which he thought must be the home of the owners of the skin boats. The Trondheim cathedral records indicate that a kayak and an umiak were indeed among its museum pieces in the fifteenth century, and the cathedral's inventory descriptions of the time make it clear they were Greenland-style boats.[85]

An increasing body of convincing evidence that the kayaks and their inhabitants seen in the waters around Orkney were North American was produced during the twentieth century.[86] The major objection to a North American origin for the mysterious strangers has been the apparent impossibility for a kayak to stay afloat in open water for nearly 1200 nautical miles, or 2000 kilometres, that being the distance from Cape Farewell at the southern tip of Greenland to Scotland. An explanation that accepted a North American origin and at the same time did away with the long sea voyage was put forward early in the twentieth century. The mysterious strangers could have been captives carried across the Atlantic by whalers, fishermen, or explorers. When the sailing ships came in sight of land, the captives could have attempted to escape in their kayaks and ended up along the Scottish coasts.[87]

The "escaping-captive" theory gained considerable support and is still being championed.[88] There is no question that while some arctic inhabitants were willing passengers to Europe, considerable numbers were taken forcibly from their homes in the sixteenth and seventeenth centuries. In addition to the Labrador woman and child kidnapped in 1566 by French fishermen for exhibition in several German cities in 1567, and the four people taken from southeast Baffin Island by Martin Frobisher's 1576 and 1577 expeditions, at least thirty Greenlanders were kidnapped by Danish, Norwegian, and Dutch ships, and taken to Europe between 1605 and 1660.[89]

At first glance, one documented incident lends support to the escaping-captive theory. In 1605 a Danish expedition took five Greenlanders to Europe. The next year three of them tried to get away in their kayaks and were caught making their way along the coast of Denmark.[90] The most serious flaw in the theory is that the majority of captives were taken, not to British waters, where all the known sightings occurred, but to Denmark and The Netherlands. Ian Whitaker has pointed out that "it is possible that one, or even two, of these escapees may have reached Scotland, [but] it can scarcely be maintained that six or more arrived in the course of fifty years. One is thus forced to the conclusion that the 'Finn-men' were in fact Greenlanders … making the journey from their homeland."[91]

If they were not escaping, how are the appearances to be explained? Whitaker concluded that "deliberate design" lay behind them, because "it is unlikely that storm would send six or more Greenlanders to Iceland, and then on to the Faeroes, and then further still."[92] The possibility that Greenlanders were deliberately trying to cross the Atlantic should not be rejected out of hand. The people of seventeenth-century Greenland had motive, means, and opportunity to seek out new resources, and information about where such resources might be found.

Environmental phenomena provided necessary motive. Lichenometric dating of moraines indicates continuous and rapid glacial advance in Greenland between 1600 and 1775.[93] Eyewitnesses also recorded the visible progress of ice rivers into Greenland fjords. Moravian missionary Otho Fabricus wrote, "The ice spreads out more and more every year … the experiment has been tried of erecting a post on the bare ground a good distance from the ice, and the next year it was found to be overtaken by it. So swift is this growth that present day Greenlanders speak of places where their parents hunted reindeer among naked hills which are now all ice. I myself have seen [caribou] paths running up towards the interior of the country and worn in bygone days but now broken off at the ice."[94]

Along with strong motives, Greenlanders had the means to make the trans-Atlantic journey. The escaping-captive theory was originally proposed because Europeans could not imagine that a kayak could survive across nearly 2000 kilometres of open ocean. The feat is, however, not impossible, or even improbable. Experiments have shown that a carefully oiled skin kayak can remain seaworthy for at least two weeks, immersed in fresh water, and a kayak in salt water will remain seaworthy much longer.[95] The small craft most commonly used by Icelandic colonists for fishing and sea-hunting in the tenth and eleventh centuries was the leather-covered coracle, or curragh. It was fully capable of crossing the narrowest part of Denmark Strait between Greenland and Iceland. A Greenland kayak in the hands of an experienced seaman such as a Greenland hunter would also be capable of crossing Denmark Strait or the southern stretches of the Norwegian Sea. The notion has more credence particularly if we remember that people following the edge of the sea ice would have spent some part of their time on the ice, and been able to dry out and repair their boats.

The nearly 2000 kilometres from Cape Farewell to Scotland are irrelevant to the argument. The most direct route from Greenland to Europe is just over 1200 kilometres: from Cape Brewster in Ammassalik territory to northwest Iceland is 260 kilometres, from southeast Iceland to the Faeroe Islands is 442 kilometres; from the Faeroes to Shetland is 200 kilometres, and from the Faeroes direct to Orkney is 322 kilometres.[96] A journey from Cape Brewster to Orkney could have been made in three or four stages, and involved at most 1230 kilometres at sea, or at the edge of the pack ice.

Opportunity was also at hand. The shift in the direction of the Gulf Stream-North Atlantic Drift from northeasterly to due easterly that accompanied the southward expansion of the polar pack between 1577 and 1800,[97] although it was an obstacle to ships sailing west, was an asset to vessels heading east. However, it is not necessary to assume the entire journey must have been by water. As Astrid Ogilvie's reconstructions of ice conditions in Denmark Strait indicate,[98] the first leg of the journey, to Iceland, could certainly have been on ice, as might the second stage, from Iceland to the Faeroes. The water portion of the trip could have been less than 500 kilometres, and possibly even in the neighbourhood of 325 kilometres. Provisions need not have presented a problem; people living and travelling along the edge of the ice pack would have been able to harvest the resources of the sea.

Finally, along with motive, means, and opportunity, several different groups in Greenland, Baffin Island, and Labrador had information, limited though it was, of inhabited lands to the east. As late as the nineteenth century, Greenlandic oral histories recalled the thirteenth-century Norse presence, and Baffin Islanders had not forgotten Martin Frobisher's expeditions of the 1570s, or meetings with Irish, Icelandic, Basque, or Portuguese in the fifteenth and sixteenth centuries. By 1650 Greenlanders, Baffin Islanders, and Labrador coast people were certainly aware of a well-populated and apparently affluent country on the other side of the Atlantic. A number of their people had been taken there; most had not returned.

Ammassalik oral histories remain the most compelling source of evidence for Ammassalik attempts to find resources and allies to the east. While the Scottish and Orkney sources do not provide unimpeachable corroboration of Inuit histories, they fit well with, and tend to support, Inuit memory of attempts to travel east from Greenland across the North Atlantic.

The environmental circumstances that forced southerly migrations of Greenland and grey seals to the latitude of Scotland, and emptied the North Sea of several varieties of fish, were favourable to southeasterly moves by Greenlanders. The increasing appearances on Scottish coasts of strangers who were clearly Greenlanders were arguably also related to events in the climatic regime of the late seventeenth century. In the conditions of the First Maunder Minimum, Greenlanders, like Baffin Islanders and the people of Labrador, were hard-pressed and highly motivated to seek relief from conditions of scarce resources and recurring periods of starvation similar to those reported for the west coast of Hudson Bay during the period. It is by no means impossible that they should have undertaken deliberate voyages in that direction, to hunt the large arctic seals that live at the edge of the ice pack, to seek new resource areas in a new country, to find their lost compatriots, or to open up trade relations with the people of the sailing ships.

Physical environments, and particularly changes within them, may act as forcing factors in human history, requiring human responses but not dictating the nature of the responses. Human beings have created an almost endless variety of subsistence technologies and techniques, and economic and social systems, in order to find and use the resources necessary to survive within particular physical environments. Rational adaptations or alterations of resource base, subsistence activities, and attitudes are strategies intended to increase both individual and societal chances of survival, and perhaps to make desirable changes in quality of life. Among the strategies designed to protect or obtain necessary resources are denial of access to resources by other groups, or the seizure of resources held by other groups. The violent hostilities undertaken by Baffin Islanders against strangers in the 1570s and 1580s can be interpreted as an example of a resident group protecting its resources against perceived competitors. Expansion to new territories, while continuing to occupy and use old territories, was a strategy that Labrador coast peoples used between 1550 and 1650 in search of new resources. Abandonment of territory and migration to new areas were apparently the choice of Coronation Gulf people in the late 1600s. The strange appearances of seal-people near Scottish islands between 1680 and 1728 may have been attempts by eastern Greenlanders to find new resource areas across the Atlantic Ocean.

Both Dorset (1000 BCE – 1000 CE) and Early Thule (1000 – 1550 CE) peoples were proficient at designing and manufacturing articles from available materials: ivory, bone, stone, wood, and baleen. Beautifully decorated toggles were used to fasten clothing, tent covers, and dog harnesses. Delicately carved amulets helped human beings to understand and control the spirit world, while articles of personal adornment, such as pendants and combs, were often exquisitely decorated. Snow goggles of bone, antler, and baleen provided efficient eye protection. (Courtesy of Manitoba Museum of Man and Nature, The John Stanners Collection)

Floe-edge sealing at Melville Peninsula (1824). When the perpetual daylight
of late spring attracted seals to sun themselves on the ice, the Inuit hunter
crawled across the ice, imitating a seal's movements and sounds, until he was
close enough to use his harpoon on his prey. (From Parry, *Journal of a Second
Voyage*)

Breathing-hole sealing at Melville Peninsula (1824). In the darkness of winter,
seals create tunnels in the ice, through which they rise to breathe. The Inuit
hunter waits above the breathing hole, and thrusts his spear into the tunnel
when a movement of the water indicates a seal is about to surface. (From Parry,
Journal of a Second Voyage)

1000 BCE – 1000 CE. All that remains of a Dorset house is a depression in the ground, and whale vertebrae used as wall and roof supports. (Hudson's Bay Company Archives [HBCA] 1987/47/221)

ESKIMAUX WOMEN.

1822. Iglulingmiut women's winter clothes included roomy boots that served as pockets and purses. The flaps at the front and back of women's parkas provided insulation when they were kneeling or sitting on snow or ice. Iglulingmiut women braided their hair around a stick or bone, and added decorative ribbons made from dyed or bleached caribou and seal skins. (From Parry, *Journal of a Second Voyage*)

Iglulingmiut winter village at Winter Island in 1822. The presence of a number of dogs indicates that this was a wealthy community. The length of the sled runners and the relative straightness of the crossbars suggest the sleds were made of wood, which had to be traded from communities as far south as Knapp's Bay. (From Lyon, *The Private Journal*)

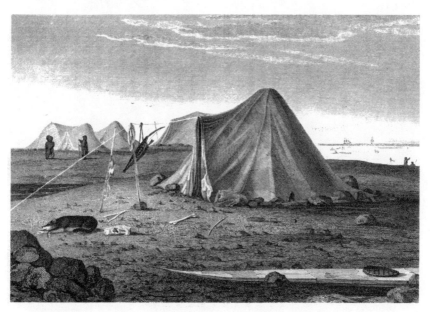

Iglulingmiut summer village at Igloolik in 1822. The wooden tent poles that support the unusually tall tupik (summer tent) had to be transported considerable distances from wooded areas inland and in the south. Only an affluent community operating within a widespread trading network would have had the necessary bartering power. (From Parry, *Journal of a Second Voyage*)

People of the Savage Islands in kayaks and umiaks met European ships in Hudson Strait to trade throughout most of the 18th and 19th centuries. By the 1820s, the arrival of any sailing ship was an occasion for merrymaking, accompanied by minor trading of souvenir items. (From Parry, *Journal of a Second Voyage*)

Umiaks such as this one, c. 1904, were multi-passenger boats, used by South Baffin Islanders crossing Hudson Strait to spend the winter in Ungava Peninsula and Ungava Bay. Baffin Island umiaks, often called "luggage boats," could carry as many as 50 people. When handled by women, the boat was rowed; when the crew was male, it was paddled. In Greenland umiaks were rowed exclusively by women, and known as "women's boats." (National Archives of Canada [NAC] PA51464)

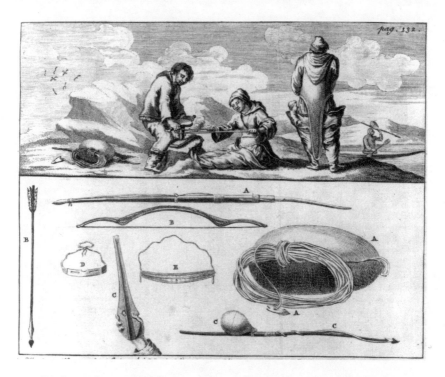

On the south coast of Baffin Island in the 18th century, people still adhered to a largely Thule way of life. Like their ancestors, they continued to hunt whales, and had perfected tools for hunting seal and caribou. Many of them wintered in Ungava, on the south side of Hudson Strait, and returned in the spring with supplies of wood for harpoons, kayak frames, and bows. The sketch by Henry Ellis, made around 1746, includes a woman with her infant tucked inside her capacious boot in the manner of the Labrador Inuit. (From Ellis, *A Voyage to Hudson's Bay*)

At first meetings with strangers, Inuit sent one of their own, usually an elderly woman, as an emissary to test the intentions of the newcomers. Correct greeting protocol required that the strangers offer proof they were unarmed. The practice was described by John Ross, George Lyon, and William Gilder. (From Gilder, *Schwatka's Search*)

Kakikigiu, an Iglulingmiut woman from Akudlik (1835), with her two Netsilingmiut husbands, Poyettak (left) and Aknalua (right). Her opinion of Parry and Lyon, whom she had met at Melville Peninsula in 1823, was instrumental in the Netsilik decision to reveal themselves to John Ross in 1830. (From Ross, *Appendix to the Narrative of a Second Voyage*)

4.

The Lands around My Dwelling: Strategies for Social Environments, 1700–1790

> *The lands around my dwelling are more beautiful from the day when it is given me to see faces I have never seen before. All is more beautiful, and life is thankfulness. These guests of mine make my house grand.*
>
> > – Inuit poem[1]

Before 1700 Thule-Historic Inuit history was marked by major demographic changes, the emergence and disappearance of many discrete societies, and periods of intense hostility or outright war. The available evidence indicates that the physical environment was a significant forcing factor in social change.

During economic 'good' times, communities maintained themselves in accustomed ways, expanding when population increase made it necessary, raising their standard of living when surpluses and favourable conditions of trade made it possible. In economic 'bad times', frequently the result of environmental conditions, people withdrew from peripheral areas, and often suffered population crashes and extinctions. When they were able to predict impending environmental-economic crises, they avoided social destruction by abandoning territory, migrating, and expanding or intruding into other regions, and they resorted to varying degrees of violence, annihilative warfare, creative innovation, and the exchange of goods and ideas.

After the cold and volatile climatic regime of the seventeenth century, a slow, steady warming began.[2] Few arctic communities were faced with

environmental conditions that threatened their continued existence or required a human response significant enough to have left traces in the archaeological or documentary records. Most communities experienced a
greater degree of affluence than had been possible during the climatically
constraining 1600s. Inuit territorial and occupational changes during the
temperate and predictable 1700s were more often responses to widening
social environments than to constraining physical ones.

The proximity of other social groups created stress when there was competition for resources, but neighbouring societies also presented opportunities in some circumstances. The major change in North American arctic
social environments after 1700 was the increasing, and increasingly permanent, presence of Europeans in Inuit homelands. European governments
and commercial interests recognized opportunities for trade, settlement,
resource extraction, and the expansion of empire in the arctic and subarctic
regions of North America. Rulers, merchants, and churches established
themselves in eastern arctic regions on a more or less permanent basis:
British traders, organized by royal charter as the Hudson's Bay Company,
opened trading posts in James Bay and Hudson Bay between 1670 and
1720; and French commercial concerns established sedentary seal and cod
fisheries on the Labrador coast in ever-increasing numbers after 1700.
Communities on both sides of Davis Strait and Baffin Bay were visited
irregularly during the second half of the seventeenth century by Dutch
whalers and traders, and annually after 1713. By 1715 west Greenlanders
were meeting Dutch whalers every year at prearranged rendezvous to exchange pelts and whale oil for metal objects.[3]

Greenland

In 1721 Danish* church and state combined forces to establish permanent
settlements and supervise resource extraction in western Greenland. Some
Greenlanders saw the broader social environments as new opportunities
for solving old subsistence problems and for satisfying needs and desires
beyond survival. By 1770 trading posts and missions had been established
along the entire west coast, and local people had begun to occupy permanent villages nearby.[4]

---

*Denmark, Norway, and Sweden operated within a number of political and economic
unions from Norse times to 1905. Scandinavian authors tend to use historically accurate,
and unfortunately confusing, designations for each of the various unions. However, the
Crown of Denmark was sovereign in all periods, so the terms Denmark and Danish, while
descriptively inadequate, will be used to refer to Scandinavian government(s) in all periods.

Two imperatives were the foundation of Denmark's official policy for Greenland: first, Greenlanders were to continue their ancient subsistence activities without interference or assistance from the (nominal) Danish government; and second, Greenland and Greenlanders were, for their own protection, to be isolated from the influences of outsiders.[5] Only two exceptions to the directives were tolerated. Individuals who could not achieve self-sufficiency in accustomed ways because of physical disability or because their communities had rejected them were permitted to live near the mission-trading posts and to take up 'non-traditional' occupations. And, missionaries were allowed to preach and to baptize willing converts, provided that such converts were not encouraged to leave their original communities or to engage in 'European' activities.

In theory, the 'hands-off' policy prevented missionaries and traders from interfering in any aspect of Greenlandic life, but local communities were quick to understand that appeal to the Christian precepts of the newcomers nearly always resulted in economic assistance. The indigent, the elderly, and the handicapped took up residence next to the missionary-traders, and were provided with housing, food, clothing, medical care, and other necessaries, as well as with the Gospel.[6] By shifting the burden of social security from their own communities to the newcomers, Inuit reduced the costs to themselves of providing for 'non-productive' members of the group, and relieved themselves of the need to make the life-and-death decisions implicit in the practices of infanticide, gerontocide, and assisted suicide.

The first converts, catechists, and interpreters were the 'non-productive' orphans, the aged, and the disabled, as well as outcasts. Outcasts included individuals identified by their communities as criminals and troublemakers. The outcast category also included many people who were of mixed descent, or who, through close association with the missions, were considered by their own people to have lost their insider identity. Greenlandic widows of Danish spouses, whether by death or desertion, were frequently assigned to the outcast category, and sought refuge at the missions from the violence and abuse they experienced in their own families and communities.[7]

By no means all such women and their mixed-blood children were driven away because of economic dependency on the community. Danish law ensured that Greenlandic wives, ex-wives, and widows, as well as the children of Danish men, had full rights to the estates and pensions of their spouses and fathers. Many of them inherited fortunes, or were provided for by annuities. Rejection was usually on the grounds that they had become 'strangers'. Some chose to become strangers, preferring the easier, safer, more sedentary life of the mission settlement to life with their own people. The managers, bureaucrats, and professionals who dominated Greenland's commercial, political, and social life in the nineteenth and twentieth centuries were descended, for the most part, from the Greenlandic mixed-blood Homeguard of the first two generations of Danish rule.[8]

Labrador

In eighteenth-century Labrador, communities and individuals continued to take advantage of the opportunities provided by the presence of Europeans, as they had done in the previous century. The territorial and occupational choices they made in the decades after the 1690s were not responses to insupportable environmental conditions, as had been the migration from Baffin Island to Labrador's Atlantic coast within 1300 to 1330. The whale populations, which were their primary subsistence resource, were not at risk,[9] and there are no indications that basic foods were in short supply, that extinctions had taken place, or that group survival was threatened.

The five- or six-fold increase in the numbers of Inuit on the Labrador coast between the early 1500s and 1700[10] stands in sharp contrast to the disappearance of whole societies from Somerset Island, Amundsen Gulf, and Coronation Gulf in the same period. The abundance of European goods in homes from Hamilton Inlet to Cape Chidley, and in storage depots waiting to be moved through indigenous trade networks, suggests that, far from being stressed by inclement climatic conditions and resource shortages, Labrador Inuit enjoyed relative affluence in the seventeenth and eighteenth centuries.[11]

While climatic change cannot be considered the major, or even a significant, forcing factor in Labrador Inuit population shifts, territorial expansion, and altered subsistence economies, it was an important factor in the movements of European populations. The steady expansion of heavy polar ice in the north Atlantic during the late seventeenth century forced large numbers of whale into summer feeding grounds in the Norwegian and Greenland seas.[12] Dutch and Basque whalers responded by moving their fleets to new, and richer, whaling grounds,[13] and the Labrador coast was open to expansion from both France and New France.

French occupation and use of the coast were vastly different from earlier seasonal use by Basque fishermen, sealers, and whalemen. The French crown allocated land in a quasi-seigneurial way, and many properties were operated throughout the year. For the Inuit, year-round access to more and better-stocked installations provided greater opportunities for trading and pilfering than had the unpredictable, seasonal Basque stations. Every year from 1716 to 1720, Inuit ransacked unoccupied shore stations. French title holders, with capital investments at stake, defended their properties and often used pre-emptive strikes against potential looters.[14] And they did so year-round.

While Inuit attacks seem to have become less frequent after 1720, they were more aggressive. Strikes against occupied stations and travelling parties in 1720, 1721, 1728, and 1742 resulted in the deaths of a number of French fishermen, as did an attack in 1757, in which the Inuit used firearms.[15] In 1743 Jean-Louis Fornel, a Canadian seigneur with concessions on the Strait of Belle Isle and Hamilton Inlet, reported hostilities on a much larger scale. A man identified only as "Laraguy from Bayonne, France" had been hunting whales near Hudson Strait in 1737, wrote Fornel, and saw "more than 400 corpses on the ice, whom he recognized as Dutch and Eskimos who were without doubt at war with one another."[16] Inuit did not always distinguish between Europeans who kidnapped their people and sent posses after their raiding parties, and traders and missionaries with more peaceful intentions. When a small Moravian mission was built at Aivertok (Hopedale) in 1752, the local people attacked it and killed seven members of the party.[17]

Some contemporary observers attributed Inuit hostility to a nature "so utterly savage and cruel that it is impossible to trade with them." Others, like Jean-Louis Fornel, believed the raiding and looting were motivated by desire for European goods and willingness to acquire them by any means, a sentiment similar to that of John Davis's when the pinnace was stolen from his ship in 1587.[18]

Most certainly, Inuit were interested in obtaining European goods, especially wooden boats and metals. However, not all raids resulted in the acquisition of items, or were directed solely to that end. For instance, in the series of winter attacks in 1718-19, the raiders took as many wooden boats as they could, and set fire to those that remained.[19] While destructive raids may have been motivated by anger at the deaths and capture of countrymen, or in order to obtain precious items, they may also have been undertaken in the reasonable hope of discouraging competitors by destroying their hunting equipment.

French activities during the period were also provocative. Kidnappings of local people can hardly have been interpreted as friendly overtures. The desire to study native bodies and languages continued to be a factor in French-Inuit relations two centuries later. Between 1717 and 1743, about a dozen Labrador Inuit, several of them children, spent periods of captivity in Quebec City.[20] Some of them were kidnapped outright, some were sold by their families, and still others were bought or ransomed from other aboriginal groups who had captured them earlier for service as slaves.

Most of the captives died from diseases in the towns of New France, especially from smallpox. A few lived and returned to their people, like the little boy who learned French and was sent back to "his people in Labrador" where, the authorities of New France hoped, he would interpret the two cultures to one another. His story had an unhappy ending; he was killed by his own people "for being half French and half stranger."[21] Rejection of the stranger and the half-stranger, implicit in the incident, echoes the Greenland experience of assigning partially acculturated wives and mixed-blood children to the category of outcast.

Violent relations with the French did not prevent Inuit from making journeys of several hundred kilometres from the north Labrador coast to the Strait of Belle Isle in order to trade at the French fisheries. By the 1730s meetings for trade at some stations had become annual affairs and peaceful trading encounters probably outnumbered hostile raids. Large quantities of European goods were being carried to more distant communities by Inuit entrepreneurs and an Inuit-French trade jargon had developed,[22] suggesting that trading contacts were both regular and extensive.

In 1763, as a result of a war and a peace far from Inuit country, the Labrador coast passed from French to British control. The new government faced two immediate problems: French competition for use of the fisheries, and hostile Inuit raids on its establishments. The British governor of Newfoundland, Commodore Hugh Palliser, tried to solve both problems by forbidding year-round occupation of the north coast by Europeans. The ban was mildly successful in eliminating French competition, but less so in stopping Inuit harassment. The indigenous inhabitants remained hostile to the point that the continued existence of British fisheries was threatened.[23]

Desperate to end Inuit depredations, Governor Palliser gave permission for a group of Moravian missionaries, among them Jens Haven, to visit communities on the Labrador coast and find out if the Inuit would agree to a truce with the trading stations. Haven's knowledge of the Greenland dialect enabled him to negotiate peace terms directly with the (male) inhabitants. They agreed to stop raiding and to hand over part of their land to the missionaries, provided their access to European trade goods was guaranteed. Each of the Inuit received a payment for his land when he signed (or put his mark on) the compact.[24]

Haven and the Moravian Mission Society got the prize they wanted: a Greenland-style monopoly on religion and the trade that would support it, as well as a land grant of 100,000 acres.[25] Palliser attained his goal: a guarantee that the Inuit would be kept away from English fisheries, trading posts, and settlements. The Inuit secured their access to European trade items and, as had happened in Greenland, the social security that went with membership in a Christian congregation. They could not have foreseen that achieving their immediate goals would, in the end, cost them their collective autonomy. Between 1780 and 1800 a few Inuit continued to come south to trade, but there were no hostilities and no raiding parties.[26]

Missionary-trader government in northern Labrador, under British supervision, differed sharply from that of Greenland. The British government's policy of 'hands-off' was in fact a policy of 'out of sight, out of mind', which gave the Danish and German missionary-traders total control of the social and economic activities of Inuit converts. Members of the congregation were encouraged to settle near the missions and were isolated from the unconverted, insofar as this was possible, given that another missionary imperative was to keep the people in 'traditional occupations' where they could be self-supporting.[27] At the same time, as had happened in Greenland, non-Christian Inuit had access to trade and relief on the same footing as their converted countrymen. By the 1790s neither Christian nor unconverted went south to trade. The result of missionary government was a rapid erosion of aboriginal self-direction and autonomous decision making.

From the time of their fourteenth-century migration from Baffin Island to the 1720s, Labrador Inuit had tempered the effects of deteriorating climate and changes in the availability of resources by relocating communities, expanding their harvesting range, and by raiding and trading. Between 1730 and 1770, in a period when fairly stable environmental conditions relieved them of serious threats to survival, they had made decisions and used strategies that enabled them to deal with broad changes in their social environment, with notable success. Their population continued to rise, their homes were filled with large quantities of luxury, as well as utilitarian, goods of European origin, and Inuit entrepreneurs were operating a trade network capable of distributing goods as far west as Hudson Bay and north to Baffin Island.[28] With the imposition of British-supported missionary government, they entered a period of nearly two centuries during which they lost control of their social, political, and economic lives.

West Hudson Bay

Early in the eighteenth century, the people of the west coast of Hudson Bay also found themselves in new social environments, but their experience differed significantly from the new circumstances of Inuit in Greenland and Labrador. In the two latter places, people long established in homelands experienced European intrusions that proved to be permanent. On the west coast of the bay, it was the Inuit who were the newcomers, and the British presence was aloof and non-intrusive.

The arrival of Coronation Gulf immigrants some time between 1650 and 1715 brought between 100 and 200 people into Chesterfield Inlet and the near coasts. The greatly augmented population required immediate access to adequate food resources, and small groups of people began moving south along the coast to harvest seal, walrus, fish, and wood. The southward expansion brought them into territories that had been used or occupied by Athapaskan people since the 1500s. Athapaskans, specifically Chipewyan, spent the winters in the boreal forest and moved north of the treeline during the summer migrations of the caribou herds, which were their major subsistence resource. According to their own histories,[29] they had, at some earlier but unspecified period, harvested the resources of the barren grounds as far north as the arctic coast, but had ceased to do so, probably because deteriorating weather forced the caribou herds to shift to a more southerly summer range.

The newly arrived Inuit moved south cautiously, keeping well out of the way of Chipewyan caribou-hunting parties by using only the most isolated parts of the coast in summer. When the Chipewyan withdrew to the south in winter, Inuit were able to move a few miles inland to harvest the fish resources of nearby lakes and to take advantage of straggler caribou who wintered on the barren grounds. Some early British observers believed the choice of residential sites was made as much out of fear of the Chipewyan as from any preference for a maritime subsistence economy. According to Andrew Graham, they chose "an insular situation [in order] to be more secure from the attacks of the Indians, who are inveterate enemies to them, and glory in their destruction."[30] Samuel Hearne agreed. "Farther North [of Churchill] hostilities continue, and most barbarous murders are perpetrated; and the only protection the Esquimaux have from the fury of their enemies is their remote situation in the Winter, and their residing chiefly on islands and peninsulas in Summer, which renders them less liable to be surprised during that Season. But even this secluded life does not prevent the Northern Indians from harassing them greatly, and at times they are so closely pursued as to be obliged to leave most of their tools and utensils to be destroyed by their enemy."[31]

The tentative Inuit expansion into Chipewyan territory was underway precisely at the time the Hudson's Bay Company established a trading post at the mouth of the Churchill River in 1717. In 1718 and 1719 the company sent boats north on voyages from which it hoped to gain geographical information relevant to the ongoing search for a northwest passage, and to the discovery of valuable mineral deposits. It also wanted to learn more about the inhabitants of the area and to persuade them to come to Churchill to trade. The Inuit, in the course of their southward expansion to the islands and peninsulas between Chesterfield Inlet and Knapp's Bay, met HBC traders for the first time.[32]

Their numbers are not known. The log of the 1718 voyage noted people on the coast in "large numbers," and the 1719 log reported "many" people at Whale Cove.[33] The company's potential customers and clients showed none of the hostility that had characterized the Baffin Island encounters 125 years earlier, and little enthusiasm for trade. They accepted gifts of metal knives and other cutting tools, and offered "some Whalebone Oyle and some Sea Horse teeth [walrus tusk]" in exchange.[34]

On the second of the voyages, the Knapp's Bay people agreed to Chief Trader Henry Kelsey's suggestion that two of their young boys go with him to Churchill, to be returned the following year. Kelsey, familiar with the Chipewyan and Cree custom of exchanging children and young people, offered to leave two "Indian" boys, Andrew and Daniel, as hostages. It is not clear whether Andrew and Daniel were Chipewyan or Cree, and although they were referred to as "slaves," their status with the Hudson's Bay Company is as mysterious as their ethnicity. Kelsey named the two Inuit boys Jerry and Sharper.[35]

Kelsey's intention was for the boys to learn English and some of the intricacies of European trading customs before being returned to the community where they would act in future as language and culture interpreters. Inuit motives in agreeing to the exchange of boys may have been precisely the same; Kelsey's offer was an opportunity for them to gain useful information about the strangers' language, customs, and technology, and a means of establishing good relations with the newcomers in order to expand the network of allies on whom they could depend for assistance in times of need.

Whatever the reason for the willingness of Jerry's and Sharper's people to let them spend a year at the trading post, their trust was not misplaced. In 1720 Captain Hancock returned them safely to their families with a good

report, both "ladds" having learned English quickly and "proved very agree-
able."[36] Andrew and Daniel, the "Indian slave" boys, did not return to
Churchill; unlike the two "ladds," they had not survived the winter in strange
surroundings.[37]

Henry Kelsey's 1721 trip north was intended to be a trading voyage, but
in the fourth year of contact, the local people continued to show a marked
lack of interest in trade.[38] In 1722 Captain Scroggs was sent north with
instructions to spread the word that a trading post had been established at
Churchill River and to invite the Inuit to come there to trade. The voyage
did not have the desired effect. No Inuit made the trip to Churchill.

After a fifteen-year hiatus, the company decided on a new attempt at
drawing Inuit to the post.[39] Its field officers questioned the policy, pointing
to the dangers inherent in having two warring groups simultaneously at
the post. Their letter of August 1, 1738, read, in part: "With submission to
your honours we think there may be danger of drawing them to Ascomay
Point [at the Churchill River], if we could, while so mortal an enmity is
subsisting between them and the Northern Indians."[40] Head office took
their point. In 1739 it ordered annual voyages as far north as ice conditions
would allow, to carry the trade to the people in their own communities.[41]

In contrast to the preceding century, all European vessels travelling the
coast between Knapp's Bay and Roes Welcome saw Inuit or signs of recent
Inuit occupation. James Isham reported "numerous" people on the coast
near Whale Cove in 1740. Captain Francis Smith was more precise, with a
count of 200 people seen on the coast between Knapp's Bay and Whale
Cove in 1744.[42]

The 1744 voyage was the last of a series of six trading visits between
1737 and 1744, and was fairly typical of the trips that had preceded it. On
July 1, 1744, Francis Smith in *Churchill* sailed from the Churchill River,
arriving at Knapp's Bay on July 8. A day later, after trading with the forty or
so people there, he moved on to a second location about thirty kilometres
to the north, where he found a community of between thirty and thirty-
five men, women, and children. On July 10, about twenty kilometres farther still, Smith found a single family. Five days later, he waited at anchor in
Whale Cove for twenty-four hours until thirty-seven kayaks appeared with
whale oil and baleen to trade.[43] The number of kayaks suggests that a very
large settlement, perhaps as many as 150 people, was somewhere in the
vicinity, although Smith and his crew did not see it.

No Inuit were at any of the usual anchorages on the coast at the moment of Smith's arrival, but they always responded to the sound of the
sloop's guns, arriving a day after the alert. The timing suggests they were

occupied at a distance from the coast, but not out of earshot of the guns. They kept the trading sessions brief, and did not remain near the sloop or the anchorage after they had run out of things to trade. Unlike the Cumberland Sound people, who danced and played football with John Davis's crews, and the Hudson Strait groups encountered by Bylot, the Keewatin people did not stay to feast, socialize, pilfer, or ask for gifts after trading had been concluded.

Thirty years and a dozen encounters with British traders apparently had had no effect on the habits of west-coast Inuit. They occupied the same summer villages during the same weeks as they had in 1718. The items they traded in the early 1750s were the same as those they had traded in 1719: whale oil, blubber, baleen, the occasional narwhal or walrus tusk, and once in a while a wolf, wolverine, or marten pelt. The items they took in trade were the same as those they had taken at every trading occasion since 1719: bayonets, hatchets, scissors, ice chisels, knives, awls, and needles, all useful in hunting and preparing skins.

The behaviour of the west-coast Inuit toward the Hudson's Bay Company's personnel was in sharp contrast to that exhibited by other arctic groups. There were no displays of hostility or overt xenophobia similar to those shown by the Baffin Islanders and Labrador coast people, and none of the long-distance raiding and trading characteristic of Labrador Inuit. Nor did they create entrepreneurial roles for themselves and distribute large quantities of European goods through their own trade networks, as the Labrador people did. The west-coasters showed no interest in settling near the traders, as the Greenlanders had done during the same period, or even in visiting them. The trading rituals associated with other groups, such as initiatory silent trade, diplomatic greetings, formal exchange of gifts between leaders, exchange of temporary hostages, and feasting, were absent, except when instigated by outsiders. Trading activity did not lead to socializing. For the west-coast Inuit, trade was a business to be carried out quickly, followed by immediate return to other occupations.

The differences in the responses of Keewatin coast communities to Europeans between 1718 and 1750, and those of more easterly Inuit groups in the same period and in the preceding centuries, can be explained by the geographical, historical, and psychological factors that pertained in different contact situations. Between 1576 and 1616, Baffin Island, Labrador, and Digges Island people had reacted with extreme violence to appearances of strangers into their country. Meetings north of Churchill, on the other hand, were mildly cordial. One reason may have been the relatively short period of Inuit occupancy. They were newcomers, tentatively intruding into territory to which the Chipewyan clearly had a prior claim. As new-comers themselves, they were in no position to protest the presence of other people who, as far as they knew, may also have been long-time in-habitants. Second, unlike the people of Baffin Island and the Labrador coast, they had not experienced repeated kidnappings and the theft of women by Europeans, and had no revenge debts to collect.

At the same time, they were probably aware that open acts of violence would almost certainly carry a high price. After the 1718 voyage, they knew that an alliance of some sort existed between the British traders and the Chipewyan. They also knew from their encounters with James Knight's shipwrecked crews, some time between 1719 and 1721, what firearms could do. They may even have known or guessed the effects of firearms on hu-man bodies from encounters with their Chipewyan neighbours. They had every reason to conclude that retaliation by armed Indians and the Indians' white allies, who together greatly outnumbered them, would almost cer-tainly follow acts of violence against the floating trading posts. Knowledge that they stood to gain little or nothing, and to lose much, by violent actions against the itinerant traders was sufficient encouragement to peace-ful relations.

Differences in geography may account for the absence of Labrador-style raiding, and for long-distance trading and settlement as they occurred in Greenland and Labrador. Churchill post, the only possible raiding target, was safe from Inuit attack by virtue of being so far from their country, continuously occupied, and well manned. The presence at the post of Chipewyan and possibly Cree enemies, combined with the high costs of travel and lost hunting opportunities, were also sufficient deterrents to at-tempts at long-distance trade. Distance between the trading post and pos-sible client communities north and east of Chesterfield Inlet, as well as the small numbers of potential customers on the barren grounds and Melville Peninsula, were other factors that militated against the adoption by Keewatin Inuit of entrepreneurial and middleman roles. In sum, the costs of a redistributive trade network would have outweighed any profits.

Settlement near the trading post was not an option. The Churchill trad-ers did not establish posts in Inuit country comparable to the fishing and whaling stations, and the missions, of Greenland and Labrador. West-coast bay people were also less pressed for resources from 1718 to 1750 than the eastern arctic communities had been between the 1570s and 1700. The presence of competitors for the limited resources of Frobisher Bay and Digges Island was an immediate and potentially serious threat. West-coast bay people, on the other hand, were not facing life-threatening resource shortages. Censuses taken by the sloop captains showed no population losses that could have been the result of periods of starvation. The people had no reason to treat the crews of *Prosperous, Success, Musquash,* and *Churchill,* the Hudson's Bay Company's sloops sailing north from Churchill post, as competitors for scarce resources.

While west-coast Inuit were apparently not hard-pressed for subsistence resources in the first half of the 1700s, they did not have unlimited supplies, either. A precondition of trade is that each party must have a surplus of at least one item desired by the other. The key word is "surplus." It does not make sense to trade necessities for non-essentials if the lack of necessities will result in fatal scarcity at a later date. And it does not make sense to take time away from acquiring necessities in order to obtain goods that are only useful for trade.

The key questions are: What constitutes surplus? and How is it acquired? The simple answer to the first question is that "surplus" is what remains after use or need is satisfied. Few individuals or social units will have difficulty predicting use or need over the short term of a season. The difficulty is in predicting the availability and accessibility of adequate resources for the period of at least a year. The problem is compounded where resources are seasonal, subject to extreme fluctuation, and limited to one or two species, which was the situation faced by the Keewatin people. For them, surplus was more complicated than the simple definition would suggest. Because they were relative newcomers to the coast, they lacked knowledge about what the worst conditions might be, and were, therefore, uncertain how much they needed to harvest and store in any particular season.

One means of minimizing risks inherent in unpredictability is to amass resources in times of abundance and store them for use in times of scarcity. Because fluctuations in availability and accessibility of resources cannot be confidently predicted, the quantities of resources sufficient to satisfy needs cannot be foreseen with certainty, either. Communities must, therefore, amass resources for storage in sufficient quantities to satisfy needs for any eventuality, including the worst case, consistent with their technological capabilities.[44]

The necessity to store resources sufficient for an entire season if the worst happens means that resources must be seized and stored at the first, and every subsequent, opportunity. If the worst does not happen (and for most arctic communities in most years, it did not), resources stored as future subsistence eventually become unneeded surplus. In other words, the creation of surplus is inherent in storage-dependency.

The Keewatin coast people visited by the sloops every year did not have much in the way of surplus, partly because the voyages always took place in July. Even in years when the spring and early summer seal and whale hunts were enormously successful, people would not yet have amassed enough oil for food, light, and fuel to see them through an entire winter. Lacking surpluses, as they defined them, they were in no position to engage in brisk trade with the sloops. The best they could do was exchange small amounts of current or potential subsistence supplies for implements that would increase their hunting and food-processing efficiency. It was probably also the wisest thing they could do.

Company personnel, accustomed as they were to dealing with Cree and Chipewyan, were mildly puzzled by the absence of excitement, social ritual, and bargaining at west-coast trading locations. Andrew Graham suggested that Inuit lacked interest because they did not perceive themselves to be in need of anything. "[Wood] seems to be the only article the Esquimaux are short of, and it is but seldom they feel a scarcity of it.... The sea is to them the treasures of the universe, affording them food, raiment and all the necessaries of life; and the surplus of their labour is sufficient to barter with Europeans for superfluities and ornaments."[45]

Graham assumed, reasonably enough, that Inuit, like Europeans, were prepared to exchange goods to acquire items of a nature or quality they could not harvest or produce for themselves. He was not correct, however, in claiming that the Inuit were indifferent to trade, or that they bartered only for "superfluities and ornaments." From the time of the first sloop voyage, they were keenly interested in acquiring metal cutting tools, whether as gifts or through trade, and in every trading year they added considerably to their store of useful items. Everything they traded for was in the nature of a capital investment—items that would increase their efficiency as hunters, tanners, and tailors, amassed slowly and steadily. They did not trade for 'luxury' goods for at least the first hundred years of trading contacts.

In the 1744 trade described earlier, eighteen men at Knapp's Bay received ten awls, eleven hatchets, twenty-five knives, eight ice chisels, and six bayonets. A pound and a half of glass beads, twenty quilting needles, twenty metal buttons, seventeen looking glasses, a brass collar, seven rings, six bells, and two ivory combs also changed hands. A day later at a camp consisting of exactly one tent, the householder exchanged one bag of seal oil for four awls, thirteen knives, and two ice chisels, along with one double-edged metal scraper, fourteen finger rings, and three-quarters of a pound of glass beads.[46] The nineteen men who engaged in trade acquired, on average, more than three knives each, and each of the households received at least one hatchet, chisel, or bayonet. One man, who acquired thirteen knives, may have been acting as a purchasing agent for an entire community, or possibly as a middleman.

These examples are typical, and do not suggest that Keewatin Inuit were indifferent to trade and the acquisition of useful items. When the company presented its newest customers with opportunities to acquire items that would make survival more certain and perhaps even more comfortable, they were ready to take advantage of the offer. Slowly and steadily, they acquired valuable metal tools at very little cost. The individual who received four awls, thirteen knives, two ice chisels, and an array of other items in exchange for one bag of seal oil was not unusual. Andrew Graham may have been right that trade was poor, but only from the company's point of view. The company's failure to realize a profit was not due to lack of interest on the part of its customers. Some of it can be attributed to Inuit lack of tradeable surpluses, but most of it was the logical outcome of the sloop captains' habits of giving gifts and accepting worthless country products in exchange for goods of much greater value. As an attempt to create consumer demand and draw customers to Churchill, the loss leaders did not work. People were not diverted from their primary goal of ensuring their own survival through harvesting the resources of their own territory.

That primary goal may, in fact, have been the source of the aloofness toward traders and trading that Andrew Graham sensed in the actions and attitudes of the west-coast Inuit. Their recent history explains why this may have been so. Like the Hudson's Bay Company, the west-coast Inuit were new to the area. They had been there three generations at the most, assuming that the migration from Coronation Gulf took place in the mid-1650s, the earliest possible date. The people who met the first sloops in 1718 and succeeding years could have been the children of the original immigrants. If the migration took place in the 1680s, the most likely possibility, or later, which is also possible, then many of the immigrants could still have been alive. Even as late as 1750, there may have been individuals alive who had actually made the trek across the barren grounds.

As immigrants, their first priority was to create appropriate ways to deal with their new physical environment, learning where the country's resources were and devising efficient systems for harvesting them. Identification of possible resource-acquisition strategies, assessment of each in terms of costs and benefits, and choice of the most appropriate ones depend on having adequate information. In hunter-gatherer societies generally, the most important kind of information is environmental; the ability to deal with "environmental variability" depends on the "ability to collect, process, and store information" about it.[47] The body of knowledge to be collected and processed by a newly arrived population was enormous. They needed to know the general lie of the land and the details of its topography to determine how and when travel was efficient, as distinct from merely possible; they needed to know its particular flora and fauna, in order to discover what resources were available, in what quantities, when and where, and the degree to which each was readily accessible; and they had to become familiar with the unique habits of particular caribou herds and seal populations. If, as Marc G. Stevenson has suggested, the ancestors of the Keewatin coast people had spent several generations on the wooded upper Thelon River after leaving Coronation Gulf, theirs would have been an inland, riparian economy, which they would have had to change drastically to wrest a living on a treeless coast where marine mammals were the primary sources of food, clothing, shelter, and fuel.

They also had to adjust all the elements within their cognitive systems. The clues by which they understood, predicted, and controlled the physical world were different in their new location. They needed to know when the salmon would spawn, the caribou would rut, the seal would den, the warble fly would hatch, and the swans would nest, not in terms of a days-and-dates calendar, but in terms of a mental almanac consisting of clues from the physical environment itself. Wind direction, temperature, topography, precipitation, insolation, daylight, and dark were all variables that affected freeze-up, break-up, flood, and the locations, numbers, and movements of animals. Each variable on its own affected weather forecasting, navigation, cartography, snowhouse construction, travel and transportation, and every other aspect of physical existence. The almost limitless combinations and permutations of the variables made their interpretation a complex undertaking indeed.

Because the animal, and other, resources on which they depended for survival were different, the newly arrived west-coasters had to make appropriate adjustments to their technology. New techniques for floe-edge sealing had to be developed to replace the breathing-hole sealing that had been the main food-harvesting method in Coronation Gulf. And, again if Marc G. Stevenson is correct about a sojourn on the Thelon River, there might not have been a hunter in any of their communities who had actually hunted and killed a seal. The almost complete absence of whalebone required the development of a new architecture. Clothing styles and fabrication techniques had to be re-thought to make better use of the available material. Cache construction and other storage technology had to be altered to suit differences in building materials, food supplies, temperature, and humidity.

These adaptations are all related to the natural world. Learning the manual skills and amassing the knowledge necessary for survival in the new physical environment required a huge investment of time and energy. The immigrants, however, also had to collect and process information about their new social environment. They needed to know if other groups of people were nearby, who they were, and how they were responding to the sudden increase in the numbers of people resident around Chesterfield Inlet. Inuit groups to the north, with their more or less similar social regulations, had to be surveyed and assessed in order to make sensible decisions about future relationships. The establishment of diplomatic relations with the less-known and unpredictable Cree and Chipewyan societies to the south, who were potentially hostile rivals for territory and resources, demanded careful collection of information and cautious overtures.

Hostility existed between Chipewyan and Inuit in the immediate post-migration period. In 1689 the possibility of Inuit attack was certainly on the mind of Henry Kelsey's native companion when he refused to go toward Inuit country for fear of meeting the enemy.[48] Immediately before and after the establishment of Churchill post, Chipewyan began reporting Inuit raids against their travelling trading parties. In 1716 a party of nine Chipewyan returning north from York Factory was attacked "in meeting of the Iskemays at Churchill River," and six of them were killed.[49] Several Chipewyan lost their lives in another incident reported in 1719.[50] In 1725 a party of 105 Chipewyan arrived at Churchill to complain that somewhere near Marble Island "the Uskuomays had been to warr with them & had Murdered Severall of them."[51]

The incidents suggest that Inuit expansion into Chipewyan territory was not entirely peaceful. There were, however, occasions when Inuit and Chipewyan met in peaceful encounters, such as in 1720, when a group of Chipewyan made peace with some "Esquimaux," probably in the vicinity of the Coppermine River, at least long enough to trade some knives and awls for copper lances and arrowheads.[52]

The Chipewyan were not the only people who had less than cordial relations with the Inuit. Like the Chipewyan, the Cree remembered ancient enmity, probably dating from the forced ejection of Inuit from the area around Churchill River a few centuries earlier. In 1724 a party of lowland Cree from York Factory was prevented by HBC personnel at Churchill from "going to warrs with ye Eskimoes."[53] As late as 1747 James Isham had to talk an "Albany Indian" out of his plan to "go to war against the Esquimaus to the Northward of here."[54] Cree and Inuit had occupied widely separated territories for several generations and could have had no quarrel over resources. However, the York and Albany Cree owned Inuit "slaves,"[55] and the aborted raids of 1724 and 1747 could have been attempts to take more captives.

Occupied as they were with physical survival and major adjustments to their social and economic lives, the Keewatin Inuit may well have seen the sloop visits as occasional, and mildly profitable, interruptions to the critical business of survival. The single-mindedness with which west-coast Inuit pursued their own interests in their own ways points to a recognition that conservatism has value as a strategy to ensure survival. Archaeological studies of the Coronation Gulf societies, direct ancestors of the Keewatin coast people, support the interpretation. "Thule sea mammal hunting strategies on Coronation Gulf ... seem to have been rather conservative, preserving and reflecting with only a few necessary modifications an economic pattern and way of life which had first developed over 1500 kilometres to the west [in Alaska]."[56]

In situations of sudden change and extreme unpredictability, conservatism can be an adaptive strategy. If something is working, changing it increases risk, and in circumstances where survival is already problematic, additional risk is unacceptable. Innovation can be safely undertaken only in conditions of security sufficient to cushion the community in the event of failure. The circumstances of the Keewatin people, in the first few generations of their occupation of the west coast of Hudson Bay, were precarious. At the time the first traders from Churchill post arrived at their summer villages, they were already dealing with an unfamiliar physical and social setting. Serious involvement with yet one more unknown may well have seemed too great a risk.

By 1750 the Keewatin Inuit had experienced a generation of sporadic contact with European trading and exploring parties, during which they had acquired trade goods and, perhaps more importantly, information about the Churchill traders, from which they could draw conclusions about the implications of the sloop trade for their own communities. Following the resumption of trade in 1750, and assurances given by Captain James Walker that in future vessels would visit the coast communities annually,[57] they experimented with new ways of acquiring European goods.

In 1753, for the first time in the company's experience on the bay's west coast, its Inuit customers were hostile and actively threatening. At Knapp's Bay between July 8 and 11, few local people were willing to trade and those who did had little to offer. They insisted that Captain Walker lend them a boat and four sailors to help them fetch their oil from a cache along the coast. After an absence of sixteen hours, the sailors and the boat returned to an anxious captain with a mere two hogsheads of oil.[58]

The almost continuous arrivals of strange Inuit from inland and the north, their repeated refusals to trade, and their demands that half the crew accompany them out of view of the sloop, worried Walker. He moved the sloop to Nevil's Bay (now Dawson Inlet), where the same scenes were repeated. By July 16 Walker was seriously alarmed by "the natives behaving so very rude to us and offering to stab one of our men." Noting growing hostility the following day, he ordered the sloop to sail.[59]

At Whale Cove on July 18, over 100 people were alongside, more than triple the usual number, and for twenty-four hours there was constant coming and going. Again Walker noted that people were "behaving themselves in so insulting a manner we were obliged to be under arms to keep them out of the sloop and not without great difficulty we could do so with them being so many in number."[60] One man managed to get on board and helped himself to a chisel. When Walker tried to stop him, he cut an inch-long gash in the captain's leg. When Walker took up a cutlass and chased him off the sloop, he picked up a lance and dared the captain to fight him. The incident ended only when Walker produced a pistol. Tension continued to mount. On July 20 "several of the natives came alongside and would be on board whether we would let them or no—in two hours after that they went on shore and made a raft of their canoes and brought all their women off and put them in our boats astern of the sloop then the men left them and went on the rocks where they stayed near an hour."[61] Only after Walker's gestures of cutting the boats loose resulted in loud screams and other signs of agitation from the women, did the men ferry them back to the beach.

A day later, nine men attempted to board the sloop. Walker's order to sink their kayaks if necessary to prevent boarding so "enraged" them that they went ashore, where they stood on the rocks, each one sharpening three or four lances and holding them up in a "daring manner." When a second and larger party consisting of twenty-two men tried to force its way on board *Churchill*, Walker hauled in the anchor and moved farther offshore, while about 150 people made threatening gestures on the rocky beach. Within hours, about 300 people were on the beach, greatly outnumbering the eight crewmen, "which might," Walker suggested, "be the reason they behaved so rudely to us."[62]

Several elements of the incident—the gathering of people, the ruse to separate crew members, the display of weapons, the taunting and posturing (*qarzuigutsaq*), and the fact that the sloop's crew of eight was greatly out-numbered—are reminiscent of the experiences of Frobisher and Davis nearly 200 years earlier, and fully consistent with other descriptions of Inuit war or pre-war activities. The motive is harder to discern. In contrast to the Baffin Island and Labrador coast people a century or so earlier, the communities of west Hudson Bay had no grounds for seeing the strangers as possible competitors for resources.

Of the nineteen British vessels that visited parts of the west coast between 1718 and 1752, fifteen were trading sloops from the Churchill post.[63] They came only in the summer, stayed only a few days, and had crews of less than ten men. Local people knew from their visits on board the sloops that the visitors brought provisions adequate for their own needs, plus surpluses of ship's biscuit and oatmeal, which they shared generously. They may also have known from the reports of Jerry and Sharper, the two Knapp's Bay boys who spent the winter of 1719-20 at the post, that the traders had stocks of food from their own country, replenished yearly, as well as access to the food resources of the Churchill area.

In the years between 1750 and 1752, however, one or two Chipewyan crew members attempted to provide the sloop with some fresh meat and fish. They hunted only along the coast, the least likely place to find either caribou or fish in the summer, leaving the more fruitful inland areas to the local people, and their hunts met with limited success. They cannot have placed any noticeable strain on resources. Nevertheless, the Inuit may have objected, not to the presence of Europeans in what had effectively become Inuit territory, but to the presence of Chipewyan hunters. While the sloop captains had shown themselves to be generous in sharing food and other resources, Inuit had little reason to expect hospitality from the Chipewyan.

If the threats and ruses of 1753 had been intended to deliver new resources to the communities, the strategy did not work. The local people succeeded only in driving the visitors away, at the cost of losing whatever chances they had of acquiring the intruders' desirable resources, at least for that year. As far as they knew, the departure of *Churchill* for the south in 1753 may have been their last opportunity to obtain valuable goods in any year.

When the sloop returned in 1754, the populations of the summer villages had returned to their more usual numbers. Walker recorded a total of 150 people on the entire coast: fewer than twenty at Knapp's Bay, about thirty at Nevil's Bay, less than forty at Whale Cove, and the rest scattered in camps of one or two families.[64] Whatever they had hoped to accomplish by their threatening behaviour in 1753, they did not repeat the tactics.

Instead, they had new tactics in 1754. They met the sloop with forty-five kilos of deer flesh and twelve tongues, which they offered for trade.[65] The meat may have represented no more than the edible parts of two caribou; nevertheless, it was a new product in their trade, indicating, first, that they had some surplus food, little though it may have been, and second, that they were thinking of subsistence resources as commodities. They may also have hoped to demonstrate that they were able to replace Chipeywan hunters as provisioners to the sloops' crews.

The second change, a demand for more control over trade goods, also indicated new ways of thinking about commodities. A few men, invited to *Churchill's* galley for a quick meal, spotted twenty-four tin cooking pots among the cook's utensils and insisted on buying thirteen of them.[66] The company responded to its customers' demands. On the next voyage, the sloop carried sixteen large and sixteen small tin pots, and a dozen saucepans in the trade goods inventory. All thirty-two pots and eight of the saucepans were sold.[67] Pots, saucepans, and kettles became staple, and very popular, trade items in succeeding years.

In 1755 at Knapp's Bay, "very kind and courteous" people met *Churchill* with "a deal of joy" and "parted very lovingly" from the crews when the sloop departed. Even so, John Bean, making his first trip as captain, wondered if their "civility was from innocence or from lack of opportunity to insult," and worried that a hundred hostile fighters might at any moment appear and threaten his boat and crew. When he visited his customers in their tents to show them samples of the kinds of items the company was interested in buying, he took five "well armed" men with him. The people responded to his visits by bringing forth five wolf and two fox skins, which they traded, along with blubber and baleen, for awls, quilting needles, files, hatchets, tin pots, and ice chisels.[68]

In the atmosphere of good will and developing commercial relations, John Bean's fears that the unusual hostility exhibited by the Inuit in 1753 might surface once more seem to have been unjustified. However, violence was loosed at Knapp's Bay in 1755, in which Inuit were the victims, a half-dozen Chipewyan were the instigators, and the company was a contributing, although unwitting, cause. Within hours of *Churchill's* departure, a party of travelling Chipewyan took murderous revenge on their ancient enemies.

Interpreting the Hudson's Bay Company's new policy of taking the trade to the Inuit as favouritism, Chipewyan had complained on several occasions at having to travel overland for distances of up to 150 kilometres in order to trade at Churchill, while the Inuit had only to wait in their camps for the floating posts to come to them.[69] In 1755 a party of Chipewyan men on their way to Churchill were on the coast a few hours' walk south of Knapp's Bay when they saw the sloop sailing north in search of Inuit. They sent up a smoke signal, their usual means of communicating at a distance. John Bean recognized it as a Chipewyan signal and, following his instructions, ignored it. He completed the usual round of trading at Knapp's Bay and Whale Cove, and sailed south.

In November several young Chipewyan men reported to the Churchill traders their version of what had taken place at Knapp's Bay on July 22, 1755. Having signalled the sloop on its way north without response, they shadowed it along the coast to Knapp's Bay. From hiding places among the boulders on the beach, they watched the trading activity and saw the sloop depart. When all the members of the little community were asleep in their tents, they struck, killing between sixteen and eighteen people. They kept one young woman alive, "which it seems some of them fancied." She eventually escaped, naked and barefoot, but was easily tracked in the treeless land, and when she tried to hide in a shallow pool, they "found her and shot her instantly in the water."[70]

While relations between Inuit and Chipewyan along most of their shared border were inflammatory and unpredictable, no hostile incidents at the coastal villages had been reported in the years between the 1717 founding of Churchill and 1755. The attack on Knapp's Bay, therefore, appears to be something of an anomaly. The reasons for the differences in Inuit-Chipewyan relations in the coastal villages and those between the two peoples in the transitional forest areas, as well as the underlying cause of the attack on Knapp's Bay, may have more to do with the Chipewyan than with the Inuit.

From the time of the first trading posts in Hudson Bay, the traders had distinguished between "Home Indians" and "Away Indians." The distinction had implications for the external relations of both groups, and for the Inuit. Home Indians or "the Home Guard" lived at or near the posts, and were employed as interpreters, hunters, and labourers. Samuel Hearne described them as "certain of the natives who are immediately employed under the protection of the Company's servants, reside on the plantation, and are employed in hunting for the Factory."[71] They learned English and were often familiar with several aboriginal languages and dialects, as well; they were skilled hunters; they had insider knowledge of the geography of the country; and they were familiar with the manners and customs of neighbouring indigenous societies and of the British traders. Some had kinship ties with trading-post personnel through female family members who had entered into country marriages with company officers and men. As a result,

Home Indians were effective as culture brokers and diplomatic agents for the company.

The particular skills and experience of the Home Indians gave them attitudes somewhat different from those of their Away compatriots. Because the Homeguard were able to maintain peaceful relations with their ancient arctic enemies does not mean that others of their countrymen were able or willing to do so. Away Indians spent their lives in their own territories and were less familiar with European manners and methods. A few visited the forts and factories occasionally in trading parties, but most never went to the posts. The Chipewyan attack on the community at Knapp's Bay in 1755, the bloodiest ever recorded for the bay coast, was the work of Away Indians.

In spite of the terrible incident at Knapp's Bay, no intensification of Chipewyan-Inuit hostilities followed, nor did the Inuit withdraw to more distant precincts. Quite the contrary: "Pacific and friendly terms [began] to dawn between those two tribes at Knapp's Bay, Navel's Bay, and Whale Cove."[72] A few Chipewyan families began spending the summers at Knapp's Bay, living amicably beside their Inuit neighbours. In 1762 they told Captain Magnus Johnston that a truce existed between their two peoples,[73] and by 1764 it was taken for granted by the company's men that the two nations were "now tolerably well reconciled with each other."[74] In 1767-68 at least two Inuit families spent the winter with a Chipewyan community on the barren grounds about 250 kilometres northwest of Churchill.[75] Again, it is worth noting that the Chipewyan were Homeguard families, whose understanding of trade and social relations between nations differed from the perceptions of Away groups.

For the next twenty-five years, Knapp's Bay was the site of bicultural summer communities in which the Chipewyan formed the larger group. In 1765 between thirty and forty Inuit in seven tents, and Chipewyan individuals "to the number of 60 or 70," made up the summer community. A year later, the community consisted of three tents of Inuit and twenty-seven of Chipewyan. By 1770 so many Chipewyan were present that Captain Magnus Johnston complained about running out of trade goods before he had finished his tour of the coast. Between 1770 and 1782 the Inuit population averaged about thirty and the Chipewyan about 100.[76]

While historic enmities may have been smoothed over, the people of the two northern nations remained distinctly different in the conduct of their economic lives. The Chipewyan continued to act as provisioners, trading caribou meat as well as fox and marten pelts, and occasional robes of black bear fur. In exchange they wanted powder and shot, woven cloth, clothing of European manufacture, brandy, and medals. The Inuit continued to bring seal oil, baleen, caribou skins, and, from time to time, a wolfskin; in exchange they wanted kettles, tin pots, bayonets, awls, and chisels. Several Chipewyan men who were well known to the Churchill traders undertook to keep the peace at Knapp's Bay, and one of them, the trusted trading captain Hissty, promised to teach the Inuit how to trap furs for trade.[77]

Inuit were also learning about white men and their style of trade from their own young people. Jerry and Sharper, who had accompanied Henry Kelsey to Churchill in 1719, were only the first of a number of teenagers who learned the language and customs of the British traders at first hand. In 1756, the year after the massacre at Knapp's Bay, the people of that community sent two youngsters to the fort.[78] Most of the company's temporary wards were boys, but at least one woman, Doll, was an interpreter for the company, sailing with Magnus Johnston in 1765 and 1766.[79]

Between 1765 and 1771 two or three arctic apprentices from Knapp's Bay, Whale Cove, and Marble Island wintered at Churchill every year.[80] Young Petee Gunn was especially valued by Magnus Johnston, as well he might be, considering his linguistic achievements and apparent familiarity with the customs of the local people. Johnston records that "Old Hogg Shoke came along side and brought along with him Pette Gun a lad about 14 years of age who has been 2 winters at the factory before and understands Southern Indian as also Eskimaux Languages very well and the Same Gun is of material service to me along the coast amongst the different tribes of natives—I then gave the old man his Gun and all other presents sent by me to him from The Governor."[81]

The capitalized word "Gun" in Johnston's report was almost certainly a deliberate double entendre. The temporary adoption of boy apprentices by the company was always accompanied by the giving of gifts, including a gun. Petee's father received a gun for his Gunn.

The company's London office hoped the boys would become familiar with its methods of trade, learn enough English to be able to act as interpreters, and "acquaint their countrymen to be ready at the seaside with what commodities of trade they can procure ... also for them to inform others whom they may meet with."[82] Company officers in the field, with the exception of the sloop captains, expressed doubt that the strategy was working to the company's benefit.[83] In the 1760s, Samuel Hearne counted off some of the pros and cons of the youth-training program.

> Though during their stay at the Fort they made considerable progress
> both in the Southern Indian [Cree] and the English languages, yet those

intercourses have not been any ways advantageous to the Company, by increasing the trade from that quarter. In fact, the only satisfaction they have found for the great expense they have from time to time incurred, by introducing those strangers, is, that through the good conduct of the upper servants at Churchill River, they have at length so far humanized the hearts of those two tribes, that at present they can meet each other in a friendly manner; whereas, a few years since, whenever they met, each party premeditated the destruction of the other.[84]

The Inuit seem to have benefitted more from the practice than did their hosts. The boys learned English faster and more easily than the company's men learned the Inuit language, partly because the post personnel had much less opportunity to hear and speak it, and partly because their linguistic priorities were Chipewyan and Cree, the languages of their principle customers and trading partners. The Inuit also learned far more about British attitudes and customs than their temporary foster parents learned about the Inuit. They picked up a good deal of technological knowledge, including the construction of traps and the best ways to prepare skins for trade. Youths returning to their families after a year or two at the post were well supplied with clothing for themselves and their families, plus a store of household goods. They also brought their families "preferred customer status" with the company. The quasi-familial relationship of the fathers of the boys, and later of the young men themselves, entitled them to gifts at every meeting and to the first chance to trade.

Another benefit of temporary adoption by the Hudson's Bay Company was skill in the care, repair, and use of firearms, which Inuit had begun to acquire in the early 1760s. Andrew Graham commented that when "their young people began to winter at Churchill Settlement, they were initiated into the use of [guns], and a few of them are now annually bartered. When I commanded Churchill Factory Anno Domini 1773, 4 and 5 I trained up four young Esquimaux to use fire-arms, and left them fully a match for our best Indians, either at an object sitting or on the wing."[85]

Graham attributed the apparently more peaceful relations with the Chipewyan to the Inuit possession of guns, rather than to a fundamental change in the attitudes of either Inuit or Away Chipewyan. One of the Inuit parents made the same point. When he put his two sons into the custody of Captain Johnston in 1765, he expressed his hope that they would return home knowing how to use guns to defend their communities from their Chipewyan neighbours.[86] His continuing mistrust of the western Away Chipewyan was well founded.

In 1769 three Chipewyan on a visit to Churchill declared their intention of going to war with the Inuit, whom they blamed for the witchcraft deaths of a number of their people during the preceding winter. HBC personnel believed they had talked the warriors out of their plan,[87] but during the winter four Inuit hunters from Knapp's Bay were attacked and robbed at gunpoint by "strange Northern Indians."[88] In July 1771, Away Chipewyan carried the attack to Bloody Falls on the Coppermine River, where they destroyed an Inuit summer settlement while a horrified Samuel Hearne looked on.[89]

In spite of attacks and hard feelings at distant places, in the bicultural community at Knapp's Bay, peaceful relations between Inuit and Home Chipewyan were the norm. Slight increases in the coast trade after 1760 were due to greater numbers of Chipewyan in the summer villages, not to increased Inuit interest and involvement. They continued to spend their summers near the coast,[90] avoided areas where fur-bearing animals were found, and disappeared to inland residences for the winter. All the encouragement of the sloop captains and the efforts of Chipewyan trading captains like Hissty, who tried to convince them to spend more time hunting for saleable animals,[91] were without effect.

Until 1775, west-coast Inuit had successfully combined conservatism and adaptation to local conditions to shape their economic and social lives. After 1775, however, factors in both the physical and social environments introduced new uncertainties and forces for change. Ocean cooling resulted in the most severe summer ice conditions in Hudson Bay since the beginning of the Little Ice Age. Caribou herds began to decline, and assistance of the kind the Hudson's Bay Company was able to provide to the Chipewyan and Cree in bad economic times was not available to the Inuit.[92]

Inuit did, however, see their trade with the company as an alternate source of necessary supplies in hard times. The Marble Island people did not wait for the sloop to come to them in 1776; they went to Whale Cove with their country products to make sure they did not miss the opportunity for trade. In 1778 and 1779 the heaviest summer ice of the century to date damaged and delayed the sloop *Charlotte* past the time when Inuit frequented the coast. No trade took place and again no relief could be offered.[93]

No more than thirty-five Inuit families were seen on the entire coast in 1780, and while they had adequate caribou skins for their own use, they had none to spare for trade. At one village, the problems of deteriorating weather were compounded by a serious loss of community members. A number of people had drowned in a boating accident caused by heavy sea ice during a move from Rankin Inlet.[94] In hunting communities with populations under thirty, the loss of even a few hunters can have catastrophic implications for the group's survival. Captain George Holt paid handsomely for some oil, to give "encouragement," but he understood that people were reluctant to trade because "all the oils I am likely to trade is part of their winter stock." He recognized that so early in the summer season, the people's stored supplies were not yet sufficient to see them through the coming winter. They were most reluctant to part with anything.

The social environment of the decades from 1750 to 1780, in which Inuit had interacted with Chipewyan in their summer villages and with sloop traders every year, also changed dramatically. In 1781-82, the Chipewyan suffered a devastating smallpox epidemic that, according to Samuel Hearne, nearly destroyed them. Hearne noted that only those Indians who were members of the sloops' crews travelled up the coast in subsequent years,[95] and it was at least fifty years before they again frequented the barren grounds.

War between England and France also had its effect on the west-coast Inuit. The seizure and occupation of Churchill by the French between 1782 and 1784 prevented all trade, and when the annual sloop voyages resumed in 1785, only a few Inuit and no more than a handful of Chipewyan greeted them. Neither group had surplus goods to trade.[96]

Two years later, a combination of factors—the deteriorating weather, the disappearance of the Chipewyan, a succession of bad caribou years, and the failure of the sloop voyages in 1778 and 1779, and between 1782 and 1784—did what no amount of encouragement and persuasion in the previous seventy years had been able to accomplish: it brought Inuit to Churchill to trade. On May 28, 1787, six men, with their wives and families, arrived at the post. They had "goods which consisted of little more than a few hairy deer skins scarce worth the duty," Samuel Hearne wrote in Churchill's daily journal, and continued: "Traded with them and gave them some presents to carry back to their friends, but they inform me they intend to kill some seals off the river mouth, and build some canoes before they return to their own country. The principal reason for their undertaking this journey was to look for old iron works in the ruins of the Stone Fort.... Early in the morning [of May 30] all the Esquimaux went from the factory to pursue the seal fishery at the mouth of the river."[97]

Two months later, Inuit were at their usual summer villages in the usual numbers, but there was still "very little trade." In the summer of 1788, population shifts were evident: the people who usually summered at Knapp's

Bay were all at Nevil's Bay, but, like their countrymen all along the coast, they had little to trade. The following year, people again appeared in unaccustomed places: half the Marble Island people were at Whale Cove.[98]

From the point of view of the Hudson's Bay Company, the attempt to develop trading relations with the Inuit was a failure. With the virtual disappearance of the Chipewyan from the coast, and no profit to be had from the Inuit trade, the company decided to end its annual visits to the coastal villages. George Taylor took *Churchill* on its last northern voyage in 1790 and informed the people that the sloop would not come again.[99]

Estimates of Inuit numbers in Keewatin at the end of the eighteenth century are speculative. Archaeological investigations have suggested a population of slightly over 100 in the Chesterfield Inlet-lower Thelon River area before 1650, to which somewhere between 100 and 200 Coronation Gulf or inland immigrants were added some time in the next fifty years.[100] The head-counts of the sloop captains between 1718 and 1780 yield numbers no more reliable than the guesses based on the numbers of ruined house sites. Between 150 and 200 people were seen on the coast between Knapp's Bay and Rankin Inlet in July of most years, but they were only part of the total. In 1753, 300 or more adult men threatened the crew of *Churchill* at Whale Cove, suggesting that at least 600 adults occupied the coast and near inland between Knapp's Bay and Rankin Inlet. Andrew Graham's estimate of 500 individuals on the coast, at Chesterfield Inlet, Baker Lake, and adjacent lakes and rivers was low.[101] By the end of the century there were probably between 800 and 1000 individuals, including children, in communities along the coast, and at Chesterfield Inlet, Baker Lake, and the lower Thelon River.

Identification of Inuit residential groups, or bands, on the coast and barren grounds north of Churchill in the eighteenth century is as problematic as estimates of population. Between 1750 and 1790 the sloop crews regularly saw, and traded with, people at Knapp's Bay, Nevil's Bay, Whale Cove, and Marble Island, which Andrew Graham identified as "summer resorts." On the basis of his experiences on board *Churchill* in 1750, 1751, and 1752, and conversations with the young men who spent winters at the fort over the next twenty years, he concluded that each coastal village was the summer headquarters of a separate "tribe." He identified the four groups as the Achuiuck at Knapp's Bay, the Tahuiuck at Nevil's Bay, the Tekotheack at Whale Cove, and the Ockshotheack at Marble Island.[102] The suffixes *-uck* and *-ack* would today be written with a final *q* or *k*, and designate place names, not ethnonyms. While Graham made no comments on the possible locations of winter villages, he agreed with the sloop captains and other HBC personnel that the people spent the winters at points inland.

Taken together, archaeological and documentary evidence for the activities of the Keewatin coast Inuit between 1670 and 1790 indicates they had made decisions and choices of both major and minor importance for their future. The first was their decision to abandon Coronation Gulf to seek new opportunities to the southeast some time between 1670 and 1717. By 1718 they had begun to extend their living and hunting range southward along the coast, risking competition and conflict with Chipewyan who used the same territory. Between 1750 and 1790, the period of regular sloop voyages, they sent young people to the trading post to learn new languages, customs, and technology; they established a working relationship with the traders, keeping their distance and refusing to accommodate them, but at the same time insisting that the company supply the kinds of trade goods they wanted; they began to replace utensils and implements of their own manufacture with metal ones of sturdier, lighter materials; they agreed to peaceful coexistence with the Chipewyan; and they not only maintained their population base in spite of losses such as the one at Whale Cove in 1780, they allowed it to expand. Adaptations in their social and cultural systems, while invisible in the archaeological and documentary records, surely accompanied the other changes.

At the same time, however, they chose not to transform their lives in other ways. Throughout most of the century they made no obvious changes in their subsistence occupations, their seasonal timetables, or the locations of their multiple residences. Except for the young people who accompanied the sloops to Churchill for a winter's experience with the company, they did not visit the trading post before 1787. No Inuit Homeguard developed around the post, and Inuit–British relations did not produce a mixed-blood generation.

5.

The Degree of Cold: Subsistence and Survival, 1790–1830

The degree of cold at one place furnishes no inference which can be relied upon as to the temperature of another place even moderately distant.
                                        – George Back, at Great Fish River[1]

The intensely cold and unstable climatic regime of 1645 to 1715, known as the First Maunder Minimum, was succeeded by roughly seventy-five years of slightly milder weather in most of the northern hemisphere. This in turn gave way to four decades of intense cold, known as the Second, or Little, Maunder Minimum, beginning about 1790 and lasting until 1830. Like the First Maunder Minimum, it was global, and in the Canadian arctic climatic deterioration was especially sudden, swift, and severe. Heavy summer rains were characteristic of the Keewatin coast in the 1790s. Temperatures at Churchill were unusually cold in every winter from 1801 to 1806, and ice conditions along the coast were particularly severe in 1802, 1808, and 1815. The eruption of the Indonesian volcano Mount Tambora in 1815 added volcanic dust to the atmosphere and further reduced levels of solar heat reaching the earth's surface, setting the stage for 1816, "the year with no summer." The eleven years from 1810 to 1821 proved to be the coldest in the entire period from 1602 to 1961.[2]

Keewatin
The severe environmental and atmospheric conditions of the Second Maunder Minimum disturbed normal animal-habitat relationships, which

in turn created conditions of extreme unpredictability for human communities. The virtual disappearance of the caribou herds along western Hudson Bay resulted in varying degrees of famine and starvation for the three aboriginal groups that frequented Churchill post. Inuit from coastal villages north of Churchill, who had been visited by the trading sloops almost every year from 1750 to 1790, began going to the post. Instead of the oil and blubber that had been their stock in trade during the sloop years, they offered animal skins in exchange for the metal tools they wanted. Trading was not the only, or perhaps even the primary, reason for their trips south, however. They went because seal and whale resources near the post represented an opportunity for long-distance harvesting of products that could be treated as subsistence goods as well as trading commodities. They traded some of the products of their hunts and took what they needed for winter subsistence back to their homes, limited only by what they could carry.

In June 1791, a year after the last sloop voyage, twenty men and their families took "50 deer skins, 6 fox skins, and a wolf skin" to trade at Churchill. The pelts would not have bought them a good used gun. The ninety-one seals they took during five weeks of hunting at the Churchill River were enough to buy them several.[3] They went again in June of 1795, in larger numbers—more than sixty men, women, and children with about 390 Made Beaver (MB)* in furs. Again they hunted seal at Churchill, and then moved about thirty kilometres north to the Seal River to hunt whale for a month. They brought in the blubber of four whales and more than sixty seals. To the disappointment of post master Thomas Stayner, they ended the hunt in mid-July and left, in order to "return to their own country as by the time they can arrive there the deer will be plenty."[4]

Eight men visited the post without their families in each of the years 1796 and 1797, arriving in August and September, later in the season than in previous years. Their deerskins and fox pelts were of little worth—only 360 MB in 1796—and again, they were anxious to return to the north, and refused to join the seal and whale hunts.[5] A pattern began to emerge, which would hold for most of the next half-century. Men who went for the seal and whale hunts arrived in May or June, and nearly always brought their families. By early to mid-August, they were on their way again, anxious to

---

*The Hudson's Bay Company's unit of barter was the Made Beaver (MB). It was not currency to be passed across the counter in exchange for furs; they were simply counters with arbitrarily assigned values, 1/4, 1/2, 1, 2, and 5, by which customers could keep track of the amount of credit they could use. One MB was equal to the value of one prime beaver skin in good condition, and its value in goods varied with the value of beaver pelts on the European market.

get home before the fall caribou hunt. Men who came late in the season, in August or September, came only to trade, did not bring their families, and left almost immediately.

Years when only a few, or perhaps no, men went to the post were often either very good, or very bad, years. In very good years, when there was an abundance of caribou and enough seal in their own country to provide adequate oil for food, light, and fuel, they had no need to take part in the company's seal hunt. In very bad years, when caribou and seal resources at home failed entirely, they were often unable to get to the post because of malnutrition-related illnesses and difficult travelling conditions.

About thirty men made the trip in June and July of 1798, singly or in small groups, and together they brought the largest harvest of furs to date— deerskins and fox pelts amounting to almost 1000 MB. Some hunted seal briefly, but on July 7, "in consequence of their numerous families [in the north, they] have been obliged to betake themselves to their own country." The same year, "strangers" appeared at the post for the first time. When fourteen men arrived between July 22 and August 26 with more than 500 MB in furs, post master William Auld specifically identified eleven of them as men who had not been seen at any of the four regular ports of call during the sloop years, and who had not visited Churchill post before.[6]

In the second decade of the forty-year pessimum, the three aboriginal nations that frequented Churchill post suffered increasingly from scarce food supplies. No Inuit reached the post in 1802, and in 1803 six arrived with "the dreadful intelligence of a great part of their tribe having perished by famine during the winter, which was remarkably cold." Churchill's Chipewyan Homeguard were likewise suffering the stresses of those years and in the fall of 1804 asked for assistance from the post master, "their families being starving." The Homeguard Cree also reported "that their families are starving having not seen any deer the whole winter." As was usually the case, conditions varied widely from place to place. A party of Away Chipewyan from the west reported that at the start of their trip "they had been amongst plenty of deer but had not seen any within 12 days journey of the factory."[7]

At Churchill, post master Auld continued to get appeals for help. In February, March, and April, 1805, Cree reported that their families were "starving and had not seen any deer during the whole winter." In April and May, Auld gave relief supplies to Chipewyan families whom he described as "almost dead for hunger. I never saw more wretched objects."[8]

Like the Chipewyan and Cree, Inuit suffered from the severity and unpredictability of the weather. Between 1802 and 1821, the numbers visiting the Churchill trading post every summer, and the quantities of furs they brought, rose and fell with the temperature. Other than the years 1802 and 1808, when no Inuit went to the post, and 1810 and 1818, when they went in larger than usual numbers, they arrived in small groups, were seldom accompanied by their families, and brought few furs, usually of inferior quality. In seven of the twenty years—1804, 1807, 1809, 1810, 1812, 1815, and 1816—they stayed to hunt seal, but only long enough to get essential supplies of oil, blubber, and skins for their own use, indicating a subsistence crisis in their own countries. Between 1813 and 1820, none remained to hunt whale.[9]

As they had done in the 1750s, they looked for ways to ease their misery and ensure their survival. Expansion of territory was one of these. Early in the century, people from the coast between Whale Cove and Rankin Inlet began using inland territories more extensively in order to hunt muskox as well as caribou.[10] Some also turned to technological upgrading. In 1807 five men convinced post master William Auld to sell them an old whaleboat, and by pooling their labour they were able to bring in the twenty-five beluga they needed to pay for it. Still others, unable to find adequate food supplies in their territory north of Whale Cove, turned to hunting for peltries. A dozen men spent part of the winter of 1806-07 hunting wolf, wolverine, and white fox, and in the spring appeared at the post, anxious to trade them for provisions.[11]

Planned relocation was yet another survival strategy used in those difficult years. In the fall of 1804, when Churchill post was already crowded with Chipewyan in need of assistance, at least four Inuit families sought relief and a winter refuge at the post, the first occasion on which Inuit other than the young apprentices of the previous century showed interest in spending a winter near the traders.[12]

Eighty men, women, and children went to the fort at the end of May 1810, with almost nothing to trade. Their appearance in such numbers may have been the first step in a planned relocation to territory where they expected to find more abundant resources. Within a week of arriving at the post, they declared their intention to go en masse to York Factory. Aware of the widespread suffering of Cree southwards along the bay, and of the heavy burden of relief already undertaken by the company, post master Thomas Topping "sent for their head men who promised they would not go." Instead they hunted seal and whale, frightened the Chipewyan, and worried Topping with their constant pilfering.[13]

Inuit remained hard-pressed in 1812, and seven families bringing only twenty-seven MB in country products to the post "complained as well as the Northern Indians of the scarcity in the winter of provisions." Long-distance harvesting of scarce resources was one of the strategies resorted to in 1814. Twenty-one men, who brought in more than 500 fox pelts, refused to hunt seal and whale, but took the time "to turn over the rubbish thrown out of the ruins for lead to convert into shot of which however they could find none." Their search is reminiscent of the 1787 incident in which Inuit came to Churchill to "look for old iron works in the ruins of the Stone Fort." In 1812 and 1814, new supplies of iron and lead could have increased the efficiency of their hunting implements. [14]

Along with requests for assistance, attempts to increase hunting and transportation efficiency, long-distance harvesting of resources, and possible attempts at relocation, the west-coast Inuit also became more heavily involved in hunting and trapping fur-bearing animals. Captain Edward Chappell, exploring Hudson Bay in *HMS Rosamond*, arrived at York Factory in September 1814, and noted that "the land to the northward of Churchill Factory, in Hudson's Bay is inhabited by Esquimaux, who, *contrary to the general customs of this people, employ themselves in hunting.* They carry their furs annually to Churchill Factory, for the purpose of traffic" [emphasis added]. [15]

Yet another economic strategy, although probably not a new one, was the exchange of country products among groups at trade meetings within Inuit territory. In 1815 the people of Knapp's Bay informed post master Adam Snodie that they planned to go "far off to trade furs with other tribes of Esquimaux whom they prevent from coming here as it enabled them to carry on an advantageous traffic at the expence of their more credilous neighbours." For post personnel, trade among Inuit communities meant potentially more clients and customers, and, with Inuit middlemen delivering both country products and trade items, none of the costs of transportation. Augustine, the company's Inuit clerk, convinced Snodie "that many of his nation are incapasitated from procuring furs" by their lack of steel traps, which, Snodie thought, "would be an essential article and which they have hitherto never been favoured with." Steel traps of the type used by the Chipewyan thereafter became regular items in the Inuit trade. During the same period, firearms continued to be the most desired item on Inuit shopping lists. [16]

The already difficult situation of Inuit, Chipewyan, and Cree became even worse following the eruption of Mount Tambora in 1815. Increased atmospheric pollution shut out sunlight and solar warmth, resulting in a further sudden drop in world temperatures. In 1816, the worst year in a century, only three Inuit families made it to Churchill, bringing a mere fourteen white fox pelts. They explained that "their hunt was very nigh to this place all the winter and no deer about them, their only subsistance was fish which occupied their time angling and prevented them from killing foxes."[17]

Cree and Chipewyan also reported "great starvation" that winter. The company sent food and transport to bring survivors to the post, noting that "their account and indeed appearance of having been in starvation is beyond discussion. Many of their relations had died during winter." By late May of 1816, 106 Chipewyan were receiving relief at Churchill.[18]

Tempers were short and intercultural tensions were high during the years of extreme cold and scarce resources. In 1807 the journal writer at Churchill had noted, "Much jealousy subsists between [the Inuit] and the other natives indeed the 3 distinct tribes are excessively jealous of the least favour being shown to any of the others so that it is with much difficulty we can please them."[19] People were on edge again in 1815, and there was trouble when a gun-trading deal between an Inuit and a Chipewyan went sour. Post master Hugh Leslie defused a potentially dangerous confrontation by taking temporary custody of all Inuit firearms and standing guard while the affronted Chipewyan left the post.[20]

In 1818 seventy-four men, the largest number of Inuit men ever to have come to the post at one time, arrived "with a quantity of white fox, wolves and deerskins etc to trade or barter into guns, ammunition, with such other articles of merchandise as they were able to procure." They came without their families, caused no trouble, and within forty-eight hours they were gone.[21]

The winter of 1819-20 was another desperate season, and in the summer that followed only sixteen men visited the post. They brought nothing to trade, "but came merely for the purpose of killing seals." They were given ammunition and powder on credit and went "off for said purpose."[22] The presence of large numbers of seals at the mouth of the Churchill River offered an opportunity for Inuit to survive 'bad' economic times in their own country by combining long-distance resource harvesting with short-term labour contracts. The costs of travel, transportation, and opportunity were manageable because the traders were prepared to outfit the potential seal hunters on credit, and undertook to feed and otherwise care for the women and children while the men hunted. Inuit recognized and used the opportunity.

The 1807 strategy by which a group of men turned accumulated savings into capital equipment was repeated in 1821. On May 11 Kootchuck and Au-we-ace-wack, hunters well known to the Churchill traders, arrived at the post, and were later joined by three other men and two or three boys.

They intended to hunt seal and whale, and requested a boat to use in transporting the oil. While the post's carpenter repaired a boat for their use, they hunted caribou, bringing in twenty-six deerskins to be put on account. Between May 22 and the end of July, they killed 258 seals and twenty-six beluga. On July 31 they used their accumulated collective credit to purchase the old whaleboat.[23]

Also in 1821, the Inuit took steps to minimize their investment in the seal and whale hunt and to maximize their profits. They warned Hugh Leslie that they would no longer transport the products of the hunts without payment, nor would they accept the physical risks created by the company's unseaworthy boats and inadequate work force. "They would only agree to it upon this condition," Leslie wrote to Governor George Simpson that fall, "namely that I would receive the blubber from them where it was killed."[24]

The following year the expected traders from the north were late arriving at the post, leading Leslie to think they may have been short of provisions and unable to spare time for a trading trip. When nineteen hunters finally arrived, they immediately locked wills with Leslie, keeping to the position they had stated the previous year by refusing to hunt whale until they were assured the company would transport the oil from the killing ground to the post. Leslie promised extra rewards and then tried to force their hand by refusing to trade with them, "the only plan I could adopt to ensure their stay," he wrote. But their seeming capitulation was short-lived. Three days and eleven whales later, they claimed to have run out of harpoon heads and prepared to depart. When accusations of breach of promise failed to move them, Leslie was forced to trade their 367 white, and five blue, fox furs, ten wolfskins, three wolverine pelts, one muskox robe, 198 deerskins, eighteen pounds of walrus ivory, and one and a half tons of whale blubber, and they left for their homes.[25]

Two days after they left, a new party consisting of twenty-four or twenty-five men, four of whom "came from beyond Chesterfield Inlet," arrived. Leslie traded with the four "far away" visitors and three others, receiving from them 150 fox, a few deerskin, wolf, wolverine, and muskox skins, and thirty pounds of ivory. His refusal to trade with the other eighteen, and an offer of necessary supplies "part gratis," were the levers he used to force them to spend two weeks reluctantly hunting whale. Before departing they traded 300 fox, 229 deerskin, sixteen muskox robes, nine wolf, four wolverine, and fourteen pounds of ivory.[26]

Unpredictable climatic changes, and their effects on animal numbers and locations, brought disaster to several communities in the mid-1820s. In

July 1825, reports of "starvation during the winter" reached the post. A year later, Utuck, whose name was always linked in the post account books with those of Augustine's brothers and nephews, and whose country products suggest concentration on marine mammal hunting, reported to George Taylor on other catastrophes experienced by his people and their neighbours.[27]

> Before the commencement of the thaw he [Utuck] received a visit from one of the subjects of his neighbour whose domains was contiguous to his own who reported to him the mortality with which they had been visited with last summer and in the fall, likewise to communicate to us their intention of not coming to the House this season, should he or any of his tribe visit us. He [Utuck] himself has had the misfortune to lose part of his tribe—I could not distinctly make out the numbers of deaths in each respective tribe, but of the two the numbers amount to 34 of which 22 were men, 10 women and 2 children—Their deaths were not caused by starvation as they were at that time living in affluence.[28]

Inuit responses to unpredictable weather and fluctuating food supplies were rapid and, on occasion, appeared inconsistent. Regular visitors to the post continued to hunt whale at Seal River, but they did so unwillingly, because the company could not supply them with whaling boats. Trusting in the company's promise that boats suitable to the work would be supplied, along with the men to handle them, thirty-eight hunters arrived in 1829, prepared to kill whale. Instead they were left on their own with only one "small boat" which was "driven on the rocks" and from which they "with some difficulty reached the shore in a half drowned state."[29] The post master's repeated requests for more men and safer boats for the whale hunt were consistently ignored by his superiors in London.

Throughout the 1820s country goods for trade were increasingly terrestrial, possibly inland, products. Walrus ivory and narwhal tusk were less and less often brought for trade, and only by the Whale Cove people, whom Leslie identified as "the farthest away Eskimaux." Also increasingly, people arrived at the post empty-handed and hunted seal before they were able to trade.[30]

Inuit shopping lists were also changing during the 1820s. The awls, chisels, bayonets, and files so eagerly desired during the sloop trade years were less frequently requested. Guns were the first priority and by 1830, a man who did not own a gun was a rare exception. The next most frequently traded items were kettles, blankets, and yard goods, closely followed by luxury purchases of shirts, jackets, decorative gartering, and tin tobacco boxes.[31]

The numbers and products suggest that the west-coast people had made significant changes in the locations of their winter and summer residences, and, as Lieutenant Chappell noted in 1814, in their occupations during the Second Maunder Minimum (1790 to 1830). During the period of coastal trade, sloop captains reported an average of about 300 people sealing and whaling on the coast during the summer.[32] Although no HBC personnel were ever on the coast in winter, they believed, on the basis of information provided by the people themselves, that the arctic communities moved inland in August and September for lake fishing and the early fall cariboo hunt. Yet, in 1821, only thirty years, or a single generation, later, Augustine said his people spent the summers at inland lakes and rivers, fishing for salmon and hunting reindeer and muskox, and the winters seal hunting on the coast, a reversal of the previous pattern of seasonal residence.[33]

Churchill post's Inuit clerk, Augustine, had come to the post in 1812, but unlike the "lads" who spent one or two winters with the traders, Augustine was a company employee for more than twenty years, with a few sabbaticals to spend the winter in the north. Much of the information we have concerning the west Hudson Bay people in the period from 1810 to 1830 came from Augustine. Exactly who he meant by his "people" cannot be determined with certainty. He described his community as living "a little to the northward of Churchill [from which they] came to the Fort with sledges in the spring."[34] However, when he first came to Churchill as a "lad" in 1812, he was identified by Thomas Topping as one of the "farther natives,"[35] which suggests his people were not part of the Knapp's Bay summer village. When he was shown a map of the west coast of Hudson Bay, Augustine recognized Chesterfield Inlet, although he himself had never been farther north than Marble Island, which he knew as the site of the "disastrous termination" of James Knight's northward voyage of 1720.[36]

His home, therefore, seems to have been north of Knapp's Bay but south of Marble Island, at Nevil's Bay or Whale Cove. His summary censuses of his people—eighty-four adult males and ninety married women,[37] sixty-four girls and sixty-two boys between infancy and adulthood,[38] totalling 300, plus an unknown number of babies—are in line with the estimates of 300 adults at the three villages visited regularly by the sloops prior to 1790, and with Andrew Graham's guess of about 500 people at the three more southerly villages and at Rankin and Chesterfield inlets as well. Augustine's comments suggest that he considered all the inhabitants of the three southerly villages to be "his people," but that he and his immediate family belonged to a group that maintained a seasonal village at Nevil's Bay or Whale Cove.

After more than a century of commercial association, the men of the Hudson's Bay Company at Churchill were reasonably well acquainted with the people of the bay's west coast as far north as Chesterfield Inlet. But during the 1820s, when "strangers" came to Churchill from Chesterfield Inlet, or "from beyond the Inlet,"[39] the Churchill traders knew almost nothing about their communities, numbers, names, territories, occupations, and social organization. Unlike eighteenth-century clerks and post masters such as Samuel Hearne and Andrew Graham, few post masters in George Simpson's reorganized company concerned themselves with gathering or publishing ethnological information.

By the 1820s, however, the British government had made the discovery of a northwest passage a high-priority national goal. At least eight major expeditions were carried out between 1819 and 1836. Members of the expeditions produced a substantial body of ethnographic literature, which adds to the documentary sources available for reconstructing Inuit demography and activities, and partially compensates for the absence of ethnographic material in the post records.[40]

Augustine was a member of both of John Franklin's overland expeditions to the Mackenzie River and the arctic sea, from 1821 to 1823 and 1825 to 1827, seconded to the position of interpreter by the British Admiralty with the permission of the Hudson's Bay Company. He also acted as an interpreter and chief informant to John West, who visited Churchill in 1823 in search of new fields for the propagation of the Christian gospel. When questioned by John Franklin and his officers—John Richardson, George Back, and Robert Hood—and by the Reverend John West, he made it clear that some of the 'far away' Inuit, so little known to his questioners, were known to him, and that they had already begun to acquire European goods, as well as information about Europeans, through trade and the exchange of news with the Knapp's Bay and Whale Cove communities.

Augustine identified one of the far away groups with which his people traded as the "Ootkooseck-kalingmoeoot,"[41] that is, Utkusiksalingmiut, People of the Soapstone Place. Franklin identified them as a "tribe" occupying territory at Franklin Lake and along the lower Back River. There was, however, another soapstone quarry near Wager Bay, known to the Melville Peninsula people in the same years as "Ootkooseeksalik,"[42] and Augustine's reference could have been to people who lived near it.

According to John Franklin, Augustine's people also traded with "one tribe, who named themselves Ahwhacknanhelett, [who] he supposes may come from Repulse Bay," and with "the Kangorrmoeoot, or White Goose Esquimaux, [who] describe themselves as coming from a great distance."[43] In the case of the former, Augustine was probably talking about people from Aivilik, the Walrus Place (Repulse Bay), whose name became seriously garbled when Franklin, who couldn't speak Inuktitut, tried to write it down. The second group seems to have been the Kanghirmiut, the White Goose People, whose territory was along the Perry River, a major nesting ground of the white, or snow, goose. During the Franklin overland expedition of 1819 to 1822, Augustine found a paddle near Perry River, which he "on examination declared to be made after the fashion of the White-goose Eskimaux a tribe with whom his countrymen had had some trading interviews."[44]

Melville Peninsula

John West's ethnographic research at Churchill in 1823 added to the information gathered by Franklin and Richardson, and supported what William Auld had been told in 1815 about trade between Inuit communities. West wrote, "They informed me that a great many of the Esquimaux meet in summer about Chesterfield Inlet....The object of the Esquimaux in meeting from different tribes at Chesterfield Inlet every year, is to barter with those principally who trade at Churchill Factory, and also with some Northern Indians, who exchange what European articles they may have for fish-hooks made of bone, and sinew lines, and skins."[45] The same "strangers" who traded at Churchill in 1823 had been at the Chesterfield Inlet gathering in 1821, and had met people "from the great lake to the north" who told a curious story. "They had seen two very large canoes when there was no ice; and when one of these canoes stood in towards the shore where they were, they were so alarmed as to run off over the rocks, and ... they did not return till the big canoes were out of sight towards where the sun rises."[46]

West speculated that the two "very large canoes" had been *Fury* and *Hecla,* under the command of Captain Edward Parry, searching for a northwest passage in 1821. Parry's own account confirmed West's guess. In August of 1821 Parry and his second in command, George Lyon, had been in Repulse Bay and had found open water in a bay known for its summer ice. A village site there appeared to be deserted, but Lyon was convinced that people had been there within the past few days, and speculated that they may have left when they saw the ships. After a brief exploration of the area,

Parry's little fleet headed east out of the bay and turned north in search of a suitable wintering site. In February 1822, while his ships were iced-in at Winter Island near the mouth of Lyon Inlet, Appokiuk, one of the residents of a nearby winter community, confirmed that she and her companions had secretly observed the crews of *Fury* and *Hecla* in Repulse Bay the previous year, as Lyon suspected.[47]

The following month, another of Parry's informants, Iligliuk, who was also his most trusted cartographer and navigator, drew a map of the Melville Peninsula on which she included "a lake of considerable size ... [where] her countrymen are annually in the habit of resorting during the summer, and catch there large fish of the salmon kind, while on the banks are found abundance of rein-deer."[48] The description and location of the lake suggest it was the "great lake to the north," now known as Curtis Lake.

Little is known of the human history of the bay coast between Chesterfield Inlet and Repulse Bay before the 1820s. When Parry and Lyon visited between 1821 and 1823, there were no permanent villages, although the Melville Peninsula people told that in earlier times there had been a principal settlement at the mouth of the Wager River, called Nuvuk. Inuit histories, recorded by whaling captain George Comer a few generations later, in 1897, also mention Nuvuk. It was destroyed, they said, in a war of extermination with a neighbouring group under the leadership of a great chief, Oudlinuk. After the downfall of Nuvuk, a community at Depot Island planned to attack Oudlinuk's village to avenge the Nuvuk people, but dropped the idea when they saw the extent of the destruction his forces could wreak.[49] As is the case with other Inuit histories, nothing indicates when the hostilities took place. On the basis of Comer's information, Franz Boas dated the attack on Nuvuk and the subsequent abandonment of Depot Island to the years immediately before 1800.[50]

The Iglulingmiut of Melville Peninsula seldom went south of deserted Nuvuk, which, they said, was the southernmost limit of their territory.[51] While it was no longer an inhabited village, it continued to be a major Inuit trading centre for the redistribution of country articles and European goods. Augustine knew about trade meetings there,[52] and some Iglulingmiut visited there for a few weeks in most summers. By 1820 most people from the Melville Peninsula communities had been there at least once to meet people from Chesterfield Inlet and trade. A major item in the trade was wood, from which they made their paddles and tent poles. Every family had a wooden tray which, they said, "had been traded north by more southerly people,"[53] probably from Knapp's Bay, where the people had access to the inland forest areas. They also had copper kettles, iron knives stamped with the names of European makers and used by all the men, iron blades in the women's knives, beads, and an iron axe.[54]

The Iglulingmiut considered the whole of Melville Peninsula, as far south as and including Repulse Bay, to be their particular territory. Although there were "no regularly established settlements along an immense extent of coast," there were "three or four which are considered as general mustering places." The main villages, in addition to deserted Nuvuk where trade meetings took place, were Aivilik, Igloolik, and Akudlit.[55]

Aivilik, at the bottom of Repulse Bay, was regarded by the Iglulingmiut as a settlement of some importance, which had once held a larger population than it did in the years of Parry's visit. Parry and Lyon saw the remains of an "immense Eskimaux settlement" there, with more than sixty tent rings, "several small fire-places covered with soot, about a dozen perfect store-houses for flesh," and nearly a hundred other structures including fireplaces, storehouses, caches, canoe stands, and route markers. By 1821 it was occupied only in the winter and by no more than sixty people at a time.[56]

Akudlit, at Committee Bay, was the western limit of occupation by Melville Peninsula people. All Parry's and Lyon's informants knew of it, most had visited there once or twice, and the general consensus was that about fifty people lived there.[57] It was, however, more common for the people of Akudlit to visit Igloolik or Aivilik than it was for the inhabitants of the two latter settlements to cross the Rae Isthmus to their western border. The route to and from Akudlit was always overland across the Rae Isthmus. "Not one of them had been by water round to Akkoolee, but several by land," Parry wrote, nor could people recall visits to or from lands farther west than Akudlit.[58]

By far the largest permanent village was Igloolik. The population in 1822 was 219, according to Parry's count, and included sixty-nine men, seventy-seven women, and seventy-three children, among whom there were eighteen deaths and nine births that winter. Most of them identified Igloolik as their birthplace. They preferred it to any other residence, and wintered elsewhere only when its resources were not adequate for their numbers. During the dark period of the winter of 1822-23, about sixty individuals moved to Aivilik near Repulse Bay in order not to put too great a strain on the resources of the main village.[59]

Around 220 people made up "nearly all the inhabitants of the northeast coast of America" between Igloolik and deserted Nuvuk at Wager Inlet at the time of Parry's and Lyon's visit.[60] They identified themselves as a single social unit occupying a particular territory, with intramural familial ties and with a history and dialect distinct from those of neighbouring peoples. The people of Akudlit, on the west coast of the peninsula, were part of the larger Melville Peninsula community, in the sense that they were not outsiders, but were less well known, and were both geographically distant and emotionally removed from the heartland village.

Trade among the Melville Peninsula communities and with other groups was reliable and capable of satisfying most resource needs. Although a soapstone quarry at Ootkooseeksalik (Utkusiksalik) near Wager Bay seemed to Captain Parry a likely source of the material for pots, the people "assured us [that] was not the case, the whole of them coming from Akkoolee [Akudlit]." One woman explained that her parents "were much employed in making these pots, chiefly it seems as articles of barter." Asbestos, used by women to trim their lamps, was found in abundance near Aivilik.[61]

The east coast of Melville Peninsula and the other lands around northern Foxe Basin, which had sustained a Dorset occupation for 2000 years, continued to provide adequate, and frequently abundant, food and other resources in the nineteenth century. Scarcity arising from environmental conditions was less frequent than in many other parts of the arctic. Between 1821 and 1823, the Igloolik community was well off enough to feed and maintain more than 100 dogs.[62] The community was, however, fully aware of exactly how many people could expect to spend the winter comfortably in a particular place. Lyon suspected that the number of people who left Igloolik to winter at Aivilik in 1822-23 would have been greater if it had not been for the presence of *Fury* and *Hecla*. "In consequence of our known intention of visiting it, [Igloolik] proved the most attractive wintering quarter, and at least half the dwellers along the coast hurried to assemble there."[63]

One of the leading men of the community, Ooyara, confided to Lyon on New Year's Eve of 1822 that because of an unexpected decline in caribou numbers, "they could not hope to support so great a number as by the recent arrivals were now assembled at Igloolik." Ooyara and other community leaders made arrangements for the crews of *Fury* and *Hecla* to take turns acting as hosts and provisioners in supplying bread and oil for the women and children and such other people as were "most distressed."[64]

Just outside the Iglulingmiut core area, resources were not always adequate. Three hundred kilometres away, the people of Akudlit suffered serious starvation in the winter of 1820-21. Two of its residents, Ooyarrakhioo and his wife Tabbi, visiting Igloolik in the spring of 1823, brought news "that during a very grievous famine which had been experienced, one party of Eskimaux had attacked, killed, and eaten another party."[65]

The Iglulingmiut maintained connections with three communities on north Baffin Island, across Fury and Hecla Strait from Igloolik. At about ten days' walking distance was the village of Tununeq, at Pond Inlet on the northeast shore of Baffin Island. Toolemak, a widely travelled man of the Iglulingmiut, described Tununeq and its people in terms that suggest that much of the classic Thule way of life still survived there. The people depended on whaling for their subsistence, and the surrounding bays and inlets provided cetacean harvests rich enough to support a year-round population in a permanent village. European whalers were attracted to the area because of its abundant resources, and by 1820 were regular visitors. The local people had not only observed them closely and passed information about them to the Iglulingmiut, but had communicated with them and accepted gifts. The Tununirmiut, People of Tununeq, had been the beneficiaries of European whaling in that carcasses from which the whalemen had cut away the fat had "frequently" been left on the beach for their use.[66]

Close to Tununeq was the village of Toonoonee-roochiuch in Admiralty Inlet. Toolemak had little to say about the community there, but Parry and Lyon gathered that its people, the Tununirisirmiut, did not differ perceptibly from the Tununeq people.[67]

The third Baffin Island community associated with the Iglulingmiut was at Peelig. Parry was unable to determine the location of the village, but in 1823 ten Peelig residents visited Igloolik. They had not known Europeans were there, but they were familiar with sailing ships like *Hecla* and *Fury* from meetings with whaleships on the northeast coast of Baffin Island.[68]

In describing the people of the north Baffin Island communities, Toolemak made it clear that although they were different from his own Iglulingmiut, they were not strangers. Their speech was the same, although in his opinion the more northerly people spoke with an accent, and there were minor differences in clothing, hairstyles, and women's tattoos. People from both sides of Hecla and Fury Strait were on friendly terms with each other and maintained social relations through visits, intermarriage, and exchanges of children. Families from each group were free to live temporarily or permanently within the other's communities.[69]

In attempting a classification of arctic peoples according to cultural characteristics, the Fifth Thule Expedition (1921-24) grouped the people of Aivilik, Akudlit, Igloolik, and Tununeq together, and identified them as Iglulik. Although Toolemak and his people did not use the term "Iglulik," or any other term as an ethnic identifier, they implicitly accepted the classification because it included the people and groups they recognized as friends and relatives, and excluded all those they saw as strangers.

During Parry's visits, people who wintered at Aivilik were an integral part of the Igloolik subgroup. They did not see themselves as separate. The woman Appokiuk, for instance, was accustomed to divide her time between Aivilik and Igloolik,[70] and could quite correctly have claimed to be Iglulingmio (a resident of Igloolik) during the fall and winter, and Aivilingmio (a resident of Aivilik) in the summer. The transformation of part of the Iglulingmiut subgroup into a distinct Aivilingmiut band centred on Aivilik in Repulse Bay did not happen until some families were drawn into permanent residence there by the attractions of American whaling fleets in the 1860s.

Iglulingmiut response to European explorers was decidedly unlike that of Baffin Islanders in Frobisher's day. The contrast may be explained by differences in the ecology of Melville Peninsula and in the amount of information Iglulingmiut had about white men. In the Foxe Basin core area, the arrival of strangers did not necessarily mean competition for limited resources, even in the difficult years of the Little Maunder Minimum. At Lyon Inlet in 1821, food supplies were adequate for the usual wintering population. The Iglulingmiut had no need to withhold hospitality or to take their guests' important resources without permission, although both Parry and Lyon complained of petty thefts of useful and attractive objects such as the officers' silver mugs. The community also had information about Qabluna ("white people"), which the Frobisher Bay people had not had 225 years earlier. The residents of Tununeq and Toonoonee-roochiuch had already had a number of encounters with whaleships, and knew from experience that much could be gained from establishing friendly relations with the strangers. Iglulingmiut had also heard descriptions of the Churchill traders from the southern groups they met at trade gatherings at Chesterfield Inlet, Curtis Lake, and Nuvuk. In 1821 they had no reason to see the strangers as a threat to their resources, as the east Baffin Islanders apparently had in the 1570s and 1580s, or to fear for their lives and freedom as the Labrador people had in the sixteenth and seventeenth centuries.

As well as maintaining familial ties and trading relations with other groups, the Iglulingmiut were part of a wide communications network through which information on both past and current events was exchanged. "They have many traditionary stories of Kabloona and Indians," Lyon wrote. They knew about the white men at Churchill far to the south, who were said to "have plenty of wood and iron." And they had a substantial store of information about Indians, whom they called "It-kagh-lie" (*itqilit*, nits, louse eggs), and of whom they spoke "with fear."[71] From the beginning of their relations with Parry, Lyon, and their crews, the Iglulingmiut eagerly sought to add to their store of information about other peoples and places. For instance, Parry described his best map-maker and pilot, Iligliuk, as "always very much entertained ... by pictures having any relation to the Esquimaux in other parts, [she] derived great entertainment from a description of any difference in their clothes, utensils, or weapons. Of these the sail in an Esquimaux boat seemed particularly to attract her notice."[72]

Hudson Strait

To satisfy Iligliuk's intense curiosity about the people of Hudson Strait, George Lyon showed her some sealskin clothing he had purchased from them. She and her husband Okotook declared the items badly made, but continued to ask Lyon and Parry for details of their makers.[73] Their descriptions embodied the first, and lasting, impression of all British explorers and traders—the Hudson Strait people were great traders "well accustomed to bargain-making." Their first experiences of Europeans were the brief arm's-length encounters with the crews of Robert Bylot in 1615 and Jens Munk in 1619. More than a century passed before they began meeting the Hudson's Bay Company supply ships at the Middle Savage Islands, Nottingham and Salisbury islands, and Cape Digges in the 1730s. By 1800 the regular visits were "a sort of annual fair" where people indulged in opportunistic pilfering and enthusiastic but minor trade.[74]

The people of the north shore of Hudson Strait wanted, above all, items such as "iron nails [and] barrel hoops," which they could use as "heads for their arrows, spears, and harpoons." They were not, however, prepared to pay a high price for what they wanted, and "displayed no small cunning in making their bargains, taking care not to exhibit too many articles at first." They refused to sell their country products "for anything of reasonable value," wrote Parry, who described an incident in which two men, unable to find buyers for their high-priced oil, started pushing sailors around "with a violence I have never seen the Esquimaux use on any other occasion."[75]

While Frobisher Bay and Cumberland Sound people had used violence to protect or acquire resources two and a half centuries earlier in their encounters with Frobisher and Davis, the people of the Strait were seldom seen to engage in violent hostilities. Their encounters with Robert Bylot in 1615 and Jens Munk in 1619 were entirely peaceful. Edward Chappell was the only observer to suggest they may have engaged in open conflict with their neighbours in the nineteenth century. They used spears and lances when hunting birds and fishing, he wrote, but preferred bows and arrows "in their wars." His account does not explain why he thought they engaged in wars, nor did he offer any reason for his opinion as to their preference in the use of hunting and fighting equipment.[76]

Whatever their military stance, they were certainly anxious to trade with all comers, and just as certainly engaged in a particularly insubstantial trade. The poverty of their trade sprang from the absence of permanent and intensive contacts that might have equipped them with the tools and support systems necessary to maintaining subsistence while also amassing tradeable surpluses. The ships' visits, while reasonably regular and predictable, took place only once a year and were limited to a few hours' duration. Crews and passengers were interested only in mild bartering. Aside from small amounts of overpriced whale oil and ivory, most of the goods they offered in trade were souvenirs. The Reverend John West's opinion of their workmanship was the opposite of Iligliuk's. "The women presented image toys, made from the bones and teeth of animals, models of canoes, and various articles of dress made of seal skins," he wrote, "all of which displayed considerable ingenuity and neatness."[77] Neither party to the trade took it seriously. Ship-time was an occasion for small-scale recreational trading in the context of a social gathering, "an annual fair," as Chappell called it. Although the gatherings were smaller, they are reminiscent of the Greenland meetings described by the missionary Henri Cristopher Glahn in the 1760s and 1770s: "To this large gathering some travel in order to see their relations; some to look for a bride among so many beauties; some to settle their litigations before this solemn gathering; some to stand their trial in wrestling, slapping and being slapped on the back; some in order to be healed by a more noted physician, who is supposed to come here; some for the sake of buying and selling, some to be spectators."[78]

In the absence of steady and reliable markets, and of social security in hard times, the Hudson Strait Baffinlanders made few noticeable changes in their way of life and were fundamentally unaffected by the brief appearances of passersby. There is no evidence they changed their territories or occupations between the seventeenth and twentieth centuries. The population of the south coast, estimated at around 300 people in the 1740s, remained stable for nearly 250 years.[79] Some of the south-coast people spent the winter in the Ungava Peninsula, crossing the strait in their umiaks, "loaded with furs and other necessarys." On the mainland they gathered wood for boat frames, tent poles, and harpoon handles, and returned to Baffin Island in the summer to trade some of their wood with their compatriots.[80] On rare occasions, goods of European manufacture were moved through interconnecting trading zones, from Labrador to Ungava Bay to the north coast of Ungava Peninsula, and eventually across Hudson Strait.

Ungava Bay and Peninsula

The people of the Ungava coast, for their part, were as eager to trade with European vessels as were their countrymen on the north side of the strait, but had even less opportunity. Ships passing through Hudson Strait were prevented from visiting them because of treacherous and difficult ice conditions on the south shore. A few Ungava Bay people acted as middlemen, taking fox pelts, bearskins, pyrites, and other country products from Ungava Bay and Ungava Peninsula to the Moravian trading post-missions on the Labrador coast. When they returned to their own communities after a two-year round trip, they sold newly acquired European goods, including firearms, "at a very advanced price."[81]

The reputation for violence and war among the Ungava Bay people, noted by Nicolas Jérémie and Bacqueville de la Potherie a century earlier, still clung to them. Among the people of Okak on the Labrador coast, Ungava Inuit were generally believed to have a "hostile disposition." Hostility was not evident, however, in their responses to the arrival of two Moravian missionaries in 1811. Instead, they greeted Brother Benjamin Kohlmeister and Brother George Kmoch with friendly overtures and, in the case of those who had not seen white men before, with considerable timidity.[82]

Their hostility was reserved for their Indian neighbours and involved more fear than malice. At one village where the women waited alone while their men chased caribou in the water, a false sighting of an Indian sent all the women into hiding places, where they stayed until they were assured by the returning hunters that no strangers were near. They constantly used their telescopes to scan the woods to the south for the smoke of Indian fires, and spoke of "bloody encounters" at the George and Koksoak rivers with Indians from the interior and from Hudson Bay.[83]

Even people from the Hudson Strait coast were constantly on the alert for Indians. Among the fourteen families camped at the mouth of the Koksoak River when the Moravian party arrived were five families from Aivertok (Stupart Bay). They had set up their tents in a cluster some distance from the others and although they had been told about the missionaries, they were nervous about having strangers in their midst. When Brother Kohlmeister walked in the direction of their tents, the Koksoak people feared "that the Eivektok people, seeing him alone, might mistake him for an Indian, and shoot at him, [and] dispatched two men to bring him back." An interesting aspect of the account is that, although neither the Koksoak nor the Aivertok people had previously been visited by Europeans, they had guns and telescopes.[84]

Fear of the Indians influenced their choices of living sites and occupations. Fourteen families who planned to winter at Koksoak in 1811 because of an abundance of game there refused to make permanent residences "by their fear of the land-Indians." They pointed out many signs of Indian occupation—places where Indian fires had burned out some of the woods, and the remains of Indian encampments. The missionaries attributed the hostility to "national jealousies" on the part of both peoples, suggesting that disputes over the resources of the untreed territory were a basic cause of conflict.[85]

The Lowland Cree on the east coast of Hudson Bay were equally nervous about meeting Inuit. When William Hendry explored the interior of Ungava Peninsula and the shores of Ungava Bay in 1828, with a view to establishing a trading post in the area, his Eastmain Cree guides were reluctant to proceed into Inuit territory, "they being evidently under fearful apprehensions of the Esquimaux." After they had ventured a few days' travel beyond their own known territory, they refused to look for caribou, "having a particular aversion to hunt in these grounds, being too much afraid of the Esquimaux." Hendry concluded that "the apprehension of being butchered by the Esquimaux would be an insurmountable obstacle" to attracting Cree to a trading post in Ungava. The murders of a Moravian missionary and five sailors in Labrador in 1752, and the killing of a Hudson's Bay Company clerk at Richmond House in 1754, remained vivid in the memories of both Cree and Europeans, even though the events had occurred more than half a century earlier.[86]

In spite of the concerns of its men on the spot, the company's London Committee ordered the establishment of a post near the mouth of the Koksoak River in Ungava Bay for the purpose of trading with the Inuit. The founding party, which left Moose Factory in June 1830, included two officers, Nicol Finlayson and Erland Erlandson, and a dozen men, among them Moses and Ullebuk, who were from the Keewatin coast and had long been employed at the Churchill post. Three others were James Bay Cree, who proved to be reluctant founders, "evidently under fearful apprehension of the Esquimaux."[87] By mid-September the party had constructed a dwelling house adequate to shelter the traders during their first winter. The following year the post was given the name Fort Chimo.

The newcomers were soon visited by "six kyaks and two large skin boats full of people ... [who] expressed their joy" in song and dance when greeted in their own language by Moses. As it turned out, they were not local people, having recently come from the east coast of Hudson Bay, "which they were forced to leave on account of the Indians whom they often see in that quarter and who sometimes unprovoked make them deplore the loss of a friend and relative."[88] They already owned some European items, including knives bought from Inuit middlemen who visited Okak, in exchange for their fox skins and seal oil, and they were eager to trade. Their eagerness, however, did not guarantee that they would have articles for barter. In 1830 they had nothing to exchange except skin boots, which Finlayson bought for his men.[89]

The Ungava people, like other communities of their distant countrymen, suffered greatly from the severe climatic conditions of the Little Maunder Minimum. Famine and starvation were frequent, and led to infanticide and cannibalism as well as to increased violence, murder, and feuding.[90] Living off the land was no easier for the fur traders. Fish and game were scarce in the vicinity of the new post, but not necessarily because of a decline in their numbers. Only a few miles away, both caribou and fish were available in good supply. They were, however, inaccessible due to the difficulties of travel and transportation.

In October 1830, Ullebuk, accompanied by Augustine, who had arrived with the supply ship in September, set up their tent at a small lake upriver from the post, where they hoped to find fish in sufficient quantities to supply the new post. The plan failed, not because of any shortage of fish, but because the erratic freezing and thawing of the river made it uncrossable and the products of the fishery could not be transported to the post. Between November 8, 1830, and January 15, 1831, communication between fishery and post was impossible. Finlayson, fearing the two fishermen might have starved, sent a relief party, which succeeded in reaching them and bringing them home. They had been living comfortably on the products of their fishery and had built up stores adequate to supply the traders as well, but they could not get the fish or themselves to the post.[91] Unable to provide for their own table, the traders tried bringing food from James Bay. However, by the end of 1831, the journey from Fort Chimo to James Bay had become so difficult due to heavy snowfalls that one of the company's Cree couriers died from exposure while attempting to reach Eastmain.[92]

The distinction between scarcity and inaccessibility of game, frequently ignored by non-Inuit observers, was understood by Nicol Finlayson. He recognized that in the particular environmental conditions of Ungava, it was impossible to track deer in the soft snow of winter, no matter how abundant the animals were. Only in the spring, "the snow being hard, [could hunters] follow the deer into the interior."[93] Finlayson put his understanding of snow conditions into practice during the first winter at Fort Chimo, when he set his men to making snowshoes at every opportunity. Two Inuit families from Hudson Strait, who were among the new post's first customers in 1831, experienced similar difficulties. They complained that the mildness of the winter had prevented them from achieving a good hunt, presumably because of soft, wet snow, which made travel difficult. Their main purpose in making the six-day journey from the north was to get a gun.[94]

Caribou were scarce or inaccessible again in the winter of 1831-32, during which temperatures varied from unusually high to very cold, and there were periodic spells of heavy rain. Desperate with hunger, small parties of Inuit arrived at the post, and Finlayson used the whale oil he had bought from them during the summer as relief supplies. The company's men were suffering from scurvy, and Indians arriving from the interior in May 1832 reported starvation among their people.[95]

In June 1832, Finlayson sent Erland Erlandson and half the men inland to set up a trading outpost, make contact with the Indians, and encourage them to trade at Fort Chimo. He was also hoping to relieve the pressure on the post's slender food supply by having men in another part of the country. In September he wrote a heavily underlined letter to Erlandson. "I had calculated on supporting six of the people in the interior on the produce of the country.... As it is, we must *fight it out the best way we can*, providence assisting ... and am confident that you will *leave no stone unturned* in endeavouring to procure provisions for the people that are with you" [Finlayson's emphasis].[96]

Relations between Inuit and Cree remained cool for some time, but there was no violence, at least in the presence of the traders. The traders encouraged friendly relations, and in his September 1830 annual report to the company's headquarters in London, Finlayson predicted that when more Inuit owned guns, "the Indians ... will not be averse to a peace, as they must know that the Esquimeaux will have it now in their power to retaliate." A year after the establishment of the post, on September 11, 1831, Finlayson noted that "the Indians appeared to be suspicious of their old enemies, but the Esquimaux on the contrary had none whatever and were as familiar and laughed as much as if they had been old friends and acquaintances." Indian suspicion was slower to fade. In November of 1832, four Indians arriving at the post were fearful of coming near the Inuit tents there, and Finlayson was still wary. He noted in his daily journal that "it was fortunate none of the Esquimaux were off today; had this band [of Indians] met with them at a distance from the fort there is no doubt that they [the Indians] would through mere levity have sacrificed them [the Inuit]." Two years later the two nations were living peacefully in tents side by side at the post.

The Inuit insisted the Indians' kind treatment of them was due to the influence of the traders.[97]

During the somewhat better hunting and trapping summer of 1833, several Inuit left credits on their accounts, promising to return to buy guns after the supply ship had visited. Others kept their furs, but planned to trade them for guns in the fall. When the supply ship could not get through the Ungava Bay ice, three umiaks of people who were expected failed to show up. Finlayson concluded that "they were informed no doubt by those I saw of my having no guns; but whether they have proceeded on to the eastward or not I have not been able to learn."[98]

The Inuit trade continued sparse and uneven during the dozen years the post was in operation. In some years people brought in a few fox pelts, and in other years they not only had nothing to trade, they were forced to rely on the post for emergency provisions. Finlayson reported to his superiors that the principal Inuit food was oil, of which they seldom had a surplus, and that it was not unusual for them to be starving when they arrived at the post.[99]

The risks to its men and the facts of no profit led the company to close its three small outposts in Ungava, and Fort Chimo itself in 1843. The local people once again had to depend on their middlemen for European goods, or undertake the long journeys to posts on the Labrador and Hudson Bay coasts.

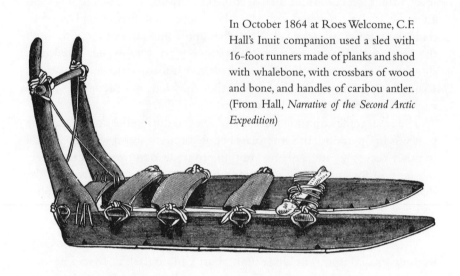

In October 1864 at Roes Welcome, C.F. Hall's Inuit companion used a sled with 16-foot runners made of planks and shod with whalebone, with crossbars of wood and bone, and handles of caribou antler. (From Hall, *Narrative of the Second Arctic Expedition*)

In February 1866, on Ooglariuk Island in Repulse Bay, Hall found a sled of less sophisticated construction, made entirely from whale jawbone. (From Hall, *Narrative of the Second Arctic Expedition*)

On July 28, 1834, Ugjulingmiut at Great Fish River met George Back with "wild gesticulations" and brandishing of spears. When Back walked up to them without visible weapons, calling to them in their own language, they accepted his handshakes and returned his greeting by patting their breasts. (From Back, *Narrative of the Arctic Land Expedition*)

Netsilingmiut and Arvilingjuarmiut arrived at Lord Mayor's Bay in 1830. Among the 100 or so residents were Ableelooktook, the first to see John Ross's *Victory* frozen in the ice; Nalungituk, an elderly woman emissary in the greeting protocol; and Illicta, the oldest hunter in the group. On January 9, they made themselves known to a surprised John Ross. (From Ross, *Narrative of a Second Voyage*)

In the fall of 1879, King William Island Inuit invited members of the Schwatka expedition to live with them. Because the snow was not yet compacted enough to build domed snowhouses, their houses were leather tents, probably caribou skin, built in typical Inuit fashion with a ridgepole sloping down from the conical entry portion. (From Gilder, *Schwatka's Search*)

At Aivilik in 1864, Tookooliktoo (left), an interpreter for Charles Francis Hall, made winter clothing and bedding for four adults: Hall, Hall's servant, her husband Ipervik (right), and herself. Even for as expert a tailor as she was, each outfit took at least 120 hours to make. When women began to sew professionally for whaling crews, their workload was greatly increased. It became impossible for them to restrict their work with caribou skins to the late fall period, as prescribed by Inuit worldview. The result was conflict between ancient religious principles and the economic interests of both Inuit and whalemen. (From Hall, *Narrative of the Second Arctic Expedition*)

Hudson's Bay Company trade goods. The cylindrical object wrapped in rope (left, middle ground) is a tobacco carrot. The copper pot, or kettle, with lid and overarching handle (right, middle ground), first traded in the Keewatin by Captain George Comer in the 1890s, later became standard stock-in-trade of the HBC. It was preferred by Inuit women because the handle made it possible to suspend the pot over the cooking lamp. The two blades, or hand dags, would have been fitted to wooden or bone handles and used for shaping snowshoe frames, sled crossbars, and other carved wooden pieces. (HBCA 1987/363/-T-37/14)

Aivilik Inuit in snowhouse, at Fullerton Harbour in 1905. The Aivilingmuit
(People of the Walrus) were the first whaling Homeguard. The kettle above the
oil cooking lamp is suspended on sinew or twine. (NAC PA38301)

A shaman wears religious symbols on his clothing to help him understand humankind's obligations within the universe. (HBCA N8366)

6.

Memories of Hunger: Windfalls, Surplus, and Scarcity, 1830-1860

There are many memories of hunger in our land, memories new and memories of byegone days. Sometimes famine is due to hard winters with unceasing snowstorms, sometimes to mild winters when the ice will not lie.

– Samik, at Boothia Felix[1]

Boothia and the Arctic Coast

People in the community at Igloolik in 1821 to 1823 had not given Edward Parry and George Lyon any information about lands and peoples west of Melville Peninsula, in spite of relentless questioning by the ships' officers. The Igloolik people were not silent on this point out of ignorance. Perhaps they were being cautious, even though their relations with the visitors were friendly and apparently trusting. In spite of what Parry and Lyon took to be Iglulingmiut denials, communities did exist at Pelly Bay and Boothia Peninsula, and the members of the more westerly communities were familiar with the villages and villagers at Igloolik, Lyon Inlet, Repulse Bay, and Akudlit. They not only had iron and tools of European manufacture traceable to Melville Peninsula, a few of them had relatives in the large village at Igloolik.[2]

A century after the Parry-Lyon explorations, Knud Rasmussen, whose travels took him into nearly every part of Greenland and the Canadian arctic over a period of thirty years, said of Boothia Peninsula: "There is scarcely any country on earth that presents more severe and inclement conditions for man ... for it lies waste and bare of all that is considered necessary to life." More recently it has been described as "one of the most desolate environments on earth, particularly inappropriate for human occupation."[3] If Boothia gave this impression to twentieth-century observers, it was even more inhospitable during most of the last millennium. Except for the three centuries of stable, temperate climatic conditions from 900 to 1200, when Thule people expanding out of Alaska settled there, human occupation of Boothia Peninsula and Somerset Island has always been problematic. The Thule who occupied Somerset Island after 1300 were gone by 1500, and the island was deserted, either abandoned by hard-pressed communities or emptied through recurring extinctions of its people. The absence of archaeological evidence for occupation suggests that Boothia Peninsula may also have been *terra desolata* for much of the period between 1500 and 1800.

The Second, or Little, Maunder Minimum, the last cohesive climate event of the Little Ice Age, was followed by a period of extremely unstable and variable weather, lasting until about 1860. The receding ice pack and expanded open-water areas released more than usual amounts of moisture to the atmosphere, resulting in more frequent summer rain and heavier winter snowfall. Winters were long and cold, and summers were short, cold, and cloudy. The last fifteen years of the period, 1845 to 1860, were characterized by especially severe sea ice, low temperatures, and unusually heavy precipitation.[4] Fluctuations in temperature and precipitation encouraged animal, fish, and bird populations to alter their schedules and habitats erratically. Indigenous pathogens, for whom humid conditions were ideal, multiplied and brought the misery of epidemic disease and parasites to human beings and to the dogs, fish, and reindeer on which they depended. Given the inhospitable nature of Boothia's physical environment, communities there after 1830 might have been expected to find conditions insupportable during the years of unpredictable weather and scarce resources. Instead they survived in greater comfort and safety than many of their fellow countrymen did.

Because of their connections with Melville Peninsula and the Keewatin coast, Boothians knew there were white men in Hudson Bay. They first met them in their own country on January 10, 1830, at Felix Harbour where Captain John Ross and his northwest-passage expedition were wintering in *Victory*. It was not, however, the first they had heard of the newcomers. Two men had seen *Victory,* locked in the ice and drifting south along the Boothia east coast, in September 1829, and had taken the news to their principal village one or two days' journey to the west. In considering appropriate responses to the appearance of strangers in their territory, community members sought information about the visits of Parry and Lyon at Melville Peninsula from a woman whose sister, Kakikigiu, had met them both in 1823. Her comments helped to convince them they could safely make their presence known to the strangers.[5]

The local people did not, however, feel any need to hurry. It was not until January 1830, after they had moved to Lord Mayor's Bay for winter sealing on the ice, that they made contact with *Victory*'s crew. The story was passed down through the generations. In 1948 Ohokto told it to a Hudson's Bay Company post manager, who recorded it.

On the morning of January 8, the hunter Ableelooktook went for a walk with his dog, which, sniffing an unfamiliar scent, strained at its leash. Thinking the animal was on the trail of a bear, Ableelooktook followed for some miles to the south of the winter village. "But suddenly he [Ableelooktook] pulled up short because what was that he saw ahead?— strange sight indeed—what appeared to be a house, but not such as he was familiar with, with smoke pouring from its roof and many human beings moving around in its vicinity." Hurrying back to the village, Ableelooktook related what he had seen, and the whole population gathered in the dance house to consider his news. After the *angakok* (shaman) had determined that there was no danger, the villagers prepared to visit the strange "house" and greet its occupants.[6]

The next morning, January 9, they were waiting near the dismantled ship under its canvas covers "by daybreak," which, in that latitude, would have been late morning. They "sent forward Nalungituk to await the arrival of some of the white men who could be seen approaching without knives or spears or anything in their hands. Soon they were all on friendly terms with one another."[7]

The account of the meeting written in his diary by John Ross does not differ in any significant detail, although it adds a few. *Victory*'s sentry was the first to spot the approaching Inuit about a mile from the ship. As the sojourners went out to meet them, thirty-one men appeared suddenly from behind blocks of ice, "forming in a body of ten in front and three deep, with one man detached, on the land side, who was apparently sitting in a sledge. Each was armed with a spear and a knife." Captain John Ross, his nephew Lieutenant James Clark Ross (whose experience included service on all three of Parry's expeditions), and *Victory*'s men all threw down their weapons and shouted greetings in Inuktitut. The Inuit responded by casting away their spears and knives of bone and antler, but they were taking no chances. They were apparently prepared to defend themselves and their families if necessary, for each man also had, tucked at the back of his parka, "a much more effective knife pointed with iron, and some also edged with that metal." James Clark Ross presented his credentials by calling out in Inuktitut, and by claiming acquaintance with the people of Igloolik and Aivilik, mentioning the names of all those he could remember. Tensions were eased. The warriors visited *Victory* and accepted gifts of iron, after which they invited the newcomers to their village.[8]

Of the thirty-one Inuit, the oldest was Illicta, who looked to be about sixty-five years old. Six others were in their forties, and twenty seemed to be between the ages of twenty and forty. Ross also counted four "boys."[9] The ability to muster a fighting force of thirty-one men suggests a community of around 100 individuals, but no village, of any size, had existed in Lord Mayor's Bay in the fall and early winter of 1829. Who, then, were the inhabitants of the newly built snowhouse settlement visited by Ross on January 9, 1830? Where had they come from, and why? There are two, slightly different, versions of events, told by different groups of people: the Netsilingmiut, whose principal village, Netsilik, was one or two days' journey to the west of Lord Mayor's Bay; and the Arvilingjuarmiut, whose village, Arvilikjuaq, was at Pelly Bay, a two- or three-days' journey south of Lord Mayor's Bay.

The Netsilingmiut version, as told to and recorded by the Rosses, states that none of their people were normally resident in the area, but they had known about the strange "house" on the ice and its inhabitants as early as the previous September, had made a deliberate effort to gather information about them, and had considered various ways of responding to their presence. Arvilingjuarmiut histories, told almost a century later, stated that it was an Arvilingjuaq hunter who first saw *Victory*, a day after his people had arrived from their village to the south, and that only one day passed before their people greeted the strangers for the first time.

The two versions are not necessarily contradictory. January was the usual time for dispersed groups to come together in large communities for breathing-hole sealing on the ice, and Lord Mayor's Bay was used by people from both Netsilik and Arvilikjuaq. It is entirely possible they came together at Lord Mayor's Bay for the large winter seal hunt at the usual time, that the people of Netsilik already knew about the wintering explorers, as James Clark Ross's informants said, but that the people from Arvilikjuaq were surprised by the presence of white men, as their histories state.[10]

The Boothia people had three principal villages or territories: Netsilik on Boothia Isthmus, which the Rosses visited; a second village somewhere on the east coast of Boothia; and a third at Owutta, an island on the Boothia coast "three days' journey to the westward of Nei-tyel-le," which the local people described. Ross thought that the place name Nei-tyel-le, sometimes written as Neitchillee and Netchillik, was used variously by the people to refer to "the land, the river, the lake, and the village, or settlements," individually or collectively.[11]

The east-coast village, which Ross did not name or identify on his charts, may have been an intermittently occupied settlement of the Arvilikjuaq people, who frequently spent the late winter months at Lord Mayor's Bay hunting seals, in communities that included Netsilingmiut from Boothia Felix and families from Pelly Bay who spent occasional periods of one or two years on the east coast of Boothia.[12] The third village, Owutta, which, like the east-coast village, was not marked on John Ross's charts, was identified by James Clark Ross as a small island between Boothia and King William Island, "one of their steady places of resort."[13]

John Ross counted ninety-nine individuals in the winter village at Lord Mayor's Bay—thirty-three men, twenty-five women, twelve elderly people, and twenty-nine children. During the following two years he met about sixty others.[14] Even assuming that the Rosses did not meet face-to-face with every resident of Boothia and Pelly Bay, the total number of people at the end of the 1820s was probably no more than 200 souls.

Boothia Felix people, like other Inuit, dealt with regularly recurring periods of short-term scarcity by separating into small groups, sometimes no bigger than one nuclear family, and dispersing widely in order to harvest the resources of large territories. John Ross's journal is filled with references to camps, settlements, villages, resorts, stations, and centres, and to continuous shifting of groups of people, suggesting that Boothia communities were highly mobile, harvesting the resources of many different areas at different seasons, sometimes for very short periods of time. The picture is consistent with the survival strategies of societies that have been described as under "continuous ecological pressure."[15]

The Netsilingmiut were well travelled outside their own country, and tolerant of strangers in their territory and society. Within a week of meeting them, Ross had been introduced to at least nine competent mapmakers, who drew charts of territories as far distant as Wager Bay, Repulse Bay, and Melville Peninsula. Visitors to the ship included a party of Netsilingmiut returning from a trip to the east, where they had seen people from Igloolik. During the same period, three men who were clearly not Netsilingmiut visited *Victory*. One "belonged to a different tribe"; one appeared to be "Indian rather than Esquimaux"; and one "was a stranger from another tribe, with his hair in a different fashion; but we could not make out the place of his residence." By the end of the second week, the crew had been host to a Netsilingmiut woman who was married to "a stranger, belonging to some southern tribe." A number of the women in Netsilingmiut society had been born in other communities.[16]

Netsilik histories contain a substantial body of information on relations between the Netsilingmiut and the Arvilingjuarmiut. The histories are not clear on whether the place name Arvilikjuaq referred to a major village or to the entire area of Pelly Bay. They are very clear, however, that in spite of, or perhaps because of, the many marriage ties between the two groups, violent confrontations were common. One series of hostile encounters, said to predate Ross's visit, began when a Pelly Bay man killed a Netsilik man with whom he shared a wife. The sons of the murdered man, along with most of their community, carried the attack to Arvilikjuaq and both sides suffered heavy loss of life.[17] The history makes the point that the Netsilingmiut had special weapons for use in war, but the Arvilikjuaq people had only their caribou-hunting implements.

The hostility that existed between Netsilik and Arvilikjuaq in spite of kinship ties and frequent communication has been attributed to quarrels over women.[18] Given the Netsilik practice of female infanticide, and consequent inequities in the sex ratio of adults, it is not surprising that violence should erupt in order to get women from other groups, or to prevent other groups from marrying Netsilingmiut women, or to maintain a favourable balance in the exchange of women. Such quarrels sometimes flared up into revenge or blood feuds involving several generations.

Other histories tell of Netsilik battles with Aivilik communities and with people living along the Great Fish River and at Garry Lake,[19] although, like most Inuit histories, they are vague about dates. Planned hostilities followed certain conventions: a messenger, always an elderly person, was sent to inform the enemy that an attack was imminent; a short truce was arranged so that both sides could prepare themselves; and when the time arrived for confrontation, the combatants arranged themselves into facing rows.[20] The object was to annihilate not just the opponents, but all their kin, as well. Netsilingmiut war parties included women.[21] It is not clear precisely what their roles in warfare were, although they were probably lightning rods. One observer wrote: "An old decrepit woman now came forward to meet us and ascertain our intentions and status. Apparently they intended her as a sacrifice for the good of the others should we be of a hostile nature."[22]

Netsilingmiut relations with their western neighbours, the Ugjulingmiut of King William Island and Adelaide Peninsula, were less tense, perhaps because they were less frequent due to the greater distance between them. Two Netsilingmiut men, Ooblooria and Awack, who crossed Boothia Felix with James Clark Ross in April 1830, told him about Ugjulik "across the salt water" where there were "great numbers of Esquimaux" in the summer.[23] As was the case with the place names Netsilik and Arvilikjuaq, "Ugjulik" was sometimes used to refer to a specific village on the west coast of Adelaide Peninsula, and at other times to refer to the whole territory occupied by Ugjulingmiut, which included the eastern and southern coasts of King William Island. King William Island was frequently referred to as "Qikirtaq," a generic word for any island.[24]

Because non-native iron, copper, and wood have been found on Boothia, some investigators have assumed the existence of a significant trade between the Boothians and neighbouring groups.[25] The supposition overlooks the question of what the Boothians might have traded in return, and assumes that non-indigenous items could only have entered the economy through trade. Given the almost total absence of surplus-beyond-subsistence goods in the Netsilik economy, it is unlikely that they engaged in regular or frequent trade.

It is not clear that women were commodities in the Netsilik economy—although Ross hints at the possibility—but the evidence indicates that women were the major import of the Netsilingmiut, and that some men emigrated in order to find wives. One man, Kanayoke, "had communications with a tribe in [the west] where the females were most numerous." Over a period of some years, he had "married" six women from "the westward," and had, at different times, given (or sold?) the first five as brides to his unmarried co-residents. Other women entered Boothian society from the east, including two sisters from Akudlit, one of whom, Kakikigiu, was married to two Netsilingmiut brothers.[26]

The exchange of people between territorial groups necessarily resulted in the creation of overlapping kinship networks. A description of the mobility and the almost impenetrable connections of just a few members of one family makes the point. "Seeuteetuar visited Ross at Felix Harbour and saw Rae at Pelly Bay, McClintock on Boothia, Hall at Keeuna, and Schwatka near Starvation Cove. In-nook-poo-zhe-jook (a Netsilingmiut) first met Rae when travelling from Boothia to Pelly Bay, and often visited Repulse Bay. Pooyetta (Netsilingmiut) had an Arviligjuarmiut wife (Tooktoocheer). Too-shoo-art-thariu (Netsilingmiut) was a cousin of Ouela and his brothers at Repulse Bay, and his mother lived at Pelly Bay. Eek-choo-archoo ("Jerry"), a native of Pelly Bay, was a cousin of Teekeeta (Netsilingmiut), and met Hall while living at Igloolik!"[27]

With family connections of this order spanning several territorial groups, material goods and ideas can be exchanged without the vehicle of trade. Among 160 Netsilingmiut, John Ross saw only three knives of European manufacture.[28] To assume they were acquired through trade is to ignore the possibility they could have been introduced by brides coming from other groups, by Netsilingmiut returning to the home village after a visit to relatives elsewhere, or by non-Netsilingmiut visiting kin in Boothia.

By 1832 *Victory* had been iced in for three winters, food stores were getting low, and Ross made a decision to abandon the vessel and make his way north to Lancaster Sound, where, he believed, correctly as it happened, that he and his crew might be rescued by a passing whaler. He gave orders that *Victory* be dismantled and its materials cached on the beach at Lord Mayor's Bay. The abandonment of the well-equipped vessel provided the Netsilingmiut with an abundant supply of their scarcest resources: metals and wood. After 1832 they began making their traditional weapons and utensils from the newly accessible materials. Slate knives, lances, and harpoons were replaced by implements with cutting edges of iron, copper, tin, and brass. Copper and iron replaced bone rivets in the manufacture of soapstone and leather items. Other items, clearly locally made, incorporated innovations from European artifacts, such as serrated-edge blades similar to surgeons' saws.[29]

One change which the Netsilingmiut might have been expected to make was in sled construction. Their sleds before 1833 were made of fish, bone, antler, and animal skins. To create runners, frozen fish were wrapped in hides, which were moulded to the appropriate shape and frozen solid. The runners were fastened together by crossbars of bone or antler. John Ross described them as "singularly rude; the sides consisting of pieces of bone tied round and enclosed by a skin, and the cross bars on the top being made of the fore legs of a deer. One of them was but two feet long, and fourteen inches wide, the others were between three and four feet in length. On the under part of the runner, there was a coating of ice attached to the skin, rendering their motion very easy."[30] The sleds were short, off balance, clumsy, fragile, and slow. In warm weather they thawed, and while runners made of fish and hides served a second purpose as emergency rations, the absence of efficient transport added to the labours of travel and limited the range and speed of movement, as well as load size.

Access to long, straight wooden planks for sled runners could have led to a revolution in Netsilingmiut transportation technology. Larger, faster sleds would have allowed them to increase their hunting range, harvest more food supplies, maintain more frequent communications between villages, expand their territories, and extend their trading contacts. Apparently they did not appreciate, or else they rejected, the possibilities.

In 1859 Leopold McClintock observed sleds in two different communities of Netsilingmiut. On the west coast of Boothia Peninsula, at the northern entrance to James Ross Strait, sleds, according to McClintock, were "wretched little affairs, consisting of two frozen rolls of sealskins coated with ice, and attached to each other by bones, which served as crossbars."[31] Construction was the same at Matty Island, in the middle of James Ross Strait. "The runners (or sides) of some old sledges left here were very ingeniously formed out of rolls of sealskin, about 3-feet long, and flattened so as to be 2 or 3 inches wide and 5 inches high; the sealskins appeared to have been well soaked and then rolled up, flattened into the required form and allowed to freeze. The underneath part was coated with a mixture of moss and ice laid smoothly on by hand before being allowed to freeze, the moss, I suppose, answering the purpose of hair in mortar, to make the compound adhere more firmly."[32]

The Netsilingmiut could have manufactured wooden sleds at this time. They were familiar with the sleds belonging to Ross's party and had used them in travels with James Clark Ross; they had access to plenty of long, straight boards from the abandoned *Victory*; and by the time of McClintock's visit, they also had access to materials from Franklin's stranded vessels, and had either visited the ships or traded with people who had. McClintock observed "from the quantity of wood chips about the huts, they probably had visited the stranded ship alluded to by the last E[s]quimaux we had met, and the route to which lies up an inlet visible from here, and then overland three or four days' journey to the westward, until the opposite coast of King William's land is reached."[33]

In spite of this knowledge and the availability of suitable materials, only one family in the more than half a dozen villages McClintock visited owned a sled. It was "made of two stout pieces of wood, which might have been a boat's keel." At Arvilikjuaq, on the other hand, people had developed a new transportation technology more than ten years earlier. By 1847 they had pieces of mahogany, sleds with oak runners and cross-braces, and iron-tipped weapons.[34] Why the Netsilingmiut did not change their sled technology remains a mystery.

It might safely be assumed that the possession of adequate supplies of wood and metals not only cushioned the Netsilingmiut from the full force of the erratic and unpredictable climatic and other environmental conditions of 1830 to 1860, but also made daily life somewhat easier and more comfortable. Their sudden acquisition of surplus wealth does not seem to have led the Netsilingmiut to expand their territory or hunting range, or to engage in more active trade with their neighbours. It does, however, seem to have made them more suspicious of outsiders than formerly, and their previously friendly relations with neighbouring groups deteriorated. In 1847 at Pelly Bay, people thought it necessary to caution John Rae that "the natives of this part of the [Boothia] coast bear a very bad character, and are much feared."[35] The worsening climatic regime of the mid-1840s, coupled with a second windfall of prized resources to the west of Netsilingmiut territory, turned hostile distrust into open violence.

The sequence of events can be reconstructed from the histories of the Netsilingmiut's southwestern neighbours, the Ugjulingmiut (People of the Bearded Seal), who occupied the southern coast of King William Island and most of Adelaide Peninsula, and the Utkusiksalingmiut (Soapstone People), who lived along the lower Great Fish River and Garry-Pelly Lakes. In 1834, near the mouth of the Great Fish River, about thirty-five Ugjulingmiut saw white men for the first time. The strangers were George Back of the British navy and his exploration party, searching for news of John and James Ross. The villagers reacted to the appearance of boat and crew by "brandishing their spears, uttering loud yells, and, with wild gesticulations, motioning to us not to land." When Back threw aside his gun and spoke a few words in their language, they responded with gestures of friendship and everyone, including the children, shook hands with the strangers.[36]

A second, larger village of between sixty and seventy people stood at the eastern end of Garry Lake. No one there seemed to have any information about the Ross expedition or the cache at Lord Mayor's Bay, and Back did not see any items from the abandoned *Victory* among them. Although Back was unable to understand much of what the villagers told him, he gathered that they had been hunting or trading along a river that flowed into Hudson Bay, and concluded they had only recently returned from a visit to Chesterfield Inlet or Wager Bay. The Utkusiksalingmiut generally were familiar with conditions on the west coast of Hudson Bay, however. They knew about the trading post at Churchill and had frequent communications with people from the bay coast. In one of their communities, people conveyed to Back, through gestures and a sketch map, that they traded at Akudlit, where they met with people from Arvilikjuaq, Igloolik, and Aivilik. They also met people from the southern Keewatin, as Augustine had told Back, Richardson, and West in the early 1820s, and supplied them with "short and rudely fashioned iron knives" and "rough iron."[37]

Like most other arctic people in the second half of the 1840s, Ugjulingmiut and Utkusiksalingmiut, as well as Netsilingmiut, were dealing with climatic stress of almost unmanageable proportions. The years from 1845 to 1859 were "one of the least favourable periods in the past 700 years."[38] Recalling the winters of 1846 to 1848 nearly twenty years later, four Netsilingmiut men who had lived through them declared, "The Innuits never knew such very cold weather—there was no summer between two winters—could catch no seals or kill any rein-deer at most of the usual places."[39] Ugjulingmiut also remembered the virtual disappearance of both caribou and seal from their country and two years of starvation and death. Three generations after the fact, people at Great Fish River spoke of the blizzards, starvation, death from exposure, and cannibalism as "the year of horror."[40]

While the people of Boothia and Adelaide peninsulas, Great Fish River, and King William Island suffered and died, strangers in sailing ships caught in the ice shared their fate. In 1845 John Franklin's massive expedition sailed into Lancaster Sound in what was intended to be a final effort to realize the British dream of discovering the North West Passage. Given the climatic conditions, the timing could hardly have been worse. A year later, *Erebus*, *Terror*, and their complement of 135 men were beset by ice off the northwest coast of King William Island. On April 22, 1848, 105 survivors abandoned the frozen ships in the hope that they could reach safety overland. Like the people of Ugjulik and Great Fish River, they met death from starvation and exposure, and ate the flesh of their companions as they faced their own "year of horror." One by one, they died, leaving wooden boats, metal fittings, cutting tools, cloth, and containers strewn mile after mile along the west coast of King William Island and the shores of Simpson Strait.

Within two years, with their survival still threatened by climatic stress, the Ugjulingmiut were assaulted on a new front: Netsilingmiut moved into their territory to harvest the littered coasts. Using the windfall of wood and metal from the abandoned *Victory*, they had increased the efficiency of their hunting technology just enough to give themselves a slight edge during the ecological disaster. Their relatively better health and higher levels of energy enabled them to take advantage of the second windfall of precious resources left by Franklin's retreating crews, and to destroy the few remaining Ugjulingmiut.

Hints of famine, war, and displacement of people surfaced from time to time over the next two decades, and were recorded by John Rae, James Anderson, and Leopold McClintock in the course of their searches for news of the lost Franklin expedition. The Ugjulingmiut account of events remained hidden from outsiders for thirty years, until it was told to members of Frederick Schwatka's expedition in 1878. Taken together, and against the background provided in the accounts of earlier visits by George Back and John Rae, the scattered clues and the Ugjulingmiut history tell a coherent story of events.

In 1845 there were no villages and no people along the Boothia Peninsula and Somerset Island west coasts. Everything was much as it had been fifteen years earlier, including reasonably peaceful relations between the Netsilingmiut and their neighbours.[41] By 1854 things had gone badly wrong. Arvilikjuaq (Pelly Bay) people, who only twenty years earlier had shared territory and winter sealing villages, and had maintained trading and marriage ties with the Netsilingmiut, refused to accompany John Rae westward in his search for news about the lost Franklin expedition, even for a day or two. They could not, or would not, give information on events taking place to the west, and they refused to act as guides in spite of generous rewards. They frightened Rae's interpreter, William Ullebuk, by warning him that "the natives in that direction were acting particularly violent."[42] A day later, a less nervous man, Innookpooshejook, travelling from Netsilik to Pelly Bay, met Rae and Ullebuk and agreed to travel west with them for a couple of days. Years later, in 1869, Innookpooshejook confirmed that Pelly Bay people had told Ullebuk if they proceeded west "the party was liable to get killed."[43]

In 1855, the year after Rae's visit, a number of curious things were noted by HBC Chief Trader James Anderson as he followed George Back's route down the Great Fish River. He recorded details that had no significance for him at the time, but which hindsight and comparison with Back's journey indicate were signs of major changes in demography and intergroup relations. The distribution of people and villages had changed. Less than a hundred people occupied several small villages, in contrast to the two larger villages of 1834. People living along the river also owned greater quantities of European articles than were noted by Back. Anderson identified the goods as Fort Churchill trading stock. Among them were several stone kettles made from five slabs of sandstone cemented together, a style Anderson recognized as being used only on the west coast of Hudson Bay.[44]

Anderson was not certain exactly who the resident people were. The similarity of their clothing and implement styles to those of the Chesterfield Inlet people led him to conclude that they were from the bay. In a critique of Anderson's journal, written nearly a century later, the anthropologist Diamond Jenness disagreed, identifying them as a Back River inland band, which had frequent contacts with the people of the Keewatin coast.[45]

By 1857-58, other changes had taken place. Nearly all the Netsilingmiut were living in villages on the west coast of Boothia and the east coast of King William Island. The villages were larger and more numerous than they had been in the 1830s. A winter settlement on Matty Island contained enough house sites for 200 or more people, and several on the east coast of King William Island were each occupied by between thirty and forty people. Every family possessed relics from Franklin's wrecked ships. Forty-five people in a village near Cape Victoria had silver cutlery and medals, buttons, iron knives, a gold chain, and pieces of wood, as well as bows and arrows made from the ships' materials.[46]

At Great Fish River in 1879, Ikinnelik-Puhtoorak, formerly the leader of an Ugjulingmiut community occupying most of the southern coast of King William Island and the western shores of Adelaide Peninsula, told his story to Frederick Schwatka. As a little boy he had seen ten white men in a boat near the mouth of the Great Fish River. He had shaken hands with all of them, and recalled that their leader's name was "Tos-ard-e-roak." Schwatka's Inuit interpreter thought he was saying "George Back." The next time he saw a white man was on "a great ship which was frozen in" after having been carried by the ice to the village of Ugjulik on the west coast of Adelaide Peninsula. The white man was dead.[47] The ship, one of Franklin's, remained grounded there until the winter of 1857-58, the last date at which Inuit are known to have visited it. Soon after, Ikinnelik-Puhtoorak's "once powerful band" was "reduced ... to a handful" by the Netsilingmiut, who had taken possession of his country in order to gain access to the valuable remains of Franklin's ships and crews. The displaced Ugjulingmiut fled as refugees to join the Utkusiksalingmiut at Great Fish River. In 1879 Ikinnelik-Puhtoorak was the headman of a community consisting of about thirty Ugjulingmiut and Utkusiksalingmiut.[48]

Given Ikinnelik-Puhtoorak's account, arithmetic suggests that the Netsilingmiut began to harvest resources from the wrecked ship some time after 1851 but before it was completely broken up around 1858. By that time, the Ugjulingmiut had been reduced by famine and cold to a remnant of their former numbers, and when they were overwhelmed by Netsilingmiut invaders, the survivors took refuge with the Utkusiksalingmiut on the Great Fish River.

The only estimates of populations of Ugjulingmiut and Utkusiksalingmiut before the mid-1850s are those of George Back, who counted thirty-five of the former, and between sixty and seventy of the latter at Great Fish River in 1834. He did not go to west Adelaide Peninsula or King William Island, and none of the inhabitants of those areas could have figured in his census. Twenty years later, the population of the lower Great Fish River was still about 100, but that number by then included all the Utkusiksalingmiut, and all the remaining Ugjulingmiut as well. A conservative guess might be that prior to the mid-1840s, the two groups together would have numbered upwards of 300 people. Among European observers, both explorers and HBC traders, George Back seems to have been one who counted all adults, not just males, but none of his comments make it clear whether he included children.

If Anderson was right[49] and the forty or so adults he saw at three villages in 1855 were from Keewatin, then the total number of Ugjulingmiut and Utkusiksalingmiut combined could not have been much over fifty. Climatic pressures and Netsilingmiut wars of expansion had been very costly in terms of human life. The particular events and specific results of those wars, although hidden from contemporary view, were of shattering significance to the people involved. The merging of Ugjulingmiut and Utkusiksalingmiut, along with the borrowing or infiltration of technology and ideas from increased contact with the Keewatin people, would explain Anderson's inability to place the people he saw in any of the ethnic categories with which he was familiar.

In addition to the blurring of group distinctiveness, another result of the events of 1848 to 1858 was the Netsilingmiut reputation for fierceness and warlike behaviour. In the 1860s Aivilik and Arvilikjuaq people repeatedly warned American explorer Charles Francis Hall not to enter Netsilingmiut country, and attempted to dissuade him with stories of murder and violence similar to those that had frightened William Ullebuk during John Rae's second expedition. Like Rae, Hall had to abandon his attempt to reach King William Island in 1866 when no one would agree to accompany him.[50] On his second attempt, in 1869, he found some willing guides, but when the party met "about fifty Netchelli hunting seal" on the south coast of the island, there were some tense moments. Ipervik (Joe Eberbing), one of Hall's interpreters, said the Netsilingmiut "showed fight when we first saw them, and had knives, and one of them the barrel of a rifle made sharp like a knife."[51] On the journey back to Repulse Bay, Hall saw the military mindset of a group of Pelly Bay men, whose reaction to seeing guns for the first time was that they would "be a good thing to kill Inuits with."[52] The word *inuit* means "people," and is not necessarily an ethnic identifier. It is likely that the remarks of the Pelly Bay men should have been translated as "a good thing to kill people with."

Other Pelly Bay people were distressed enough over the continuing conflicts in their land to consider permanent emigration. At least one family moved to Aivilik in the 1860s to escape the violent hostilities between their people and the Netsilingmiut.[53] The oral evidence of Aivilik people in the 1860s suggests that even Aivilik was not a safe refuge. They maintained that "the natives of Pelly bay ... are a hostile tribe, who occasionally come and make a raid on the Iwilli [Aivilik] tribe of Repulse bay, and take everything away from them."[54] Utkusiksalingmiut shared the fear and passionate dislike, making it clear to Schwatka's 1878-79 searching party that they regarded the Netsilingmiut with extreme hostility.[55]

The available evidence suggests that the Netsilingmiut were neither more nor less warlike or inhospitable to strangers than other Inuit groups before 1832. In spite of periodically violent relations with the Arvilikjuaq people, they maintained communications and kinship ties with them, and shared territory, settlements, and resources at Lord Mayor's Bay. They had friends and relatives at Igloolik and Aivilik, and many of their women were Ugjulingmiut from King William Island. They included in their community a number of men and women who were not Netsilik-born, and at least one who was not Inuit. They did not object to the presence of John Ross's party in their country. They were not territorially expansive, nor did they attempt to exploit the resources of other territories.

By 1847, however, as John Rae's experience showed, they had a growing reputation for belligerence, apparently born out of their willingness to use violence in protection of resources they already possessed. And after the abandonment of *Victory* in 1832, they had resources worth protecting. Their activities after 1850 suggest that by then they were also prepared to fight in order to acquire new resources. Their expansion to the west and southwest was motivated by desire to gain access to the abundant supplies of useful articles at Ugjulik and along the western and southern coasts of King William Island.

The abandonments of *Victory*, *Erebus*, and *Terror* in 1832 and 1848, and the windfall of resources they contained, were of major significance in the ability of the Boothia Peninsula people to survive environmental stress in the forty middle years of the nineteenth century. Efforts to gain access to valuable resources and the need to protect them led to changed relations among the groups of the larger Netsilik society, including expansion of territory and warfare.

Keewatin

On the west coast of Hudson Bay, the people of southern Keewatin were faced with similar environmental degradation, but without the windfalls to which the Boothia people had fallen heir. Because of the distance between their places of residence and the post at Churchill, their long association with the traders was only minimally useful in helping them through the crisis. Instead they relied on their ancient strategies of increased mobility, community dispersion, long-distance harvesting, expansion of territory, relocation, intensification of labour, and a switch to new food resources. Their ability to choose appropriate strategies to deal with diverse problems ensured their survival and supported a minor, but steady, increase in population.

Fluctuations in the numbers and locations of caribou created special problems for the people of southern Keewatin because of their high degree of dependence on caribou for food, clothing, bedding, tenting, and kayak coverings. All caribou herds experience unpredictable cycles of population increase and decline, and shifts in migratory habits, for reasons not yet clear to wildlife scientists. Even in stable environmental conditions, caribou are not a reliable resource over the long term. Caribou-dependent human communities can expect to face a major change in the migratory patterns and distribution of herds at least once in every fifteen to twenty years, and more frequent minor fluctuations in numbers and location.[56]

In unstable environments, caribou numbers and locations become even more unpredictable. Numbers fall in periods of higher than usual humidity and when snow cover is icy or unusually deep, and tend to increase in drier conditions.[57] Migration routes are affected by the quality and depth of snow cover, and the condition of underlying vegetation. An early or late freeze or thaw, a sudden storm on an inland lake, a snowdrift in a valley between eskers, indeed, almost any change in topography or atmospheric conditions is enough to divert a moving herd, making its whereabouts uncertain at any given time.

Keewatin communities depended on two herds, the Kaminuriak herd, whose summer range was (and is) south of Baker Lake between the Kazan River and the coast, and the Beverly herd, which spent the summers along the Dubawnt River as far north as Beverly Lake. Both herds wintered south of the treeline, but in most winters stragglers remained on the tundra in groups of between ten and fifty.[58] Their numbers and movements were highly unpredictable. For the people of the southern Keewatin, who depended on the stragglers for winter food, access to caribou was a probability, but never a certainty.

As the numbers of caribou and fur-bearing animals declined in the early 1830s,[59] Inuit communities along the southern Keewatin coast continued to combine opportunities for long-distance resource harvesting and for trade, which were offered by the post at Churchill. Although the trade in country products in 1832 was the best since 1798—fifty-five men brought more than 1000 fox pelts and over 700 deerskins[60]—in most years trade was decidedly sparse. The seal hunt at Churchill River was a more dependable means of acquiring surplus products than hunting for luxury furs was, and a more certain source of subsistence supplies.[61] It was also cheaper in terms of time and transportation because subsistence hunting, acquisition of surplus, and conversion of surplus to goods were all available at the same time and place.

Although Inuit came to depend on the Churchill seal hunt in times of caribou shortages, they were reluctant to take part in the whale hunt. It was often unprofitable and always dangerous, largely because of the company's inability to supply adequate whaleboats. Forty-five hunters in 1835 lost "a great deal of the oil by lying exposed to the sun" because they lacked efficient transport. The death by drowning of a woman during the 1838 hunt was also attributed to unsafe watercraft, and the accident "put a stop to their whaling." Except in years when a crisis of scarce resources at home gave them no alternative, they avoided the whale hunt.[62]

Tough times were not limited to the nearby communities that regularly traded at Churchill. People began coming from much farther afield and, like their more southerly countrymen, they did not come primarily to trade; they came to get subsistence supplies by hunting seals near the mouth of the Churchill River. Small groups came from "a considerable distance to the Northwards" in 1836 and 1837, and in 1838 and 1840, there were visitors "from a great distance to the northward."[63]

The presence of caribou at specific locations was erratic. In 1836 and 1840, the people from "northwards" worried over shortages of deer, while more southerly people had adequate supplies. In the winter of 1840-41 and the spring that followed, the "northwards" people reported plenty of caribou in their country; in the fall of 1841, and throughout the winter of 1841-42, they faced a serious shortage.[64]

In 1841 unknown people arrived at unusual times of the year. In February three visitors "from some distance to the northward" complained of the "late stormy weather" and difficult travel conditions. Between the early fall of 1840, when their community separated into small family groups for winter hunting, and their arrival at the post in February 1841, they had seen only two other human beings. In April another six families reported they too had "seen no other Esquemaux since last summer." In December three travellers arriving "from some distance" reported continuing scarcity of fox and caribou.[65]

A sudden decrease in the number of dogs belonging to the northern people is another signal of increasingly bad economic times in the 1840s. A decade earlier, the company had regularly bought dogs from the Inuit. After 1840 Inuit often did not have dogs. In 1841 three of the five small parties that went to the post were man-hauling. Post master Robert Harding routinely sent dogs north to assist starving and weakened families in reaching the post. Travel to resource locations and hunting sites, and delivery of stored foods from caches to homes and of country products to the post, were difficult or impossible because of reduced transportation efficiency. The few groups of two or three men who managed to reach the post in most years were limited in the amount of time they could spend hunting seal, as well as in the quantities of blubber, oil, and meat they could take away with them.[66]

The winter of 1843-44 took a heavy toll in health and life. All the Inuit who managed to reach the post were in serious trouble for lack of dogs and provisions. In January 1844, a family visiting the post reported a recent death.[67] Another party trying to reach the trading post split into two groups while still "some distance away" at Egg River. One family moved on ahead, but at North River all but two individuals were too weak to continue. On February 10, a father and son succeeded in reaching the post, where they requested "a little provisions for [their] family to enable them to reach here, they being much in want." Two days later, when they arrived back at North River with emergency supplies, they found that "another of his sons who was fairly wore out ... [had died] which has caused great distress to the poor father who with his son that came with him are in a very low state from sheer starvation. His two surviving sons with the women and children yet remain near Egg River and most of them are unable to walk and tis not unlikely that more of them may perish ere we can assist them."[68]

Assistance was delayed because of bad weather, but on February 15 the company's Inuit clerk, Ullebuk, set out for Egg River with "5 dogs and 30 salt geese for the Esquimaux besides provisions for himself & dogs for 7 days." Ten days later he was back with "3 men, a boy, 3 women, and 3 children some of whom unable to walk and hauled by the dogs." Another man, along with his son and two widows, were still north of Churchill, being "unable to walk and fairly knocked up by sheer hunger." On February 27, Ullebuk brought the last of the travellers to the post.[69]

The strain of a winter on short rations and the gruelling journey took its toll. On March 10, one of the babies died, "owing to the mother being unable to suckle it." Post master Harding recorded his desperation at not having dogs to perform the usual work of the post and to assist Inuit families in trouble. His only hope was that Chipewyan would come so that he could borrow a team.[70]

In April Hoomeneshak, who had been hunting seal at Churchill regularly since at least 1829, brought his family safely to the post, but within a day or two his son died, having "been in a very low state since last autumn brought on by want of food, since which he has not been able to walk." By the end of April, four more were dead and at least twenty-five people suffering from starvation, malnutrition, and exposure were being cared for at the post.[71]

Three new arrivals in June reported that although they had spent the winter within seven days' journey of the post, they had been "starving all winter" and unable to reach the post for assistance. In August, as the seal hunters prepared to start north for their homes, "two of them fell over, one dying immediately and the other not expected to live."[72]

Only one family reached the post during the spring of 1845. Five other families, with whom they had spent the winter, were unable to make the trip, being "pinched for provisions."They had not seen any other members of their usual community during the entire winter. At the same time, news from nearby Chipewyan indicated starvation among them, and post master Harding began to worry about the state of food supplies at Churchill. "Our means will not admit of rendering them assistance to the extent of their need," he wrote, "and with them can only hope for a change of weather to benefit us and themselves."[73]

The activities of the Keewatin Inuit over the next ten years were a series of rapid responses, some successful, others not, to a high degree of environmental fluctuation in specific places, and extreme variability of conditions in different locations. A single community could experience extremes of starvation and satiation within a few months. At the same time, scarcity and abundance often existed in communities separated by only a few miles. As George Back noted in 1834, "the degree of cold at one place furnishes no inference which can be relied upon as to the temperature of another place even moderately distant."[74] His comment could refer equally well to the presence of game resources as to temperatures.

While Inuit and Chipewyan families living near Churchill were "pinched for provisions," the "more distant Esquimaux," who reached the post on August 1, 1845, after sixteen days' travel, were a healthier lot, "having been fortunate in meeting with deer all winter." Game was also more abundant, weather was less severe, and trade marginally better in 1846 and 1847. No cases of starvation were recorded in the post journals. The Inuit had dogs again and were willing to sell some to the post, which by then had only six, and of them, two were "not sound."[75]

The somewhat more abundant food resources were apparently not being found on the coast. When Doctor John Rae, Ullebuk Senior, his son William Ullebuk, and a dozen men sailed from Churchill to Repulse Bay in July 1846, they found the coast almost deserted. There were no signs of villages north of Knapp's Bay,[76] where the sloop captains had regularly seen around 300 people a year in the previous century. Their disappearance from the coast was consistent with Augustine's information that his people had been spending the summers inland since early in the century.[77]

Rae and his party did not find an occupied village until they reached Fullerton Bay. Ten families were in residence there, and were engaged in hunting inland along the northern shores of Chesterfield Inlet. Their summer hunt had been good, and one man already had a stock of wolf, fox and parchment (hairless) deerskins, but he had been at Churchill the previous year and intended to wait one more year before making another visit.[78]

Four families, consisting of twenty-six individuals, who were actually making their living on the coast, were spending the summer at Aivilik. None of them had ever been south to Churchill, but all had connections with Igloolik and Akudlit, the same villages that, along with Aivilik, had been occupied by the Iglulingmiut twenty-five years earlier. Like the community at Fullerton Bay, the Aivilik people had had a good summer caribou hunt, and were well supplied with skins and venison. One late September day, a local hunter sold Rae sixty caribou tongues, and Rae himself brought down seventeen caribou. His men killed sixty-three deer a day later, along with five hares, 172 partridges, and 116 salmon and trout.[79]

The winter of 1846-47 was warmer than previous years had been, at least on the bay coast north of Chesterfield Inlet. As George Back had noted while at Great Fish River in 1834-35, conditions varied considerably between places. The warmer temperatures north of Chesterfield Inlet were in sharp contrast to conditions at King William Island, where famine was destroying the Ugjulingmiut, and where the crews of the Franklin expedition, their ships frozen solidly into pack ice, were experiencing lethal cold. At Repulse Bay, there was a noticeable increase in the amount of snowfall. Anticipating a poor caribou hunt in conditions of deep, soft snow, several families left Aivilik to join Arvilingjuarmiut relatives at Simpson Peninsula.[80] By the end of October, the wisdom of their decision was obvious; Rae's hunters, trying to follow a small herd of caribou, spent eight hours covering a mere eight miles, and ended the day exhausted and un-successful. At Aivilik, the exploration party and the remaining Inuit had adequate, although not abundant, provisions from the land throughout the year.[81]

Communities just north and south of Aivilik were not so fortunate. At Wager Bay there was near starvation. Three men who reached Aivilik in the fall of 1846 were "so much reduced that they could not walk." At Igloolik, food was so scarce that two members of the community saved themselves only by resorting to cannibalism. A smaller community near Igloolik did not suffer shortage of provisions, but many people fell victim to a fatal disease that caused the deaths of twenty-one adults, although no children were affected. On hearing a description of the symptoms, Rae tentatively diagnosed some form of influenza. Near Rankin Inlet, a disease, which the Churchill post master thought might be measles, proved fatal to "many" people.[82]

Few travellers managed to reach Churchill in the summers of 1846 and 1847,[83] although one of Ullebuk's sons walked from Rankin Inlet to the post during the intervening winter.[84] Four men made the trip at the end of December 1847, driven to desperate acts because "they had not a single ball to shoot deer." When they met a small herd of muskox on their way south, they improvised, and "broke a stone kettle and made ball of it, with which they killed 3."[85]

The first three visitors of 1848 reported another bad caribou year. They had survived their journey only by eating frozen deerskins they had planned to trade. The post master was disappointed that they brought no meat, as the Churchill winter hunt had also failed and the provisions shed was nearly empty. He also expressed surprise that the visitors had "started so far with so very little," but again it was a case of desperation; the purpose of their trip was not to trade, but to kill seal and whale for their own winter use and to ask for relief supplies, which they were given.[86] Four men who arrived on the first day of May likewise had "nothing eatable amongst them" and for two months hunted seals without success. Only at the end of June did they begin to kill seals in quantities large enough to supply their immediate needs. By mid-July they were whaling, and in a week they had taken ninety-two beluga whales.[87]

Rae's observations of 1846-47 and the post records for 1846 to 1848 suggest that caribou were scarce around Churchill and the southern Keewatin, but rather more plentiful to the north. According to the post journal, thirty or forty "Distant Esquimaux" who reached the post at the end of July had not only found adequate supplies of caribou during the winter, but brought "a quantity of white foxes and wolves."[88]

The erratic distribution of game resources continued over the next few years. Fewer than thirty Inuit went to Churchill in 1849. The nearer people brought almost nothing to trade, and the more distant ones had skins but no surplus meat. The early visitors of 1850 arrived with empty sleds, reporting that "foxes are scarce & have been so all winter." Their complaints were echoed by the Chipewyan Homeguard, who experienced "a miserable hunt, [and] complain of starvation." Ullebuk's people north of Whale Cove had kept themselves alive by eating deerskins, and ten newly arrived "distant homeguard Esquimaux" were as badly off.[89]

Throughout the 1850s scarce game and hunger were frequently reported to the post. Dogs were in short supply again, and the heavy, soft snow of milder winters made hunting and travelling difficult. Only small quantities of fox, wolf, and wolverine pelts were traded, and they were of poor quality, as were the muskox skins brought by northern hunters in increasing quantities. Deer continued to be scarce in most years, and when they were more abundant, the seal and whale hunts failed. Messengers from some of the communities in 1852 reported they had been forced to separate into small groups, and, as happened throughout the 1840s, had lost touch with each other for the entire winter.[90]

In 1852 there was no scarcity of seal, but the animals were inaccessible. Fifteen hunters on their way to the sealing grounds were stopped short of their goal by early melting snow and ice, which made travel impossible. The only Inuit to reach the post that year were twenty-seven "Homeguards," probably from around Knapp's Bay, who managed to get to Seal River by sea for a short whale hunt, and nine "distant Esquimaux" who also went in kayaks. The latter took the precaution of borrowing one of the company's whaleboats to return home in, thus equipping themselves to make the next year's journey more easily and safely. Unfortunately, none of their preparations were of use in 1853. Although travel conditions on the land allowed the hunters to get to the sealing grounds, they found very few seal. The entire summer's hunt produced less than half the usual amount of blubber.[91]

Again people reported "starving lately on account of the want of ammunition."[92] The post master increased the amount of ammunition he gave as presents, and instead of buying meat from the regular visitors, he gave what he could from the post's stores. In addition to getting emergency rations and other supplies from the post, and hunting seal and whale for subsistence and trade, people tried other survival strategies, including dispersion of communities, expansion of harvesting range, relocation to new territory, and the unilateral sharing that the post masters called pilfering.[93]

In 1851, for the first time in more than two decades, the traders complained of pilfering. Iron handles were removed from a soup kettle, the cook's fire tongs went missing, and lead was cut away from the roof of a shed. More roofing lead disappeared in 1854, a year of extraordinary cold.[94]

William Ullebuk's community north of Whale Cove lost all its dogs "from want of meat" in the winter and spring of 1855. After "starving most of the winter, [because of] no deer in their quarter," they opted for temporary relocation. Led by a man the Churchill traders called The Chief, all but three families moved "to the Northward & inland from there" in the spring of 1855. Sickness among them during the winter took the lives of The Chief and at least eight others. Their exact location remains unknown, but the messengers who carried the news to Churchill in February 1856 were "2 1/2 moons coming to the post, which is 45 days."[95] It may be more than an interesting coincidence that July 20 to 22, 1855, were the days on which Chief Factor James Anderson saw people at Great Fish River whom he strongly suspected were from Hudson Bay. Those he met on July 20 gave him the impression they had come from Chesterfield Inlet and down the McKinley River, which agrees with the messengers' comment to the Churchill traders that they had gone "to the Northward and inland." The forty-five-day travel period also seems reasonable. A group of people that included the elderly, the sick, and the babies, travelling without dogs to bear some of the burdens, and hunting as they went, might easily take that long to cover the distance.

Wherever they were, they found caribou sufficient for their own food and clothing needs, and a surplus for trade. In March 1856, William Ullebuk, fifteen other men, and two women brought three sleds heavily loaded with 1603 pounds of venison, eleven whole reindeer, sixty-one reindeer hearts, twenty-one tongues, 336 parchment deerskins, and seven heads with antlers attached. They also brought 378 fox furs, twenty-two prime and staged (lesser grade) wolves, seven wolverine, and five arctic hare pelts. The post master noted with some surprise that although they were coastal people, they brought only inland products. A week after Ullebuk's arrival, two more members of his community brought some coastal products, explaining that they had separated from the main party while on the way to make a side trip "to the coast for oil." With the exception of fifty pounds of seal, the products the later arrivals traded were also all inland items, including venison, parchment deerskins, caribou hearts and tongues, a few white fox, and caribou sinew.[96]

Some communities began bringing trade items consisting entirely, or almost so, of inland products. In 1855 the Churchill journalist noted that the trade of one group of "the more distant" people was all inland products. In February 1858, William Ullebuk and seven other hunters made a midwinter visit to deliver 135 fox furs, a few prime wolf and wolverine, venison, tongues, hearts, kidneys, whole heads and horns, and even two whole deer. Not only were the products all inland items, but most were provisions for the post.[97]

By 1858 post personnel were aware that some people had become "inland Esquimaux that never visit the coast in summer."[98] So many were at the post in 1861 that the post master was nervous: "34 men and 7 wives, with nine sledges heavy laden with parchments [but] very little meat.... This is all the inland Esquimaux, there is too many of them here at one time and have set 2 men to watch them all night for fear of them stealing the lead of the houses."[99]

The Homeguards continued to hunt seal when caribou were scarce and fell back on the whale hunt in times of acute crisis. In good economic times, they became increasingly involved in trading provisions, but this does not signal a change in occupation. It was an extension or intensification of existing activities, in which they traded food to the post only after their caches were sufficient to sustain them throughout the next winter. By 1860 the Churchill traders were heavily dependent on the food they bought from their northern suppliers.[100]

In March 1860, the post was short of provisions again. On the 12th, the post master wrote, "I do not know what we are to do for provisions & no appearance of any Esquimaux ... there is now about 40 souls of us at this place & nothing to eat." By far, Chipewyan families were the greater part of the forty souls forced by the scarcity of game in their own lands to depend on the trading post for subsistence. On March 18, one of the traders killed a caribou and on March 19, the emergency was over, at least for the moment, when eleven Inuit arrived with 2220 pounds of venison, thirty hearts, forty kidneys, twenty-five tongues, and seven livers taken during their caribou hunt.[101]

Venison from the north did not, however, alleviate the suffering of the Chipewyan living near the post. In May, "half the Indians are starving, bad news." The meat brought in during March was gone and the weather was so bad that the post master feared for the Inuit who were hunting seal. The seal hunt was a failure on account of "so much water on the ice" and the whale hunt yielded only nine animals. The post master handed out oatmeal and carefully rationed venison.[102]

The recurring descriptions of starvations in the post journals, if taken at face value, indicate a people at the mercy of a cruel environment and on the edge of extinction. The suffering was real and widespread, but Inuit communities were surviving without appreciable loss of numbers. The Keewatin population north of Churchill as far as, and including, Chesterfield Inlet at the beginning of the eighteenth century has been tentatively estimated at between 200 and 300. Trading sloop censuses and the comments of Andrew Graham suggest at least 600 individuals living at Chesterfield Inlet and south of it by 1790. Forty years later, at the end of the Little Maunder Minimum, about 160 men from the coast south of Rankin Inlet were identifed by name in the Churchill journals, suggesting a minimum population of 700 people. In 1850 the population was holding steady, at about 732 souls.[103] In that period of one generation, births and deaths must have been almost equal. If the number of births was high, then deaths (in raw numbers) must have been almost equally as high.

The apparent contradiction between actual head-counts of a population holding its own, neither increasing dramatically nor declining, and reports in the post journals of deaths from starvation, accident, or disease in at least one year out of every four between 1791 and 1881 can be explained by an assumption of the Churchill fur traders. Their population estimates were based on the number of adult males who came to the post, and because most of the traders assumed that all productive adult males came to trade, they consistently underestimated the populations of their client communities. A second, and related, assumption led to another sampling error. The traders tended to believe that a report of bad conditions from one community meant that all other communities were in the same condition. The traders' own account books indicate that such was not the case.

The starvation periods resulting from scarcity of caribou, so carefully noted by HBC post masters, were usually local. In years when one or two communities experienced life-threatening shortages, people in other places were reporting adequate or even plentiful supplies. The reports of death by starvation in the post records for the most part describe the sufferings of individuals and families from communities who frequented the trading post. The suffering was real and dreadful, but famine was not severe enough to cause a population crash, or even to prevent population increase.

Two facts of the physical environment in the period from 1830 to 1860 made it possible for the Keewatin people to maintain almost constant numbers in the face of fluctuating and uncertain food supplies: unoccupied territory nearby, and an underused food resource. As Keewatin coast populations increased and caribou herds declined or became less accessible in the first half of the nineteenth century, families began to hunt farther inland than previously. The expansion of hunting territory brought them within reach of a second food resource, the muskox herds. Although there is no evidence that muskox was or was not a regular part of Inuit diets in the eighteenth century, it was important enough by 1821 for Augustine to mention it in the top three when he told George Back that his people "obtained abundance of musk-ox, reindeer, [and] salmon, sufficient for their winter consumption" at inland rivers and lakes during the summer. By 1844 post master Robert Harding recognized muskox as a staple food resource of the northern communities. "Their means of subsistence in all seasons are Deer, Musk ox, Fish of many kinds," he wrote to George Simpson. "Deer, Musk oxen and Fish are said to be in general plentiful and abundant enough to serve more people than themselves and families."[104]

Between 1820 and 1840, muskox wool and skins were a regular, if minor, item in the Inuit trade at Churchill, and the hunters who brought them also brought marine products. During the 1840s and 1850s, the fur traders recorded increasing numbers of people who brought only inland products to the post.[105] In maintaining their numbers during a period of frequent failures of the seal and whale hunts, people who, for more than a century, had spent their summers on the coast harvesting marine resources, expanded inland, spending less time sealing and whaling and more time hunting caribou and muskox.

The emergence of an inland community of people was only one of the significant changes in location and social organization made by the Keewatin people between 1830 and 1860. In 1821, according to Augustine, the coastal people south of Rankin Inlet were a single community with villages at Knapp's Bay, Nevil's Bay, and Whale Cove. North of them at Chesterfield Inlet was a second community where the inhabitants were not "Augustine's people." The observations of Fort Churchill's traders agree with Augustine's description; like him they distinguished between only "two tribes.... The one from towards Chesterfield Inlet and the other from Knapp's Bay." By 1825, following a sharp drop in the price of white fox furs, the Chesterfield Inlet people had stopped going south except on rare occasions.[106]

In the 1840s the traders began referring to "Augustine's people" as the "near" and the "more distant Esquimaux,"[107] implying that they were no longer a single social unit, but were geographically separate and in some sense identifiably distinct groups. The "near Esquimaux" had their principal residence at Knapp's Bay, and went to the post more frequently and in larger numbers than did the northern group. The "more distant" people lived between Whale Cove and Rankin Inlet, and brought larger quantities of coast products to trade, including ivory. Augustine, Utuck, and the Ullebuks were identified by the traders as members of the "more distant" community. At the beginning of the 1850s, the traders adopted the terms "Homeguard" and "distant Homeguard" to refer to the two groups they now thought of as discrete bands.[108]

The separation of Augustine's single "people" into inland and coastal groups is not surprising. For centuries, their ancestors had survived short-term scarcity every year by fragmentation and dispersal of communities. Two instances are described in exploration literature. During the winter of 1822-23, while Parry was wintering at Igloolik, fifteen or so families left the larger community to spend the winter at Aivilik, and in 1846, several Aivilik families opted to spend the winter at Simpson Peninsula. In both cases the dispersion was a means of lessening the strain on local food resources. The constant reports of the Inuit themselves, recorded in the Churchill journals, illustrate how frequently the strategy was used and how successful it was in ensuring the survival of small family groups.

About the same time that the single society of southern Keewatin was splitting into three geographically separate groups, Churchill's traders began to note the existence of leaders or chiefs among them. During the 1850s there were frequent journal entries concerning the activities of The Chief or The Eskimaux Chief. He was always mentioned in connection with a member of the Ullebuk family,[109] and always in connection with hunters who took part in the seal hunt, the whale hunt, or both. He can, therefore, be identified with the Distant Homeguard whose territory was north of Whale Cove, and possibly extended to Rankin Inlet.

In 1851 a reference was made to two chiefs, one who was already at the post, and another, Uchuputack, who was expected at any time.[110] A few clues exist in the *Eskimo Trading Books* of 1823 and 1828-32 as to the identity of the second chief. Although the same names occurred over and over among people of different communities and in different generations, two people in the same residential group seldom shared a name. It is, therefore, not unlikely that the references in the trading books to Uchuputack, Utchiputak, and Utchapetahk are all to the same person. If so, Chief Uchuputack had a reputation of long-standing as a good son, a good hunter, and a good provider. In 1823 he was identified as "a boy, Atahoona's son." Atahoona was a close companion of Utuck and Ullebuk the Elder, indicating that he was a member of their community, possibly a relative. Of the thirty seals traded by Atahoona that year, six had been taken by "his boy."

The son, however, also had his own account with the company. In addition to the six seals he handed over to his father, he traded twenty-four on his own behalf, in exchange for one white jacket, one copper kettle, a cloth capot, a bayonet, a knife, and a tobacco box. His name appeared again six years later in the second *Eskimo Trading Book*, when he bought a new gun. The evidence suggests that the families of both chiefs were part of the community north of Whale Cove that came to be known as the Distant Homeguard.

Through the Little Maunder Minimum and the fluctuating environmental conditions of the thirty years that followed, communities in southern Keewatin solved problems of long-term shortages by using ancient strategies singly and in combination. In the last years of the eighteenth century they began to make regular trips to the post at Churchill. In the first two decades of the nineteenth century, they coped with the terrible years of the Second Maunder Minimum by increasing their long-distance harvesting of seal and whale at killing-grounds near Churchill, and transported most of the oil supplies back to their winter homes. In the same period they apparently spent more time and energy trapping the fur-bearing animals that brought them the best returns at the post. By 1820 they were regularly hunting muskox, an inland animal, in contrast to the previous century, when muskox does not seem to have been a staple food. Throughout the 1820s, the people whom Augustine had regarded as a single community were arriving at Churchill in three distinct waves. Each of the three groups brought a different combination of marine, inland, or mixed country products to trade, and each arrived at a different season. By the end of the 1850s, the single community of "Augustine's people" had become three communities, recognized by the Churchill traders as the Near Homeguard, the Distant Homeguard, and the Inlanders.

7.

Skin for Soles, Moss for Wicks: The Search for Predictability, 1860–1940

You, louse-like; you, long legs; you, long ears; you with the long neck hair. Do not run past below me. Skin for soles, moss for wicks, you shall look forward to. Come hither, come hither.

> – Orpingalik's magic words to bring luck
> on a caribou hunt, at Netsilik, 1923[1]

Like the southern Keewatin peoples and the Netsilingmiut of Boothia Peninsula, communities in Cumberland Sound on Baffin Island's east coast were faced with problems of long-term resource shortages during the Little Maunder Minimum and the highly unstable climatic conditions that followed. In each region, the people found different solutions to their problem. In Keewatin, people moved into unoccupied inland territories in order to harvest new kinds of resources. As a result of the relocation, at least three new and discrete communities were created. The Netsilingmiut found a temporary solution in the eagerly sought, and fought-over, resources left by the Franklin disaster, but these were, of course, lucky windfalls. They were uncertain and unpredictable, and did not offer long-term solutions to problems of scarcity, or permanent affluence to their finders. As a result of their readiness to protect their property, through force of arms if necessary, they gained a reputation for ferocity and within twenty years were socially isolated from their compatriots. Communities at Cumberland Sound recognized commercial whaling activities in their waters as opportunities for longer term security, and seized them.

Cumberland Sound

After the three brief visits of John Davis to Cumberland Sound in the 1580s, few European vessels visited the area and fewer still left records of their visits. Almost nothing is known of the activities of local people in the next 250 years. In July 1824, however, Inuit near Merchants Bay on northern Cumberland Peninsula encountered British whaleships. At the first meeting, the Inuit approach was cautious but threatening, according to the crew of the Scottish whaler *Ellen*. During a second meeting the following year, local people tried to intimidate one of *Ellen's* officers with bows and arrows,[2] but neither episode resulted in open violence.

The suspicions and tension of the meetings of 1824 and 1825 disappeared quickly, perhaps because local communities recognized the economic possibilities offered by the whaleships. First were the trading opportunities. Inuit were quick to initiate trade, offering baleen from their own whale hunts and provisions from their seal hunt. In return, they received metal items, needles, and food supplies such as bread and molasses.[3] They also benefitted from whale carcasses left on the beach by the whaleships, as had the Tununeq communities of northern Baffin Island a few years earlier.[4] With so much to be gained, the Inuit apparently decided that their best course of action was to make the newcomers welcome.

Cumberland Sound people began going to the northern coast of the peninsula every fall when the whalers were expected, and a few moved permanently to areas near the whaling stations. The economic opportunities were, however, still of a windfall nature, and local people took steps to make their relations with the whalemen more permanent and predictable as a hedge against recurring hard times. Throughout the 1830s, they tried to bring the ships into Cumberland Sound by showing the captains what a rich whaling ground it was. In 1840 one man, Inuluapik, persuaded the Scottish captain William Penny to begin whaling in the Sound.[5]

In spite of the climatic changes that had affected wildlife resources during the centuries between the arrival of Thule people on Baffin Island and the mid-nineteenth century, whaling was still an important subsistence occupation. Communities at the head of the Sound killed between eight and twelve whales every year in the 1830s, providing themselves with abundant oil for fuel, baleen for utensils and tools, and bone for sleds, kayak frames, and houses. At the same time, seal hunting remained a principal occupation and seal meat was the dietary staple, supplemented by whale meat, blubber, fish, and caribou. In most years seal were plentiful, even after the Inuit became provisioners to the whaling fleet. The relative abundance of food resources supported a population of about 1000 people in 1840.[6]

In 1846 and 1847, the same years in which the Franklin expedition met disaster in Victoria Strait, and the Ugjulingmiut of King William Island were reduced to a tiny remnant of their former numbers, bad ice years on the east coast of Baffin Island resulted in failure of the seal hunt. Whalers returning to east Baffin stations in 1848 found communities with populations reduced by as much as ten percent from starvation in the preceding winter. Desperate people from other parts of the coast made their way to Cumberland Sound, hoping to find relief among the whaling fleet. Most were disappointed when the whaleships were unable to enter the Sound because of the severe ice conditions.[7]

The Inuit solution to the hard times of 1845 to 1848 was to continue efforts to bring whalers permanently to the rich bowhead grounds of Cumberland Sound. They were finally successful in 1851. That year, American whaling captain William Quayle of *M'Clellan* left a volunteer crew to overwinter near Niantilik. Inuit from the nearby community of Kingmiksok acted as teachers, guides, provisioners, and boatmen, and ensured themselves of more or less reliable and steady access to necessary resources. Wintering was also profitable from the whalemen's point of view; the men at the Niantilik station had seventeen whales waiting when *M'Clellan* returned in 1852.[8]

The Scottish captains William Penny and George Brown wintered *Lady Franklin* and *Sophia* at Niantilik in 1853-54, and employed fifty Inuit as boatmen, hunters, and transportation labourers. Other vessels also wintered in the Sound in the 1850s and by 1857 every local man who wanted work with the whaleships—and nearly all did—was sure of employment. Women also joined the whaling workforce, as professional seamstresses, laundresses, provisioners, and tanners. Inuit and whalemen communicated with each other on matters of work and daily routines by using a mixture of words from Inuktitut and English.[9]

As the economic environment changed, so did the social environment. Material culture was greatly expanded; every household had tools and utensils unimaginable a generation earlier. Inuit acquired many European items as payment for their labours and through trade of country products. They also increased their material wealth by recycling items discarded by the whaling crews; for example, transforming broken oars into tent poles. New techniques and technologies eased the labour of some kinds of work. Hunting and butchering were more easily and quickly done after the introduction of rifles and metal flensing tools, and shears and hand-operated sewing machines lightened the burden of skin preparation and sewing. The British government and many of the whaling captains provided relief and other kinds of social security,[10] including medical care, all of which had their effects on Inuit family life and other social arrangements.

Most whaling captains who had long-term relationships with the indigenous people respected local customs and social arrangements, and were committed to act in the best interests of the host community. Others, however, were unconcerned about the welfare of their employees. They introduced alcohol into communities, cheated local people when they could, and made no attempt to restrain their crews from conduct that was considered immoral by most people in both European and Inuit societies. Liaisons with Inuit women were commonplace and children were the inevitable result. The impact of such children on the societies of Cumberland Sound was probably negligible. Few mariner fathers took an interest in them, or, indeed, even knew they had become fathers. Most of the children were raised in their mother's families. Their European genetic inheritance was of little consequence in their lives.

Other changes arising from increased Inuit involvement in European whaling were unintended and unforeseen by both Inuit and whalemen, and benefitted no one. The late 1840s were particularly nasty for the diseases that sickened and killed local people. In spite of the almost continuous arrivals of people from other parts of Baffin Island looking for work with the fleet, the population dropped from an estimated 1000 souls in 1840 to about 350 in 1857.[11] Some illnesses were the result of contagion when people with no immunity came in contact with pathogen-laden sailors. Others sprang from inadequate home hygiene, a problem Inuit had not had to deal with when they maintained mobile residences, constructed clean, new snowhouses every winter, and occupied tents and the open air in the other seasons. Sedentary village life, centralization, and cramped quarters gave rise to conditions in which disease was easily spread.

West Hudson Bay: North of Chesterfield Inlet

Although Keewatin Inuit, like the people of Cumberland Sound, had encouraged Europeans to establish stations closer to their homes, they had not met with any success. In the 1860s, the Hudson's Bay Company still had no plans for establishing permanent posts in Inuit country. A significant non-Inuit presence north of Whale Cove came from a different and unexpected direction. The climatic warming of the mid-1800s brought whales in large numbers into Hudson Bay. The opportunities for commercial whaling, particularly in the strait known as Roes Welcome, between Southampton Island and the mainland, were too good to be ignored by the whaling fleets of New England. Two American whaleships wintered at

Winchester Inlet, just north of Chesterfield Inlet, in 1860-61. They were followed by other commercial whalers, who brought new social and economic environments within which some of the "most distant Esquimaux" sought security against the vagaries of an unpredictable physical environment.

From the late eighteenth century, when the villages at Nuvuk and Pikiulaq (Depot Island) were destroyed or deserted in local wars, until 1860, when the first whalers wintered in Roes Welcome, the coast and inland areas from Chesterfield Inlet to Repulse Bay constituted an empty buffer zone between the Melville Peninsula people and the people of Chesterfield Inlet.[12] Almost immediately after the arrival of the first whalers, however, Inuit began moving to the uninhabited coast near the winter whaling stations, as Baffin Islanders had done.

The first event in the discourse with American whalers was an Inuit request for relief supplies. The log of *Syren Queen*, one of the two ships at Winchester Inlet, recorded at least three incidents of Inuit families applying to the captain for assistance during March of 1861. Less than a month later, "the old natives" built houses beside the ship, assuming that necessary help would be forthcoming, a move reminiscent of the Greenlanders' shifting of responsibility for unproductive members of society from the indigenous community to the newcomers. Inuit continued to ask for, and obtain, relief throughout the whaling period.[13]

Inuit also took employment with the whalers in the first season of Roes Welcome commercial whaling. By the spring of 1861, they were hunting to supply not only their own subsistence needs, but also the needs of the whaling crews for fresh meat,[14] and transporting blubber from the flensing station to the ships. In succeeding years, men continued to work as labourers around the ships in winter, and in the boats during the whale-hunting season. Women found employment tanning skins and sewing winter outfits for sale to the whalers, as had happened in Cumberland Sound.[15]

The southern Iglulingmiut, whose summer village was at Aivilik, were the first whaling homeguard. They began moving south into the formerly unoccupied coast between Wager Inlet and Fullerton Bay immediately after the arrival and overwintering of the first whaleships. They established new year-round villages at Depot Island and Wager Bay. To maintain contact with the whaling fleet, they continued their southward move. Within a decade the old site at Nuvuk, which had been abandoned after the hostilities at the beginning of the century, was occupied summer and winter. One new summer settlement was at the exact midpoint of the whaleships' range, which, according to George Comer, captain of the whaler *Era*, was the most productive whaling ground of the entire coast.[16] The physical and occupational separation of the Roes Welcome people from their Iglulingmiut parent community on Melville Peninsula encouraged their emergence as a separate band. By the end of the century, they perceived themselves as a new social entity, centred at Aivilik and self-identified as Aivilingmiut.

Although nearly all the whaling fleet homeguard, according to Captain George Comer, came "from the vicinity of Repulse Bay," that is, Aivilik, others came in smaller numbers from the south and west. People from the coast between Rankin Inlet and Chesterfield Inlet began wintering near the whalers at Depot Island, and working as casual labourers and provisioners as early as 1864-65. In 1866 several Pelly Bay families moved to Repulse Bay, seeking to exchange the uncertainties of life on the land in an unpredictable physical environment for assured, year-round work and social security.[17]

As was the case with the south-coast hunters who became provisioners to the trading post, the Roes Welcome people did not change their occupations. They adjusted them to fit new circumstances. In continuing to hunt caribou, seal, and walrus, they used the same skills and knowledge they used for subsistence. The work of transporting blubber and meat from kill sites to flensing, rendering, and storage areas also depended on old skills and the familiar equipment of dogs and sleds.

Although the activities themselves remained basically the same, their timing and duration did not. Roes Welcome Inuit, whether they worked as independents or as hired hunters, were not selling surpluses created as by-products of storage for subsistence. Meat sold to the whaling captains ranged from the "3000 pounds" of venison purchased by the chief steward of *Isabella* in 1878-79, to "16,000 pounds" of caribou, walrus, and seal meat, as well as fish, purchased for *Abbie Bradford*'s crew of fifteen over a fifteen-month period in 1886-87.[18] The quantities indicate deliberate attempts to increase the harvest through intensification of effort or increased periods of time spent hunting.

As tanners and tailors, women also used accustomed skills to produce familiar articles in traditional ways. But their work—preparing skins and sewing winter outfits—was greatly increased when they began to market their products to the whalers. At Aivilik in 1864, Tookooliktoo, one of the interpreters to Charles Francis Hall, made winter clothing for herself, her husband, Hall, and Hall's servant. She "labored for thirty days, fifteen hours out of the twenty-four, during which time ... she had made up, besides bedding, seven complete fur suits."[19] Tookooliktoo, an expert seamstress, spent a minimum of sixty hours on each suit, and about 120 hours on a complete winter outfit for one adult. The period within which sewing of new clothing was done was short; sewing could begin only after skins were taken in the fall hunt and had to be completed before the onset of winter. Women who became professional tailors in addition to producing clothing for family needs had greatly increased workloads.

As the men of Aivilik became more involved in whaling activities during the summer, they had less time for caribou hunting. Whaling captains looked farther afield for hunters and provisioners, and hired men from Rankin Inlet and Chesterfield Inlet to supply meat for their crews. Increasingly, during the last thirty years of the century, Aivilingmiut involvement in whaling prevented them from taking enough meat and skins for their own subsistence. Whaling captains had to provide meat for the families of their employees and, by the turn of the century, were also buying skins from the Qairnirmiut of Rankin Inlet so that Aivilingmiut women could clothe their families as well as the whale crews. "We have now collected about 75 deer skins for winter clothing and spring use," wrote Captain George Comer of *Era* at the end of September 1903. "If our natives are not successful we will let them have some of these skins we have got from outside natives *who have not been in boats looking for whale*" [emphasis added].[20]

The Roes Welcome Inuit did not undervalue their products and services. Independent provisioners consistently charged a high price for meat.[21] They were paid with immediate goods or with credit, which could be turned into goods at a later date. Hired hunters were similarly compensated, but, in addition, many whaling captains recognized social obligations, which local people invoked in times of resource shortage. Food, powder, and ammunition were nearly always provided when needed. Other perquisites of association with the whaling fleet, accessible to all community members, were medical services, repairs to guns and other implements, and access to carcasses left on the beach after baleen and oil had been removed. The abandoned carcasses were a major source of oil for lighting and heating, and of meat for human consumption as well as for dog feed. After 1870, winter villages on the coast of Roes Welcome were invariably located near flensing stations to facilitate access to the whale cache.[22]

While work in the provisioning trades resulted in greater economic security evenly spread throughout the year, it did not guarantee affluence. The buying power of hunters varied from year to year, depending on the number and needs of wintering vessels, and the availability of game. Farther south at Rankin Inlet, unreliable ice frequently prevented travel between the whaleships at Marble Island and the mainland, and many vessels were dangerously undersupplied.[23] The provisioners suffered a loss of buying power at the same time.

Instead of spending the late summers inland, local people began going to the whaling stations in time to greet the ships arriving in August.[24] The decision to tie their economic lives to commercial whaling had the immediate effect of limiting the seasons of Inuit mobility. Because the whalers were in harbour for nine months of the year, so were the local families whose livelihood was linked to them. They adjusted their timetables in order to take advantage of the whaler presence.

Among the whaling fleet homeguard, starvation times became less frequent and less severe than in earlier decades.[25] It is a given of hunter-gatherer life in the arctic that all communities suffer periodic shortages in their own territories, due to fluctuations in the availability of game. There was a general reluctance to take necessary resources from the territories of other groups because open hostilities might follow and be costly in terms of group survival. After more than a century of interaction with British traders and explorers, most communities were confident that requests for food would be met with at least minimal generosity, and never with hostility. The worst that could happen was refusal. Involvement in commercial whaling guaranteed even more reliable access to food at all seasons of the year.

Some changes in social and cultural life, although they are largely invisible in the historical record, must be assumed. Village life and a decrease in residential mobility, increased economic security, and provisioning and labouring as male occupations, for example, imply changes in family and social life. Separation of communities into small groups during seasons of scarcity was no longer so necessary or so frequent. The separation of family members on a daily basis, however, became more common as men began to work apart from wives and children. Child-rearing, of boys as well as girls, which had earlier been a family responsibility in which men were fully involved, more and more became the province of women.

The professionalization of women's labour in skin preparation and clothing manufacture required adjustments in religious understanding and spiritual imperatives. Powerful religious tenets restricted the sewing of new clothing to the period between the fall caribou hunt and the beginning of winter sea-mammal hunting. Ancient wisdom attributed the sewing timetable to a need to separate land and sea animals; that is, sewing caribou-skin clothing must be completed before seal hunting began, lest one or the other become jealous and withhold its gifts. Underlying the ideology was an economic necessity—a soundly constructed winter wardrobe was a prerequisite to travel and hunting in the bitterly cold, dark winter months. Women had to finish their sewing before men could begin winter hunting. The expression of the economic necessity as a divine imperative helped to ensure the work was done on time. As the number of people to be outfitted grew, however, there were occasions when new clothing had to be made at other times of the year. Sometimes sufficient skins were not available in the early winter; often more outfits were required than could be completed during the allotted time. Women's domain thus became an arena where Inuit religious principles, Inuit economic self-interest, and the physical needs of both Inuit and whalemen were in conflict.

Other changes are better documented. Less than two decades after the beginning of commercial whaling, Aivilingmiut living between Wager Bay and Chesterfield Inlet had "added to their language so-called pidgin-English, that is, a mixture between their own language and English."[26] Inuktitut itself expanded to include new words for new things: *tii* (tea), *sigaliaq* (cigarette), and *siorauyak* (sugar). Square dancing and new forms of music became popular recreations, and a mid-winter festival of feasting and revelry was introduced and adopted[27] before the Christian meaning of Christmas was preached in their midst.

The presence of the whaling fleet gave local people opportunities and motives for adapting and adding to their material culture. Before the 1860s few north-coast Inuit had owned watercraft larger than kayaks, although the idea of multi-passenger boats was not new to them. Iglulingmiut had seen them during the long visits of Parry, Lyon, and Rae, and in their contacts with people from the southern Keewatin coast who had been using whaleboats acquired at Churchill since early in the century. They did not, however, begin to build, use, or own umiaks or ship's boats before 1861.

At least one whaleboat was left for the use of the community at Winchester Inlet when *Syren Queen* and *Northern Light* sailed from Roes Welcome after the first year of whaling (1861). By 1865 three men in a community of about a dozen families at Wager Bay owned wooden boats. In 1874 ten Marble Islanders arrived at Churchill in three whaleboats, which they said they had received as wages in kind for their work as harpooners, provisioners, labourers, and seamstresses for the American fleet at Roes Welcome. Thirteen "faraway" Inuit in two boats made the trip the following year. In 1878 Roes Welcome people began using wooden boats to make annual trips to Churchill. The same year, William Ullebuk, after three years' employment with the whaling fleet at Marble Island, owned a small schooner, which he used for freighting goods and transporting people along the coast.[28] While employment encouraged a more settled residence among whaling fleet homeguard families and limited the seasons in which they could travel, possession of multi-passenger boats increased their ability to move entire households safely and quickly between widely separated resource sites in summer.

Firearms were a technological commodity familiar to most central and eastern arctic communities before the beginning of the whaling period. Southern Keewatin Inuit were using guns a century before the first whalers entered Hudson Bay and by 1830 every hunter from the communities south of Rankin Inlet probably owned one. After the beginning of commercial whaling in Roes Welcome, more northerly groups at Repulse Bay, Chesterfield Inlet, and Rankin Inlet began to acquire firearms in greater numbers. Gun ownership not only increased hunters' ability to harvest some subsistence resources, it was a prerequisite to provisioning as an occupation. Because the whalers, like the Churchill traders, were dependent on local people for fresh meat, it was in their interest to see to it that their hired hunters were well equipped. And see to it they did. *Syren Queen* supplied guns, powder, and shot to local people during its first wintering, and by 1867 firepower materials were staples of the whaler-Inuit trade and remained so until the end of the whaling era.[29]

The Iglulingmiut proper, who still occupied Melville Peninsula north of Lyon Inlet as they had during the 1820s, were not drawn to Roes Welcome by the presence of whaleships. There were at least three reasons for their decision not to participate in commercial whaling. First, commercial whalers did not frequent Foxe Basin. Second, severe, long-term shortages were less frequent in the lands around Foxe Basin than in most other arctic environments. Caribou, walrus, and seal, which had maintained Dorset communities in their heartland for almost 2000 years, continued to sustain Iglulingmiut communities in the late nineteenth century. And, finally, by 1867 they were getting guns, metal cutting tools and kettles, and wood passed on to them by families at Aivilik. They also had frequent trading contacts with their countrymen at Tununeq (Pond Inlet), who, like the people at Aivilik, saw whalers nearly every year.[30] They apparently did not perceive a need for greater access to European goods, and the presence of whalers to the south did not tempt them. In the relatively unthreatening physical environment of Melville Peninsula, opting for the status quo was a rational strategy.

West Hudson Bay: South of Chesterfield Inlet

Among the first items purchased by an Inuit in 1861, the first year of American whaling at Roes Welcome, was a gun. The Hudson's Bay

Company learned of the American presence—and the gun—the following year. The Churchill post report that year informed company headquarters that "it appears there has been some ship or vessel visiting [the distant Esquimaux] last summer as they ... has got sailors clothing on some of them. I think it has been American ships as I got a gun from 1 of the Esquimaux made in Boston, most likely they seen whalers."[31]

Concerned that the whalemen were buying furs, threatening its charter rights, and destroying the Churchill trade, the company sent its *Ocean Nymph* to Marble Island and Repulse Bay in 1866-67 to protect its interests. Its fears were, for the moment, unfounded: whalemen were not yet conducting a commercial trade with local Inuit, and fur and skin returns at Churchill were not down. Over 1200 fox were taken to the post in 1866, more than in either of the two record years, 1798 and 1832, and the post reported, "We have now more parchment than we have room for."[32]

Throughout the 1860s, with the exception of firearms, powder, and shot, whaler trade with local people was of the souvenir-trinket variety.[33] As long as whale remained abundant and prices in Europe justified the long, expensive voyages, whaling firms focussed on taking baleen and oil. As the number of whales began to decline in the 1870s, however, owners instructed their captains to engage in commercial fur trading as well as whaling.[34] Inuit used their buying power to get the kinds of goods they wanted. The 1892 log of the whaleship *A.R. Tucker* noted that men agreeing to work wanted assurances beforehand that they would be paid with lumber, axes, lances, guns, powder, boat masts, and wooden poles. In the 1890s, one astute captain, George Comer of *Era*, was supplying his customers with exactly what they wanted: guns, ten-inch knives, fish hooks and lines, telescopes, buttons, scissors, planks and shoeing for sled runners, and roasting pans that could be hung over a cooking lamp.[35]

In the southern Keewatin, people were faced with problems of subsistence and survival similar to those of their northern neighbours, but fewer possibilities for solutions. For them, no new social environment offered economic opportunities. While Rankin Inlet and Repulse Bay people were becoming involved in commercial whaling, the southern people continued to respond to the pressures of the physical environment in more familiar ways: hunting caribou and muskox for subsistence and a trading surplus; occasionally relocating temporarily to better game areas; and participating in the Churchill seal and whale hunts.

Caribou and fox distributions continued to be erratic throughout the second half of the century. A dozen "distant" Inuit went to the post in 1859 and 1860, and described caribou in large numbers in the north. At the same time, some Homeguard Inuit reported "no deer to be seen," others could find "no foxes among them ... but deer is plentiful," and still others declared "foxes extremely scarce—Deer only made their appearance a short time ago." Post masters continued to comment on the small number of Homeguard who went to the post and on their pitiful trade, described as "not worth them coming so far with."[36]

Seal, once a staple of the coast communities, were in seriously short supply during the 1860s and so were the sealskin boots the company usually bought in large quantities. In 1862 the Homeguard seal hunters did not find or kill a single animal, and in 1866 seals were so rare all along the coast that the Inuit "are so scarce themselves nowadays for boots that no bribery will scarcely induce them to part with any."[37]

In conditions of scarce game and consistently poor whale hunts, the Homeguard used what power they had as consumers to ask for better prices for their country produce. Post master William Simpson blamed William Ullebuk for creating unrest in the early 1860s by "telling them lies" that caused them to abandon the whale hunt and prevented the Little Chief from coming to the post. "They say it is very hard work killing whales. William Ullebuk I suspect has put that in their heads."[38]

Both Near Homeguard (Knapp's Bay) and Distant Homeguard (Whale Cove) hunters were prepared to take advantage of competition between post and whaler almost from the moment the first whalers appeared. Thirty-five "distant Esquimaux" went to the post in the summer of 1862 with "a good quantity of clothing which they traded from the Americans.... This was given them for assisting them in killing of whales, of course they gave them everything they had in the shape of furs and parchment." Sixty men visited Churchill the following winter and reported that no "Yankies" were wintering over, but the whaleships were back in the summer of 1863 and "none of the distant Esquimaux visited" Churchill. The distant people did not show up again until 1869, when thirty of them made the long trip to Churchill in three American whaleboats with nearly 400 white fox, sixty-four pounds of ivory, fifty-seven muskox skins, and over 500 parchment deerskins. Again they reported "the entire absence of any American whalers in our northern waters."[39] By 1868 the "distant" people visited the trading post only when whaleships were not around to provide employment and trading opportunities.

The numbers of Near Homeguard going to Churchill also continued to drop off. In January 1868, the post master wondered about "the entire desertion from this place of all my Esquimaux during the past year. 18 Esquimaux! were all that visited the post during the twelvemonth just ended."William Ullebuk, somewhat mysteriously, attributed "the desertion of all the hunters ... to bad news brought them by the distant Esquimaux."[40] In 1869 there was more bad news for post master William Simpson. "My Chipewyans told me a long rigmarole story about a Priest and some 'Indian Chief' having been amongst these Homeguards of mine last summer and endeavoring to induce them all to go to Deers Lake [Lac du Brochet]. They don't seem to have succeeded very well in their machinations, as regards my Chipewyans, but managed to induce five of my Inland Esquimaux to go at which I am exceedingly annoyed, evidently from all I hear too, [they] had no wish to go but in the simplicity of their hearts allowed themselves to be enveigled into going and have left their families a drag on the movements of my Chipewyans."[41]

To add to his problems, Simpson foresaw bad times ahead and, on the first day of January 1870, he wrote:"I am greatly afraid my poor Esquimaux will be put to their shifts* this winter, for it seems the deer all left the coast very prematurely last fall, they passed here early in October and instead of their going, as in former years east and south of this, went south a short distance and then made a detour to the westward."[42]

His fears were well founded. The Homeguard Inuit began to arrive in January, and during March people sought refuge and relief at the post almost every day. At the end of the month, "no less than 46 Esquimaux [arrived] all in one band, they gave us no rest night or day." Between January and April 1, eighty-eight men, thirty-four women, and thirty-five children were at the post. The summer seal and whale hunts were poor, the fall fishery was "a mere apology for one," the goose hunt was "the most wretched affair I ever have seen," and deer were "unprecedentedly rare this winter everywhere."[43]

The next year, 1871, was worse. Over thirty men, many with their families, went to the post for the spring seal hunt, and fell victims to diarrhoea and dysentery, which "carried off nearly, if not quite, two thirds of this number of men, besides a great many women, and children." After two months of misery and death, the survivors, including the Little Chief and Wot Wot, the leader of a party from Rankin Inlet, left early in August, using one of the post boats in an attempt to reach their homes before fall. "They were all then, with but two or three uncertains, either dangerously ill or so very reduced and prostrated by illness without proper or sufficient nourishing food either, that really its marvellous how they got off as well as they did."[44]

---

*That is, in nothing but their underwear, because there had not been enough caribou for new winter clothing.

Nothing more was heard of them until August 28, when William Ullebuk arrived. He reported leaving his community north of Whale Cove with eight other men in a kayak brigade. The travellers, except for Ullebuk, lashed their canoes together and set up a sail of parchment deerskin. When a sudden squall hit, they were unable to control the raft and all eight drowned. Ullebuk, paddling alone close to shore, landed his kayak safely and survived.[45]

Continuing south, Ullebuk met the Little Chief, who had left the post three weeks earlier, and "all that was then left of his party … very ill and perfectly helpless, in fact, starving." The Little Chief's wife, oldest son, and brother Tatiak were dead. The others were "all lying there perfectly helpless on the beach, some too ill to do anything, those that were in any way or the least convalescent so weak and exhausted that they could neither hunt or fish nor yet scarcely able to assist the helpless."[46]

Throughout the fall, reports of deaths continued to reach the post. A day or so after leaving the Little Chief, Ullebuk saw Wot Wot and his people "in a dying state."[47] In October, two travellers found Wot Wot's body, "starved to death, died in his very tracks in endeavoring apparently to reach here, the men say he was reduced to a ghastly skeleton, fearfully emaciated. Strange too, he had a fur nearly new, ammunition, firebag, etc, etc, but we fancy he was too weak and reduced by illness to attempt killing anything for himself. His wife must be there or thereabouts somewhere too, of course dead, or he never would have left her."[48]

The last grim news of the year arrived on December 29, and on New Year's Eve, post master Charles Griffin summed up the year in his journal. "All Inland Esquimaux arrived this morning early, no meat, no deer, starving, no ammunition, no nothing…. These fellows report that all our Homeguards are dead but five! out of 30 odd!

"Last day! last entry for 1871! take it all together, one of the most disastrous, unfortunate, miserable years I ever passed in my life—one thing with another, I never experienced its equal."[49]

Griffin also summed up Inuit activity in relation to the trading post in his 1871 New Year's letter. The "Distant Esquimaux" (at Chesterfield Inlet and Roes Welcome) were "entirely alienated" by the American whaleships that supplied all their trading and other needs in their own country. The "middle Esquimaux" (between Rankin and Chesterfield inlets), suffering the aftermath of epidemic disease and high mortality, were uncertain customers with an undependable trade. The Homeguards or "Coast Esquimaux" (between Knapp's Bay and Whale Cove) were "truly the main support" of the post, supplying all the oil and blubber, but "fearfully reduced in numbers now." The Inlanders continued to go to the post in their usual numbers, but they brought and bought little. They traded only parchment deerskins and their purchases did not go beyond ammunition, files, saws, and knives.[50] Once again the names that the traders used to identify various groups had changed, and possibly so had their locations. The Distant Homeguard had become the "middle Esquimaux" and occupied territory somewhat north of their former home. The Near Homeguards or "Coast Esquimaux" were described as living between Knapp's Bay and Whale Cove instead of at Knapp's Bay only.

The new year, 1872, brought very little in the way of an easier life to Churchill's regular clients. To begin with, there was unusually heavy snow, "perfectly startling to behold." Twenty-two Inlanders went to the post "in a miserable plight" with no food and having seen no deer. The traders could not spare food for them, although they gave them "plenty of ammunition."[51]

Only five men, one woman, and one girl made the trip from the coast communities. Two of the men tried to hunt at Seal River, but whale were scarcer than anyone could remember, and the travellers went home empty-handed. Whale were still absent in 1873 and the fall fishery was a failure on account of high water.[52]

In 1874, for the first time in thirty years, no Inlanders went to Churchill.[53] The "long rigmarole story" post master William Simpson had heard in 1869 was true. The missionary priest Alphonse Gasté, spending the summer of 1868 with a band of Churchill Homeguard Chipewyan, had visited a community of Inland Inuit on the Dubawnt River. Through a Chipewyan interpreter, he encouraged them to trade at Reindeer Lake, also known as Deer Lake and Jackfish Lake.[54]

The Hudson's Bay Company station at Reindeer Lake was originally intended "for procuring provisions for District use." It was established in 1858, two years after Roman Catholic missionaries opened a small trading post there. By 1871 the company's meat depot had begun trading furs and, in order to compete with the mission post, offered store goods at lower prices, paid higher tariffs for country products, and gave credit on easier terms than were available at Churchill. The Inuit who accepted Father Gasté's invitation to go to the Brochet post recognized an economic opportunity when they saw one, and began to trade, not at the Catholic trading post but at the company's inland depot, in greater numbers. "Were the Company an opposing force," raged Charles Griffin at Churchill, "they could not more determinedly conspire to ruin the trade here than they have done by the establishment of Deers Lake."[55]

Inuit trading loyalty, however, was not blind; it depended on customer satisfaction of one kind or another. In 1869 "many" Churchill hunters went to Reindeer Lake because "they had no furs by which to pay their debts [at Churchill]." In 1873 twenty-two switched their accounts back to Churchill because they suspected the Deer Lake trading posts of "swindling" them,[56] but the switch was a temporary one. In 1881 nearly one-third of the hunters who had accounts with HBC were trading at the company's inland post,[57] while an unknown number sold their produce to the missionaries.

In 1885 they were still trading at Reindeer Lake, where, they said, they could "get so much more for their furs." Some responded to Churchill post's efforts to offer them a customer-sensitive inventory. A four-sled party took a good hunt of white fox, wolves, wolverines, muskox robes, and deerskin to Churchill in 1886 because they liked Churchill's merchandise better than what was available at Brochet. "If it was not for our larger tin kettles, hand dags, and carrot tobacco* it is a question if they would ever come to Churchill," wrote the post master.[58]

After the severe winter of 1887, when many Inlanders suffered "considerable sickness and a great want of food," they began going to Churchill again in larger numbers. More Inlanders followed after the bad winter of 1889-90 when deer were scarce and both Chipewyan and Inuit were forced to go farther afield in search of food animals and furs.[59]

The resumption of HBC trading voyages along the coast in 1882, in an attempt to reclaim some customers from the whaling fleet traders, gave the coast Inuit an opportunity to take advantage of competing markets. The returns from the Marble Island boat in 1886 were good, in spite of a hard winter and sixteen reported deaths from starvation. Like the more southerly groups, the Marble Islanders explained that customer satisfaction was the reason for their change of heart. They complained that "the Americans used to take their furs and pay them without consulting their requirements."[60]

In addition to a preference for Churchill goods and dissatisfaction with whaler disregard for their autonomy, the Rankin Inlet people found their choice of traders limited after 1886. As whale became increasingly scarce near Marble Island, the fleet moved farther north into Roes Welcome.[61] Local communities had to decide whether to follow the whalers north, go to the post at Churchill, or trade with the Marble Island boat.

---

*A "hand dag" was a short, broad-bladed, double-edged hunting knife. Tobacco for shipping was rolled into a carrot shape; hence "carrot tobacco" or "a tobacco carrot."

The first option cannot have been seriously considered. Roes Welcome communities were already providing adequate country products and labour for the whaling fleet, and straining the resources of the mainland for subsistence. In 1887 some people chose the second possibility and went to the post, partly for trade and partly for the seal hunt. But they made it clear they would no longer use their own kayaks or boats for the journey. If they came to the post at all, they wanted to return north on the Marble Island trading vessel or spend the winter at Churchill. Their preference was for a coastal boat, and their gentle blackmail ensured they got it. The generally profitable nature of the Marble Island boat trade, its popularity with local communities, and alarm at the thought of a hundred or so Inuit spending the winter at the post were all factors in the company's decision to continue to send trading boats north every year. The company also established a number of "pick up places" where the boats stopped regularly to trade for furs,[62] reminiscent of the sloop trade of the previous century.

Throughout the nineteenth century, Inuit took fox pelts to Churchill post in most years, but no Keewatin hunter was deeply involved in the fur trade, as such. The principal country products were venison for trading-post provisions and parchment deerskins for Europe's tanneries. After mid-century, Inuit hunters added a second staple skin to their trade goods: muskox.

The Muskox Trade

The abundance of muskox in the interior was a major attraction for coastal people in the years of growing population and declining caribou and seal. Faced with shortages of their preferred food staples, they increased their use of muskox meat, going farther and farther inland in search of it. They seldom bothered to take the skins to the post, however, because they were heavy, cumbersome to transport over long distances, and had little trading value. In the 1850s the growing demand for muskox robes in Europe prompted the Hudson's Bay Company to request more skins of the huge animals. Within a few years Inuit began to oblige, bringing at least twenty-two in 1862. When the price went up in 1865, they brought more—over fifty in 1866, and nearly 150 in 1869. They also sold muskox skins to the whalers, probably in quantities at least as great as what the company purchased. Over one-third of the skins taken to Churchill in 1869 came from Marble Islanders who would have traded with the whalers, had any showed up.[63]

The increase in muskox skins being traded does not indicate an increase in the total number of muskox kills, nor does it mean that animals were being killed solely for their skins. Muskox were already a staple food of the southern Keewatin coast people in 1821, according to Augustine's testimony, and they continued to be hunted as food when caribou were in short supply. In 1885–86, a community of about a hundred people from near Rankin Inlet spent the winter inland, hunting muskox, "deterred through fear of starvation" from coming to the coast.[64] The presence of traders and whalers willing to buy muskox skins allowed Inuit to turn the formerly useless by-products of the subsistence hunt into trade goods in much the same way they turned unused subsistence stores into trading surpluses.

When caribou were available, few muskox skins were taken for trade. In 1862, for instance, hunters brought 2800 parchment deerskins, over 5400 pounds of venison, 1765 prime fox pelts, and twenty-two robes; in 1863, they brought more than 3000 parchment deerskins, 6400 pounds of venison, 3500 fox furs, and only two muskox skins.[65]

Unlike the southern Keewatin peoples, Aivilingmiut living at or near whaling stations and beaching sites were seldom hard-pressed for basic food supplies. They became specialists in the muskox hunt because there was a reliable market for both meat and robes in the American whaling fleet. As the demand for whale products declined in the 1870s, demand for muskox robes continued to rise, and whaling firms, facing reduced profits from whale products, began to develop a trade in muskox skins. The Roes Welcome Aivilingmiut, the people most closely allied with the whalers, became the primary procurers. Their commercial hunters ceased to hunt seal and walrus in the deep winter and spring months, and became muskox hunters instead. By the beginning of the 1890s, they were hunting muskox from December to May, whale from May to September, and caribou from September to December. With the decline of both caribou and whale after 1900, they spent even more time inland, hunting muskox, sometimes from December right through to the autumn. From a beginning of four animals taken in the years 1860 to 1862, the number of robes bought by whalers reached at least 150 every year between 1899 and 1912.[66]

Change in Communities and Inter-Community Relations

Throughout the nineteenth century, all west-coast Inuit south of Lyon Inlet responded to population increases and the constraints of the physical environment by changing locations, principal food resources, and seasonal activities. Their communities were in a state of continuous flux. Early in the century, the Churchill traders had perceived all the communities south of Rankin Inlet as a single social entity, which they called "Augustine's people." All others they referred to as "Distant Esquimaux." By 1860 they recognized that Augustine's people had become three more or less discrete societies occupying different territories. The "Near Homeguards" occupied the coast between Whale Cove and Eskimo Point-Knapp's Bay (Arviat). The "Middle Esquimaux" or "Distant Homeguard" lived around Rankin Inlet, probably as far south as Whale Cove, and possibly some distance north of Rankin as well. Augustine and the Ullebuk family were mentioned most often in connection with them. The third group, the "Inlanders," expanded out of Augustine's people as their population grew. Over the course of two generations they became year-round residents of the upper Kazan River area, distinct from the parent community.

The Churchill traders, with their long experience of aboriginal peoples, recognized Keewatin residential groups as fluid and voluntary communities associated with particular locations and subsistence activities. Other nineteenth- and twentieth-century European observers were more inflexible thinkers, and made attempts to fit Inuit societies into categories based on European concepts of nation, state, ethnicity, and territorial allegiance, which did not reflect Inuit reality. Franz Boas classified what he called the "tribes" of southeastern Baffin Island after a year of observation in 1882-83, and in succeeding years he arranged the peoples of west Hudson Bay and Boothia Peninsula into categories based on his reading of Heinrich Klutschak's and John Ross's memoirs, and on information from the whaling captain, George Comer. The members of the Fifth Thule Expedition of 1921-24 conceived of all Keewatin Inuit south of Repulse Bay as a single "tribe," to which they gave the name "Caribou Eskimo," and constructed a neat taxonomy of "bands" within it. They applied the model retroactively to Keewatin Inuit of earlier periods.

Scholars ever since have used the Boas and Fifth Thule classifications, artificial, oversimplified, and sometimes just plain inaccurate as they are, because they provide a concept and a vocabulary that allows for generalization. The conceptual framework is tempting and sometimes useful because it facilitates discussion about social and historical processes, but it does not reveal how Inuit thought about their societies or their identity. What needs to be stressed is that Inuit who were assigned to particular categories, say Ahiarmiut, did not always consider themselves to be irrevocably Ahiarmiut; nor did they inevitably and necessarily behave the way Ahiarmiut in general have been described as behaving.

The Fifth Thule taxonomy identified five bands in the so-called Caribou Eskimo group. The Distant Esquimaux of the Hudson's Bay Company journals were called Kinepetu by the whalers, a mistaken and meaningless identification. Their own designation for themselves, identified by the Fifth Thule Expedition, was Qairnirmiut, People of the Rocks. The communities around Rankin Inlet and probably as far south as Whale Cove, known to the Hudson's Bay Company as the Distant Homeguard, were identified by the Fifth Thule as Hauniqtormiut, People of the Place of Bones. Because of an s/h consonant shift in some dialects, they also appear in the literature as Sauniqtormiut. Between Whale Cove and Eskimo Point were the Near Homeguards, known to Fifth Thule observers as Padlirmiut, People of the Willow Thicket.

The assignment of the name Padlirmiut is problematic. In 1922 Kaj Birket-Smith and Knud Rasmussen of the Fifth Thule Expedition agreed that the Near Homeguard were self-identified as Padlirmiut (Willow People), but they recognized two subgroups among them, one with an inland orientation and the other more focussed on the coast and marine activities. Rasmussen, a lifelong speaker of Greenlandic Inuktitut, suggested that the self-designation of the coast dwellers, whose principal village was at Eskimo Point, was actually Paatlirmiut, similar in sound to Padlirmiut (at least to non-Inuit ears), but derived from a root word meaning "river mouth." Rasmussen's position has received support from recent linguistic studies by Thomas C. Correll, which suggest that Paatlirmiut, People of the River Mouth, is a more likely designation for both coast and inland groups. On the other hand, oral testimony gathered by R.G. Williamson (also a fluent Inuktitut-speaker) in the 1960s and 1970s favours Birket-Smith's conclusion that the Padlirmiut, People of the Willow, was the name used by the people themselves, and suggests that a small community at the river mouth called themselves Avviamiut.[67]

The third group recognized by the Churchill traders before 1860 was the Inlanders living along the upper Kazan River. They were later identified as the Ahiarmiut (or Asiarmiut, depending on the speaker's dialect), People from Out of the Way.

Two other groups are known to have emerged towards the end of the nineteenth century. The Harvaqtormiut (or Savaqtormiut), People of the Rapids, occupied the lower Kazan River just south of Baker Lake by 1890.[68] They probably represented an expansion of the Qairnirmiut, whom they closely resembled. By 1915, the Tassiujormiut, People of the Place Like a Lake, had winter residences inland on the shores of Kaminak Lake just west of Whale Cove and spent their summers hunting seal on the coast around Dawson Inlet.[69]

Throughout the nineteenth century, Inuit responded to changes in social environments, such as the presence of whalers, relocation, and expansion and emergence of communities, and to the increase in their own numbers by adjusting their trading and social relations. In the period before commercial whaling, Chesterfield Inlet had been the site of a market at which European goods were passed by Churchill's Homeguard to the southern Iglulingmiut (later Aivilingmiut) in exchange for walrus hides and sinew.[70] The Homeguard also moved goods to Akilineq at the western end of Beverly Lake, where they met with people from Chantrey Inlet and the arctic coast.[71]

Knapp's Bay people were middlemen between the Churchill post and groups farther to the north since at least the beginning of the nineteenth century. According to Augustine, by 1815 Homeguard middleman activities were important enough in their economies that they "prevented" more distant people from trading directly at Churchill. The means of prevention were not made clear in post master Adam Snodie's report of his conversations with Augustine, but he was certain that profit was its motive. John Rae's experiences of 1846-47 and 1852 to 1854 made him equally certain of both the prevention and the profit, although, like Snodie, he did not record details. He noted only that the people within "350 English miles" of Churchill preferred "to barter all their own half-worn weapons, tools, cooking utensils [to more northern and western groups] … at a much higher price than would be paid for new articles at the trading post, and thus secure a double profit."[72]

After 1862, Aivilingmiut and Qairnirmiut had direct access to European goods from the whalers and were no longer interested in the trade of second-hand articles from the south. They were also ideally placed to act as middlemen between the whaling fleet and the communities of Melville Peninsula, Pelly Bay, Great Fish River, and the Keewatin interior. Wage labour and provisioning enabled them to amass surpluses of the European goods most desired by other groups, and whaling captains and firms were willing to buy the furs and muskox robes that made up the bulk of the resources offered by more distant bands.

The Churchill Homeguards found themselves shut out of the trade.[73] Not only did they lose the profits of their brokering activities, they no longer had access to walrus hides and bearded sealskins in sufficient quantities to meet their own footwear needs. By the 1890s the only trade taking place between groups north and south of Chesterfield Inlet was the transfer of furs at Baker Lake from the Keewatin Inlanders to Aivilik middlemen, and that trade was organized and supervised by Captain George Comer.[74]

The Homeguards also lost what little trade they had with Ahiarmiut, who had begun to meet with Qairnirmiut and Aivilingmiut middlemen at Akilineq and Baker Lake by the 1890s. Families in a dozen small camps along the Dubawnt River in 1893 owned tin kettles, old guns, and clothing of European manufacture, acquired at Akilineq from coast people who traded with the HBC at Fort Churchill and with whalers at Marble Island and Roes Welcome.[75]

Aivilingmiut and Qairnirmiut trading activity was in itself an encouragement to greater mobility and inter-band contact among more distant people, who were unwilling to pay inflated prices to middlemen. The people of Great Fish River occasionally bypassed the intermediaries; instead of meeting them at Akilineq as they had done before 1870, they followed the Quoich River to Chesterfield Inlet and dealt with the whalers directly. Copper Inuit from as far away as Bathurst Inlet were part of the summer community at Rankin Inlet in various years during the 1890s, along with visitors from Repulse Bay, Cape Fullerton, and Baker Lake. The Ahiarmiut also undertook to buy goods at the source at times, bypassing Aivilingmiut and Qairnirmiut at Akilineq and Baker Lake. Inspector E.A. Pelletier of the 1908 Royal Northwest Mounted Police Thelon River Patrol reported communities occupied solely by women and children, in the absence of the men, who had gone to Cape Fullerton to trade directly with the whalers.[76]

Because of their location, the Keewatin Inlanders had frequent contact with Chipewyan. A meeting between Chipewyan and Inland Inuit near Dubawnt Lake in 1868, described by Father Gasté, was apparently a regular occurrence. The Chipewyan knew enough of the language of their northern neighbours to exchange news, transact business, interpret Gasté's sermons, and convince the Inuit to trade at Lac du Brochet instead of at Churchill.[77] The Inlanders' decision to trade at Reindeer Lake after 1868 led to even closer association with Chipewyan and a slow expansion southwards into the forest fringe.

Farther north, Aivilingmiut and Qairnirmiut were also dealing with the problems of boundaries. Communities that in earlier times had been geographically separated by unoccupied land found themselves in a tense situation in 1879. Two visiting Qairnirmiut took part in a target-shooting contest in an Aivilingmiut village, during which one of the host community accidentally wounded one of the guests. The Qairnirmiut demanded compensation and were refused. The two groups then each selected three men and charged them with continuing the vendetta, while the remaining members of each group maintained their usual peaceful, if somewhat wary, relations. As the observer who reported the incident noted, neighbouring communities had to identify new borders between their altered territories and work out ways of crossing boundaries "with the approval of their neighbours."[78]

Relations between some communities remained unchanged. The fear and suspicion with which the Aivilik people had regarded Netsilingmiut in the 1840s were still there a generation later. During the 1870s members of an Aivilingmiut family did not hesitate to undertake a journey of 650 kilometres to Boothia Peninsula to take revenge on their Netsilingmiut opposite numbers in a blood feud.[79]

Although responses of Inuit communities to the long-term presence of Europeans and Americans in Hudson Bay had resulted in permanent changes in social and economic organization by 1900, the short-term incursions of non-Inuit into Boothia and King William Island had few lasting effects. By the beginning of the twentieth century, the peoples of King William Island, Adelaide Peninsula, and Boothia Peninsula had reverted, to a large extent, to the territorial distribution that had prevailed prior to the abandonments of *Victory* in 1832, and *Erebus* and *Terror* in 1848. The Netsilingmiut had withdrawn from Adelaide Peninsula and the south coast of King William Island. Ugjulingmiut, descendants of people who had fled to the Great Fish River during the famines and Netsilingmiut invasion of the 1850s, were again living in their former territories. The east coast of King William Island was shared territory, Netsilingmiut and Ugjulingmiut villages being interspersed. In a few settlements, people from both groups lived together. There were other signs that the enmities that had sprung up in the 1840s and 1850s had become less important. The Netsilingmiut of Boothia Isthmus, the Utkusiksalingmiut of Great Fish River, the people of Lord Mayor's Bay on the east coast of Boothia Peninsula, and the Ugjulingmiut, while maintaining their separate communities, regarded themselves as a single social unit, in which they included the Kidlinirmiut of the lower Coppermine River. Their dress, customs, and habits were similar, and they routinely intermarried and exchanged children.[80]

Unlike the Hudson Bay whaling communities, which were created to facilitate occupational activity, Netsilik villages were based on kinship. In the summer and fall of 1904, fifteen families related by blood, marriage, or spouse exchange, and two families of temporary residents were living at the principal Netsilingmiut village. One of the visiting families was from Ugjulik. The other family was from Ittuaqturvik. The place name Ittuaqturvik, at Lord Mayor's Bay where John Ross spent the years from 1829 to 1833, and the band designation Ittuaqturvingmiut appeared for the first time in the expedition memoirs of Roald Amundsen in 1908.[81]

Contacts between Netsilik and Hudson Bay were greatly reduced, although three or four men occasionally went to Aivilik to trade. In the first decade of the twentieth century, only three of the women whom Roald Amundsen interviewed had ever seen white men or had been outside their own territory. They were all elderly individuals whose only trip east had been to Aivilik with their husbands in their youth.[82]

In the 1920s Pelly Bay people were living much as they had a century earlier. They continued to spend the winters in villages on the sea ice, occupied in breathing-hole sealing. They had two villages, each with a population of about 100 people. In 1938-39, the same number of people were distributed among five winter villages.[83]

As commercial whaling declined around the turn of the century, Aivilingmiut and eastern Netsilingmiut, who made up the bulk of the whaling fleet homeguard, were increasingly faced with economic uncertainty. In 1897, when Captain George Comer built a whaling station on Southampton Island, 125 Aivilingmiut agreed to live there and operate the station. Although his accounts are vague on the exact dates of occupation, the station does not seem to have operated continuously. In 1899 a second attempt at settlement was made, with 100 Inuit from the mainland coast of Roes Welcome. Again in 1903 Comer took "the greater number of my natives (Eskimos from Repulse Bay)" to the island, "hoping that they might procure a quantity of fox-skins." In 1908 he left about seventy Aivilingmiut on Southampton.[84] Recognizing that commercial whaling was coming to an end, and faced with inadequate supplies of walrus, whale, and caribou around Repulse Bay, between fifteen and twenty families chose to remain there more or less permanently.

The end of commercial whaling in Hudson Bay in 1915 coincided with the onset of highly variable climatic conditions. The receding ice pack introduced more moisture into the atmosphere, resulting in heavier winter snowfalls and wetter summers. The period from 1910 to 1920 was characterized by rapidly alternating, short periods of cooling and warming every year.[85] Increased precipitation and fluctuating temperatures created conditions particularly inhospitable to caribou. The herds disappeared in search of a more congenial climate, and it was a decade before they began to reappear.

The Iglulingmiut were able to compensate for climatic conditions more effectively than were their southern countrymen. Their strategies included separation into smaller communities and relocation of about a quarter of the population to Steensby Inlet on the northwest coast of Baffin Island. As caribou resources declined, they became more dependent on sea mammals for subsistence. The potentially serious consequences of lost caribou resources were avoided, primarily because walrus and seal numbers remained adequate for the population. A second important factor in their success was possession of whaleboats. More efficient transportation technology allowed them to harvest larger territories, hunt more safely, and transport greater quantities of marine mammal resources over greater distances.

Iglulingmiut continued to occupy more or less permanent coast villages close to their cached food supplies. In 1922 there were three principal settlements: Igloolik with a population of seventy-three; Steensby Inlet with thirty-five souls; and a village at the northern end of Roes Welcome, occupied by twenty-eight people. Most Igloolik families owned five or six sled dogs and most hunters were able to put together teams of ten or more animals.[86] The relatively large number of dogs they were able to support attests to their success at compensating for loss of caribou through more efficient sea-mammal harvesting and dispersion of population.

After 1915, when the last whaleship left Hudson Bay, coastal communities turned to more intensive sea-mammal hunting. Extension of hunting territory, storage, increased seasonal mobility, and dispersion into smaller, separated villages were their major survival strategies. Hunters searched for food resources over larger areas, remaining near their cached food supplies only when few game animals were available.[87] They abandoned the large settlements at flensing and beaching stations, and created more dispersed, smaller villages of between fifteen and twenty-five souls.[88]

The establishment of trading posts at Chesterfield Inlet and along Roes Welcome between 1911 and 1925[89] made trapping a viable option for Qairnirmiut and Aivilingmiut after 1915, when opportunities offered by commercial whaling were gone and caribou was no longer an adequate food source. They turned increasingly to fox trapping, and some found employment with the trading posts, missions, and RCMP detachments, although in fewer numbers than had worked for the whalers. The high price of fox throughout most of the 1920s and 1930s assured them of economic security and even a degree of prosperity.

Like the Melville Peninsula communities, Inuit of the southern Keewatin had always put a higher priority on hunting for subsistence than on trapping animals for resale or working for external agencies. They had also always understood that subsistence hunting required their presence in their own territories, and was incompatible with long journeys to trading posts and trapping areas. The failure of the fur trade companies to establish posts near their hunting territories effectively prevented Inuit from taking the fur trade seriously as a full-time occupation. Trapping was incidental to hunting for subsistence.

As James VanStone pointed out in connection with the Snowdrift Chipewyan, trappers have two options: to stay on the trapline for weeks at a time, depending on chance-met game for subsistence; or, to go to the trading post frequently to drop off furs and pick up supplies.[90] The first plan requires fairly abundant game, accessible almost everywhere in the trapping area, a rare situation on the barren grounds and one which certainly was not the case for Keewatin communities after 1900. The second strategy can only be used if the post is within easy reach of the trapping territory, which again was not so for any Keewatin community before 1911, or for the Ahiarmiut and Paatlirmiut, or Padlirmiut, before the mid-1920s. Both arrangements, of course, have another serious drawback. During the absence of hunters on the trapline or en route to the post, families are left without support for long periods of time.

Southern Keewatin communities responded to the disappearance of food resources with the old and usually reliable storage strategy. It was not enough. The disappearance of game too often resulted in half-empty caches. According to oral sources, they tried, sometimes running traplines of a hundred miles or more radiating out from the cache site,[91] but with limited success.

The final disappearance of the caribou herds after 1915 pushed the two southern Keewatin bands into a decade of catastrophic famine. There was no rhetoric, exaggeration, or misunderstanding about this famine; starvation was real and mortality was high. From a probable total of around 1200 people on the coast south of Chesterfield Inlet and inland on the upper Kazan River at the turn of the century, the population had fallen to about 500 in 1922.

After 1920 the only means of survival left was trapping and the only certainty was the Hudson's Bay Company post. Survival was, however, relatively certain only when trading posts were within reasonable distance of trapping areas. The establishment of trading posts at Eskimo Point (formerly Knapp's Bay and now Arviat) in 1921, Maguse Lake in 1925, Padlei in 1926, Tavani in 1928, and Nunalla in 1929 gave a degree of economic certainty. People survived, continued to occupy their accustomed territories, and, until the massive government interventions after the Second World War, maintained their collective autonomy.

For the inland communities, even the presence of trading posts nearer to their country did not ease uncertainty. In the 1920s and 1930s, at least a dozen small posts were operated for periods of one to five years in

Chipewyan territory around Ennadai and Nueltin lakes. Some belonged to the well-established fur trade companies, such as the Hudson's Bay Company, Lamson and Hubbard, and Revillon Frères; others were operated by independent trapper-traders.[92]

Although the small posts often proved to be a lifeline for hard-pressed, isolated Kazan River communities, they could not be counted on. Most were manned by one person and were operated by independents without sufficient capital to buy or transport a large, or even sufficient, inventory. Inuit got information about opening and closing of posts only when they deliberately sought out one of the traders. When Inuit had not been to a post for a while, a trapper-trader might move his post, hoping to be closer to his customers, but because communication was almost impossible, the result on several occasions was that Inuit could not find a trader when they needed one. The problems of the one-man post were not limited to independents. In 1926 between fifteen and twenty Inuit died of starvation at the HBC's one-man outpost at Poor Fish Lake during the absence of the operator, who had gone to Brochet to pick up supplies.[93] The tragedy was not a rare event.

None of the few options available was adequate to answer the needs of the Inlanders. They could not survive as subsistence hunters because of game shortages and the impossibility of laying up stores sufficient for a season's needs. They could not enter fully into the fur trade because the trading posts were too far from their caches and traplines, and were all too often temporary and unpredictable. The same factors of distance and unpredictability made the few missions and police detachments unviable as sources of relief. By the end of the 1930s, the Ahiarmiut and inland Padlirmiut were on the edge of extinction.

8.

The Experience of Dead Generations: Social Organization, Worldview, and Survival

Anyone who keeps his eyes and ears open and remembers what the old people relate, has a certain knowledge that can fill the emptiness of our thoughts. Therefore we are always ready to listen to those who get their knowledge from the experience of dead generations. And all the old myths we got from our forefathers are dead men's talk. In these speak those who long ago were wise. We, who think we know so little ourselves, listen eagerly to them.

– Apakak, in Alaska[1]

Eskimo and Inuit activities over several thousand years were closely linked to physical environments. Archaeological investigation has shown a direct and powerful relationship between climatic change and the emergence and disappearance of paleo- and neo-Eskimo communities throughout the North American arctic from about 2000 BCE to 1700 CE. Linguistic, archaeological, and documentary evidence supports the conclusion that human activities in the arctic during the following centuries, from about 1700 CE to 1940, were also often responses to alterations in climatic regimes and the resulting disappearance or relocation of food and other necessary resources. The fundamental problem of Eskimo and Inuit life has always been how to ensure access to necessary resources. Sub-disciplines in eco-archaeology and ecological anthropology have developed to examine human responses to resource shortages and scarcity resulting from events in the physical environment.

Other explanations of sociocultural change have been used less frequently in arctic historiography, largely because of the nature of the available evidence, but factors other than the physical environment have always played a part in social change. Individual choices are known to have been catalysts for cultural and demographic change, and have been based on such things as food preference, involvement in blood feuds, curiosity about distant places, and desire for adventure. Threats to resources are also present in social environments, as different social units compete for resources or seek ways to share them. Contact with outsiders sometimes introduced new technology and ideas, necessitated new kinds of social organization, or led to conflict. Thule adoption of Dorset techniques and technology in the decades following the Thule expansion into the central arctic is an obvious example. The hostile relations and more frequent violence of communities in the Boothia and King William Island regions, which followed the sudden and unexpected acquisition of additional resources by the Netsilik people after the abandonment of *Victory* in 1832, is another. Open hostilities erupted again in the 1850s when the Boothia people attempted to claim the larger share of the resources left by the Franklin expedition. The clash had major consequences for the social organization of the Utkusiksalingmiut of Great Fish River and the Ugjulingmiut of Adelaide Peninsula, and gave the Netsilingmiut a reputation for violence and evil intent, which still clung to them more than a hundred years later. Opportunities offered by the presence of commercial whalers and trading posts also acted as catalysts for changes in subsistence systems, location, and both material and intellectual culture.

Yet another explanation for sociocultural change is the "idealist paradigm (i.e., that human behavior is a function of ideas, values, beliefs, wills, etc.)."[2] For arctic peoples, physical effort was one of life's givens, without which survival was impossible. But mental strategies were as important to achieving the goal of an ordered and orderly society. Social units, from the microsociety of a nuclear family to the macrosociety of a world community, create systems to understand and organize their physical and social environments, means to predict their events, and strategies to control their impacts. In the harsh physical environments of the arctic, explanation, anticipation, and stratagem operated as mutually supportive systems to reduce uncertainty, which is the ultimate threat to survival, however defined. Worldview, social organization, and value system prescribed and explained the behaviours best calculated to reduce subsistence uncertainties and to enhance survival by creating an orderly society.

Human activity is, at the most fundamental level, designed to reduce uncertainty about survival and to ensure access to adequate resources for both individuals and communities. The first step in reducing uncertainty is to recognize threats to essential resources. Hunting-gathering societies, which are typically subject to both short- and long-term economic uncertainty, predict periods of scarcity through close familiarity with their physical environments. On the basis of detailed information about the environment, arctic hunting societies developed a variety of responses (identified in the vocabulary of social theory as "buffering" or "coping mechanisms" or "risk-reducing strategies") that alleviate or guard against shortages. Mobility, diversification, storage, exchange, technical innovation,[3] and attempts to alter or modify the environment itself are basic responses to the problems of scarce or inaccessible resources.[4]

Each of the broad categories of possible strategies covers a wide range of activities. They are, for the most part, complementary. Mobility strategies among arctic hunting-gathering societies, for example, have included routine seasonal movements between resource sites, long-distance harvesting, trading journeys, timely visits to relatively affluent kin and allies to seek relief or to reinforce ties against the day when relief should be needed, and temporary relocation during short-term scarcity. Mobility has also enabled territorial expansion and, in extreme cases, permanent abandonment of territory and relocation elsewhere. Diversification, maximization, and optimization strategies have ranged from the habitual use of different resources in season, to temporary or permanent substitution of one food staple for a former one, and, if necessary, change of occupation. In arctic societies, storage has involved the caching of food supplies, the creation of techniques for preserving harvested food, taboos against killing certain animals in some seasons, the reuse and recycling of scarce building materials, and overeating in times of abundance as a hedge against impending hunger. Storage has also been an encouragement to trade when surpluses amassed for the worst case prove to be unnecessary. Exchange strategies have included sharing and trade, among many others. Some theorists have identified as "exchange" the unilateral and unequal changes of ownership that accompany war and theft: "Interactions that are characterised by 'negative reciprocity', such as raiding, theft and appropriation, can also be placed under the broad heading of exchange."[5] Technical innovation among hunting-gathering peoples has been a frequent accompaniment to relocation into regions where the harvesting of different resources requires new tools, or where some necessities must be fashioned from unfamiliar materials. Some strategies could not be invoked simultaneously: the fundamental and ultimately insoluble problem faced by Keewatin Inlanders after 1915 was the incompatibility of storage-dependence with the mobility requirements of trapping, long-distance harvesting, and trade.

The first five of the six strategies for reducing uncertainty—mobility, storage, diversification, exchange, and technological innovation—imply human adaptation to the environment. Individuals and societies learn the rules of the natural world and live within them. A precondition of successful use of any one of the strategies is, then, an investment of intellectual effort in order to understand natural law, and to shape social and technological behaviour so that human beings might take the resources necessary for survival without disturbing the rights of non-human persons who share the land, and without endangering their own collective survival by depleting limited resources.

The sixth named strategy involves adapting the physical environment to suit human needs. Among indigenous arctic societies, alterations to the physical world have included the temporary damming of rivers and construction of fish weirs, but these activities have tended to result in insignificant modifications of the physical environment. Instead of changing the physical world, Inuit of the central arctic prior to the mid-twentieth century concentrated on changing the metaphysical world to meet their needs. Their worldview identified animals as the ultimate source of human subsistence, and characterized them as other-than-human persons with immortal souls, self-consciousness, omniscience, the ability to reincarnate, and a charitable imperative powerful enough to require self-sacrifice. For Inuit, land and animals in their physical and spiritual manifestations were central to human survival. As late as the 1960s, most Inuit, no matter what their occupations, continued to believe that "survival of the whole society depended upon intense and unceasing concentration on [hunting]."[6] Their belief system also acknowledged the influence of the spirits that animate weather and land. Inuit societies, therefore, have made huge investments of psychic capital to understand the natural order of things and to learn how to manipulate the metaphysical world, as well as to bring themselves into harmony with it. Because of their "severe and demanding" physical environment, Keewatin people in particular recognized that "simple physical exertion for the sake of survival would be insufficient," and turned to "the primacy of thought" as a means of manipulating the environment, "something which requires considerable intellect and spiritual strength."[7]

Knowledge of the environment and information about current conditions were as important to choosing appropriate strategies as they were to identifying threats to survival. Seasonally recurring, short-term, predictable shortages of some resources were always assumed and planned for by arctic peoples. Decisions about storage and diversification in these times of seasonal scarcity depended on current information, such as precisely where caribou were at the moment.

Knowledge of similar situations in the past was critical to predicting the consequences of particular choices, and knowledgeable individuals with relevant information were highly valued in Inuit communities. People who spoke other dialects or languages, for instance, and could collect information from and about neighbouring communities, were assets to the group. Often they attained "positions of power" because of their usefulness to the group and because they controlled the spread of information.[8] Well-travelled women and men were esteemed for their contributions to geographical knowledge, mapping skills, and information about other societies. As George Lyon noted, "The importance assumed by a great Eskimaux traveller is fully equal to that displayed by Europeans who have seen the world."[9]

Shamans often achieved status and power, and, except in rare cases, were highly valued by their communities because of the special knowledge that enabled them to predict environmental conditions and to manipulate the metaphysical world. Given the Inuit belief that human success and survival depended on human beings occupying their proper places in an orderly universe, shamanistic ability to identify sources of disharmony with the spirit world and to restore the balance was essential to effective subsistence activities. Although shamans dealt with social conflict and physical and spiritual healing, most shamanistic work focussed on "the basic function of the Eskimo society, that upon which their whole survival depended—hunting."[10]

As was the case with linguists, travellers, navigators, and shamans, elderly "uncertainty specialists" were appreciated as repositories of knowledge that contributed to the security and survival of the community. Contrary to the widespread and inaccurate notion that Inuit societies routinely practised gerontocide, mature and elderly individuals in many Inuit communities had "important roles as educators, experienced persons, and decision makers when [the community was] faced with uncertainty."[11]

In the course of growing up, every Inuit lived through a dozen or more periods of short-term scarcity, and even as a child would have been able to predict recurring seasonal shortages and choose the correct course of moving from fish camp to caribou crossing, or from winter sealing village to spring bird-nesting site. Environmental fluctuations, such as the once-in-five-years average failure rate of the whale hunt and the fifteen-to-twenty-year distribution cycle of caribou, also occurred frequently enough that most members of a community would have been able to predict the consequences in terms of food availability and accessibility, and decide on appropriate action. Other periods of scarcity were less frequent, sometimes occurring only once or twice in a single lifetime.[12]

Whether the cycle of recurrence was as short as a season or as long as a generation, most communities had someone who remembered similar events. As repositories of essential information, who knew from experience how to recognize threatening situations, how to predict their consequences, and how to choose suitable responses, they were life-saving assets in communities faced with a threat to resources. Information within living memory could be transmitted verbally throughout the community, and appropriate decisions made with a fair degree of certainty that the chosen strategies would work. Recognizing a developing problem, and knowing the options in cases of sudden catastrophic shortage or when a situation was so rare that it occurred only once in every three or more generations, was another matter.

The ability to store and transmit information about potentially dangerous situations is critical to long-term survival. Societies that do not save information in written records must develop means by which infrequently needed but essential information can be stored and retrieved by future generations when required. Transmitting knowledge through several generations is more problematic than the face-to-face transfer of data from experienced teacher to inexperienced learner, not least because intervening generations do not always recognize the importance of passing on information they may not have any use for in their own lives. A method used by Historic Inuit, and probably by their cultural ancestors as well, was the elegant one of encoding information in stories.

Oral tradition differs from ordinary verbal transfer of information in that it is institutionalized. In Historic Inuit societies, the rules required that narrators meet three conditions when relating stories. First, narrators were expected to tell more than one story at a session, thus increasing the number of tales in circulation and providing multiple opportunities for them to be heard. Second, they were expected, at least in theory, to tell the stories exactly as they had heard them, thus reducing the chances of error. And, third, they were required to preface each story by a statement of its degree of factuality. Among Yup'ik, Inupiat, and Greenlanders, the third requirement was considered to be especially important.[13]

Although the Fifth Thule Expedition collected oral traditions and histories from most central arctic communities, as well as from Greenland and Alaska, and published them in both Inuktitut and English, no analysis of the literature as a whole has been done and, to date, no studies have been published on the encoded prescriptive meanings of the oral literatures of Canadian Inuit. The ancient stories of the central arctic peoples, however, parallel stories known to Yup'ik, Inupiat, and Greenlanders, and follow the same storytelling rules. It is useful to make some comparison as a means of understanding Inuit oral literatures.

The degree of factuality in Yup'ik, Inupiat, Inuit, and Greenlandic stories is directly related to the age of the story and to its prescriptive character. The oldest stories were not intended, or relied on, as historical fact; their purpose was to convey truths about the nature of the universe and the relations of living things to one another, and to prescribe rules for proper living, which, in turn, would ensure survival. Stories of more recent times were more likely to be based on the actual experiences of their narrators, or to have been told to the narrators by participants in the action.

The oldest Yup'ik stories, the *qulirat*, were expected to contain "part of the experience of ancient ancestors and never involve particular individuals definitely believed to have existed."Yup'ik true stories, *qanemcit*, on the other hand, are historical narratives "grounded in the experience of a particular person, whether that person is living or dead." They are "based on the narrator's personal knowledge, either direct or transmitted by persons to whom living men and women can trace a relationship." In Inupiat stories, as in Yup'ik ones, time depth is the indicator of sacred or secular truth. The most ancient stories, the *unipqaq*, tell about the earliest days of creation, and are clearly not intended to convey accurate information about the past. Instead, they embody metaphysical explanations of the past and contain divinely sanctioned imperatives about proper living. Inupiat true stories, *oqaluktoq*, are placed in historical time as "very early days," "early days," or "personal memory" of the narrator. Greenlandic stories are more likely to contain mixtures of fact and fiction than Yup'ik and Inupiat stories, but are nevertheless understood to be grounded in historical fact. The most ancient tales, the *okalugtuat*, like the Yup'ik *qulirat* and the Inupiat *unipqaq*, have no time reference, and are estimated to be anywhere from 200 to 1000 years old. Like the ancient tales of other Eskimoan peoples, they embody broad truths about broad topics, even if the details are fictional, partly fictional, or a combination of elements from different factual histories. The *okalualarut* are stories whose origins can be traced to actual historical events within six generations, and fall into the same category as Yup'ik *qanemcit* and Inupiat *oqaluktoq*.[14]

What to do in times of food shortage is a constantly recurring theme in Eskimo and Inuit stories from Greenland, the Canadian central arctic, and Alaska.[15] The suggested responses depend on whether the shortage is seasonal, inter-annual, or long term. "Seasonal" refers to the predictable and regularly recurring short periods every year when a particular resource was scarce; for instance, the period of two months or so in early winter after the caribou had gone but before sealing could begin. "Inter-annual" refers to the more serious scarcity of an expected resource that was inadequate for the community's needs, was inaccessible in a particular year, or did not appear at all. The complete failure of the seal hunts along the southern Keewatin coast in 1860 and 1862 are examples. "Long-term crisis" refers to periods of longer than a year in which the total of all available resources was insufficient, such as deprivation on the scale that prompted the migration of Coronation Gulf people to west Hudson Bay at the end of the seventeenth century, and the near-fatal scarcity experienced by their descendants in the Keewatin interior after 1915.

An analysis by Leah Minc of fifty-four Inupiat stories identified three, constantly recurring themes, which reflected "strategies and social mechanisms for coping with environmental stress."[16] Seasonal shortage was the most frequent experience for arctic peoples, and the fifty-four stories contain more than 450 references to ways of dealing with it. The suggested solutions were storage, pooling of resources, and sharing within the community. Inter-annual shortages—failures of a primary food source during an entire year—happened less often than seasonal shortages, but were still frequent enough that the stories contained seventy-eight references to the problem. The prescribed behaviours for these emergencies were expansion of hunting range, temporary relocation to nearby territory, increased use of alternative resources, and application for relief from kinsmen in other communities. Shortages expected to last more than a few years were even more infrequent, but potentially more serious. Fifty-nine references to long-term crises were contained in the stories, and suggested a single solution to the problem: migration and permanent relocation to new territory. These stories contained warnings about the possible dangers of relocating to territory already occupied or used by other communities, and made it clear that even temporary use of the resources of unrelated communities depended on pre-existing diplomatic, trade, and feasting relationships.

One creation story, found in different versions in several communities, encoded specific environmental information as well as solutions to the problem. It identified a slowing down of the growth rate of spruce trees as a reliable indicator of deteriorating climate, linked declining numbers of inland animals to increasing cold, pointed out that under these conditions caribou herds were likely to disappear from a large area for a long time, and recommended relocation to the coast and reliance on marine mammals as appropriate action.[17]

To ensure that the economic options and the rules for proper living prescribed by the stories would be heard and heeded, Eskimo and Inuit societies embedded imperatives in their belief systems. The need to store supplies in quantities large enough to carry a community through a period of scarcity was reinforced by a worldview that denied the possibility of overkill. In Inuit cosmology, death was not an end to life, but, rather, a recurring event in a continuous existence in which individual essences (souls) were constantly reborn. Yup'ik metaphysics laid down that animals, like human persons, had souls capable of being constantly reincarnated. Animals were, therefore, an "infinitely renewable resource" for Yup'ik communities.[18] In the Inuit and Yup'ik, as in Inupiat and Greenlandic, belief systems, animals offered themselves repeatedly as sustenance to humankind. Their gifts of themselves came out of their spiritual goodness, and in return for the respect and gratitude of human beings. Disrespect, mistreatment, or refusal of an animal spirit's gift were insults that inevitably caused it to withdraw its offer, and may have resulted in other animals withholding themselves from human beings as well. Only if their gift of life was respectfully accepted would animals continue to make themselves available for killing. In practice, the ideology required that all animals who came within the purview of the hunter had to be killed in order not to offend the animal world.

Belief in the infinite renewability of animal resources was, to some degree, part of Eskimo and Inuit worldviews from Siberia to Greenland,[19] and remains so among many groups. As Ann Fienup-Riordan pointed out in her discussion of Yup'ik hunting practices, the belief that animals could not be overhunted was correct throughout most of aboriginal times, but only because human demands on herds were limited by relatively small numbers of people.[20] When material circumstances change and the worldview that supports economic imperatives does not, the practical intent of the ideology may be subverted to the point of contributing to disaster.

Precisely such a situation occurred among the communities of the west coast of Hudson Bay during the second half of the nineteenth century. By 1850 the slow, steady increase of the human population that began with the arrival of immigrants from Coronation Gulf some time after 1680 had resulted in a population in the southern Keewatin large enough to require separation into three discrete bands. After 1850 the increased needs of even larger numbers of southern Keewatin people, as well as of Qairnirmiut, Aivilingmiut, and immigrant Netsilingmiut in the north, led to the routine use of muskox as a substitute for caribou. Motivated by severe deprivation and confident of the continuous renewability of the herd, the west-coast bay people pushed the muskox herds to the edge of extinction. As a result, there was a real possibility after 1915 that the southern Keewatin Inlanders also might disappear. The ideology that had prescribed hunting practice for thousands of years, and which was credited with the survival of numerous small societies over millennia, was counterproductive in the face of larger populations and extreme environmental crisis.

Social Behaviour and Survival

As well as recommending mobility, diversification, storage, and exchange as effective economic strategies for getting through seasonal scarcities, Inuit oral literature has identified some kinds of social behaviour as having greater survival value than others. The prescribed behaviours, taken together, come close to the long-standing popular image of Eskimo and Inuit: be cheerful, show respect for others, cooperate, work hard, maintain good relations with the spirit world, marry in order to have someone to help with the work, have children to comfort and care for you in old age, stay on friendly terms with all your relatives, be charitable when you can, be suspicious of strangers, and, if possible, stay out of unknown territory.

Inuit informants assisting in anthropological fieldwork after the mid-twentieth century have reported that sharing and hospitality were among the most highly valued traits of their societies. The survival value of generosity and open-handedness in times of food shortage is obvious, provided that sharing serves to redistribute quantities of food sufficient to sustain life among all participants. As triage it is inadequate. When food supplies are insufficient to provide a minimum number of calories for all members of the community, unrestricted sharing is more likely to ensure death or permanent disability for everybody than to guarantee the survival of either individuals or social units. Sharing as a universal and open-ended imperative becomes counterproductive under some circumstances.

Unlike some Inuit informants after the mid-twentieth century, nineteenth-century eyewitnesses to Inuit activities noted sharing in the breach more often than in practice. When it occurred, it was in the context of public obligation, rather than of private morality. Edward Parry described the reciprocal nature of sharing among Iglulingmiut. "Anything like a free gift is very little, if at all, known among them. If A gives B a part of his seal today, the latter soon returns an equal quantity when he is the successful fisherman. Uncertain as their mode of living is, and dependent as they are upon each other's exertions, this custom is in the evident and unquestionable interest of all. The regulation does credit to their wisdom, but has nothing to do with their generosity."[21]

Parry's observations also suggest there were well-defined limits to the sharing unit. Hospitality, he thought, would not be freely extended to strangers or destitute persons "unlikely soon to repay them."[22] John Davis's experience in 1586 indicates that the people of Cumberland Sound did not expect free gifts, either; when Davis gave them knives at their first meeting, they tried to give him skins in exchange. When John Ross presented the men of Netsilik and Arvilikjuaq with iron hoops at their first meeting in 1829, they immediately reciprocated by inviting him and his crew to feast in their homes.

In Greenland in the 1720s, communities refused to help one another in famine times, leading Claus Pars, governor of the Danish Greenland colony in 1728-29, to complain about large welfare expenses accruing to his government. At Cumberland Sound in the 1880s, Franz Boas also expressed scepticism about sharing as a universal imperative. He witnessed sharing mainly in the context of hunting partnerships in which several men hunted together and shared the catch. Shares, however, were not necessarily equal; there were rules to decide which of the hunters actually owned the animal, and how much he was obliged to give away. Beyond the hunting partnerships, meat and blubber were shared within extended family groups, but only when food was scarce. Rules in seal-sharing partnerships at Pelly Bay in the twentieth century were essentially the same as those observed by Boas at Cumberland Sound, and sharing outside the regulated partnerships was rare. Members of the Second Canadian Hudson Bay Expedition to the Ungava Peninsula north coast in the 1880s also noted the absence of sharing within communities in times of severe stress. "It was a matter with many of life and death and every man looked out for himself and his family. If he secured a seal it was hidden as quickly as possible."[23]

Diamond Jenness came to similar conclusions during the investigations of the Canadian Arctic Expedition, 1913-1918, among the Copper Inuit, noting that "a thing would not be offered unless it was expressly asked for, and then the transaction would become ordinary barter." Among northern Alaskans, sharing was "limited to the household ... rare between households." Investigations of sharing among hunter-gatherer societies in general indicate that "widespread day-to-day sharing" is neither practised nor practical because it "may preclude the storage of food to counter seasonal shortages."[24]

What, then, is the source of the widespread belief among both Inuit and non-Inuit that arctic societies were open-handed and generous with possessions and resources? Another look at the myths and folktales, with attention to their time frames, suggests some possible answers. The stories address problems of resource scarcity in three time periods: seasonal, inter-annual, and long-term. Stories that advised sharing and generosity did so only in reference to the regularly recurring (and therefore predictable) local scarcities of a season's duration. Sharing was never suggested as an appropriate response to inter-annual or long-term shortages, or to geographically widespread scarcity. The cultural ideal for conduct within the residential family group in times of mild deprivation over the short term did not apply in times of abundance or in times of serious deprivation over the long term; and it never applied to strangers. The cruel necessity to enhance one's own chances of survival, even if it meant withholding assistance from strangers in need, may be the reason that several dozen people were able to watch the 130 or more officers and men of John Franklin's last expedition die from starvation and exposure without intervening.

Of course, the cultural ideal in any society is always tempered by human emotion. People love, and they share because they love. In their families and in face-to-face societies they know each other, care about each other, and, out of love, they give. However, for Inuit, specifically the people of west Hudson Bay, love has implications beyond affective relations. It also implies commitment and acceptance of responsibility for the well-being of the loved ones. The reverse is also true: to be unable to take care of someone is expressed as being unable to love them.[25] Because it cannot be separated from commitment to care for, love must necessarily involve sharing. Inability to share or care for, which is expressed as being unable to love, does not mean that affective emotion is missing. Being unable to love or care for is a source of intense grief and emotional pain to parents, children, spouses, and companions in times of extreme deprivation when there are simply not enough resources to go around.

The imperative to share, and therefore to love and take responsibility for, cannot be extended without limits. Wise Inuit in past generations were fully aware of this and did not prescribe sharing outside the familial and communal group. On the contrary, open-handedness beyond the local community was proscribed by assigning unrelated people to the category of 'strangers' and requiring that they be treated with aloofness. Within the limits of coresidential kin groups, refusal to share was seen as a threat to the internal security of Inuit communities. Outside these limits, willingness to share was recognized as an equally serious danger. Both sides of the sharing dilemma were institutionalized in Inuit law and taught to successive generations through the medium of stories.

Inuit law was a reality in spite of the statements of some observers that Inuit did not possess a coherent body of law or a system of enforcement;

for example, Diamond Jenness's statement that Copper Inuit society was "without law-courts, judges or chiefs, without laws even," and "for minor offences, therefore, such as theft and abduction, there is no remedy"; and Boas's comment that "there is no way of enforcing these unwritten laws and no punishment for transgressors except the blood vengeance."[26] The purpose of Inuit law was not to ensure justice for individuals, but to maintain harmony within the community, and between the community and the spirit world. The importance of maintaining correct relations with the spirit world was obvious. Behaviour that offended animals or weather spirits put the community at immediate and life-threatening risk of losing its food supply.

Continuing harmonious relations of individuals within the community were equally important. Most Inuit communities consisted of a dozen or so individuals living in constant close contact, often under conditions of uncertainty and stress. Minor disagreements, grudges, or even the annoying personal habits of one person could lead to open animosities and failures of cooperation, which could be dangerous to the community. Liars, layabouts, braggarts, loudmouths, know-it-alls, misers, debtors, and whiners were as likely to be classed as "social nuisances" as murderers were, because they made "life uncertain and their unpredictable attitude [worked] disruptively in the daily routine."[27]

Means of enforcing peace and harmony within communities included shaming, shunning, banishment, abandonment leading to death, and execution. Public ridicule and ostracism were the most frequently used methods of social control, and generally had the desired effect of keeping people cooperative.[28] Harsher means, such as banishment and execution, were resorted to only in cases where antisocial behaviour was perceived as a continuing threat to the community.

Banishment was common enough among Netsilingmiut in the extremely harsh physical environment of Boothia Peninsula that an outcast community existed at Bellot Strait. Some of the (male) murderers and wife-abductors who lived there with their families had been exiled by their communities; others were fugitives hoping to escape the vengeance of their communities or their victims' relatives.[29] Murderers were cast out of the community, not out of desire for retribution, but in order to prevent enmity and vengeance from escalating to the point where the community might be distracted from its primary business of earning a living, or might even suffer the loss of needed hunters, seamstresses, and child-bearers.

Among the several dozens of murder cases described in the ethnographic literature, social sanctions were never taken against a murderer if the community believed that she or he would not do it again. A case in point is that of Idjuadjuk, a Padlirmio, who killed an entire family who had opposed his marriage. The community did not act against him, on the grounds that after he had found a wife he was satisfied and was unlikely ever to commit a similar offense. A second, and different, illustrative case is that of Krittark, an old Netsilingmio, who was killed because the community suspected her of sorcery that caused her son-in-law to have bad luck in the hunt. While both of the above incidents took place at the beginning of the twentieth century, the attitudes they imply were noted in the eighteenth by Andrew Graham. "They punish no transgressors with death, [except for] murtherers and such conjurers and witches as are reported to have bewitched others to death."[30]

Crime and punishment were not relevant ideas in the Inuit justice system. The maintenance of an orderly society was. The Inuit attitude towards law and order was summarized by Birket-Smith. "In essence it is not the mission of the community to execute law and justice, but exclusively to restore peace…. On this basis the settlement may, for instance, combine in killing a man or a woman suspected of witchcraft, for such persons are a menace to the peace of the community. The killing is not, however, a *punishment* for the practising of witchcraft, for the community may in the same manner get rid of a man with a wild and brutal temperament, or of old or sick people who are a burden upon the settlement" [original emphasis].[31]

In addition to rules for correct living, order in the community requires leaders. Much of the scholarly literature describing Inuit social organization has remarked on the absence of institutionalized leadership. Inuit historians think otherwise. Inuit historian Kananginak Pootoogook confirmed that "there were bosses way before the white man ever came," but they did not rule or enforce rules. They were chosen because their skills enhanced the community's chances of survival. "The best hunter in a camp would automatically be boss because he was the main support."[32] Usually a leader's influence was restricted to his own residential kin-based communities, and lasted only as long as the physical community did.[33] New leaders appeared when extended families moved away from band aggregations in seasons of scarcity, and set aside their limited authority when dispersed groups came together again. When chiefs were chosen to deal with special problems, their tenure was often of even shorter duration. Catchoe assumed authority as a leader, for instance, only after the events at Jackman Sound had confirmed that Martin Frobisher's 1577 mining expedition was well and truly a threat. George Best's description of the 1577 encounter clearly portrays the concerted action of men following the plan and the

orders of their military leader, Catchoe, but suggests that Catchoe's authority was limited to conditions of war.

Close to two and a half centuries later on the west coast of Hudson Bay,
Augustine described "two great chiefs, or *Ackhaiyoot* ... who directed the
movements of the party ... [with the help of] the *Attoogawnoeuck*, or lesser
Chiefs ... [who were] respected principally as senior men. The tribe seldom suffers from want of food, if the Chief moves to the different stations
at the proper season."[34]

The *ackhaiyoot* may actually have been *angakot*, shamans. A shaman's ability
to create harmonious relations between humans and the spirits on which
their lives depended was a solid basis for the recognition of authority. If
they were personally popular, they were respected and had considerable
prestige. If they were successful in finding necessary resources for the community and attracting animals to the hunters, they attained great power
within their communities, whether they were personally much liked or
not.

Most eyewitnesses noted the existence of chiefs, headmen, and other
leaders in Inuit communities in periods before outside influences were
present. "The Eskimo respect for power is not a post-Kabloona phenomenon," wrote one observer.[35] Throughout the nineteenth century the Hudson's Bay Company traders at Churchill made frequent mention of chiefs
among the southern Keewatin communities, and in the 1890s Captain
George Comer noted leadership roles among the Aivilingmiut. One chief,
Coonic Charley (Kunuksialuk?), was succeeded by his son Albert, and then
by a grandson, Tesiaq. The latter was recognized as a leader "on account of
his ability," wrote Comer, but Tesiaq had also apparently been nominated as
a future leader by his grandfather.[36]

Generally, leaders were experienced adults who had proven themselves
to be good providers and who managed their own families well. They were
physically strong, skilled in hunting or in the spiritual manipulation of
animals and the environment, knowledgeable in matters pertaining to subsistence, and able to maintain peaceful relations within the community. In
short, they were people who had made or were capable of making significant contributions to the security and prosperity of the community. They
were usually, but not always, male. In south Baffin Island, a woman was the
chief or leader of a band for many years in the 1920s and 1930s.[37]

Among central arctic Inuit, a man's material wealth was an indicator of
his suitability for leadership. On their journey to the Labrador coast and
Ungava Bay in 1814, the missionaries Kohlmeister and Kmoch described
their companion, Johnathan of Hopedale. "He was a man of superior

understanding and skill, possessed of uncommon presence of mind in difficulties and dangers, and at Hopedale considered as the principal person, or chief of his nation." He also "possessed a shallop, with two masts," and this worldly wealth was directly related to his status as a leader.[38] He fit the description of what it took to be a leader, given by Inuit historian Kananginak Pootoogook. "I have known that for many generations here in the North that when a man was rich in food, when he was the best hunter in the camp, that he was known to be the boss."[39] A man of means, such as Johnathan of Hopedale, had proved his worth in amassing personal wealth, and was therefore recognized as having leadership qualities that could benefit the community.

According to the ideal, leaders could suggest but not command, and enforcement of customary law was not their business. In the end, all decisions were made by the community, but leaders could be asked, or instructed, to carry out the community's judgements. For example, "people who have made themselves obnoxious are disposed of by common consent," wrote Franz Boas, but leaders, according to F.F. Payne, were often "sought for in the settlement of disputes and sometimes [to] act as public executioners."[40]

Leadership was provisional, lasting only as long as the community required the special skills of an individual and approved his actions. Public recognition of an individual's proven ability, wealth as an indicator of competence, reputation for honesty and wisdom, and non-abrasive leadership style were factors that predisposed communities to choose a particular leader, but chieftainship lasted only as long as it reflected public opinion.

Law and leadership in Inuit communities, like economic activity and social attitudes, were intended to increase the chances of survival by reducing the risks. The goal was an orderly society that operated within the physical environment so that the needs of human beings were met, but did not outstrip available resources. Interpersonal relations, social behaviour, and, to a large extent, economic strategies are matters that affect members of the residential group and can be handled without interference from outsiders. Inuit, however, were sometimes faced with situations that could not be managed within the immediate community or even within the confines of its territory. The behaviour of strangers, unlike that of coresidents, was unpredictable and often dangerous. How to deal with strangers was a major problem requiring a complex set of strategies.

Meetings with strangers before the arrival of the first Europeans in Inuit homelands most often happened during inter-annual and long-term crises caused by resource shortages. The prescriptive stories recommended the expansion of hunting range into nearby territories, preferably unoccupied ones, or relocation, either temporary or permanent, to nearby territories, again preferably unoccupied ones. The stories assumed that intrusion or relocation to unoccupied zones was not likely to create insurmountable problems, but that contact with strangers would. The social mechanisms suggested by the encoded instructions for use of new territories were all concerned with the problems of strangers.

The great majority of stories dealing with encounters between Inuit and strangers identify strangers as murderers or monsters intent on doing harm.[41] Eyewitness accounts readily and consistently confirm that attitude. Inuit reactions to the appearance of Europeans in their homelands in the sixteenth and seventeenth centuries were immediate and violent, as were their responses to their Indian neighbours. As a Copper Indian warned Robert Hood in 1821, "the Esquimaux had never met a stranger who they did not find an enemy." The conviction that strangers were always danger-ous applied to other Inuit as well as to Indians and Europeans. After the 1850s, Copper Inuit communities described Netsilingmiut as "cruel, blood-thirsty people," as did the Aivilingmiut, and in both cases the feeling was returned in full measure. Fear of strangers was so strong that it was com-mon practice for people to carry amulets as protection.[42]

"One would think that in these waste and desolate regions," wrote Knud Rasmussen, "they would feel pleasure when they came across people who could be company for them; far from it."[43] Like sharing, friendly social relations were restricted to coresidents and kinsmen. In situations where food supply was often limited, and always a source of concern, the mere presence of strangers could have been seen as competition for resources, both on the hoof and in the cache. The extension of sharing privileges beyond the small circle of procurers and their families could reduce sup-plies and endanger the community. While insiders, that is, members of the immediate community, could hunt anywhere within the bounds of the territory a collective considered its own, strangers could not.[44]

The underlying reason for the worldview that proclaimed strangers to be dangerous was apparently economic. To keep strangers away was equiva-lent to safeguarding food and other important resources for one's own use. Inuit did not usually carry food with them when they travelled; they hunted as they went. If the people of Frobisher Bay in the 1570s assumed that their visitors planned to do the same, they had solid grounds for anxiety. Taking Frobisher's boat in 1576 may have been an attempt to protect resources by taking away the strangers' ability to hunt seal or whale. By preventing Frobisher's men from setting foot on the mainland, which they did with great success in 1578, they made sure the strangers could not take food resources, or gather information about the nature and extent of local resources. The demolition of John Davis's boat at Cumberland Sound in 1587 was another case of people destroying the means by which strangers could harvest the resources of the country, had they wanted to do so. Both responses were similar to the actions of Labrador people during the attacks of 1718 to 1720, when their destruction of boats and other hunting equipment effectively prevented Europeans from pursuing whale and seal.

Recognition of strangers was easy; the histories identified a stranger as any person who was not a member of the face-to-face community. However, cultural wisdom and pragmatism also insisted that in periods of long-term or critical food shortages, the only means to survival might very well be through interactions with strangers. The problem then became how to make strangers into non-strangers. The solution, again according to the prescriptive stories, was to accommodate the largest possible number of individuals in the category of family, and to recognize or create kinship outside the genetically related group.

Most Eskimoan kinship systems included members of the father's family, mother's family, spouse's family, and adopted child's family, to the greatest extent that they were known. Kinship was also recognized in naming practice and spouse-exchange. Individuals who shared a name shared a soul and were therefore related, as were elders who chose a name for an infant; individuals who exchanged spouses did so in order to widen their kinship circle by accepting responsibility for each other and for children born or adopted by any of the participants; individuals who were delivered by the same midwife, "she who makes," were related at the in-law level, and also had special lifelong relationships with their "cultural mother" and her kin in all categories. Every member of a familial network, fictive or otherwise, could, at least in theory, turn to every other member for assistance in time of need.[45]

In addition to the relationships recognized as familial, Inuit created economic alliances that bound individuals together in non-stranger relationships. Among Netsilingmiut, unrelated men entered into seal-sharing partnerships; Copper Inuit males created partnerships for hunting, seal sharing, and rifle sharing, and like other Inuit made socially recognized agreements of friendship, endorsed by dancing, singing, joking, or sparring; among Mackenzie and Copper Inuit, trading partnerships were of primary importance in creating safe ways to approach men from other groups. The nature of relationships and partnerships varied from group to group across the arctic. Keewatin Inuit, for instance, emphasized biological, adoptive, and in-law kinship, and gave less importance to partnerships with non-kin than some other groups did. They did, however, create some relationships that involved reciprocal sharing and obligation when they formed collectives to buy whaling boats, as groups of hunters did in 1807 and 1821 at Churchill.[46]

While recognition of different degrees of kinship and the creation of friendship agreements made it possible to function among known strangers by converting them into non-strangers, there remained the problem of unknown strangers. Means were needed for dealing with the unexpected appearance of strangers with whom there was no pre-existing rationale for laying aside suspicion. A greeting protocol for just such situations has been widely described by eyewitnesses. It required that the strangers show evidence of friendly intent by laying aside their weapons or otherwise offering proof that they were unarmed. Local people then tested the intentions of the strangers by sending one of their own as an emissary-*cum*-hostage, or as George Lyon put it, "a kind of herald."[47]

The emissary was usually an old woman, sometimes an old man or a lame person, and occasionally a child. Observers believed they were chosen because they were relatively non-productive members of the community. "If our designs had been hostile, and we had killed the old woman," concluded William Gilder of the Schwatka expedition, "their fighting strength would not have been reduced, and it would only have been one less old woman to care for."[48] Gilder was probably correct that the community wanted to keep its hunters out of harm's way until they knew what the strangers' intentions were, but his suggestion that the choice of an old woman was callously made does not square with the usual Inuit practice. As a member of the wisdom generation, and possibly also a loved individual, the "old woman" may have been highly valued. She may have been chosen as emissary because of a previous acquaintance with white men, or because she was well travelled. She may also have nominated herself for the potentially dangerous job as a way of loving and caring for her community.

The greeting protocol was called into play only when meetings took place between people who were genuinely uncertain about each other's intentions. People who were already known to each other, if only by reputation, were not bound by the rules, even when formal alliances or kinship did not exist between them. Inuit greeted John Rae at Repulse Bay in 1846 and Leopold McClintock at Admiralty Inlet and Boothia Peninsula in 1857-58 casually and without ceremony, because, as McClintock noted, "they evidently knew us to be friends."[49] In some communities, even those that had never before met Europeans, white men were accepted as non-strangers. William Gilder described the meeting of Schwatka's party with Utkusiksalingmiut in 1879: "They carried their bows in their hands, with arrows fixed to the strings; but when the old woman [emissary] shouted back that the strangers were white men, they laid aside their arms, and received [us] in a friendly fashion."[50]

Before the meeting, one of the members of the party, Equeesik, had suggested that a gun be fired to signal their approach. Gilder concluded that it was the firing of the gun, and "the knowledge of the effect of the white men's fire-arms [which] protected [us] from attack."[51] It could also have been because white men had never been known to cause bodily harm to Inuit, and were generally accepted as friendly and peaceful, albeit marginally human, persons. It helped a great deal if the strangers showed some familiarity with the local language. Bylot and Munk at the Lower Savage Islands in 1615 and 1619, George Back on the Great Fish River in 1834-35, Moses at Fort Chimo in 1830, and James Clark Ross at Lord Mayor's Bay in 1830 all found that speaking a few words in Inuktitut resulted in smiles and friendly greetings from otherwise apprehensive Inuit.

Correct greeting etiquette in all its prescribed detail was adhered to, in most cases by chance, in the peaceful encounters between Inuit and Munk in Hudson Strait, Bylot at the Savage Islands, Parry and Lyon at Melville Peninsula, Lyon at Southampton Island, the Rosses in Boothia Peninsula, Back and Anderson at Great Fish River, and McClintock and Schwatka at King William Island. In each case, although the Inuit were meeting white men for the first time, they had previous knowledge of them and quickly exempted them from the category of strangers to be feared.

The parties of John Davis near Cape Chidley in 1586, John Knight at Cape Grimington in 1606, and Thomas Button at Digges Island in 1612, all of which were attacked by local people, did not follow correct greeting procedures. As well, the Inuit were meeting white men for the first time and probably did not have prior information about them. In each case, the new arrivals were taking the food resources of the country—the Davis and Knight parties had been fishing just offshore, and the Button crew had been collecting eggs and netting birds—without the permission of the owners and without having established their credentials as friends and allies. The Inuit would not have known, nor would it have mattered to them, that the strangers were unaware that the land was inhabited. An encounter that does not fit the pattern was that of the Digges Island people and Abacuck Prickett's party in 1611. When *Discovery* arrived at the island, its crew apparently observed correct greeting procedures, and went bird hunting at the invitation of the local people. The attack on the English sailors the next day took place during trading, and seems to be an exception to usual Inuit hospitality toward invited guests who, a day earlier, had been accepted as non-strangers.

Some communities had mechanisms for converting their own people into strangers. The banishing of partly acculturated women and their mixed-blood children from Greenlandic societies is one example, as is the killing of the little Labrador boy by his people "for being half French and half stranger." Another incident, which also took place in Labrador, was described by the priest Francis de Crespieul. On a journey up the Saguenay River in 1671, he met a family of "Christian Eskimo" who said "they had fled from the other Eskimo to escape being strangled for having become converts."[52] Explanation of the rejections on economic grounds fails to convince: many of the outcast Greenlanders had rights in their husband's and father's estates guaranteed by the Danish government; no evidence suggests the little Labrador boy was unwelcome because he returned to his family in bad economic times, or that the Christian family fleeing down the Saguenay were unproductive members of the community. The practice does not seem to have been widespread—either it did not occur elsewhere, or it was unobserved and unrecorded. The young apprentices who wintered at Churchill post in the eighteenth century, and the men who were employed there in the nineteenth, were certainly not repudiated by their communities. Nor were the dozens of people who willingly accompanied ships' captains to London, New York, Boston, Edinburgh, Copenhagen, and other European and American cities over several centuries. One possible explanation for the anomalies, unsupported by evidence and purely speculative, comes to mind: the half-strangers may have been rejected because they were not educated in Inuit ways. It may have been assumed that, because of their ignorance, they would prove unproductive and become burdens on the community, or introduce disharmony that could put the community at risk. Alternatively, the incidents may have been the results of events or conditions specific to the people and communities involved.

Economic and social strategies for reducing uncertainty and ensuring community survival carried with them implications for both change and continuity. Prior to 1860, inter-group trade among the communities of Melville Peninsula, the southern Keewatin, and Boothia and Adelaide peninsulas enhanced survival, as the cultural wisdom encoded in stories intended, but had little influence for change in opinions or in practice. Because of the widespread uniformity of worldview, trade between Inuit communities was an unlikely vehicle for the introduction of new ideas. Meetings between Indians and Inuit were also poor vehicles for changes in intellectual culture: they were either violent encounters in which material items might change hands at the same time that negative emotions were reinforced, or they were so fraught with suspicion and anxiety that little exchange of ideas was possible. The introduction of new ideas in the course of trade with Europeans was also extremely limited because of the brevity and infrequency of contact.

Because of similarities in environment and in subsistence practices, the exchange of material goods did not encourage change in customary practices, either. For example, from the beginning of the eighteenth century, the communities of Melville Peninsula exchanged walrus hide and sinew with the people of Chesterfield Inlet, in return for wood. As a result the more northerly groups were able to make kayak frames, harpoon handles, and tent poles more easily and in greater quantities. However, even without the trade, they would still have managed to make whatever implements they needed, using bone. Chesterfield Inlet communities benefitted from the longer-wearing boots and tougher walrus cord they received in trade from the north, but had there been no exchange, they could still have provided for their needs by making thread, ropes, and laces from seal sinew. The goods traded from Churchill post were similarly insignificant as agents of change. The knife blades, metal awls, and kettles acquired through trade allowed for more efficient performance of work, but in no case did the introduction of new material goods lead to changes in subsistence practices or social organization.

Extensive use of storage as a survival strategy encouraged continuity rather than change. One of the consequences of storage-dependence was a high degree of sedentarization, which reduced opportunities for trade and travel, and supported relative isolation. There was always some travel undertaken by individuals and families in order to trade, seek spouses and children, exchange information, and keep up friendship and kinship ties, but no large-scale mingling of distinct communities.

Of all the survival strategies employed by Inuit, the practice of mobility arguably had the greatest potential for significant social change in the period between 1650 and 1940. The strategic objective of mobility, whether seasonal, or in connection with temporary or permanent relocation, was to bring people and resources together in one place. The permanent relocation of Coronation Gulf people to Chesterfield Inlet in the late seventeenth century and the subsequent peopling of the southern Keewatin is one example.

Division of communities in times of shortage, implicit in seasonal mobility, encouraged permanent separation in times of increasing population and the search for additional resources. Residence by portions of a community at alternate locations sometimes became permanent, as happened to Augustine's people between 1820 and 1860. In the case of the Keewatin Inlanders, relocation meant new sources of subsistence and the loss of connections with the sea. Significant changes in intellectual, as well as material, life were the result.

The temporary relocations of Netsilingmiut to areas close to abandoned ships in the 1840s and 1850s, and of Ugjulingmiut to Great Fish River as a result of famine and Netsilingmiut incursion in the same period, were facilitated by the Inuit recourse to mobility as a first response in cases of deprivation. Netsilingmiut efforts to protect the windfall represented by the abandonment of John Ross's *Victory* left their mark in attitudes of hostility and increased suspicion towards other arctic groups, opinions other groups returned in full measure. In 1830 Netsilingmiut villages had included many women and men from other groups, as spouses, immigrants, and visitors. By 1870 the Boothia people were generally feared and disliked. In the 1920s Takornaq, an Aivilingmio, told Therkel Mathiassen of the Fifth Thule Expedition that "if she were to have a new husband, it was all the same to her whether he was an Aivilingmio, an Iglulingmio or a Tununermio; if need be, a Qairnermio or an Akudnermio might do; but a Netsilingmio—never!"[53]

As late as 1951, Cape Dorset families who had emigrated to Boothia Peninsula in the mid-1930s refused to let their children marry Netsilingmiut. Their stated reason was that "while the Nechilik men have shown that they would like to marry [Cape] Dorset girls, and have done so in a few cases to the girl's detriment, no [Cape] Dorset father will willingly allow a daughter to marry into the tribe."[54]

The movement of the surviving remnant of the Ugjulik community to Great Fish River in the 1850s was reversed by the 1870s, after the withdrawal of Netsilingmiut from Adelaide Peninsula and the return of the Ugjulingmiut to their former territories. After a generation of sharing territory, communities, and subsistence activities with the Utkusiksalingmiut, Ugjulik people (re)assumed their self-perceptions of difference and distinctiveness. Between 1832 and 1860, the practice of going where the resources were resulted in temporary demographic change for the Netsilingmiut and their neighbours, and in the creation of long-lasting suspicion, but not in fundamental changes in social organization and worldview.

After 1860 strategic mobility drew some Melville Peninsula people to Roes Welcome, and led to the rapid emergence of the Aivilingmiut as a distinct community. The Qairnirmiut did not have to move in order to increase their access to resources; the whaleships arrived on their doorstep. Both groups became sources of relief and hosts to immigrants from Boothia Peninsula and Great Fish River anxious to participate in the new affluent societies. People had to reconcile old attitudes about strangers and group distinctiveness with new realities of culturally mixed communities. Group identities, which previously had been taken for granted, perhaps because they were not threatened, became more noticeable. Aivilingmiut, Netsilingmiut, and Qairnirmiut maintained their sense of difference. The Netsilingmiut practice of infant betrothal between kin, for example, made it unlikely that there would be enough women within the group to marry out. Ahiarmiut also maintained their sense of distinctiveness by refusing to marry outside their own dialect group, although it was common practice for families to spend periods of one or two years living in other communities.[55]

Occupational specialization also contributed to the maintenance of group distinctiveness and mental boundaries. The Aivilingmiut were more involved in summer whaling activities than were other groups, and spent less time in the caribou hunt, with the result that whaling captains depended on the Qairnirmiut for summer meat supplies and on Aivilingmiut as a labour force.[56]

Inuit societies in the eighteenth and nineteenth centuries tended to be egalitarian within their own confines, but each was convinced of its own superior position relative to all other groups defined as strangers, including other Inuit. As communities expanded into previously unoccupied territory, and the empty buffer zones between them disappeared, ideologies were created in order to maintain distinctions. By the beginning of the twentieth century, each of the whaling homeguard societies—Aivilingmiut, Qairnirmiut, and eastern Netsilingmiut—saw itself as an elite community, superior to all the others.[57]

After 1940, when government initiatives created more communities and drew in people from many different regions, a hierarchy of west Hudson Bay bands was widely recognized among Inuit. The Aivilingmiut were at the top. They were more deeply involved with white men, at an earlier date, than any other group. They formed the first Inuit homeguard and were the first to become employees of white men on a large scale, the first to live in wooden houses, the first to learn English, and the first to produce a mixed-blood generation. In other words, the Aivilingmiut had made the most changes in their way of life, and were the first group to be identified by their compatriots as Qallunamiut, People of the White People. The mockery implicit in the name did nothing to prevent members of other groups from giving them first place in the hierarchy of Inuit peoples, or from adopting, or aspiring to adopt, Aivilingmiut vocabulary and accent.

By the 1960s, at Chesterfield Inlet, Baker Lake, and Rankin Inlet, most Keewatin Inuit accepted social rankings in which the top place was still occupied by the Aivilingmiut, followed by Qairnirmiut, Utkusiksalingmiut, and other Great Fish River people.[58] The Paatlirmiut, Padlirmiut, and Ahiarmiut, whose biological and cultural ancestors were the first to meet and treat with Europeans, were in general the last to give up complete dependence on the land, the last to move into government communities (which they did unwillingly), and, in the opinion of their fellow country-men, came to occupy the lowest rung on the Inuit social ladder.

The most obvious differences between the high-ranking Aivilingmiut and the low-ranking Ahiarmiut were their relative economic positions and the degree to which they had instituted or accepted change. By the end of the nineteenth century, the Aivilingmiut were wealthy in terms of material possessions, and because they owned whaling boats, rifles, long wooden sleds, and relatively large dog teams, they had achieved economic security. They had been in the right place at the right time when commercial whal-ers appeared on their doorsteps, and they had made changes in their ways of living and earning a living in order to take advantage of the opportuni-ties implicit in the presence of Qallunat. As the whalers withdrew, traders, police, and missionaries took their place as employers, trading partners, and occasional providers of health care and relief. Aivilingmiut and, to a lesser extent, Qairnirmiut created relations with Qallunat that ensured individual and societal survival. They attained the Inuit cultural ideal of economic certainty by reinterpreting the sanctified rules for life embodied in their ancient oral literature. In short, apostasy led to relative prosperity, and achieved the economic certainty that an earlier ideology in different cir-cumstances had promised, but had been unable to deliver when physical and social environments changed.

On the other hand, the southern Keewatin people—the Ahiarmiut, Padlirmiut, and Paatlirmiut—continued to respond to the pressures of the physical environment with behaviours that were validated and reinforced by past successes, sacralized in their ideology, and embedded in their pre-scriptive cultural lore. The responses proved to be inadequate as survival strategies in post-1915 conditions, when deteriorating climate and declin-ing herds could no longer support the greatly augmented population. In other words, fidelity to cultural imperatives and ancient worldview was maintained at great cost in individual lives and brought their societies close to extinction.

For hundreds of years, the individual and social survival of Inuit depended on faithful adherence to old strategies made emotionally bearable by an ancient ideology. The old behaviours were created in order to maintain small, face-to-face societies of fifteen to thirty people. They required acceptance of early and painful death, occasional cannibalism, and strict population control. The relative prosperity experienced by most central Canadian Inuit in the nineteenth century relieved them of the dreadful necessities implicit in limiting their numbers through 'infanticide', 'geronotcide', and 'assisted suicide'.[59] Increased population and environmental pressures were central facts in the disasters that befell the post–1915 generation.

On the surface, the greatest of the disasters (as seen by outsider observers) was the cost in human lives. Less obviously, the catastrophic events led to the traumatic realization that the ancient ideology was out of step with new aspirations. The results were a crisis of religious faith, growing doubts about ancestral wisdom, and loss of confidence in ancient sociopolitical institutions. People began to question their understanding of the natural order, and the correctness of their views on the relations of human beings with each other and with other-than-human persons. The emotional strain that accompanied the destruction of the belief system was expressed by Aua, a shaman of the Iglulingmiut in 1922.

> We fear the weather spirit of the earth, that we must fight against to wrest our food from land and sea. We fear Sila. We fear dearth and hunger in the cold snow huts. We fear ... the great woman down at the bottom of the sea, that rules over the beasts of the sea. We fear the sickness that we meet with daily all around us; not death, but the suffering. We fear the evil spirits of life, those of the air, of the sea and the earth.... We fear all the creatures that we have to kill and eat, all those we have to strike down and destroy to make clothes for ourselves ... and which must therefore be propitiated lest they should revenge themselves on us for taking away their bodies.[60]

Aua's summation, "We do not believe. We fear,"[61] was as descriptive of southern Keewatin and arctic coast societies in the years after 1915 as it was of the Iglulingmiut.

The contradictions between new social goals and old beliefs and practices are obvious. Old sociopolitical institutions, created to meet the needs of face-to-face communities in which decision making was ideally a consensual process, were no longer efficient in residential groups four and five times the size of traditional ones. Measures to reduce numbers were no longer emotionally or socially acceptable. But the new aspirations and expectations were in conflict with the divinely sanctioned view of the cosmos, which defined animals as an infinitely renewable resource and human soul-names as capable of endless reincarnation. The ideology was incompatible with increased populations in a deteriorating physical environment, and an increasingly crowded social environment. The cosmic order that Inuit intellectual and spiritual leaders had struggled for centuries to understand was called into question.

The transition from Thule to Historic Inuit in the centuries between about 1250 and 1600 involved permanent socioeconomic transformation. Historic Inuit subsistence occupations, architecture, residential patterns, and resource use were profoundly different from those of their biological ancestors. In contrast, between about 1550 and 1900, most self-directed change in Historic Inuit societies and economies were surface oscillations, not long-term transformations. In the greatly altered environments after 1915, old strategies failed, and physical survival was possible only through extraordinary measures taken by non-Inuit agents. Since the mid-twentieth century, Modern Inuit have been seeking ways to transform their societies in ways appropriate to a greatly altered demographic regime within a new world economic order, while at the same time in ways that are ideologically, socially, and economically compatible with their cultural past.

Appendixes

Appendix 1

Collective Naming Practice

Considerable debate has taken place among scholars and in the popular media in the past twenty years on the origin and meaning of the word "Eskimo." One of the abiding myths that clings to the indigenous peoples of the central arctic is that the word is of Algonquian origin, and that it means "raw-meat eaters." No linguistic evidence supports such an interpretation, but a case has been made for its origin in the Montagnais *ayaskime*, or the proto-Algonquian *ayacimew*, both of which mean "snow-shoe netter."[1] European visitors to the lower St Lawrence and the Labrador coast learned the word from the St Lawrence Montagnais. Its first appearance in English print was in Richard Hakluyt's treatise of 1584, which described the indigenous people of "graunde baie" as "Esquimauwes," but was not clear on where the word came from.[2]

Samuel de Champlain believed it to be the people's own word for themselves. "There is an Indian tribe inhabiting this territory," he wrote, "*who call themselves Eskimos*" [emphasis added].[3] Linguistic analysis suggests that he may have been correct. As an agglutinative language, Inuktitut assigns a conceptual meaning to each syllable. *Asi-* (in some dialects, *Ahi-*)[4] indicates otherness, difference, or uniqueness, as in *asi* (another than him), *asiani* (elsewhere), and *asirqupaa* (takes another path, goes by another way). The idea of distance or otherness appears in the word *Asiarmiut* or *Ahiarmiut*, People of the Far Away Place, or People from Beyond. *Ko* (also written in older orthographies as *qu, qo, or qua*) can express slipperiness, especially slipperiness due to ice, and occurs in words such as *koak* (frozen hard meat), *koaiyakrikpok* (slips on ice), *koasak* (newly formed lake ice), *quaq* (frozen stiff), and *quaqauti* or *quakkuvik* (refrigerator). *Miut* is a suffix meaning "people of," as in Sikimiut, People of the Ice Place, and Netsilingmiut, People of the Seal Place.[5] The word rendered as *Esquimawes* by Hakluyt, *Exquimaux* by Champlain, and *Eskimaux* or *Esquimaux* by various fur traders, missionaries, explorers, and adventurers might also be rendered as *Asikomiut, Asiquamiut, Esiquomiut* (and a number of other variations), and would mean something like "People from Another Frozen Place," or "People of a Distant Icy Land."

Whatever the people of Grand Bay called themselves, the autonym would have applied only to them. Prior to the emergence of a Pan-Eskimo movement in the 1970s, indigenous arctic people of neo-Eskimo ancestry and language did not use any designation that included all of them. Many communities did not use group designators at all, and when they did it was to identify local and sometimes temporary groups of co-residents, usually in terms of territory and resources; for example, *Aivilingmiut*, People of the Walrus Place, and *Napartormiut*, People of the Tree Place. The self-designations were highly flexible and seldom implied self-conscious ethnic or sociopolitical identity. As late as 1921, Therkel Mathiassen noted that group names were "more geographical than ethnographical."[6] If Champlain was correct that *Eskimo* was a word used by the people themselves, usage would have been local.

All Eskimoan languages and dialects contain a word, such as *yup'ik, yuit, inuit*, or *inupiaq*, that means "authentic people" (that is, real persons), and that served to differentiate them from their non-Eskimoan neighbours, who, in Eskimoan cosmology, were not fully human. While they might look like human beings, Eskimoan worldview assigned all people (that is, persons) except Eskimos to subhuman categories.[7] While the generic terms translate into English as person (singular) and people (plural), they refer to *persons* as individuals, not to *peoples* as nations or ethnic communities.

In West Greenland, people of Thule Eskimo ancestry called themselves *Kalaallit* (singular *kalaaleq*; in older orthographies, *kaladlit*) at least since the mid-1700s.[8] With the emergence of Greenlandic nationalism, the word has come into general usage as an autonym used by all Greenlanders of Eskimoan ancestry. Danish philologist William Thalbitzer concluded that it derived from *skraelingar*, Old Norse meaning "scrawny," which was applied to all North American indigenous peoples by the first Norsemen to reach North America. More recently, Dirmid Collis has suggested that the term derived from the Icelandic phrase *skinn kloedast*, meaning "those who wear skin clothing," and was not indigenous to Greenland.[9]

In western Alaska, the self-designation of Eskimoan people "has always been, and remains to this day, Yup'ik, from the base *yuk*, person, plus *-pik*, genuine or real, hence 'a real or genuine person'." However, all individual persons and all communities of people have a variety of affiliations, and bear many categorical names. Within the group of Yup'ik-speaking societies are subgroups who accept Yup'ik as a general designation but also retain ethnic identifiers for local groups, such as Yupigit on St Lawrence Island and Yupiit in southwest Alaska.[10]

In the 1970s, in response to the demands of Canadian Inuit political groups, the name "Inuit" began to be more commonly used in Canada. In 1977, at the suggestion of Canadian Inuit delegates, the Inuit Circumpolar Conference "officially adopted Inuit as a designation for all Eskimos, regardless of their local usages."[11] However, the use of the term to include peoples outside the Canadian central arctic, and some people within it, is inappropriate and incorrect. It is also ahistorical when used to refer to most Canadian arctic peoples prior to the second half of the twentieth century. "Inuit" has until recently been used only by Inuktitut-speakers of West Greenland and eastern Canada, and even then was not a proper noun. As a proper noun, it "is properly applied only to the Canadian Eskimos ... but excluding the Mackenzie Delta Inuvialuit."[12] The Committee for Original Peoples' Entitlement has explicitly rejected the appellation "Inuit" to designate the Inuvialuit of western Canada.[13] Other Canadian western arctic people, for instance, many Holman Islanders, have also rejected the term Inuit, and continue to identify themselves as Eskimo. Western Alaskans do not use "Inuit" as their own ethnic category on the grounds that they belong to the Yup'ik-speaking, not the Inuit/Inupiaq-speaking, branch of the Eskimoan linguistic family.

Aside from denying the self-designations of the Inuvialuit and of all non-Canadian Eskimos, the term Inuit is inadequate to describe the genetically and culturally related social groups who hold different nationalities. In northern Alaska, "Inupiaq" is the preferred term, both for the people and for their language. Since 1977, in a spirit of Pan-Eskimo cooperation following the Inuit Circumpolar Conference, the Inupiaq have increasingly used a hyphenated construction, "Inuit-Inupiaq," in verbal and written communications intended for international audiences. Locally, they continue to identify themselves as Inupiaq. Siberian Eskimo groups identify themselves locally as Chaplinski and Sirenikski, and collectively as Yuit, Yugyt, or Eskimosy.[14] "Eskimo" continues to be used by Greenlanders, Yuit, Yup'ik, Inupiaq, and Siberians, among others, as an overall designation for all speakers of Eskimoan languages, and for arctic peoples prior to the seventeenth century.

Problems of ethnic identification are not the only naming issue that faces arctic scholars. They, especially historians, also must deal with a people, or peoples, whose genetic inheritance has remained more or less constant for at least a thousand years, but whose economic and cultural institutions have changed several times during that period. The first people to hold an Eskimoan way of life emerged from an Asiatic Mongoloid ancestry in Siberia. They brought their arctic-adapted lifestyle to North America at least 4000, and possibly 5000, years ago. From them developed a number of cultural complexes that succeeded one another, and that were, to greater and lesser degrees, either culturally or biologically similar. In 1973 the Joint Project of the National Museums of Canada and the School of American Research adopted the term "paleoeskimo" to refer to all arctic occupations between 3000 BCE and 1000 CE. In the context of the Canadian arctic, all the cultural complexes subsumed under the term, including the Arctic Small Tool tradition and the Dorset, were *culturally* Eskimoan.[15] There is no evidence to suggest that ASTt or Dorset people spoke any Eskimoan language, and probably no way to find such evidence. We simply do not know anything about their language or languages. In addition, ASTt and Dorset people were not biologically ancestral to the Thule and Inuit peoples of the last 1000 years.

Shortly before 1000 CE, the Dorset disappeared, by assimilation or extermination, during the advance across North America of an invading people from Alaska, the Thule, also biological and cultural descendants of an Asiatic group. They have been categorized as the first of the Neo-Eskimo peoples. The Eskimoan peoples of Siberia, the Aleutian Islands, Bering Strait, and Alaska experienced similar histories. While the Thule were biologically ancestral to today's Inuit peoples, their descendents are socially, culturally, and economically very different. The only words that adequately subsume all the arctic peoples of the past, as well as all the related contemporary societies in Siberia, Alaska, Canada, and Greenland, are "Eskimo" and "Eskimoan."[16]

While it is illogical to use the term "Inuit" to describe Thule peoples and the social groups noted in the preceding paragraph, it is appropriate to use it in discussions of the inhabitants of Greenland and the Canadian eastern and central arctic since the seventeenth century. The differences between Thule and Inuit societies are clear. The Thule people of arctic Canada and Greenland were largely coast-dwelling people who occupied relatively large, permanent winter villages, and depended on whales as their chief resource. During the fifteenth, sixteenth, and seventeenth centuries, the Thule peoples of what are now Greenland and the central and eastern

Canadian arctic made enormous changes in their subsistence economies, territories, and sociocultural institutions, largely in response to climatic change. Their descendants of the eighteenth, nineteenth, and twentieth centuries were, and are, so different from their ancestors that they must be recognized as a new people. They are appropriately called Inuit.

The problem of naming is complicated to an even greater degree by the increasing use in both scholarly and popular works since 1970 of the designations Historic, Recent, and Modern Inuit to identify post-Thule peoples. While most work on arctic peoples hints at a distinction between Historic and Recent/Modern Inuit, the differences have never been clearly stated and the designations have not been defined. General meanings are, however, implicit in the way the terms have been used. "Historic Inuit" most often refers to post-Thule societies in which economic, demographic, social, and cultural change was self-directed. "Recent Inuit" or "Modern Inuit" are terms most often applied to people who experienced change through the coercive efforts of a permanent non-Inuit presence, and who have, since the early 1970s, been searching for ways to reclaim autonomy. A few studies have used the term "Government Era" to refer to the period of imposed change.

In scholarly studies, Eskimo and Eskimoan identify an ethno-linguistic category that includes Inupiaq-Inuktitut and Yup'ik speakers, as well as societies that "cannot specifically be affiliated with either language group" and which antedate the Historic Inuit period. They are the only words that identify precisely who is included and who is excluded. They include all the peoples of the circumpolar arctic who share certain genetic, linguistic, and cultural characteristics, their ancestors and their descendants, and they specifically exclude everybody else.[17]

Appendix 2

'Gerontocide' and 'Infanticide'

Some Eskimo and Inuit social behaviours, such as infanticide and gerontocide* have been characterized by some observers as cruel necessities that allowed people to survive in extremely hostile environments. Other

---

*Most scholarly literature uses the word "senilicide" to describe the killing of elderly members of the community. "Senilicide" carries with it the connotation of senility and mental incompetence. In my experience most aged people, whether Inuit or other, are neither senile nor mentally incompetent; they are just old. I prefer the more accurate word "gerontocide." But, as Appendix 2 is intended to make clear, gerontocide among Inuit does not actually involve killing.

observers have seen them as criminal and immoral. They were none of these things.

The 'gerontocide' myth sprang originally from the observations of European explorers that in their brief encounters with Inuit communities, they saw few old people. The absence of the elderly in situations the Inuit might well have considered dangerous does not mean there were no aged persons in the community; it might as easily have meant that members of the wisdom generation were so highly valued that they were hidden in places of safety. The myth was reinforced by accounts given by the Inuit themselves of having helped an elderly parent, grandparent, or seriously wounded companion to die. Assisted suicide at the behest of a suffering individual may be a question for public debate in some societies, but in others, including Inuit communities, it is an act of compassion toward a loved and valued companion.

The Inuit practice of 'leaving people to die' has been misunderstood by being taken out of context. At least one government official noted that in times of community stress, elderly people sometimes "*voluntarily* elect to be left to starve, or die of cold."[1] An observer in Labrador in the 1880s, while not disagreeing that voluntary election sometimes took place, had a more profound understanding. "At this time [of severe food shortage] the old and those weakened by starvation and unable to move from place to place were left to their fate, though should a party be so successful as to capture more than would supply their immediate wants they returned at once with food to those they had left behind."[2] My own discussions of this point with Leo Ussak at Rankin Inlet in the 1960s led me to believe that in times of crisis, when speed of travel is essential to the survival of the community, the strongest individuals often made the difficult decision to leave those who would slow them down, in order to make all possible speed to a source of relief. Among the many instances described in the documents of the Hudson's Bay Company and other observers, the stronger travellers invariably sent assistance, or returned themselves, as soon as they could, to rescue the weaker members. Sometimes, the return was too late to save all those who had been left, as happened just north of Churchill in 1844. In that instance a father and son arrived at the post, having left companions who were too weak to travel at about two days' journey to the north. When they returned with food and blankets, they found at least one member of their family dead, and another died within a few days of a rescue that came too late.[3] Occurrences of this nature were tragically frequent, but they are not gerontocide, abandonment, neglect, or in any way uncaring or abusive behaviour.

The idea that infanticide was routine among arctic peoples is also a mistaken one. Only one group of arctic dwellers, the Netsilik, seems to have institutionalized the practice, although other communities were, from time to time, forced to it by circumstances.

Both words—"infanticide" and "gerontocide"—are misnomers. Within the context of Inuit ideology, 'infanticide' and 'gerontocide' were logical and socially responsible acts, which did not involve killing.

The key to this paradox lies in the ancient Inuit ideology of existence. In the belief of most Inuit before their general conversion to Christianity, all living creatures (as well as some things considered by non-Inuit to be non-living things) were invested with souls. Souls were immortal, and capable of infinite reincarnation into new physical bodies.

In people, the soul resided for all eternity in the name, and was synonymous with it. At birth, a physical body was an empty shell, which, although it had the appearance of being human, did not yet contain an immortal soul-name, and was therefore not human. At death, a person's body again became an empty shell of no importance, while the soul-name continued to exist unseen by living human beings, as it had throughout all of time past. Where the soul-name existed when not dwelling in a body is unclear. It may have been in another realm, or it may simply have been in the realm where all existence takes place. Occasionally a soul-name made itself known to living people in a ghostly form.

Because soul was inherent in name, it would be difficult to overestimate the importance of personal names in Inuit religious and social life. The significance of names explains why Ikinnelik-Puhtoorak at Great Fish River in 1879 was able to tell Frederick Schwatka the name of the leader of a group of white men whom he had met as a small child more than forty years earlier. And why the woman who acted as navigator for Captain McClintock at Pond Inlet in 1858 was able to recall the name of an English sailor she had heard about who died at Igloolik in the early 1820s. She told McClintock that "one of the crew died, and was buried there, and his name was Al-lah or El-leh." McClintock checked up on her memory, and found that she had precise recall of names she had heard only briefly some thirty years earlier. In McClintock's words: "On referring to Parry's 'Narrative,' I found that the ice-mate, Mr. Elder, died at Igloolik!... The Esquimaux take considerable pains to learn, and remember names; this woman knows the names of several of the whaling captains and the old chief at De Ros Islet remembered Captain Inglefield's name, and tried hard to pronounce mine."[4]

According to Inuit understanding of the metaphysical world, death was of little importance, and certainly not the end for the soul-name. In this, ancient Inuit ideology was similar to Christian belief about death and the continued existence of the soul. However, in Inuit philosophy, a soul-name could be plucked from the death state and established in a new physical body at will. To put it another way, human life did not begin until the soul-name was breathed into the physical body.* The bringing together of a new physical body and an old soul-name was entirely at the discretion of the community.

Among the Netsilik, it was fairly common practice, as late as 1920, to withhold life and humanness from female bodies born in bad economic times; and among Netsilik many times were bad, or at least difficult. It was less common to withhold human existence from male bodies, which, if all went well, would eventually become valued hunters in the community, but it did happen. Most other Inuit groups experienced fewer occasions when a new life would place the entire community in jeopardy.

In Europe and North America today, there is considerable debate about when human life begins. The ancestors of today's Inuit accepted that human life begins when society says it does. And for them, it usually began on the third or fifth day after the appearance of a new physical body (depending on whether that body had the characteristics of a male or a female), at the moment when the community called an immortal soul-name to inhabit a newly born physical body and animate it with humanity and personality.

Another choice involving life and death, which had to be made by Inuit communities faced with resources too limited to sustain the entire community, was the decision to reduce the numbers of people in whom soul-names already resided. Close observers, such as Birket-Smith, Stefansson, Rasmussen, and Williamson, all fluent Inuktitut speakers, and Inuit informants themselves believe that in such crisis situations, elderly people were generally the first to offer to leave their bodies in order to enhance the survival chances of the rest of the community. Some of them deliberately placed their bodies in situations where death of the body would inevitably result, such as walking away from the village during a blizzard or remaining on an ice floe about to be swept out to sea. Some asked family members or community leaders to help them.

When help was given, it was not gerontocide, or assisted suicide, or even killing. It was simply the temporary withdrawal of a soul-name from a physical body. Those who assisted, or merely watched, were undoubtedly

---

*I cannot imagine a more literal acting out of the theological concept, "The Word Was Made Flesh."

grieved by the loss of parent, spouse, or companion, and comforted by the thought that the individual continued to exist at some other level. Similarly, to speak of infanticide is to give the wrong name to an act that did not, in Inuit ideology, involve the killing of a human being.

I would argue that most ideologies arise from one of two sources. Some are deliberately created by one group of people in order to control and manipulate another group. Others are intuitive and perhaps involuntary creations of society that serve to make reality more bearable. The ideology of the immortal soul-name and its constant reincarnation is one of the latter.

Appendix 3

Climatic Episodes and Arctic Human History

Most studies describing and sequencing past climates have been based on reconstructions of climatic events for northern Europe. The data is applicable to arctic regions in the western hemisphere, however. The marked and consistent congruence between the climatic trends of northern Canada-Iceland-Greenland and those of northwestern and central Europe over the last 7000 years has been amply demonstrated by Harvey Nichols, with the following caveat, noted by H.H. Lamb: the onset of cooling and warming trends in Greenland have sometimes been between 100 and 200 years earlier or later than in Europe. Among studies of North American past climates, the Mill Creek (Iowa) investigations of Reid Bryson, Thomas Murray, and David Baerreis confirmed that studies based on the parallelism of North American and European climatic episodes show a high degree of reliability over periods of more than a century.[1]

---

c. 7000 – 6000 BCE

Boreal Climatic Episode: global warming; North American ice sheets disappear[2]

Human History: North American arctic regions unoccupied

---

c. 6000 – c. 3000 BCE

Atlantic Climatic Episode: warmest postglacial period, also known as the Postglacial Climatic Optimum or Hypsithermal; most of the world about two degrees Celsius warmer than present; a brief colder period between about 3500 and 3000 BCE[3]

Human History: possible Paleo-Indian occupation of the central Canadian barren lands at the end of the period, or slightly later[4]

---

c. 3000 - c. 700 BCE

Sub-Boreal Climatic Episode: extremely variable climate, but with colder periods of a few centuries' duration[5]; southward movement of treeline, increase in precipitation, local glacial advance, decline in land animal populations, sea ice thicker and longer-lasting[6]

Human History:

2500-2000 BCE: emergence of Arctic Small Tool tradition, first Paleo-Eskimo occupation

2000-1000 BCE: emergence of a series of Paleo-Eskimo variants, and re-occupation of barren lands by Paleo-Indians

c. 1600 BCE: emergence of Paleo-Eskimo variants; 1600-1500 BCE: forest-tundra fire in central barren lands and withdrawal of Paleo-Indians[7]

1500-1000 BCE: expansion of Igloolik Paleo-Eskimo to Churchill and Upper Thelon River[8]; new pre-Dorset communities on western arctic coast[9]; Canadian tundra tradition[10]

1000 BCE: re-occupation of barren lands by Paleo-Indians, and withdrawal of Paleo-Eskimos to the north

1000-500 BCE: emergence of Dorset, appearance and disappearance of Dorset outliers; rapid culture change across arctic[11]

---

550 BCE - 400 CE

Sub-Atlantic Climatic Episode: significant global cooling, some glacier advance, probably mild winters and cooler summers; increased precipitation[12]

Human History: disappearance of Dorset outliers, re-occupation of barren lands by Paleo-Indians; significant population decrease in arctic; Dorset migrations from Baffin Island to Labrador and Newfoundland[13]

400 – 900 CE

Scandic Climatic Episode: mild cooling to about 800, then mild warming

Human History: expansions and florescence of Dorset at end of period[14]; Birnirk (north Alaska) people adapting to whale hunting, combined ice-lead whaling, sealing, and walrus hunting[15]

900 – 1250 CE

Neo-Atlantic Climatic Episode: pronounced warming throughout northern hemisphere; mean summer temperatures in northern Europe up by about two degrees Celcius; North American boreal forest about 100 km farther north, reduction of drift ice in North Atlantic, pack ice farther north, fewer seals and walrus near mainland coasts, Pacific whales entering Beaufort Sea and Amundsen Gulf[16]

Human History: whaling people from northern Alaska move east into arctic as far as Greenland; Dorset people experience environmental stress; Greenland Dorset migrate southward; Norse arrive in North America, establish Greenland colonies

1250 – 1550 CE

Pacific Climatic Episode: serious cooling, increased pack ice[17]

Human History: increased diversity of Thule communities in Amundsen Gulf, Foxe Basin, Hudson Bay, Baffin Bay, and Labrador; disappearance of Norse colonies from Greenland; expansion of Eskimoan people from northwest coast of Hudson Bay to Churchill River and subsequent retreat to Chesterfield Inlet; expansion from northeast coast of Hudson Bay to Eastmain River and subsequent retreat to northern Ungava Peninsula; abandonment of Somerset Island; migration from south Baffin Island to the Labrador coast

---

1550 - 1850 CE

Neo-Boreal Climatic Episode, Little Ice Age: severe climatic deterioration; glacial advance, sea temperatures to three degrees lower, pack ice extending into North Atlantic and eastward flow of Atlantic Drift; changes in whale migration routes in the west; 1645-1715 First Maunder Minimum; 1790-1830 Second Maunder Minimum; 1816, The Year with No Summer

Human History: cultural variation highly evident across the arctic; Thule whale-hunting lifestyle disappears and Historic Inuit emerge; subsistence economies increasingly diverse; first encounters with Europeans, and great changes in indigenous social, economic, and cultural complexes of indigenous arctic peoples

Endnotes

Abbreviations

HBCA: Hudson's Bay Company Archives

HBRS: Hudson's Bay Record Society

PAM: Provincial Archives of Manitoba

Front Matter

1. Aua, at Lyon Inlet. In Knud Rasmussen, *Report of the Fifth Thule Expedition, 1921-24*, vol. 7: 1, *Intellectual Culture of the Iglulik Eskimos* (1929), 56.

Preface

1. Stuart E. Jenness, Preface and Prologue, in *Arctic Odyssey: The Diary of Diamond Jenness* (1991), xxx.

2. For authors of some of the many studies done, see Bibliography under Bird, Clark, Collins, Dumond, Fitzhugh, Gordon, Harp, Hickey, Linnamae, Maxwell, McCartney, McCullough, McGhee, Meldgaard, D. Morrison, Nash, Savelle, Schledermann, Spiess, W.E. Taylor, J.V. Wright, and Yorga. A few of the institutions that supported archaeological research were The Arctic Institute of North America, National Museums of Canada, The Royal Ontario Museum, The Smithsonian Institution, The American Museum of Natural History, *Meddelelser om Grønland*, and various universities.

3. For broad surveys of Dorset occupation, see Bibliography under Maxwell; for archaeological studies of the pre-1800 period, see McGhee; and for more geographically limited investigations see Brenda Clark, and McCartney. Western arctic coast peoples have been investigated by David Morrison. For the eastern high arctic, see Karen M. McCullough. For the archaeology of Labrador peoples, see entries under Fitzhugh, Kaplan, and J. Garth Taylor.

4. The *Handbook of North American Indians*, vol. 5, *The Arctic* (1984) summarized anthropological research and conclusions prior to 1984 in chapters by a number of arctic specialists, and contains a comprehensive bibliography of earlier works. Morris Zaslow's histories of the Canadian arctic, *The Opening of the Canadian North, 1870-*

1914 (1971) and *The Northern Expansion of Canada, 1914-1967* (1988), are narrowly focussed on the activities of non-Inuit in the north since Confederation. Two, more recent, publications, Olive Dickason's *Canada's First Nations* (1992) and Arthur J. Ray's *I Have Lived Here Since the World Began* (1996), are welcome works of synthesis and survey in aboriginal history. Neither, however, deals with Inuit except by passing reference. Two authors, Guy Mary-Rousselière and Ernest S. Burch, are exceptions; both have produced works that focus on the self-directed activities of Inuit peoples, rather than on their responses to European actions.

5. Raymond D. Fogelson, The ethnohistory of events and nonevents, *Ethnohistory* 36, no. 2 (Spring 1989): 134.

6. Histories of indigenous societies that serve as models for a multidisciplinary approach to evidence include Ernest S. Burch's reconstruction of the seventeenth-century peopling of the Keewatin, in Caribou Eskimo origins: an old problem reconsidered (1978), and The Thule-Historic Eskimo transition on the west coast of Hudson Bay (1979); Guy Mary-Rousselière's studies of nineteenth-century Inuit migrations from Baffin Island: Eskimo migrations (1959), The Paleoeskimo in northern Baffinland (1976), The Thule culture of northern Baffin Island (1979), and *Qitdlarssuaq: The Story of a Polar Migration* (1991); and Bruce Trigger's *The Huron: Farmers of the North* (1969), and *The Children of Aataentsic: A History of the Huron People to 1660* (1976).

7. James Axtell, The ethnohistory of early America: a review essay, *The William and Mary Quarterly* 35, no. 4 (1978): 118-19.

8. Ibid., 119. The same general point was made by Ernest S. Burch in The Thule-Historic Eskimo transition on the west coast of Hudson Bay, 190; and by William W. Fitzhugh, A comparative approach to northern maritime adaptations (1975). Rather less succinctly, but more demonstrably, Fernand Braudel devoted three volumes to the same idea in *The Mediterranean and the Mediterranean World in the Age of Philip II* (1976-1981).

9. Eleanor Leacock, Comments on symposium, *Ethnohistory* 8 (1961): 256-59.

10. Catalysts for change have been identified as: environmental pressures, including disease (Bryson & Murray 1977; Claiborne 1970; Crosby 1986; Lamb 1972, 1982, 1988; McGhee 1972; McNeill 1989); the discovery of new resources and the creation of new technologies (Bernard & Pelto 1972; Burke 1985; Crosby 1972, 1986, 1997; Diamond 1997); contact between societies, both peaceful and violent, and the subsequent introduction of technological innovations and new ideas (Helm 1968); the internal emergence of new religions and ideas through the influence of charismatic leaders (Mary-Rousselière 1991); and the human urge to satisfy particular needs within specific environments (Fischer 1981; Maslow 1973; W.E. Taylor 1963, 1966). Speculations about *how* societies change also abound, including hypotheses about optimal foraging (Nudds 1988; Winterhalder and Smith 1981); time-stability (Hardesty 1980); evolutionary ecology (E.A. Smith 1991); and cultural ecology (Binford 1978; Hodder 1986; Steward 1955). Comparative studies that both generate and test theories of change and continuity have appeared in a number of works dealing with the origins and cultural meanings of war (R.B. Ferguson 1984; Keeley 1996); the range of economic strategies (Halstead & O'Shea 1989; Halstead et al. 1984); the causes and implementation of migration and abandonment of territory

(Cameron & Tomka 1993); the social uses of information (Miracle et al. 1991); and social strategies for ensuring survival (Laughlin & Brady 1978).

11. Moreau S. Maxwell, Introduction, in *Eastern Arctic Prehistory: Paleoeskimo Problems* (1976), 1.

12. Burch, The Thule-Historic Eskimo transition on the west coast of Hudson Bay, in *Thule Eskimo Culture: An Anthropological Retrospective* (1979), 190.

13. Marc Stevenson, *Inuit Whalers and Cultural Persistence* (1997), xxi, 16-22; 301-305.

14. Lionel Gossman, *Towards a Rational Historiography*, vol. 79, part 3, no. 1, *Transactions of the American Philosophical Society* (1989).

Introduction

1. The chronology of the Icelandic sagas suggests the year was 982 CE.

2. Henrik M. Jansen, A critical account of the written and archaeological sources' evidence concerning the Norse settlements in Greenland, *Meddelelser om Grønland* 182, no. 4 (1972).

3. The Augsburg version of the handbill appears, with an English translation, in William C. Sturtevant, The first Inuit depiction by Europeans, *Études/Inuit/Studies* 4 (1980): 38-50.

4. Joyce Appleby et al., *Telling the Truth about History* (1994), 307.

5. Ann Fienup-Riordan, *Eskimo Essays: Yup'ik Lives and How We See Them* (1990), 44.

6. Ikinilik. In Knud Rasmussen, *Report of the Fifth Thule Expedition, 1921-24*, vol. 8, *The Netsilik Eskimos, Social Life and Spiritual Culture* (1931), 501.

Chapter 1

1. Knud Rasmussen, *Report of the Fifth Thule Expedition, 1921-24*, vol. 7: 1, *Intellectual Culture of the Iglulik Eskimos* (1929), 41-42.

2. Don E. Dumond, *The Eskimos and Aleuts* (1977); Robert McGhee, The peopling of the arctic islands, in *Canada's Missing Dimension: Science and History in the Canadian Arctic Islands*, vol. 2 (1990), 667.

3. The Sub-Boreal Climatic Episode lasted from around 3000 BCE to 700 BCE. For further discussion of the climatic episode see H.H. Lamb, *Climate, History and the Modern World* (1982), 121-22; H. H. Lamb, *Weather, Climate & Human Affairs: A Book of Essays and Other Papers* (1988), 87; and A.A. Dekin, Climatic change and cultural change: a correlative study from eastern arctic prehistory, *Polar Notes* 12 (1972): 15.

Paleo-Indian use of tundra lands during the period is described in William C. Noble, Archaeological surveys and sequences in Central District Mackenzie, N.W.T., *Arctic Anthropology* 8 (1971); Elmer Harp, *The Archaeology of the Lower and Middle Thelon, Northwest Territories* (1961); W.N. Irving, Prehistory of Hudson Bay: the barren grounds, *Science, History and Hudson Bay* 1 (1968): 26-54; Robert McGhee, Climatic change and the development of Canadian arctic cultural traditions, in *Climatic Changes in Arctic Areas During the Last Ten-Thousand Years* (1971); McGhee, The peopling of the arctic islands, 667.

4. For studies establishing the Siberian origins of the Arctic Small Tool tradition, see Emöke Szathmary, Blood groups of Siberians, Eskimos, and subarctic and northwest

coast Indians: the problem of origins and genetic relations, in *The First Americans: Origins, Affinities and Adaptations* (1979); Szathmary, Genetic markers in Siberian and northern North American populations, *Yearbook of Physical Anthropology* 24 (1981): 37–73; Szathmary, Human biology of the arctic, in *Handbook of North American Indians*, vol. 5, *Arctic* (1984), 64–71; Szathmary, Peopling of North America: clues from genetic studies, in *Out of Asia: Peopling the Americas and the Pacific* (1985), 77–100; Brian Fagan, *The Great Journey: The Peopling of Ancient America* (1987), 120–21; McGhee, The peopling of the arctic islands, 667.

For archaeological evidence of expansion of ASTt people across the arctic, see Dumond, *The Eskimos and Aleuts* (1977); W.N. Irving, The Arctic Small Tool tradition, *VIIIth International Congress of Anthropological and Ethnological Sciences* 3 (1970), 340–42; Robert McGhee, *Canadian Arctic Prehistory* (1978), 23–24; Robert McGhee, A current interpretation of central Canadian arctic prehistory, *Inter-Nord* nos. 13–14 (December 1974): 172; McGhee, The peopling of the arctic islands, 667.

5. See Douglas Anderson, A stone age campsite at the gateway to America, *Scientific American* 218 (June 1968): 24–33; Fagan, *The Great Journey*; McGhee, The peopling of the arctic islands, 667.

6. Each new variant, or apparent variant, was given a unique name by its discoverer. For descriptions of Independence I, Independence II, Sarqaq, Canadian Tundra, Pre-Dorset, Dorset, Carlsberg, Buchanan Complex, Aurora River Complex, and others, see William Fitzhugh, Paleo-Eskimo cultures of Greenland, in *Handbook of North American Indians*, vol. 5, *Arctic* (1984), 529–30; Eigil Knuth, *Archaeology of the Musk-Ox Way* (1967); McGhee, A current interpretation of central Canadian arctic prehistory, 172–73; McGhee, Paleoeskimo occupations of central and high arctic Canada, in *Eastern Arctic Prehistory: Paleoeskimo Problems* (1976) 15–39; McGhee, *Canadian Arctic Prehistory*, 32–36; McGhee, The Norse in North America, in *The Vikings and Their Predecessors* (1981), 56–60; Moreau S. Maxwell, Pre-Dorset and Dorset Prehistory of Canada, in *Handbook of North American Indians*, vol. 5, *Arctic* (1984), 359; Noble, Archaeological surveys and sequences; W.E. Taylor, Summary of archaeological field work on Banks and Victoria Islands, Arctic Canada, *Arctic Anthropology* 4, no. 1 (1967): 221–43; Christian Vibe, Arctic animals in relation to climatic fluctuations, *Meddelelser om Grønland* 170, no. 5 (1967): 153. For details of the Joint Project, see Moreau S. Maxwell, Introduction, in *Eastern Arctic Prehistory: Paleoeskimo Problems, Memoirs of the Society for American Archaeology* #31. (1976).

7. Weston Blake, *End Moraines and Deglaciation Chronology in Northern Canada with Special Reference to Southern Baffin Island* (1966).

8. Ronald Nash, *The Arctic Small Tool Tradition in Manitoba* (1969); Nash, Dorset culture in northeastern Manitoba, Canada, *Arctic Anthropology* 9, no. 1 (1972): 10–16; Nash, Cultural systems and culture change in the central arctic, in *Eastern Arctic Prehistory: Paleoeskimo Problems* (1976), 150–55.

9. Jorgen Meldgaard, Origin and evolution of Eskimo cultures in the eastern arctic, *Canadian Geographic Journal* 60, no. 2 (1960): 75; Maxwell, Introduction, in *Eastern Arctic Prehistory*; Maxwell, Pre-Dorset and Dorset Prehistory of Canada, 359–68.

10. Maxwell, Introduction, in *Eastern Arctic Prehistory*, 3.

11. Dorset occupations in Dolphin and Union Strait are described in: Noble, Archaeological surveys and sequences; Robert McGhee, Excavations at Bloody Falls,

N.W.T., Canada, *Arctic Anthropology* 6, no. 2 (1970): 53-73; McGhee, A current interpretation of central Canadian arctic prehistory, 175. Dorset occupations of the west coast of Hudson Bay as far south as Churchill are described in Nash, Dorset culture in northeastern Manitoba, Canada. Labrador and Newfoundland Dorset archaeology has been investigated and described by Elmer Harp, *The Cultural Affinities of the Newfoundland Dorset Eskimo* (1964); and Urve Linnamae, *The Dorset Culture: A Comparative Study in Newfoundland and the Arctic* (1975).

12. McGhee, Paleoeskimo occupations of central and high arctic Canada, 29.

13. Maxwell, Introduction, in *Eastern Arctic Prehistory*, 5.

14. Reid A. Bryson and W.M. Wendland, Tentative climatic patterns for some late glacial and post-glacial episodes in central North America, in *Life, Land and Water* (1967).

15. J.V. Wright, *The Aberdeen Site, Keewatin District, N.W.T.* (1972); J.V. Wright, *The Grant Lake Site, Keewatin District* (1976).

16. McGhee, The peopling of the arctic islands, 671.

17. Charles D. Arnold and Karen McCullough, Thule pioneers in the Canadian arctic, in *Canada's Missing Dimension: Science and History in the Canadian Arctic Islands* (1990), 678.

18. Robert Claiborne, *Climate, Man and History* (1970), 356.

19. Else Roesdahl, *The Vikings* (1987), 271-73.

20. R.R. Milton Freeman, Arctic ecosystems, in *Handbook of North American Indians*, vol. 5, *Arctic* (1984), 42.

21. Allen P. McCartney, *Thule Eskimo Prehistory Along Northwestern Hudson Bay* (1977), 23; Robert McGhee, Speculations on climatic change and Thule culture development, *Folk* 11/12 (1970).

22. Moreau S. Maxwell, *Prehistory of the Eastern Arctic* (1985), 249-50.

23. Dorset-type subsistence is also known as 'Netsilik-type hunting' or 'Netsilik adaptive pattern' by arctic scholars when referring to hunter-gatherer communities that use a variety of resources in different locations at different times of the year. The name was derived from the observations of Knud Rasmussen (1931) and identified as one of five basic models of arctic cultural ecology by the Oulanka-Kevo Conference on Climatic Changes in Arctic Areas During the Last Ten-thousand Years. See conference proceedings in Y. Vasari, ed., *Climatic Changes in Arctic Areas During the Last Ten-Thousand Years* (1972).

24. McGhee, The peopling of the arctic islands, 672.

25. Rasmussen, *Report of the Fifth Thule Expedition, 1921-24*, vol. 7: 1, 256-57.

26. Franz Boas, *The Central Eskimo* ([1888] 1964), 634-36.

27. Knud Rasmussen, *Report of the Fifth Thule Expedition, 1921-24*, vol. 8: 1-2, *The Netsilik Eskimos, Social Life and Spiritual Culture* (1931), 113, 116, 425-26.

28. Therkel Mathiassen, *Report of the Fifth Thule Expedition, 1921-24*, vol. 4, *Archaeology of the Central Eskimos II: Analytical Part* (1927); G.I. Quimby, The Manitunik culture of east Hudson Bay, *American Antiquity* 6, no. 2 (1940): 148; Henry B. Collins, Vanished mystery men of Hudson Bay, *National Geographic* 110 (1956); William E. Taylor, Hypotheses on the origin of Canadian Thule culture, *American Antiquity* 28 (1963): 4;

William E. Taylor, The Arnapik and Tyara sites: an archaeological study of Dorset culture origins, *Memoirs of the Society for American Archaeology* #22 (1968); Peter Schledermann, *Thule Eskimo Prehistory of Cumberland Sound, Baffin Island, Canada* (1975), 11-12.

29. John Kirtland Wright, *Human Nature in Geography: Fourteen Papers, 1925-1965* (1966), 203.

30. Robert H. Claxton, Climate and history: the state of the field, in *Environmental History: Critical Issues in Comparative Perspective* (1985), 104.

31. Lucien Febvre, *A Geographical Introduction to History* (1932).

32. Joseph Petulla, Environmental values: the problem of method in environmental history, in *Environmental History: Critical Issues in Comparative Perspective* (1985), 43.

33. Ibid.

34. David Hackett Fischer, Climate and history: priorities for research, in *Climate and History: Studies in Interdisciplinary History* (1981), 248.

35. McGhee, *Canadian Arctic Prehistory*, 113-15; W.E. Taylor, Pre-Dorset occupations at Ivugivik in northwestern Ungava, in *Prehistoric Cultural Relations Between the Arctic and Temperate Zones of North America* (1962), 80-91.

36. James Savelle and Allen P. McCartney, Geographical and temporal variation in Thule Eskimo subsistence and economies: a model, *Research in Economic Anthropology* 10 (1988): 67.

37. Changes in whale habitats are discussed in Peter Schledermann, The effect of climatic/ecological changes on the style of Thule culture winter dwellings, *Arctic and Alpine Research* 8, no. 1 (1976): 41. Habits of Boothia Peninsula caribou herds are discussed in Savelle and McCartney, Geographical and temporal variation in Thule Eskimo subsistence and economies, 35, 62, 66-67.

38. Thule subsistence in Somerset Island is discussed in Savelle and McCartney, Geographical and temporal variation in Thule Eskimo subsistence and economies, 46, 66. For evidence of abandonment of Somerset Island, see McGhee, Speculations on climatic change and Thule culture development.

39. H.H. Lamb, Climate changes and food production: observations and outlook in the modern world, *Geo-Journal* [Weisbaden] 5, no. 2 (1981): 323.

40. David Morrison places the abandonment between 1400 and 1450; Robert McGhee dates it to the early 1400s; and Harvey Nichols suggests the mid-1500s. See Morrison, *Iglulualumiut Prehistory: The Lost Inuit of Franklin Bay* (1990), 116; McGhee, *Copper Eskimo Prehistory* (1972); Nichols, *Palynological and Paleoclimatic Study of the Late Quaternary Displacement of the Boreal Forest-Tundra Ecotone in Keewatin and Mackenzie, N.W.T., Canada* (1975).

41. L.D. Williams, An energy balance model of potential glacierization of northern Canada, *Arctic and Alpine Research* 11 (1979).

42. William Fitzhugh, Indian and Eskimo/Inuit settlement history in Labrador: an archaeological view, in *Our Footprints Are Everywhere: Inuit Land Use and Occupancy in Labrador* (1977), 3.

43. Christian Vibe, Arctic animals in relation to climatic fluctuations, *Meddelelser om Grønland* 170, no. 5 (1967): 96-97.

44. Mathiassen, *Report of the Fifth Thule Expedition, 1921-24*, vol. 4.

45. Patrick Plumet, Thuléens et Dorsetiens dans l'Ungava (Nouveau-Quebec), in *Thule Eskimo Culture: An Anthropological Retrospective* (1979), 111.

46. Ibid., 110, 112.

47. McGhee, *Canadian Arctic Prehistory*, 105.

48. Don E. Dumond, Eskimo-Indian relationships: a view from prehistory, *Arctic Anthropology* 16, no. 2 (1979): 8; also William Fitzhugh, Early contacts north of Newfoundland before A.D. 1600: a review, in *Cultures in Contact: The Impact of European Contacts on Native American Cultural Institutions, A.D. 1000-1800* (1985), 25-26.

49. Locations of site-specific copper and iron deposits were identified in Allen P. McCartney and D.J. Mack, Iron utilization by Thule Eskimos of central Canada, *American Antiquity* 38, no. 3 (1973): 336; also see McCartney and Mack, p. 329, for their study of meteoritic iron origins and trade. For trade routes, see Mathiassen, *Report of the Fifth Thule Expedition, 1921-24*, vol. 4, *Archaeology of the Central Eskimos II*, 25, 82-83; Henry B. Collins, Excavations at Thule culture sites near Resolute Bay, Cornwallis Island, N.W.T., *Annual Report of the National Museum of Canada for 1949-50*, Bulletin #123 (1951), 51; and R. Cole Harris, *Historical Atlas of Canada*, vol. 1, *From the Beginning to 1800* (1987), plate 14.

50. The pendant is described by Elmer Harp, A late Dorset copper amulet from southeastern Hudson Bay, *Folk* 16 (1974). European items in Greenland Thule sites are noted by Finn Gad, *The History of Greenland*, vol. 1, *Earliest Times to 1700* (1970), 161, 183-216. Trade routes are mapped in R. Cole Harris, *Historical Atlas of Canada*, vol. 1, plate 14. Movement of European whaling vessels into North American waters is in G.M. Asher, *Henry Hudson, the Navigator; from the Original Documents* ... (1860), xcvi, clxxi.

51. Harris, *Historical Atlas of Canada*, vol. 1, plate 14; McCartney and Mack, Iron utilization by Thule Eskimos of central Canada, 331, 336; Mathiassen, *Report of the Fifth Thule Expedition, 1921-24*, vol. 4, 82-83; Moreau S. Maxwell, *An Archaeological Analysis of Eastern Grant Land, Ellesmere Island, Northwest Territories* (1960), 87; J.V. Wright, *Thule Eskimo Prehistory Along Northwestern Hudson Bay* (1977), 81.

52. McCartney and Mack, Iron utilization by Thule Eskimos of central Canada, 329; Wendell H. Oswalt, *Eskimos and Explorers* (1979), 279-80.

53. Observed during first Frobisher expedition in 1576. George Best, *A True Discourse of the Late Voyages of Discoverie, for the Finding of a Passage to Cathaia*. New edition trans. and ed. Walter A. Kenyon, *Tokens of Possession: The Voyages of Martin Frobisher* ([1578] 1975), 116.

54. McGhee, *Copper Eskimo Prehistory*, 19; McGhee, *Canadian Arctic Prehistory*, 103-17.

55. McGhee, *Canadian Arctic Prehistory*, 11.

56. Ibid., 109.

57. Fitzhugh, Indian and Eskimo/Inuit settlement history in Labrador, 3.

58. McGhee, *Canadian Arctic Prehistory*, 108.

59. J.G. Taylor, Demography and adaptations of eighteenth-century Eskimo groups in northern Labrador and Ungava, in *Prehistoric Maritime Adaptations of the Circumpolar Zone* (1975).

60. John D. Jacobs and George Sabo, Environments and adaptations of the Thule culture on the Davis Strait coast of Baffin Island, *Arctic and Alpine Research* 10, no. 3 (1978): 608, 612.

61. Best, *A True Discourse*, 113.

62. Jacobs and Sabo, Environments and adaptations of the Thule culture, 605-06.

63. Best, *A True Discourse*, 89.

64. McGhee, *Canadian Arctic Prehistory*, 86.

65. H.H. Lamb, *The Changing Climate* (1966), 65.

66. John T. Andrews, Radiocarbon dating obtained through geographical branch field observation, *Geographical Bulletin* 9, no. 2 (1967): 39.

67. Williams, An energy balance model of potential glacierization of northern Canada.

68. P. Bergthorssen, An estimate of drift ice and temperature in Iceland in 1000 years, *Jokull: Journal of the Icelandic Glaciological Society* 19 (1969): 98; Reid A. Bryson and Thomas J. Murray, *Climates of Hunger: Mankind and the World's Changing Weather* (1977), 77.

69. Jean M. Grove, *The Little Ice Age* (1988), 417-18; H.H. Lamb, Climatic variations and changes in the wind and ocean circulation: the Little Ice Age in the northeast Atlantic, *Quaternary Research* 11 (1979): 15.

70. Peter Schledermann, *Thule Eskimo Prehistory of Cumberland Sound*, 255-56.

71. Erik Holtved, Archaeological investigations in the Thule District, parts I and II, *Meddelelser om Grønland* 146, no. 3 (1944): 177-80; Gwyn Jones, *The Norse Atlantic Saga: Being the Norse Voyages of Discovery and Settlement to Iceland, Greenland, America* (1964), 59; H.H. Lamb, *Climate: Present, Past and Future*, vol. 2, *Climatic History and the Future* (1977), 461-73.

72. Dekin, Climatic change and cultural change: a correlative study, 12.

73. Ester Boserup, *The Conditions of Agricultural Growth* (1965); R. Brian Ferguson, Introduction: studying war, in *Warfare, Culture, and Environment* (1984), 55; Barbara J. Price, Shifts of production and organization: a cluster-interaction model, *Current Anthropology* 18 (1977); Barbara J. Price, Competition, productive intensification, and ranked society: speculations from evolutionary theory, in *Warfare, Culture, and Environment* (1984), 211.

74. Price, Competition, productive intensification, and ranked society.

Chapter 2

1. Vilhjalmur Stefansson, *The Friendly Arctic: The Story of Five Years in Polar Regions* ([1921] 1943), 426.

2. Robert McGhee, *Canadian Arctic Prehistory* (1978), 99.

3. George Best, *A True Discourse of the Late Voyages of Discoverie, for the Finding of a Passage to Cathaia*. New edition trans. and ed. Walter A. Kenyon, *Tokens of Possession: The Voyages of Martin Frobisher* ([1578] 1975), 40, 59.

4. Ibid., 40.

5. Luke Foxe, *North-West Fox, or Fox from the North-West Passage*, in *The Voyages of Captain Luke Foxe of Hull, and Captain Thomas James of Bristol, in Search of Northwest Passage in 1631-32* ([1635] 1894), 42.

6. Best, *A True Discourse*, 40.

7. Foxe, *North-West Fox*, 42.

8. Best, *A True Discourse*, 41.

9. Charles Francis Hall, *Life with the Esquimaux: A Narrative of Arctic Experience in Search of Survivors of Sir John Franklin's Expedition* ([1864-66] 1970), 247.

10. Best, *A True Discourse of the Late Voyages of Discoverie, for the Finding of a Passage to Cathaia, by the Northwest, Under the Conduct of Martin Frobisher, General, Divided into Three Bookes*, 1578, Early English Books Before 1640 microfilm series, reel 196, 50.

11. William C. Sturtevant and David Beers Quinn, This new prey: Eskimos in Europe in 1567, 1576, and 1577, in *Indians and Europe: An Interdisciplinary Collection of Essays* (1987), 72.

12. Best, *A True Discourse*, 51.

13. Ibid., 52.

14. Ibid., 56.

15. Ibid., 58, 62, 59.

16. Ibid., 59.

17. Ibid., 63-64.

18. Vilhjalmur Stefansson, *The Three Voyages of Martin Frobisher in Search of a Passage to Cathay and India by the North-West, A.D. 1576-8. From the Original 1578 Text of George Best, Together with Numerous Other Versions, Additions, etc*, vol.1 (1938), 161.

19. Best, *A True Discourse,* 63-64, 66.

20. Ibid., 67, 68.

21. Ibid., 68-69.

22. Ibid.

23. Neil Cheshire et al., Frobisher's Eskimos in England, in *Indians and Europe: An Interdisciplinary Collection of Essays* (1987), 36, 37-38.

24. Best, *A True Discourse*, 106; Edward Fenton, The Canadian arctic journal of Captain Edward Fenton, *Archivaria* 11 (1981): 194-95.

25. Fenton, The Canadian arctic journal of Captain Edward Fenton, 198.

26. John Janes, The first voyage of Captain John Davis of Sandruge in Devonshire 1585 to the North-West, in Foxe, ed., facsimile edition (1965), 35. Accounts of the three Davis voyages were written by the English merchant John Janes, who accompanied Davis, and originally published by Richard Hakluyt, London (1589). In 1635, when Luke Foxe published the narrative of his 1631 voyage to Hudson Bay, he included Janes's diaries.

27. Ibid., 36.

28. Peter Schledermann, *Thule Eskimo Prehistory of Cumberland Sound, Baffin Island, Canada* (1975), 20.

29. Janes, The first voyage of Captain John Davis, 37.

30. Ibid., 38.

31. Ibid., 38, 39.

32. Ibid., 41.

33. Ibid., 43-44.

34. Ibid., 35, 38.

35. Schledermann, *Thule Eskimo Prehistory of Cumberland Sound*, 257.

36. John Knight and Oliver Brownel, *Journal of the Voyage of John Knight to Seek the North-West Passage 1606*, ed. Clement R. Markham ([1877], facsimile edition 1965), 291. After Knight's death at Cape Grimington in 1606, Oliver Brownel (or Brunel) kept *Hopewell's* log. It was included by Luke Foxe in *North-West Fox from the North-West Passage*.

37. Ibid., 293.

38. Ibid.

39. Abacuck Prickett, A large discourse of the said Voyage, and the success thereof, written by Abacuk Pricket, who lived to come home, in *North-West Fox,* 152.

40. Ibid., 153.

41. Ibid., 154-55.

42. Miller Christy, ed., *The Voyages of Captain Luke Foxe of Hull and Captain Thomas James of Bristol in Search of Northwest Passage in 1631-32* (1894), 162, 164; Foxe, *North-West Fox*, 119.

43. Foxe, *North-West Fox,* 139-40.

44. Jens Munk, *The Journal of Jens Munk, 1619-1620* (1980), 9-10 (originally published in *Danish Arctic Expeditions, 1605 to 1620*, ed. C.C.A. Gosch, 1897).

45. Foxe, *North-West Fox*, 43.

46. Ernest S. Burch, War and trade, in *Crossroads of Continents: Cultures of Siberia and Alaska* (1988), 229.

47. Frederica de Laguna, *Under Mount Saint Elias: The History and Culture of the Yakutat Tlingit* (1972), 257; R. Brian Ferguson, A reexamination of the causes of Northwest Coast warfare, in *Warfare, Culture, and Environment* (1984), 274.

48. Nelson H.H. Graburn and R. Stephen Strong, *Circumpolar Peoples: An Anthropological Perspective* (1973), 121; also Ann Fienup-Riordan, *Eskimo Essays: Yup'ik Lives and How We See Them* (1990), 157.

49. On Yup'ik warfare, see Fienup-Riordan, *Eskimo Essays,* 160. On Inupiat hostilities, see Burch, War and trade, 229; and Ernest S. Burch and Thomas C. Correll, Alliance and conflict: inter-regional alliance in north Alaska, in *Alliance in Eskimo Society* (1972), 33.

50. Ernest S. Burch, Eskimo warfare in northwest Alaska, *Anthropological Papers of the University of Alaska* 16 (1974): 2, 8-10; Burch, War and trade, 231; Edward W. Nelson, The Eskimo about Bering Strait, in *Eighteenth Annual Report of the Bureau of American Ethnology for the Years 1896-1897* ([1899] 1984), 327-30.

51. Nelson, The Eskimo about Bering Strait, 327.

52. Burch, Eskimo warfare in northwest Alaska.

53. Ibid., 10.

54. Ibid., 8, 9, 11; Fienup-Riordan, *Eskimo Essays*, 158-60; Burch, War and trade, 231.

55. Fienup-Riordan, *Eskimo Essays*, 158.

56. On Yup'ik tattooing, see Fienup-Riordan, *Eskimo Essays*, 159-60; on Hudson Strait tattooing, see HBCA, PAM, Little Whale River Post Journals, B373/a/3:93d; and F.F. Payne, *Eskimo of Hudson's Strait, Extract from Proceedings of the Canadian Institute*, series 3, vol. 6 (1889), 11.

57. Burch, War and trade, 234.

58. Burch, Eskimo warfare in northwest Alaska, 2, 4; Dorothy Jean Ray, Land tenure and polity of the Bering Strait Eskimos, *Journal of the West* (1967): 374; E. Weyer, *The Eskimos: Their Environment and Folkways* (1962), 157.

59. The prevalence of interpersonal violence, as distinct from war, in Eskimo and Inuit societies is noted by Asen Balikci, *The Netsilik Eskimo* (1970), 173-82, and Margaret Mead, Warfare is only an invention, in *War: Studies from Psychology, Sociology, Anthropology* (1964), 270. Denials of Inuit warfare appear in E. Adamson Hoebel, *The Law of Primitive Man: A Study in Comparative Legal Dynamics* (1961); in Mead, Warfare is only an invention, and Margaret Mead, Alternatives to war, in *War: The Anthropology of Armed Conflict and Aggression* (1968); also William Graham Sumner, War, in *War: Studies from Psychology, Sociology, Anthropology* (1964).

60. Lawrence H. Keeley, *War Before Civilization* (1996), 113.

61. R. Brian Ferguson, Introduction: studying war, in *Warfare, Culture, and Environment* (1984), 3-5.

62. Keeley, *War Before Civilization*, 29.

63. Ferguson, Introduction: studying war, 5.

64. Burch, Eskimo warfare in northwest Alaska; Burch, War and trade; Fienup-Riordan, *Eskimo Essays*; Daniel Francis and Toby Morantz, *Partners in Furs: A History of the Fur Trade in Eastern James Bay, 1600-1870* (1983); Marvin Harris, *Cannibals and Kings* (1991); Victor Lytwyn, Distant enemies: the Inuit, Chipewyan and Iroquois, in *The Hudson Bay Lowland Cree in the Fur Trade to 1821: A Study in Historical Geography* (1993), 154.

65. Battle armour is discussed in Burch, War and trade, 227, 230; and in Fienup-Riordan, *Eskimo Essays*, 156. Ancient battlefields are discussed in Knud Rasmussen, *Across Arctic America* (1927).

66. Fienup-Riordan, *Eskimo Essays*, 153, 156.

67. McGhee, *Canadian Arctic Prehistory*, 87.

68. Harris, *Cannibals and Kings*; and R. Brian Ferguson, ed., *Warfare, Culture, and Environment* (1984).

69. Burch, Eskimo warfare in northwest Alaska, 8; Burch and Correll, Alliance and conflict, 24; David Riches, *Northern Nomadic Hunter-Gatherers: A Humanistic Approach* (1982), 71; Bernard Saladin d'Anglure, L'Organisation sociale traditionelle des Esquimaux de Kangirsujuaak (Nouveau-Québec), *Centre d'Études Nordique Travaux* 17 (1967): 148; Sumner, War, 210.

70. Stefansson, *The Friendly Arctic*, 426.

71. Susan Rowley, Population movements in the Canadian arctic, *Études/Inuit/Studies*, no. 1 (1985): 16-17.

72. Balikci, *The Netsilik Eskimo*, 183; HBCA, PAM, Churchill Post Journals, B42/a/41:14; Frederick Schwatka, *The Long Arctic Search: the Narrative of Lieutenant Frederick Schwatka, U.S.A., 1878-1880...*, ed. E.A. Stackpole ([1880] 1965), 66.

73. Burch, War and trade, 234.

74. Gert Nooter, *Old Kayaks in The Netherlands* (1971), 10-11; Ian Whitaker, The Scottish kayaks reconsidered, *Antiquity* 51 (March 1977): 43-44.

75. Finn Gad, *The History of Greenland*, vol. 2., *1700-1782* (1973), 12, 88, 158-62; Whitaker, The Scottish kayaks reconsidered, 44.

76. Burch, Eskimo warfare in northwest Alaska, 11; Fienup-Riordan, *Eskimo Essays*, 158-59; Lucien M. Turner, On the Indians and Eskimos of the Ungava District, Labrador, *Transactions of the Royal Society of Canada* 2 (1887): 109.

77. Harris, *Cannibals and Kings*, 51-52.

78. Burch and Correll, Alliance and conflict, 33.

79. Kerry Abel, *Drum Songs: Glimpses of Dene History* (1993), 31-32, 96-97; Robert Bell, Legends of the Slave Indians of the Mackenzie River, *Journal of American Folklore* 14 (1901): 26-29; Vilhjalmur Stefansson, *Hunters of the Great North* (1922), 12-13.

80. Foxe, *North-West Fox*, 38.

81. de Laguna, *Under Mount Saint Elias*, 257.

Chapter 3

1. Knud Rasmussen, *Report of the Fifth Thule Expedition, 1921-24*, vol. 9, *Intellectual Culture of the Copper Eskimos* (1932), 168.

2. Richard H. Jordan and Susan Kaplan, An archaeological view of the Inuit/European contact period in Central Labrador, *Études/Inuit/Studies* 4, nos. 1-2 (1980): 38; and Susan Kaplan, European goods and socio-economic change in early Labrador Inuit society, in *Cultures in Contact: The Impact of European Contacts on Native American Cultural Institutions, A.D. 1000-1800* (1985), 50.

3. G.M. Asher, *Henry Hudson, the Navigator; from the Original Documents* (1860), xcvi, clxxi; Finn Gad, *The History of Greenland*, vol. 1, *Earliest Times to 1700* (1970), 183-216; William C. Sturtevant and David Beers Quinn, This new prey: Eskimos in Europe, in *Indians and Europe: An Interdisciplinary Collection of Essays* (1987), 64; Alan Cooke and Clive Holland, *The Exploration of Northern Canada, 500-1920* (1978), 23.

4. Cooke and Holland, *The Exploration of Northern Canada*, 30-31; *Dictionary of Canadian Biography* 1, 111-13.

5. Sturtevant and Quinn, This new prey, 64; J. Garth Taylor, Historical ethnography of the Labrador coast, in *Handbook of North American Indians*, vol. 5, *Arctic* (1984), 509.

6. William C. Sturtevant, The first Inuit depiction by Europeans, *Études/Inuit/Studies* 4, nos. 1-2 (1980); Sturtevant and Quinn, This new prey.

7. William Fitzhugh, Indian and Eskimo/Inuit settlement history in Labrador: an archaeological view, in *Our Footprints Are Everywhere: Inuit Land Use and Occupancy in Labrador* (1977), 38; Richard H. Jordan, Inuit occupation of the central Labrador coast since 1600 AD, in *Our Footprints Are Everywhere: Inuit Land Use and Occupancy in Labrador* (1977) 43; Sturtevant and Quinn, This new prey, 64; Réginald Auger,

Probabilities for a late eighteenth century Inuit occupation of the Strait of Belle Isle, *Études/Inuit/Studies* 11, no. 1 (1987); C.A. Martijn, The 'Esquimaux' in the 17th and 18th century cartography of the Gulf of St Lawrence: a preliminary discussion, *Études/Inuit/Studies* 4, nos. 1-2 (1980).

8. Samuel de Champlain, *The Works of Samuel de Champlain,* vol. 5 ([1632] 1933), 168-69.

9. N. Clermont, Les Inuit de Labrador méridional avant Cartwright, *Études/Inuit/Studies* 4, nos. 1-2 (1980): 151-52; Jordan and Kaplan, An archaeological view of the Inuit/ European contact period, 39; C.A. Martijn, The Inuit of southern Quebec-Labrador: A rejoinder to J. Garth Taylor, *Études/Inuit/Studies* 4, nos. 1-2 (1980): 196; J. Garth Taylor, Indian-Inuit relations in eastern Labrador, 1600-1675, *Arctic Anthropology* 16 (1979): 49.

10. Antoine Silvy, Journal of Father Silvy from Belle Isle to Port Nelson, in *Documents Relating to the Early History of Hudson Bay* ([1684] 1931), 79.

11. Taylor, Historical ethnography of the Labrador coast, 510. Also see Kaplan, European goods and socio-economic change, 59.

12. Kaplan, European goods and socio-economic change, 60.

13. Champlain, *The Works of Samuel de Champlain*, 177.

14. Lucien M. Turner, On the Indians and Eskimos of the Ungava District, Labrador, *Transactions of the Royal Society of Canada* 2 (1887): 109.

15. Arthur Dobbs, *An Account of the Countries Adjoining to Hudson's Bay in the North-West Part of America* (1744), 49; Joseph Robson, *An Account of Six Years Residence in Hudson's Bay, from 1733 to 1736 and 1744 to 1747* (1752), 63; Nelson H.H. Graburn and R. Stephen Strong, *Circumpolar Peoples: An Anthropological Perspective* (1973), 119.

16. Robson, *An Account of Six Years Residence,* 63-64.

17. John Oldmixon, The history of Hudson's Bay, in *Documents Relating to the Early History of Hudson Bay* ([1708] 1931), 381-82.

18. Ibid., 305-89.

19. Bacqueville de la Potherie, Letters of La Potherie, in *Documents Relating to the Early History of Hudson Bay* ([1722] 1931), 279.

20. Daniel Francis and Toby Morantz, *Partners in Furs: A History of the Fur Trade in Eastern James Bay, 1600-1870* (1983), 75.

21. Henry Ellis, *A Voyage to Hudson's Bay by the Dobbs Galley and California* ([1748] 1967); Andrew Graham, *Observations on Hudson's Bay, 1767-91* (1969), 213; Samuel Hearne, *A Journey from Prince of Wales's Fort in Hudson's Bay to the Northern Ocean* ([1795] 1958). James Isham, *James Isham's Observations on Hudsons Bay, 1743* (1949), 181; James Knight, Journal kept at Churchill River, 14 July to 13 September, 1717, in *The Founding of Churchill* (1932); Robson, *An Account of Six Years Residence.*

22. Knight, Journal kept at Churchill River, 116.

23. Isham, *James Isham's Observations,* 181.

24. Robson, *An Account of Six Years Residence,* 63-64.

25. Graham, *Observations on Hudson's Bay,* 213-14.

26. Ships' journeys along the coast of Hudson Bay between Chesterfield Inlet and the Churchill River in the relevant time period were made by: Thomas Button in 1612

and 1613, Jens Munk in 1619-20, Luke Foxe and Thomas James in 1631-32, Henry Kelsey in 1686, William Stuart and Henry Kelsey in 1689, Nicolas Jérémie between 1694 and 1714, Bacqueville de la Potherie between 1697 and 1703, William Stuart in 1715, and James Knight in 1717.

Henry Kelsey, A Journal of a Voyage and Journey Undertaken by Henry Kelsey, June the 17th, 1689, in *The Kelsey Papers* (1929). Description of Chipewyan canoe is on page 26.

The map known as *Native Map Seventeen Rivers Beyond Churchill*, based on information from Chipewyan and drawn by James Knight, is reproduced in John Warkentin and Richard I. Ruggles, *Historical Atlas of Manitoba* (1970), 86-87. Some details of Captain Christopher Middleton's 1741-42 journey north of Wager Inlet were added to the map later. The note identifying "Usquemays" territory is unlikely to have been a late addition. By the 1740s, Inuit communities existed as far south as Knapp's Bay (Arviat). See Christopher Middleton, Extracts from the log [of H.M.S. *Furnace*, 1741-42], in William Coats, *The Geography of Hudson's Bay* (1852). See also Arthur Dobbs, *An Account of the Countries Adjoining to Hudson's Bay in the North-West Part of America* (1744); and Ellis, *A Voyage to Hudson's Bay by the Dobbs Galley and California*.

27. Ernest S. Burch, The Thule-Historic Eskimo transition on the west coast of Hudson Bay, in *Thule Eskimo Culture: An Anthropological Retrospective* (1979), 192, 194; Brenda Clark, *The Development of Caribou Eskimo Culture* (1977); Brenda Clark, Thule occupation of west Hudson Bay, in *Thule Eskimo Culture: An Anthropological Retrospective* (1979), 93-97; Elmer Harp, *The Archaeology of the Lower and Middle Thelon, Northwest Territories* (1961); Elmer Harp, The culture history of the Central Barren Grounds, in *Prehistoric Cultural Relations Between the Arctic and Temperate Zones of North America* (1962); Elmer Harp, Archaeological evidence bearing on the origin of the Caribou Eskimo, in *Proceedings of the International Congress of Anthropological and Ethnological Science* 2 (1963); Allen P. McCartney, *Thule Eskimo Prehistory Along Northwestern Hudson Bay* (1977).

28. Burch, The Thule-Historic Eskimo transition, 192, 194; Clark, Thule occupation of west Hudson Bay, 93-97; Harp, *The Archaeology of the Lower and Middle Thelon*; McCartney, *Thule Eskimo Prehistory*.

29. Climatic evidence is presented by H.H. Lamb, Atmospheric circulation and climate in the arctic since the last ice age, in *Climatic Changes in Arctic Areas During the Last Ten-Thousand Years* (1972), 464; H.H. Lamb, *Climate: Present, Past and Future*, vol. 2, *Climatic History and the Future* (1977), 461-73; A.A. Dekin, *Models of Pre-Dorset Culture: Towards an Explicit Methodology* (1975), 111; Bryan Gordon, *Of Men and Herds in Barrenland Prehistory* (1975), 50; and Harvey Nichols, The post-glacial history of vegetation and climate at Ennadai Lake, Keewatin, and Lynn Lake, Manitoba (Canada), *Euszeitalter und Gegenwart* 18 (1967): 187. Eyewitness accounts of starvation are in HBCA, PAM, Churchill Post Journals, B42/a/37; and John Oldmixon, The history of Hudson's Bay. The population estimate for the second half of the 1600s is from Ernest S. Burch, Caribou Eskimo origins: an old problem reconsidered, *Arctic Anthropology* 15 (1978): 26.

30. Burch, Caribou Eskimo origins; Burch, The Thule-Historic Eskimo transition.

31. The effects of climate and unstable environments were as significant for people in Europe as they were for North American arctic peoples. The cod fisheries of the Faeroe Islands, which had supplied a substantial proportion of the fish consumed in Europe, collapsed by 1600 as schools of cod migrated away from the edge of the advancing ice and the increasingly cold polar waters. The fish did not reappear in sufficient quantities to make commercial fishing viable until the 1820s. Whaling, however, was greatly improved in the area, especially in the period from 1717 to 1739. See H.H. Lamb, *Climate: Present, Past and Future*, vol. 2, *Climatic History and the Future* (1977), 511.

32. Lamb, *Climate: Present, Past and Future*, vol. 2, 512.

33. Astrid Ogilvie, The past climate and sea-ice record from Iceland, part 1: data to A.D. 1780, *Climatic Change* 6 (1984); Ogilvie, Documentary evidence for changes in the climate of Iceland, A.D. 1500 to 1800, in *Climate Since A.D. 1500* (1992).

34. H.H. Lamb, *Climate, History and the Modern World* (1982), 179.

35. Statistics for Iceland are from Ogilvie, Documentary evidence for changes in the climate of Iceland, 108. For descriptions of climate events in other parts of North America and Europe, see Lamb, Atmospheric circulation and climate in the arctic since the last ice age; and H.H. Lamb, *Weather, Climate & Human Affairs: A Book of Essays and Other Papers* (1988).

36. Jean Grove, *The Little Ice Age* (1988), 255.

37. John A. Eddy, The Maunder Minimum, *Science* 192 (1976).

The reduction in solar radiation is related to a relative absence of sunspots. Periods of reduced or absent sunspot activity were noted and recorded by astronomical observers in China, Japan, and Korea at least as early as the first century BCE. See Sigeru Kanda, Comprehensive list of sunspot sightings from ancient records of Japan, Korea, and China, 28 B.C. through A.D. 43, *Proceedings of the Imperial Academy (Tokyo)* 9 (1933).

It was, however, only after the invention of the telescope in the early seventeenth century that sun-gazers were able to make deliberate studies of the phenomenon, and see a connection between fewer or no sunspots and reduced solar radiation. German astronomer Gustav Spörer recognized the relationship and published his historical data in 1887 and 1889, shortly before his death. Edward Walter Maunder, of the Solar Department of the Greenwich Observatory, published a summary of Spörer's work in English in 1890, and carried on the research to identify at least one more period of "prolonged sunspot minimum," in the years 1790 to 1830. Maunder also suggested a connection between long-term sunspot activity and climatic regimes in: Summary of Spörer's sunspot studies, *Notes to the Royal Astronomical Society* 50 (1890), 251; A prolonged sunspot minimum, *Knowledge* 17 (1894): 173; and, A prolonged sunspot minimum, *Journal of the British Astronomical Association* 32 (1922).

Maunder's conclusions were largely ignored, in spite of supporting evidence from Agnes M. Clerke's auroral studies, which appeared in *Knowledge* 17 (1894). More recently, Maunder's identification of a direct relationship between "prolonged solar minimums" and periods of extreme terrestrial cooling has received new corroboration from a series of carbon 14 studies of plant materials. See Bibliography for studies by Minze Stuiver (1961, 1965); Hans E. Suess (1965, 1968); Paul E. Damon et al. (1966);

I.U. Olson, ed. (1970), as well as tree-ring studies by A.E. Douglass (1919, 1928); E.N. Parker (1973, 1975); and W.L. Gates and Y. Mintes, eds. (1976). The connection between prolonged sunspot minimums and colder climatic regimes is now generally recognized by historical climatologists. See Gordon Manley (1961); Hans E. Suess (1968); J. Roger Bray (1971); Stephen H. Schneider and Clifford Maas (1975).

38. H.C. Fritts and X.M. Shao, Mapping climate using tree-rings from western North America, in *Climate Since A.D. 1500* (1992), 281.

39. Oldmixon, The history of Hudson's Bay, 392.

40. Grove, *The Little Ice Age*, 417-18.

41. Emmanuel LeRoy Ladurie, *Times of Feast, Times of Famine: A History of Climate since the Year 1000* (1972), 91.

42. Lamb, *Climate, History and the Modern World*, 207-08; Lamb, Climatic variations and changes in the wind and ocean circulation: the Little Ice Age in the northeast Atlantic, *Quaternary Research* 11 (1979): 15; Ogilvie, Documentary evidence for changes in the climate of Iceland, 110.

43. Cited in Grove, *The Little Ice Age*, 21.

44. Astrid Ogilvie, The past climate and sea-ice record from Iceland, part 1: data to A.D. 1780, *Climatic Change* 6 (1984): 145; Ogilvie, Documentary evidence for changes in the climate of Iceland, 109-10; J.D. Ives, Indications of recent extensive glacierization in north-central Baffin Island, N.W.T., *Journal of Glaciology* 4 (1962); Lamb, *Climate, History and the Modern World*, 230.

45. Robert McGhee, *Copper Eskimo Prehistory* (1972), 122-23; Robert McGhee, *Canadian Arctic Prehistory* (1978) 113-15; David Morrison, *Thule Culture in Western Coronation Gulf, N.W.T.* (1983), 278.

46. Ice conditions in Coronation Gulf and their effects on ringed seal are described in McGhee, *Copper Eskimo Prehistory*, 122-23, and Robert McGhee, Paleoeskimo occupations of central and high arctic Canada, in *Eastern Arctic Prehistory: Paleoeskimo Problems* (1976). Effects of ocean cooling on beluga whale populations is in Peter Schledermann, The effect of climatic/ecological changes on the style of Thule culture winter dwellings, *Arctic and Alpine Research* 8 (1976): 41. Caribou herd responses to cooling are discussed in James Savelle and Allen P. McCartney, Geographical and temporal variation in Thule Eskimo subsistence and economies: a model, *Research in Economic Anthropology* 10 (1988): 36.

47. Charles W. Amsden, Hard times: a case study from northern Alaska and implications for arctic prehistory, in *Thule Eskimo Culture: An Anthropological Retrospective* (1979), 404-05; J.L. Anderson, History and climate: some economic models, in *Climate and History: Studies in Past Climates and Their Impact on Man* (1981), 339. The possible human reactions to resource shortages resulting from environmental degradation suggested by Anderson and Amsden, in spite of claims to the contrary, do not adequately encompass the "infinite variety" of human behaviour, nor are the responses noted in the present discussion by any means comprehensive.

48. Burch, Caribou Eskimo origins; McGhee, *Copper Eskimo Prehistory*, 57-58; David Morrison, *Iglulualumiut Prehistory: The Lost Inuit of Franklin Bay* (1990); Harvey Nichols, *Palynological and Paleoclimatic Study of the Late Quaternary Displacement of the Boreal Forest-Tundra Ecotone in Keewatin and Mackenzie, N.W.T., Canada* (1975).

49. McGhee, *Copper Eskimo Prehistory*, 57.

50. Burch, Caribou Eskimo origins; and Burch, The Thule-Historic Eskimo transition.

51. Ellis, *A Voyage to Hudson's Bay by the Dobbs Galley and California*, 147-48, 232.

52. Burch, Caribou Eskimo origins; Burch, The Thule-Historic Eskimo transition, 196; Urve Linnamae and Brenda Clark, Archaeology of Rankin Inlet, N.W.T., *Musk Ox* 19 (1976): 57; McGhee, *Copper Eskimo Prehistory*, 40, 53, 66-67; Therkel Mathiassen, *Report of the Fifth Thule Expedition, 1921-24*, vol. 4: 2, *Archaeology of the Central Eskimos: Analytical Part* (1927), 133.

53. David Damas, The Eskimo, in *Science, History, and Hudson Bay* (1968), 155.

54. Burch, The Thule-Historic Eskimo transition, 197.

55. Ibid., 201-02.

56. Burch, Caribou Eskimo origins, 26.

57. Burch, Caribou Eskimo origins; James G.E. Smith, Chipewyan, Cree and Inuit relations west of Hudson Bay, 1714-1955, *Ethnohistory* 28, no. 2 (Spring 1981); William E. Taylor, Hypotheses on the origin of Canadian Thule culture, *American Antiquity* 28, no. 4 (1963).

58. Marc Stevenson, *Inuit Whalers and Cultural Persistence: Structure in Cumberland Sound and Central Inuit Social Organization* (1997), 320-23.

59. Samuel Hearne, *A Journey from Prince of Wales's Fort* ([1795] 1958), 217n; Nicolas Jérémie de la Montagne, *Twenty Years of York Factory 1694-1714* ([1720] 1926). Henry Kelsey, A Journal of a Voyage and Journey Undertaken by Henry Kelsey.... June the 17th, 1689, in *The Kelsey Papers* (1929), 25.

60. Burch, Caribou Eskimo origins; Steve A. Tomka and Marc G. Stevenson, Understanding abandonment processes: summary and remaining concerns, in *Abandonment of Settlements and Regions: Ethnoarchaeological and Archaeological Approaches* (1993), 191-95.

61. Burch, Caribou Eskimo origins, 23; Ernest S. Burch and Thomas C. Correll, Alliance and conflict: inter-regional alliance in north Alaska, in *Alliance in Eskimo Society* (1972), 31-32.

62. Tomka and Stevenson, Understanding abandonment processes, 192.

63. Fitzhugh, Indian and Eskimo/Inuit settlement history in Labrador, 3.

64. Irving Rouse, *Migrations in Prehistory: Inferring Population Movement From Cultural Remains* (1986), 9.

65. Burch and Correll, Alliance and conflict, 32.

66. For a discussion of various applications of curation theory, see Tomka and Stevenson, Understanding abandonment processes, 191-95. The term originates in the Latin *curare*, to preserve or guard, and is related to words such as "cure," meaning to restore to health; "curator," meaning to care for; "cure," meaning to preserve (meat); and "cure," meaning a group of human souls entrusted to a religious leader, or curate.

67. R.F. Jones, The Keewatin Inuit and interband trade and communication, 1717-1900, MA thesis (1989), 132-36.

68. Finn Gad, History of Colonial Greenland, in *Handbook of North American Indians*, vol. 5, *Arctic* (1984), 569; Eigil Knuth, Singajuk's family saga, *Folk* 5 (1963): 209.

69. Knud Rasmussen, Posthumous notes on East Greenland legends and myths, *Meddelelser om Grønland* 109 (1939): 111; Hinrich Rink, *Tales and Traditions of the Eskimo* ([1875] 1974), 83; Knuth, Singajuk's family saga, 210.

70. Rink, *Tales and Traditions of the Eskimo*, 169.

71. Gustav Holm, Ethnological Sketch of the Angmagsalik Eskimo, English edition, ed. William Thalbitzer, *Meddelelser om Grønland* 39, no. 1 ([1888] 1914): 84, 112.

72. Holm, Ethnological Sketch of the Angmagsalik Eskimo, 232; Rink, *The Eskimo Tribes: Their Distribution and Characteristics, Especially in Regard to Language, with Comparative Vocabulary and Sketch Map*, 2 vols., *Meddelelser om Grønland* 11 (1887-91): 311.

73. Holm, Ethnological Sketch of the Angmagsalik Eskimo, 288-89; see also Rink, *The Eskimo Tribes*, 316.

74. Holm, Ethnological Sketch of the Angmagsalik Eskimo, 256-57.

75. Rink, *Tales and Traditions of the Eskimo*, 83.

76. [Reverend] James Wallace, *Descriptions of the Isles of Orkney* (1693), 28.

77. Ibid.

78. [Doctor] James Wallace, *An Account of the Islands of Orkney* (1700), 60-61.

79. John Brand, *A Brief Description of Orkney, Zetland, Pightland-Firth and Caithness* (1701), 50-51.

80. Dale Idiens, Eskimos in Scotland: c. 1682-1924, in *Indians and Europe: An Interdisciplinary Collection of Essays* (1987), 164.

81. G.F. Black and Northcote W. Thomas, *Examples of Printed Folk-Lore Concerning the Orkney & Shetland Islands,* County Folk-Lore Series, 3, no. 5 ([1901] 1967); Ernest W. Marwick, *The Folklore of Orkney and Shetland* (1975).

82. Black and Thomas, *Examples of Printed Folk-Lore,* 172, 180-81; Marwick, *The Folklore of Orkney and Shetland*, 28-29.

83. George Best, *A True Discourse of the Late Voyages of Discoverie, for the Finding of a Passage to Cathaia*, trans. and ed. Walter A. Kenyon, in *Tokens of Possession: The Voyages of Martin Frobisher* ([1578] 1975), 115.

84. Finn Gad, *The History of Greenland*, vol. 1 (1970), 173.

85. Ibid., 174.

86. Kaj Birket-Smith, *Ethnography of the Egedesminde District with Aspects of the General Culture of West Greenland* ([1924] 1976), 266; Idiens, Eskimos in Scotland, 162-63; Ian Whitaker, The Scottish kayaks and the 'Finn-men,' *Antiquity* 28, no. 110 (June 1954); Ian Whitaker, The Scottish kayaks reconsidered, *Antiquity* 51, no. 201 (March 1977).

87. David MacRitchie, Kayaks of the North Sea, *Scottish Geographical Magazine* 28 (1912): 502.

88. William Clark Souter, *The Story of Our Kayak and Some Others* (1933), 17; E. Mikkelsen, Kajakmandan fra Aberdeen, *Grønland* (1954); Gert Nooter, Old kayaks in the Netherlands, *Mededlingen van het Rijksmuseum voor Volkenkunde* no. 17 (1971): 10; Idiens, Eskimos in Scotland, 163-64.

89. Gad, *The History of Greenland*, vol. 1, 238.

90. Idiens, Eskimos in Scotland, 163; Whitaker, The Scottish kayaks reconsidered, 43; Wendell Oswalt, *Eskimos and Explorers* (1979), 43.

91. Whitaker, The Scottish kayaks reconsidered, 102.

92. Ibid., 103.

93. Grove, *The Little Ice Age*, 260.

94. Ibid.

95. Nooter, Old kayaks in the Netherlands, 9; Vilhjalmur Stefansson, *Greenland* (1942), 24.

96. Knud Rasmussen, *Greenland by the Polar Sea: The Story of the Thule Expedition from Melville Bay to Cape Morris Jesup* (1921), 319; Whitaker, The Scottish kayaks and the 'Finn-men', 103.

97. Lamb, *Climate: Present, Past and Future*, vol. 2, 512.

98. Ogilvie, The past climate and sea-ice record from Iceland, part 1; Ogilvie, Documentary evidence for changes in the climate of Iceland.

Chapter 4

1. Guy Mary-Rousselière, *Beyond the High Hills* (1961), 23.

2. P.M. Kelly, J.H.W. Karas, and L.D. Williams, Arctic climate: past, present and future, in *Arctic Whaling* (1984), 31.

3. Finn Gad, History of colonial Greenland, in *Handbook of North American Indians,* vol. 5, *Arctic* (1984), 557.

4. Ibid., 558-59, 562.

5. Finn Gad, *The History of Greenland, 1700-1782* (1973), 370.

6. Gad, History of colonial Greenland, 563.

7. Gad, *The History of Greenland,* 369-70.

8. Gad, *The History of Greenland*, 358, 360, 369-70; and Helge Klievan, Greenland Eskimo: Introduction, in *Handbook of North American Indians*, vol. 5, *Arctic* (1984), 525. Klievan cites Hans-Erik Rasmussen, *Social endogami og symbol-brug i Vestgrøland [Social Endogamy and Symbol Use in West Greenland],* unpublished MA thesis, Copenhagen University, Institute for Eskimology.

9. Robert McGhee, *Canadian Arctic Prehistory* (1978), 108.

10. Susan Kaplan, European goods and socio-economic change in early Labrador Inuit society, in *Cultures in Contact: The Impact of European Contacts on Native American Cultural Institutions, A.D. 1000-1800* (1985), 60.

11. Norman Clermont, Les Inuit de Labrador méridional avant Cartwright, *Études/Inuit/Studies* 4, nos. 1-2 (1980): 153; Richard H. Jordan, Archaeological investigations of Hamilton Inlet, *Arctic Anthropology* 15, no. 2 (1978); J.Garth Taylor, Demography and adaptations of eighteenth-century Eskimo groups in northern Labrador and Ungava, in *Prehistoric Maritime Adaptations of the Circumpolar Zone* (1975).

12. H.H. Lamb, *Climate: Present, Past and Future,* vol. 2 (1977), 511.

13. Richard Vaughan, Historical survey of the European whaling industry, in *Arctic Whaling* (1984).

14. Kaplan, European goods and socio-economic change, 58; François Trudel, *Inuit, Amerindians and Europeans: A Study of Interethnic Economic Relations on the Canadian South-Eastern Seaboard (1500-1800)* (1981).

15. Charles A. Martijn, The 'Esquimaux' in the 17th and 18th century cartography of the Gulf of St. Lawrence, *Études/Inuit/Studies* 4, nos. 1-2 (1980); François Trudel, The Inuit of southern Labrador and the development of French sedentary fisheries, 1700-1760, in *Papers from the Fourth Annual Congress, Canadian Ethnology Society, 1977* (1978).

16. Jean-Louis Fornel, Relation de la découverte qu'a faite le Sieur Fornel en 1743 de la Baye des Eskimaux nommée par les sauvages Kessessakiou, in *Rapport de l'Archiviste de la Province de Québec, 1920-21* (1921), 74.

17. J.K. Hiller, The Moravians in Labrador, 1771-1805, *The Polar Record* (1971): 840.

18. Quotation from "Letters of Claude C. LeRoy Bacqueville de la Potherie," *Histoire de l'Amerique Septentrionale*, vol. 1 ([1722] reprinted in *Documents Relating to the Early History of Hudson Bay*, 1931), 279; Fornel, Relation de la découverte qu'a faite le Sieur Fornel, 73. Description of John Davis's 1587 experience is in Luke Foxe, *North-West Fox, or Fox from the North-West Passage* ([1635] 1965), 43.

19. Martijn, The 'Esquimaux' in the 17th and 18th century cartography.

20. Marcel Trudel, *L'Esclavage au Canada francais* (1960).

21. Ibid., 81.

22. J.Garth Taylor, Indian-Inuit relations in eastern Labrador, 1600-1675, *Arctic Anthropology* 16, nos. 1-2 (1979): 49-58; and J. Garth Taylor, Historical ethnography of the Labrador coast, in *Handbook of North American Indians*, vol. 5, *Arctic* (1984), 510-11.

23. J.Garth Taylor, *Labrador Eskimo Settlements of the Early Contact Period* (1975), 7; Trudel, *Inuit, Amerindians and Europeans*, 383; Kaplan, European goods and socio-economic change, 64.

24. Hiller, The Moravians in Labrador, 841-42; J.G. Taylor, Eskimo answers to an eighteenth century questionnaire, *Ethnohistory* 19, no 2 (1972): 135-45; Trudel, *Inuit, Amerindians and Europeans*, 383, 384.

25. Hiller, The Moravians in Labrador, 841.

26. Trudel, *Inuit, Amerindians and Europeans*, 392.

27. Hiller, The Moravians in Labrador, 844-45, 848.

28. Archaeological evidence from Kaplan, European goods and socio-economic change; Taylor, *Labrador Eskimo Settlements*, 15; J. Garth Taylor, Demography and adaptations, 276. Eyewitness accounts of Inuit crossing Hudson Strait in order to trade in Baffin Island are in Andrew Graham, *Observations on Hudson's Bay, 1767-91* (1969), 213; and in Theodore Swaine [Clerk of the *California*], *An Account of a Voyage for the Discovery of a North-West Passage by Hudson's Streights, to the Western and Southern Ocean of America: Performed in the Year 1746 and 1747, in the Ship California, Capt. Francis Smith, Commander*, vol. 1 (1749), 33.

29. George Back, *Narrative of the Arctic Land Expedition to the Mouth of the Great Fish River, and Along the Shores of the Arctic Ocean, in the Years 1833, 1834, and 1835* (1836), 85-86.

30. Graham, *Observations on Hudson's Bay, 1767-91*, 213.

31. Samuel Hearne, *A Journey from Prince of Wales's Fort* ([1795] 1958), 217.

32. HBCA, PAM, York Factory Correspondence Books, B239/b/1:17, 25; B239/b/3:9.

33. Ibid., Logs of *Good Success* (1718) and *Prosperous* (1719), in York Factory Correspondence Books, B239/b/1:2, 17.

34. Ibid., B239/b/1:17, 25.

35. Ibid., B239/b/1.

36. Ibid., B239/b/1:25.

37. Ibid., York Factory Post Journals, B239/a/5.

38. Log of *Prosperous* (1721), B239/b/2:3.

39. Letter #66, from George Spurrell and others at Prince of Wales Fort, August 1, 1738, to London Committee, A6/6:4-5.

40. K.G. Davies, Introduction, in *Letters from Hudson Bay, 1703-40* (1965), 245.

41. HBCA, PAM, London Letter Books, A6/6:44-50.

42. James Isham, *Observations on Hudsons Bay* ([1743] 1949), 181; and HBCA, PAM, Log of *Churchill* (1744), B42/a/26.

43. HBCA, PAM, Log of *Churchill* (1744), B42/a/26.

44. Charles D. Laughlin and Ivan A. Brady, Introduction: diaphasis and change in human populations, in *Extinction and Survival in Human Populations* (1978), 27-28; Peter Rowley-Conwy and Marek Zvelebil, Saving it for later: storage by prehistoric hunter-gatherers in Europe, in *Bad Year Economics: Cultural Responses to Risk and Uncertainty* (1989), 45.

45. Andrew Graham, Indians, in *James Isham's Observations on Hudson's Bay, 1743, and Notes and Observations on a Book Entitled A Voyage to Hudsons Bay in the Dobbs Galley, 1759* (HBRS 1949), 229.

46. HBCA, PAM, Log of *Churchill* (1744), B42/a/26.

47. A.S. Keene, Optimal foraging in a nonmarginal environment: a model of prehistoric subsistence strategies in Michigan, in *Hunter-Gatherer Foraging Strategies* (1981), 192.

48. Henry Kelsey, A Journal of a Voyage and Journey Undertaken by Henry Kelsey ... June the 17th, in *The Kelsey Papers* ([1689] 1929), 27-28.

49. Richard Glover, Introduction, in *Letters from Hudson Bay, 1703-40* (1965), 63; James Knight, Journal kept at Churchill River, 14 July to 13 September, 1717, in J.F. Kenney, *The Founding of Churchill* (1932), 59.

50. HBCA, PAM, Churchill Post Journals, B42/a/1.

51. Ibid., B42/a/5:25.

52. Ibid., B42/a/1:81, 127d.

53. Ibid., B42/a/4:33.

54. Ibid., York Factory Post Journals, B239/a/29.

55. Ibid., B239/a/5.

56. David Morrison, *Thule Culture in Western Coronation Gulf, N.W.T* (1983), 277.

57. HBCA, PAM, Churchill Post Journals, B42/a/35.

58. Ibid., Log of *Churchill* (1753), B42/a/41:13.

59. Ibid.

60. Ibid., 14.

61. Ibid.

62. Ibid., 15.

63. The Hudson's Bay Company trading voyages north of Churchill between 1718 and 1752 were:

> 1718 David Vaughan in *Good Success*;
>
> 1719 Henry Kelsey in *Prosperous* and John Hancock in *Good Success;*
>
> 1720 John Hancock in *Prosperous* and James Napper in *Good Success*;
>
> 1721 Henry Kelsey and Richard Norton in *Prosperous*;
>
> 1722 John Scroggs in *Whalebone*;
>
> 1737 James Napper in *Churchill* and Robert Crow in *Musquash*;
>
> 1738-40 and 1742-44 Francis Smith in *Churchill*;
>
> 1750-52 James Walker in *Churchill*.

The other four voyages were: James Knight's disastrous passage and shipwreck ordeal of 1719 to 1721, with George Berley in *Albany* and David Vaughan in *Discovery*; the 1742 summer voyage of Christopher Middleton in *Furnace* and William Moor in *Discovery*; and the brief summer visits of William Moor in *Dobbs* and Francis Smith in *California* in 1746 and 1747, respectively.

64. HBCA, PAM, Churchill Post Journals, B42/a/43.

65. Ibid.

66. Ibid., B42/a/43.

67. Ibid., B42/a/45.

68. Ibid.

69. Ibid., B42/a/45, B42/a/47:2.

70. Ibid., Log of *Churchill* (1755), Captain John Bean's report, B42/a/47:2. An account of the incident is also given in a footnote in Hearne, *A Journey from Prince of Wales's Fort*, 217-18. Hearne's information is at odds with Captain Bean's logbook entries. Bean's account is more reliable, and is used here.

71. Hearne, *A Journey from Prince of Wales's Fort*, lxv.

72. Ibid., 217-18.

73. HBCA, PAM, Churchill Post Journals, B42/a/58.

74. Richard Glover, Introduction, in *Andrew Graham's Observations on Hudson's Bay 1767-1791* (1969), xiii; HBCA, PAM, Churchill Post Journals, B42/a/62.

75. James G.E. Smith and Ernest S. Burch, Chipewyan and Inuit in the central Canadian subarctic, 1613-1977, *Arctic Anthropology* 16 (1979): 82.

76. For 1765 head-count see HBCA, PAM, B42/a/63; for 1766, see B42/a/65; for 1770, B42/a/81. Average populations for years 1770 to 1782 are from logs of *Churchill*, and B42/a/78.

77. HBCA, PAM, Churchill Post Journals, B42/a/62.

78. Hearne, *A Journey from Prince of Wales's Fort*, 218n.

79. HBCA, PAM, Churchill Post Journals, B42/a/63, 65, 77.

80. Ibid., B42/a/63-82; Graham, *Observations on Hudson's Bay, 1767-91*, 215, 241; Hearne, *A Journey from Prince of Wales's Fort*, 218n.

81. HBCA, PAM, Churchill Post Journals, B42/a/78, August 14.

82. Ibid. Also Graham, *Observations on Hudson's Bay, 1767-91*, E2/12:611-612; Graham, *Observations on Hudson's Bay, 1767-91* (1969), 239.

83. HBCA, PAM, London Letter Books, A11/14.

84. Hearne, *A Journey from Prince of Wales's Fort*, 218n.

85. Graham, *Observations on Hudson's Bay, 1767-91*, 236.

86. HBCA, PAM, Churchill Post Journals, B42/a/54, July 26.

87. Ibid., B42/a/74:29d.

88. Ibid., B42/a/78.

89. Samuel Hearne described the Chipewyan's July 17, 1771, attack against the Inuit camp in *A Journey from Prince of Wales's Fort in Hudson's Bay*, 98-101. Fifty years after Hearne's visit, another British traveller, George Back, arrived at the site of the Bloody Fall massacre (on July 13, 1821), and made a note in his diary that cast doubt on Hearne's description of events. One of Back's guides, White Capot, who had been with Hearne in 1771, told Back that Hearne "was two days march from them at the time of their (the Indians) attacking the Esquimaux," and did not witness the events. George Back, *Arctic Artist: The Journal and Paintings of George Back, Midshipman with Franklin, 1819-1822* (1994), 141.

90. HBCA, PAM, Churchill Post Journals, B42/a/65:13.

91. Ibid., B42/a/101.

92. Sea ice data in A.J.W. Catchpole and Marcia-Anne Faurer, Summer sea ice severity in Hudson Strait, 1751-1870, *Climatic Change* 5, no. 2 (1983): 137. Caribou herd data in HBCA, PAM, Churchill Post Journals, B42/a/101.

93. Presence of Marble Islanders at Whale Cove in 1776 is noted in HBCA, PAM, Churchill Post Journals, B42/a/93:32d. Ice data comes from A.J.W. Catchpole, Hudson's Bay Company ships' log-books as sources of sea ice data, 1751-1870, in *Climate Since A.D. 1500* (1992), 33. The state of the Inuit trade in 1778 and 1779 is described in HBCA, PAM, Churchill Post Journals, B42/a/97, and in the London Letter Books, A6/12:126.

94. HBCA, PAM, Churchill Post Journals, B42/a/101:23d, *passim.*

95. Ibid., London Letter Books, A11/15:118.

96. Ibid., Churchill Post Journals, B42/a/108; London Letter Books, A11/15:118.

97. Ibid., Churchill Post Journals, B42/a/108, May 28-30.

98. Ibid., B42/a/109; B42/a/111; B42/a/113.

99. Ibid., London Letter Books, A6/14:105d; Churchill Post Journals, B42/a/115.

100. Ernest S. Burch, Caribou Eskimo origins: an old problem reconsidered, *Arctic Anthropology* 11 (1978): 26.

101. Graham, *Observations on Hudson's Bay,* 213.

102. Ibid., 238.

Chapter 5

1. George Back, *Narrative of the Arctic Land Expedition to the Mouth of the Great Fish River, and Along the Shores of the Arctic Ocean, in the Years 1833, 1834, and 1835* (1836), 240.

2. Gordon C. Jacoby and Rosanne D'Arrigo, Reconstructed northern hemisphere and annual temperatures since 1671 based on high-latitude tree-ring data from North America, *Climatic Change* 14 (1989): 1; A.J.W. Catchpole, Hudson's Bay Company ships' log-books as sources of sea ice data, 1751-1870, in *Climate Since A.D. 1500* (1992), 33; J.M. Lough and H.C. Fritts, An assessment of the possible effects of volcanic eruptions on North American climate using tree-ring data, 1602 to 1900 A.D., *Climatic Change* 10, no. 2 (1987): 225; H.C. Fritts and J.M. Lough, An estimate of average annual temperature variations for North America, 1602 to 1961, *Climatic Change* 7, no. 2 (1985): 221; Timothy F. Ball, Historical and instrumental evidence of extreme climatic conditions in central Canada, 1770-1820, *Annales Geophysicae* (1988): 66.

3. HBCA, PAM, Churchill Post Journals, B42/a/116.

4. Ibid., Churchill Account Books, B42/d/111; B42/d/139. The value of the Made Beaver as the standard of trade was flexible. In the 1820s, seal and fox pelts were each valued at one-half MB; used guns cost between two and twelve MB, new guns between twelve and sixteen MB; two "good" dogs were worth one gun; ten caribou tongues were worth a credit of one MB, and thirty tongues would purchase a "checkered shirt" and some tobacco; ten deerskins would buy a small knife, while one deerskin was worth "some tobacco."

5. HBCA, PAM, Churchill Post Journals, B42/a/122, 15; B42/a/123, 16; B42/a/124, 1-1d.

6. Ibid., B42/a/124, 20, 21-23d.

7. Ibid., B42/a/126; 1803, B42/a/128:4d; 1804, B42/a/130:2d, 4d, 3d. British fur traders and the aboriginal peoples who learned English from them used the word "starve" to mean wither or die from lack of some essential, such as oxygen, food, warmth, or companionship. Using it only in its nutritional sense is a modern and mainly North American usage. In parts of Scotland today, many people still speak of starving from cold or disease. In the fur trade journals and letters, the word is often used to indicate malnutrition and death from lack of food, but could also mean a lack of preferred food. When the traders admonished their customers for not bringing in any furs, Cree and Chipewyan sometimes spoke of "starving" when they wanted to suggest that they had no spare time for trapping because they had to spend all their time fulfilling their first priority, acquiring food. "Starving" is used in this work in its modern meaning of hunger for lack of food, except when context and other evidence suggest that a different meaning was intended. In those cases, its use is qualified by a comment.

8. Ibid., B42/a/130:5d, 6d, 7d, 9.

9. Ibid., B42/a/126-148. Repeated references to hunger and starvation throughout.

10. George Back, *Arctic Artist: The Journal and Paintings of George Back, Midshipman with Franklin, 1819-1822* (1994), 119; John Richardson, *Arctic Ordeal* (1984), 28.

11. HBCA, PAM, Churchill Post Journals, B42/a/132, 19, 20.

12. Ibid., B42/a/130, 1, 2d, 4d.

13. Ibid., B42/a/135:7-8.

14. Ibid., B42/a/108, May 29-30 [1797]; B42/a/137, 10 [1812]; B42/a/140, 29d [1814].

15. Edward Chappell, *Narrative of a Voyage to Hudson's Bay* (1817), 80.

16. HBCA, PAM, Churchill Post Journals, B42/a/142:13d-14. In August 1812, an Inuit trading party left a teenaged boy at the fort, following the custom of sending boys to the post on the trading sloops in the previous century. The traders called him Augustine, after the month in which he came to Churchill. During more than twenty years with the Hudson's Bay Company, Augustine worked at Churchill, York Factory, and Fort Chimo, and acted as interpreter on both of John Franklin's western arctic land expeditions. He was the source for most of the descriptions of Keewatin coast people recorded by John Richardson, George Back, and John West.

17. HBCA, PAM, Churchill Post Journals, B42/a/142, 19d.

18. Ibid., B42/a/142, 17-18. Because the word "starving" had multiple meanings for the British traders and for the members of the London Committee, and could easily be misunderstood, Churchill post managers in this period took pains to make it clear to the Committee that they meant actual physical starvation from lack of food, by adding phrases like "beyond discussion" and by noting numbers of deaths.

19. Ibid., B42/a/132, 18.

20. Ibid., B42/a/141, 18ad-18b.

21. Ibid., B42/a/144, 2.

22. Ibid., B42/a/145, 5.

23. Ibid., B42/a/146, 9-10, 11d; B42/a/148, 98; B42/a/146, 6; B42/a/148, 95; B42/a/146, 10d; B42/a/148, 97.

24. Ibid., B42/a/147, 1, 14. Also, Joseph Robson, *An Account of Six Years Residence in Hudson's Bay, from 1733 to 1736 and 1744 to 1747* (1752), 6. When Joseph Robson accused the Hudson's Bay Company in 1752 of being "asleep by the frozen sea," his intent was to mock it for lack of energy and ambition. Another way of interpreting HBC policy is as a ploy to force its customers, the aboriginal trappers and middlemen, to bear the costs of collection, transportation, delivery, local marketing, and local good will. In addition, the company preferred not to send its servants inland or to establish posts there, out of reluctance to interfere in the internal affairs of indigenous societies, and fear of becoming embroiled in intertribal relations, to the detriment of the company's interests.

25. HBCA, PAM, Churchill Post Journals, B42/a/147, 28; HBCA, B42/a/147, 31-33.

26. Ibid., B42/a/147, 32-33.

27. Ibid., B42/a/154; Churchill Account Books, B42/d/111.

28. Ibid., Churchill Post Journals, B42/a/153, 3. This is another instance of a post master making a clear distinction for the benefit of the London Committee between death from starvation due to lack of food, and deaths from other causes. A number of explanations of the mysterious deaths can be advanced. Contagious disease may have been the cause, but in that case, Taylor's inquiries should have resulted in further

comments in his journal. Another possibility is gastric distress caused by overeating after a period of enforced fasting, such as was noted among the people of Melville Peninsula by Mr. Edwards, a surgeon on Captain Edward Parry's 1823 expedition. See Edward Parry, *Journal of a Second Voyage for the Discovery of a North-West Passage* (1824), 543. A third possibility is trichinosis, a disease caused by parasitic infestation contracted by eating infected meat. Inuit, of course, are aware of the danger, and under normal circumstances avoid the most likely sources of contamination. However, incidents have been reported in which people have added variety to an all-fish diet by eating polar bear, wolf, or dog meat, all possible sources of contamination. One such case occurred as recently as 1958. After receiving reports that eighteen Garry Lake people had died of starvation, officials of the Department of Northern Affairs and the Hudson's Bay Company requested their arctic personnel to make inquiries. A post manager, in a chance meeting with a Garry Lake woman he had known for many years, obtained the following description and explanation of the incident. "She said they [the people of the community] were not really hungry having plenty of fish but wanted meat. The natives that died ate dog meat, their bodies got badly swollen and the skin started to peel off. The local nurse here says it was trichiniasis [sic]." Reported in HBCA, PAM, Letter from H.W. Sutherland to B.G. Sivertz, May 30, 1958, Native Welfare Files, General Correspondence for 1958, RG7/1/1753.

29. HBCA, PAM, Reports on Districts, B42/e/7, 4; Churchill Post Journals, B42/a/157, 4d, 5d, 6, 7.

30. Ibid., Churchill Post Journals, B42/a/149, 45; Churchill Account Books, B42/d/111.

31. Ibid., Churchill Account Books, B42/d/139.

32. Ibid., Churchill Post Journals, B42/a/93, 30; B42/a/107, 13.

33. Back, *Arctic Artist*, 119; Richardson, *Arctic Ordeal*, 28.

34. Back, *Arctic Artist*, 119.

35. HBCA, PAM, Churchill Post Journals, B42/a/138, 2d.

36. John Franklin, *Narrative of a Journey to the Shores of the Polar Sea in the Years 1819-20-21-22* (1823), 264.

37. Ibid., 263.

38. John West, *Substance of a Journal During a Residence at Red River Colony, British North America in the Years 1820-1823* (1824), 179-80.

39. HBCA, PAM, Churchill Post Journals, B42/a/147, 32; Churchill Account Books, B42/d/111; West, *Substance of a Journal*, 181.

40. Major expeditions of the period were John Franklin's first overland journey from York Factory to the Coppermine River and eastern arctic coast from 1819 to 1822, with John Richardson as surgeon and naturalist, and the two midshipmen, George Back and Robert Hood; Edward Parry's 1819-20 voyage to the east coast of Baffin Island in *Hecla* and *Griper*; Parry's voyage from 1821 to 1823 to northwest Hudson Bay and Melville Peninsula in *Fury* and *Hecla*, with George Lyon as second in command; Franklin's second overland journey to the mouth of the Mackenzie River and the far western arctic coast from 1825 to 1827, with John Richardson as surgeon; Parry's voyage from 1824 to 1827 in *Fury* and *Hecla* to Melville Peninsula; John Ross's exploration of the east coast of Boothia Peninsula in *Victory* from 1829 to 1833; the overland journey of George Back down the Great Fish River (now Back River) from

1833 to 1835; and the explorations of Thomas Simpson and Peter Warren Dease of the Mackenzie River and arctic coasts from 1836 to 1839.

41. Franklin, *Narrative of a Journey to the Shores of the Polar Sea*, 264.

42. Edward Parry, *Journal of a Third Voyage for the Discovery of a North-West Passage From the Atlantic to the Pacific: Performed in the Years 1824-1827 in His Majesty's Ships Fury and Hecla* (1828), 153.

43. Franklin, *Narrative of a Journey to the Shores of the Polar Sea*, 264.

44. Richardson, *Arctic Ordeal*, 108.

45. West, *Substance of a Journal*, 182-83.

46. Ibid.

47. George Lyon, *The Private Journal of Captain G.F. Lyon of H.M.S. Hecla During the Recent Voyage of Discovery Under Captain Parry* (1824), 71; Parry, *Journal of a Second Voyage*, 56, 175, 184.

48. Parry, *Journal of a Second Voyage*, 198.

49. George Comer, A geographical description of Southampton Island and notes upon the Eskimo, *Bulletin of the American Geographical Society* 42, no. 1 (1910): 88.

50. Franz Boas, *The Eskimo of Baffin Land and Hudson Bay* (1901), 6.

51. Lyon, *The Private Journal*, 344; Edward Parry, *Journal of a Second Voyage*, 341, 513.

52. Franklin, *Narrative of a Journey to the Shores of the Polar Sea*, 264.

53. Parry, *Journal of a Second Voyage*, 501; Parry, *Journey of a Third Voyage*, 170.

54. Lyon, *The Private Journal*, 123; Parry, *Journal of a Second Voyage*, 503, 504; and Parry, *Journey of a Third Voyage*, 154-55.

55. Lyon, *The Private Journal*, 160-61, 341; Parry, *Journal of a Second Voyage,* 185, 279, 423, 492.

56. Lyon, *The Private Journal*, 52, 160-61; Parry, *Journal of a Second Voyage*, 51.

57. Parry, *Journal of a Second Voyage,* 513, 549.

58. Parry, *Journal of a Third Voyage*, 170; Parry, *Journal of a Second Voyage*, 171, 198.

59. Parry, *Journal of a Second Voyage*, 160, 492; Lyon, *The Private Journal*, 160-61.

60. Lyon, *The Private Journal,* 307, 437.

61. Parry, *Journal of a Third Voyage*, 153.

62. Ibid., 515.

63. Lyon, *The Private Journal*, 341-42.

64. Ibid., 303.

65. Ibid., 411-12. The incident was also described by Parry, *Journal of a Second Voyage*, 550.

66. Lyon, *The Private Journal*, 293-94; Parry, *Journal of a Second Voyage*, 549.

67. Ibid., Parry, 549.

68. Ibid., 430.

69. Lyon, *The Private Journal,* 344.

70. Parry, *Journal of a Second Voyage*, 175, 184.

71. Lyon, *The Private Journal*, 345-46; also Parry, *Journal of a Second Voyage*, 513-14.

72. Ibid., Parry, 210-11.

73. Lyon, *The Private Journal*, 136-37, 150.

74. Bargaining skills of Hudson Strait people were noted by Parry, *Journal of a Second Voyage*, 13. First encounters in Hudson Strait in the 1730s are described in Richard Glover's introductory notes to *Andrew Graham's Observations on Hudson's Bay 1767-1791*, HBRS edition (1969), xiii. For descriptions of north-coast Hudson Strait people in the early 1800s and the "annual fair," see Edward Chappell, *Narrative of a Voyage to Hudson's Bay in His Majesty's Ship Rosamond* (1817), 58.

75. Desired trade items noted in Chappell, *Narrative of a Voyage*, 58, 62-63. Bargaining strategies are described by Franklin, *Narrative of a Journey to the Shores of the Polar Sea*, 17, and Parry, *Journal of a Second Voyage*, 13-15. The incidents described by Parry took place in 1821, but by the time he wrote up his notes in 1823 or 1824, he had spent two years with the Iglulingmiut and was making direct comparisons between the manners and attitudes of people he knew well as individuals and people he saw only briefly and who had a very different history of contact with Europeans.

76. Bylot's account in Luke Foxe, *The Voyages of Captain Luke Foxe of Hull, and Captain Thomas James of Bristol, in Search of Northwest Passage in 1631-32* (1894), 139-40; Jens Munk, *The Journal of Jens Munk, 1619-1620* (1980), 9-10; Chappell, *Narrative of a Voyage*, 64.

77. West, *Substance of a Journal*, 7.

78. Kaj Birket-Smith, *Ethnography of the Egedesminde District with Aspects of the General Culture of West Greenland* ([1924] 1976), 238.

79. Simple head-count censuses were reported in the 1740s by Henry Ellis, *A Voyage to Hudson's Bay by the Dobbs Galley and California in the Years 1746 and 1847 for Discovering a North West Passage....* ([1748] 1967); in the 1880s by Franz Boas, *The Central Eskimo* ([1888] 1964); between 1814 and 1825 by Chappell, *Narrative of a Voyage*, 98; Franklin, *Narrative of a Journey to the Shores of the Polar Sea*, 18; George Lyon, *A Brief Narrative of an Unsuccessful Attempt to Reach Repulse Bay, Through Sir Thomas Rowe's "Welcome," in His Majesty's Ship Griper in the Year MDCCCXXIV* (1825); and West, *Substance of a Journal*, 7. The stability of numbers between the 1740s and the 1970s was investigated both archaeologically and from historical documents by Moreau S. Maxwell, The Lake Harbour region: ecological equilibrium in sea coast adaptation, in *Thule Eskimo Culture* (1979).

80. Chappell, *Narrative of a Voyage*, 98. Similar descriptions of Baffin Islanders crossing to Ungava appear in Franklin, *Narrative of a Journey to the Shores of the Polar Sea*, 19; Andrew Graham, *Observations on Hudson's Bay, 1767-91* ([1791] HBRS 1969), 213; Theodore Swaine, *An Account of a Voyage for the Discovery of a North-West Passage by Hudson's Streights ...* (1749), 33; and Alexander McDonald, *A Narrative of Some Passages in the History of Eenoolooapik* (1841), 120.

81. Benjamin Kohlmeister and George Kmoch, *Journal of a Voyage from Okkak, on the Coast of Labrador, to Ungava Bay, Westward of Cape Chudleigh* (1814), 47, 67.

82. Kohlmeister and Kmoch, *Journal of a Voyage*, 39-40; Nicolas Jérémie de la Montagne, *Twenty Years of York Factory 1694-1714* ([1720] 1926), 16; Claude C. LeRoy

Bacqueville de la Potherie, Letters of La Potherie, in *Documents Relating to the Early History of Hudson Bay* ([1722] 1931), 279.

83. Kohlmeister and Kmoch, *Journal of a Voyage*, 57, 67.

84. Ibid., 71-72.

85. Ibid., 57, 74, 76.

86. William Hendry's journal, July 14th and 17th, in *Northern Quebec and Labrador Journals and Correspondence* (HBRS 1828), 69-99; and HBCA, PAM, Rupert House Correspondence Books, B186/b/15, 10-11. For 1752 attack on Moravian missionaries, see Glyndwr Williams, Introduction, in *Northern Quebec and Labrador Journals and Correspondence, 1819-1835* (HBRS 1963), xxiv, xxxv; and for the 1754 incident, see HBCA, PAM, Fort Richmond post journals, B182/a/6, 33.

87. HBCA, PAM, Journal of Nicol Finlayson, B38/a/1, July 27, 1830; also in K.G. Davies, *Northern Quebec and Labrador Journals and Correspondence, 1819-1835* (HBRS 1963), 108.

88. Ibid., Journal of Nicol Finlayson, B38/a/1, August 31 to September 3, 1830. Also in Davies, *Northern Quebec and Labrador Journals and Correspondence*, 115, 116-17.

89. Ibid., Journal of Nicol Finlayson, September 3, 1830; and Davies, *Northern Quebec and Labrador Journals,* 116-17.

90. Bernard Saladin d'Anglure, Inuit of Quebec, in *Handbook of North American Indians,* vol. 5, *Arctic* (1984), 480.

91. HBCA, PAM, Journal of Nicol Finlayson, B38/a/1, entries for October 21, November 8, 1830, and January 10 and 15, 1831; also Davies, *Northern Quebec and Labrador Journals,* 125, 130-31.

92. Williams, Introduction, in *Northern Quebec and Labrador Journals and Correspondence,* lxiii.

93. HBCA, PAM, Letter from Nicol Finlayson at Fort Chimo to Chief Factor George Mactavish, February 14, 1831, B239/c/29. Also Davies, *Northern Quebec and Labrador Journals,* 183. In 1888 Franz Boas made much the same point, noting that "I do not know of any cases of famine arising from the absolute want of game, but only from the impossibility of reaching it." See Boas, *The Central Eskimo,* 19. Boas probably overstated the case. His explanation is not necessarily applicable to situations where people are dependent on caribou for winter food. Because caribou numbers and routes vary unpredictably, scarcity, famine, and starvation could and did result from the absolute absence of game.

94. HBCA, PAM, Journal of Nicol Finlayson, B38/a/1, May 19 and 20, 1831; Davies, *Northern Quebec and Labrador Journals,* 143.

95. Ibid, Journal of Finlayson, December 1831 to May 1832; Davies, *Northern Quebec and Labrador Journals,* 161-66.

96. HBCA, PAM, Letter from Nicol Finlayson to Erland Erlandson, September 12, 1832, B38/b/1; Davies, *Northern Quebec and Labrador Journals*, 190.

97. HBCA, PAM, Letter from Nicol Finlayson to Governor and Committee of the Hudson's Bay Company, B38/b/1, September 20, 1830; and Davies, *Northern Quebec and Labrador Journals,* 157, 160-61, 179, 227; HBCA, PAM, Journal of Nicol Finlayson,

B38/a/1, B38/a/1, September 11 and November 20, 1831; HBCA, PAM, Letter from Nicol Finlayson to George Simpson, March 31, 1834, B38/a/3.

98. HBCA, PAM, Letter from Nicol Finlayson to George Simpson, March 31, 1834, B38/a/3; Davies, *Northern Quebec and Labrador Journals,* 225.

99. HBCA, PAM, Letter from Nicol Finlayson to George Mactavish, February 14, 1831, B239/c/2; Davies, *Northern Quebec and Labrador Journals,* 185.

Chapter 6

1. Knud Rasmussen, *Report of the Fifth Thule Expedition, 1921-24,* vol. 8: 1-2, The Netsilik Eskimos, Social Life and Spiritual Culture (1931), 135.

2. Edward Parry, *Journal of a Second Voyage for the Discovery of a North-West Passage From the Atlantic to the Pacific: Performed in the Years 1821-22-23 in His Majesty's Ships Fury and Hecla* (1824), 513; Parry, Account of the Esquimaux of Melville Peninsula and the adjoining islands, in *Journal of a Third Voyage for the Discovery of a North-West Passage From the Atlantic to the Pacific: Performed in the Years 1824-27 in His Majesty's Ships Fury and Hecla* (1828), 153, 170-71; John Ross, *Narrative of a Second Voyage in Search of a North-west Passage and of a Residence in the Arctic Regions During the Years 1829-30-31-32-33* (1835), 252, 254; Therkel Mathiassen, *Archaeology of the Central Eskimos, I: Descriptive Part* (1927), 25, 82-83; James Savelle, Effect of nineteenth century European exploration on the development of the Netsilik Inuit culture, in *The Franklin Era in Canadian Arctic History* (1985), 205.

3. Rasmussen, *Report of the Fifth Thule Expedition,* vol. 8: 1-2, 131; Asen Balikci, *The Netsilik Eskimo* (1970), xviii.

4. B.T. Alt et al., Arctic climate during the Franklin era as deduced from ice cores, in *The Franklin Era in Canadian Arctic History, 1845-1859* (1985), 69, 70, 73.

5. John Ross, *Narrative of a Second Voyage,* 309. 'Netsilik', like 'Iglulik', is an umbrella term applied by the members of the Fifth Thule Expedition to the more or less culturally related communities at Pelly Bay, Boothia Peninsula, the Great Fish River, and parts of King William Island and Adelaide Peninsula. Boothia people seem to have used the word as a place name, not as an ethnic identifier. Like the so-called Iglulik people, the Netsilik, if they identified themselves as ethnic units at all, used the names of the villages they regarded as their principal residences: Netsilingmiut at Netsilik Lake, Arvilingjuarmiut at Arvilikjuaq (Pelly Bay), and so on.

6. Ohokto [Inuit account of meeting between Netsilik and John Ross, 1830], in L.A. Learmonth, Ross meets the Netchiliks, *The Beaver* (September 1948): 10.

7. Ibid., 11.

8. Ross, *Narrative of a Second Voyage,* 242, 244.

9. Ibid.

10. Ibid., 309. The Arvilingjuarmiut history of the meeting, passed down through nearly a century, was also described in Rasmussen, *Report of the Fifth Thule Expedition,* vol. 8: 1-2, 27-28.

11. Ross, *Narrative of a Second Voyage,* 355, 389, 423, 427.

12. Rasmussen, *Report of the Fifth Thule Expedition,* vol. 8: 1-2, 23.

13. Ross, *Narrative of a Second Voyage,* 423.

14. John Ross, *Appendix to the Narrative of a Second Voyage in Search of a North-West Passage* (1835), 60. Franz Boas's estimate, in *The Central Eskimo* ([1888] 1964), 46, which has been widely cited since publication, was based on Ross's, but the two do not agree. Boas assumed that the thirty-one men who made the first approach to Ross were all Arvilikjuaq people living at Lord Mayor's Bay, and extrapolated from this a total Arvilingjuarmiut population of 120. He also assumed that each of the twenty-one winter houses Ross saw at Netsilik was occupied by about eight people, and he arrived at a total figure for the Netsilingmiut of 170. To those figures he added his guess (and it was no more than that) of sixty people at Owutta, to conclude that the total population was about 350 persons in the 1820s. By assuming that none of the people in the winter village at Lord Mayor's Bay were Netsilingmiut, Boas effectively counted them twice, once as residents of the winter village and once as residents of Netsilik. Ross's *Appendix*, published separately from his *Narrative*, contains biographical information on families and households that allows for closer identification of individuals and makes it clear that Boas had counted some people twice.

15. Asen Balikci, Female infanticide on the arctic coast, *Man: The Journal of the Royal Anthropological Institute* 2 (1967): 618.

16. Ross, *Narrative of a Second Voyage*, 259-62, 266, 273, 274. Leopold McClintock searched for Owutta during his visit in May 1859, but was unable to find it due to thick fog. Leopold McClintock, *The Voyage of the 'Fox' in the Arctic Seas: A Narrative of the Discovery of the Fate of Sir John Franklin and His Companions* (1859), 258.

17. Guy Mary-Rousselière, The grave of Kukigak, *Eskimo* 57 (December 1960): 22; Balikci, *The Netsilik Eskimo*, 182-83; Rasmussen, *The Netsilik Eskimos*, 440, 444-45; Geert van Steenhoven, *Legal Concepts among the Netsilik Eskimos of Pelly Bay* (1959), 55-57.

18. Balikci, *The Netsilik Eskimo*, 147; Charles Francis Hall, *Narrative of the Second Arctic Expedition Made By Charles F. Hall: His Voyage to Repulse Bay, Sledge Journeys to the Straits of Fury and Hecla and to King William's Land, and Residence Among the Eskimos During the Years 1864-69* (1879), 258-59.

19. Balikci, *The Netsilik Eskimo*, 184.

20. Geert van den Steenhoven, A 'Good Old Days' Eskimo story at the Netsilike, *Eskimo* (March-June 1962): 12.

21. Balikci, *The Netsilik Eskimo*, 183-84.

22. Frederick Schwatka, *The Long Arctic Search: The Narrative of Lieutenant Frederick Schwatka, U.S.A., 1878-1880, Seeking the Records of the Lost Franklin Expedition* ([1880] 1965), 66.

23. Ross, *Narrative of a Second Voyage*, 307, 308.

24. *Qikertaq* is an obvious variant of *Kekerten*, the name of one of the islands in Frobisher Bay.

25. Balikci, *The Netsilik Eskimo*; Boas, *The Central Eskimo*; James Savelle, The nature of nineteenth century Inuit occupations of the High Arctic islands of Canada, *Études/Inuit/Studies* 5, no. 2 (1985).

26. Ross, *Appendix to the Narrative of a Second Voyage*, 39, 43, 52.

27. David C. Woodman, *Unravelling the Franklin Mystery: Inuit Testimony* (1991), 295.

28. Ross, *Narrative of a Second Voyage*, 244; and Ross, *Appendix to the Narrative of a Second Voyage*, 2.

29. James Savelle, Effect of nineteenth century European exploration, 204.

30. Ross, Narrative of a second voyage, *The Beaver* (September 1948): 13.

31. McClintock, *The Voyage of the 'Fox'*, 235.

32. Ibid., 257-58.

33. Ibid., 258.

34. Netsilik sleds in 1857-58 described by McClintock, *The Voyage of the 'Fox'*, 233. Arvilikjuaq sled construction described by John Rae, *Narrative of an Expedition to the Shores of the Arctic Sea in 1846 and 1847* (1850), 124.

35. Rae, *Narrative of an Expedition*, 121.

36. George Back, *Narrative of the Arctic Land Expedition to the Mouth of the Great Fish River and Along the Shores of the Arctic Ocean in the Years 1833, 1834, and 1845* (1836), 197, 198, 202. The Great Fish River is known to the Chipewyan as Thlew-ee-choh, and to the Inuit as Irqalikjuak. The meaning of the name is the same in all three languages. After George Back's mapping of the river from 1833 to 1835, it became known as Back River, which is now the official designation.

37. Ibid., 200-01, 227.

38. Alt et al., Arctic climate during the Franklin era, 69.

39. Hall, *Narrative of a Second Arctic Expedition*, 589.

40. Rasmussen, *Report of the Fifth Thule Expedition*, vol. 8: 1-2, 120.

41. James Clark Ross, Narrative of the proceedings of Captain Sir James C. Ross in command of the expedition through Lancaster Sound and Barrow Strait, *Great Britain, Parliament, House of Commons, Sessional Papers, Accounts and Papers* 35 (1850): 58-64.

42. Woodman, *Unravelling the Franklin Mystery*, 287. John Rae gives a similar account in *Arctic Correspondence with the Hudson's Bay Company on Arctic Exploration, 1844-55* (1855), 273-74.

43. Woodman, *Unravelling the Franklin Mystery*, 24-25. "Innookpoozhejook" is Charles Francis Hall's spelling of the man's name; John Rae's transliteration of the same name was "Imikepahugiuke."

44. James Anderson, Chief Factor James Anderson's Back River Journal of 1855, *Canadian Field Naturalist, Part 2*, 55 (March 1941): 25. George Lyon had earlier described kettles made by Iglulingmiut women in the same general style. "[The women] have an ingenious method of making lamps and cooking-pots of flat slabs of stone, which they cement together by a composition of seal's blood applied warm, the vessel being held at the same time over the flame of a lamp, which dries the plaster to the hardness of a stone." Lyon added in a footnote that the blood is combined with a whitish clay and some dog's hair. In George Lyon, *The Private Journal of Captain G.F. Lyon of H.M.S. Hecla During the Recent Voyage of Discovery Under Captain Parry* (1824), 320.

45. James Anderson, Chief Factor James Anderson's Back River Journal, *Canadian Field Naturalist, Part 1,* 54 (May 1940): 135; Diamond Jenness, Comments on James Anderson's Back River Journal of 1855, *Canadian Field Naturalist* 54 (May 1940): 135.

46. McClintock, *The Voyage of the 'Fox'*, 232, 257, 260.

47. Ikinnelik-Puhtoorak described himself as a little boy at the time of Back's descent of the Great Fish River in 1834, which could mean he was anywhere up to fourteen years old at the time. When he saw the dead man on the ship, he was an adult with a seven-year-old son of his own. Schwatka guessed the son's age at about thirty-five in 1879, and he would have been seven sometime between 1847 and 1851, which coincides with the period in which Franklin's ships were abandoned.

48. William Gilder, *The Search for Franklin: A Narrative of the American Expedition Under Lieutenant Schwatka, 1878 to 1880* (1882), 30–32; Heinrich Klutschak, *Overland to Starvation Cove: With the Inuit in Search of Franklin, 1878-1880* ([1881] 1987), 65, 131; McClintock, *The Voyage of the 'Fox'*, 227, 236-37; Schwatka, *The Long Arctic Search*, 61–62.

The expedition led by Frederick Schwatka from 1878 to 1880 produced three narratives of events. First to appear was that of William Gilder, a reporter for the *New York Herald*. His paper ran his serialized account in September and October of 1880, and in 1881 he produced a book. Also in 1881, Heinrich Klutschak, an interpreter on transatlantic steamers and a freelance journalist, published his account in German. It was a major source for Franz Boas's material on the Netsilik, and appeared in its first English edition, translated and edited by William Barr, in 1987. Frederick Schwatka's diary was not published until 1965 under the editorship of E.A. Stackpole.

The accounts of Gilder and Schwatka agree in nearly all details. Klutschak's contains two significant differences: he identified Ikinnelik-Puhtoorak as Utkusiksalingmiut, not Ugjulingmiut, and claimed that it was the former who had been attacked and nearly destroyed by the combined efforts of Ugjulingmiut and Netsilingmiut. The accounts of Charles Francis Hall support the Gilder and Schwatka versions of events, as does the rather slim evidence recorded by James Anderson.

49. There is a real possibility that Anderson was right. In 1856 a group of people from Whale Cove-Rankin Inlet told the Churchill traders that they had spent 1855-56 far to the west, and that their journey there had occupied 45 days (HBCA, PAM, Churchill Post Journal, 1856, B42/a/188, 26d, 27d), details which fit with their having been at Great Fish River during Anderson's visit.

50. Hall, *Narrative of the Second Arctic Expedition*, 258–59.

51. Ipervik (Joe Eberbing), Appendix No. 1, Joseph Eberling's statement, *Journal of the American Geographical Society of New York* 12 (1880): 279.

52. Hall, *Narrative of the Second Arctic Expedition*, 274.

53. Ibid., 259.

54. Thomas F. Barry, Appendix No. 1, Thomas F. Barry's statement, *Journal of the American Geographical Society of New York* 12 (1880): 278. Barry may have attributed hostility to the people of Pelly Bay (not the Netsilingmiut specifically) through misunderstanding, or his comment may indicate that larger numbers of Netsilingmiut were living at Pelly Bay than previously, perhaps even making up the majority of residents there.

55. Gilder, *Schwatka's Search*, 77.

56. R.R. Baker, *The Evolutionary Ecology of Animal Migration* (1978), 44–52, 170–71; Ernest S. Burch, The caribou/wild reindeer as a human resource, *American Antiquity* 37 (1972): 359; C.H.D. Clarke, *A Biological Investigation of the Thelon Game Sanctuary* (1940), 63; D.R. Kelsall, *The Migratory Barren-Ground Caribou of Canada* (1968), 205;

G.R. Parker, Biology of the Kaminuriak population of barren-ground caribou, Part I, *Canadian Wildlife Service Report* Series 20 (1972), 23; Douglas R. Stenton, Caribou population dynamics and Thule culture adaptations on southern Baffin Island, N.W.T., *Arctic Anthropology* 28, no. 2 (1991); William Fitzhugh, *Environmental Archeology and Cultural Systems in Hamilton Inlet, Labrador: A Survey of the Central Labrador Coast from 3000 BC to the Present* (1972), 185; Leah Minc, Scarcity and survival: the role of oral tradition in mediating subsistence crises, *Journal of Anthropological Archaeology* 5 (1986): 58; Arthur E. Spiess, *Reindeer and Caribou Hunters: An Archaeological Study* (1979), 66.

57. Christian Vibe, Arctic animals in relation to climatic fluctuations, *Meddelelser om Grønland* 170, no. 5 (1967): 165; Minc, Scarcity and survival, 5.

58. David Hoffman, Inuit land use on the barren grounds: supplementary notes and analysis, in *Report: Inuit Land Use and Occupancy Project*, 2 (1976), 71; Spiess, *Reindeer and Caribou Hunters,* 44.

59. HBCA, PAM, Churchill Post Journals, B42/a/159, 1d, and B42/a/160, 28d; Reports on Districts, B42/e/7.

60. Ibid., Churchill Post Journals, B42/a/160, 8.

61. Ibid., B42/a/159, 179.

62. Ibid. B42/a/165, 7 reports on the loss of oil in 1835. A description of the drowning incident is at B42/a/172, 6d-7; B42/a/165-166. Reports on Districts, B42/e/8:3d, records the Inuit's consistent refusals to participate in the whale hunt.

63. Ibid., Churchill Post Journals, B42/a/165, 24d (1836); B42/a/166, 21 (1837); B42/a/165, 172 (1838), and B42/a/167, 23 (1840).

64. Ibid., B42/a/165 (1836), 172 (1840); B42/a/172-173 (1841–42).

65. Ibid., B42/a/173, 19d (February 1841); B42/a/173, 23b-23bd (April 1841); B42/a/173:17d (December 1841).

66. Ibid., B42/a/157, 3; B42/a/173, 23b-25; B42/a/175, 16-16d; B42/a/175; B42/a/177.

67. Ibid., B42/a/179, 17.

68. Ibid., B42/a/179, 18.

69. Ibid., B42/a/179, 18d-19. Ullebuk, or Ouligbuck the Younger, later called Ouligbuck Senior, along with Augustine, was a member of John Franklin's second overland expedition to the mouth of the Mackenzie River in 1825. On his return, he worked at Churchill and Fort Chimo. Between 1838 and 1843, he was with Thomas Simpson and Peter Warren Dease on their exploration of the western arctic coast, after which he returned to the post at Churchill. He died there in 1852. See E.E. Rich, ed., Appendix B: biographical B1 lists, in John Rae, *John Rae's Correspondence with the Hudson's Bay Company* (1953), 370-73.

70. HBCA, PAM, Churchill Post Journals, B42/a/179, 19-20.

71. Ibid., B42/a/179, 22.

72. Ibid., B42/a/181, 1, 8.

73. Ibid., B42/a/181, 25-25d.

74. Back, *Narrative of the Arctic Land Expedition,* 240.

75. HBCA, PAM, B42/a/183, 30d, 42d, 44d.

76. Ibid., B42/a/183:52-52d; Rae, *Narrative of an Expedition*, 23-28.

77. George Back, *Arctic Artist: The Journal and Paintings of George Back, Midshipman with Franklin, 1819-1822* (1994), 119; John Richardson, *Arctic Ordeal: The Journal of John Richardson, Surgeon-Naturalist with Franklin, 1820-1822* (1984), 28.

78. Rae, *Narrative of an Expedition*, 27.

79. Ibid., 69, 73, 75.

80. Ibid., 89-90, 124.

81. Ibid., 76, 78, 99.

82. Ibid., 169 (Aivilik), 178 (Igloolik), 173 (influenza); HBCA, PAM, Churchill Post Journals, B42/a/183, 70 (possible measles).

83. HBCA, PAM, Churchill Post Journals, B42/a/183.

84. Rae, *Narrative of an Expedition*, 182, 188-89. Ullebuk Senior had at least three children: a son Donald, the only known child of his first marriage; and a daughter and son from his second marriage, according to Letitia Hargrave, *The Letters of Letitia Hargrave (1838-52)* (1947), 164. The younger son was William, also known as Marko, and referred to in the 1860s Churchill journals as Buck. William was with his father and Rae in Repulse Bay during the winter of 1846-47, so the son who walked from Rankin Inlet to Churchill was probably Donald. Donald's presence at Rankin Inlet is an indication that Augustine and the Ullebuks were from somewhere between Whale Cove and Chesterfield Inlet.

85. HBCA, PAM, Churchill Post Journals, B42/a/185, 5d.

86. Ibid., B42/a/185, 8d-9.

87. Ibid., B42/a/185:82-9; 14-15, 20-22.

88. Rae, *Narrative of an Expedition*, 89-90; HBCA, PAM, Churchill Post Journals, B42/a/185, 22d-23.

89. HBCA, PAM, Churchill Post Journals, B42/a/185 (1849); B198/a/97, 6, 8-8d (1850); B198/a/97, 9b (Chipewyan); B198/a/97, 17 (north of Whale Cove); B198/a/97, 26d (distant Homeguard).

90. Ibid., B42/a/186-188; B220/a/17.

91. Ibid., B42/a/186, 39d, 48-50 (1852); B42/a/187, 11 (1853).

92. Ibid., B42/a/186, 74.

93. Ibid., B42/a/186, 25, 74; B42/a/189, 42- 43; B42/a/188, 4.

94. Ibid., B220/a/17, 21d; B42/a/187, 35-36.

95. Ibid., B42/a/186, 23d-24d, B42/a/188, 26d, 27d, 31d; B42/a/188, 27d.

96. Ibid., B42/a/188, 32, 33.

97. Ibid., B42/a/188, 6d (1855); B42/a/188, 76d (Ullebuk's trade).

98. Ibid., B42/a/189a, 33.

99. Ibid., B42/a/189b, 35.

100. Ibid., B42/a/189b, 42; B42/a/189a, 31.

101. B42/a/189b, 32d (March 12); B42/a/189b, 33d-34.

102. B42/a/189b:43d (bad news); B42/a/189b:47, 55 (whale hunt); B42/a/189b:44d (relief rations).

103. Population estimates in: 1720, Ernest S. Burch, Caribou Eskimo origins: an old problem reconsidered, *Arctic Anthropology* 15, no. 1 (1978): 26; from 1767 to 1791, Graham, *Observations on Hudson's Bay*, 213; in 1823 and from 1828 to 1832, HBCA, PAM, *Eskimo Trading Book*, B42/d/111, 139, Churchill District Reports, B42/3/5-8; in 1844, Churchill District Report, D5/12; 1881, Fort Churchill Census Books, B42/z/3; 1885, Cumberland House District Report, B49/e/9.

104. Back, *Arctic Artist*, 119; HBCA, PAM, Churchill District Reports, D5/12, 129.

105. HBCA, PAM, Churchill Post Journals, B42/a/142-189a.

106. Ibid., Reports on Districts, B42/e/4, 5.

107. Ibid., Churchill Post Journals, B42/a/173-181; Churchill District Reports, D5/12, 130.

108. Ibid., Churchill Post Journals, B42/a/186-189a; Churchill Post Journals, B42/a/169, 6.

109. Churchill Post Journals, B198/a/97, B220/a/17 17d, 26d; B42/a/186-189a.

110. Ibid., B220/a/17:21d.

Chapter 7

1. Knud Rasmussen, *Report of the Fifth Thule Expedition, 1921-24*, vol. 8: 1-2, *The Netsilik Eskimos, Social Life and Spiritual Culture* (1931), 279-80.

2. Philip Goldring, Inuit economic responses to Euro-American contacts: southeast Baffin Island, 1824-1940, in *Historical Papers* (1986), 158.

3. Ibid., 159.

4. George Lyon, *The Private Journal of Captain G.F. Lyon of H.M.S. Hecla During the Recent Voyage of Discovery Under Captain Parry* (1824), 293-94.

5. Alexander McDonald, *A Narrative of Some Passages in the History of Eenoolooapik* (1841).

6. Whale numbers: McDonald, *A Narrative of Some Passages*, 118. Seal numbers: Henry Toke Munn, The economic life of the Baffin Island Eskimo, *Geographical Journal* 59 (June 1922): 269. Human population: Goldring, Inuit economic responses, 156.

7. Goldring, Inuit economic responses, 159-60.

8. E. Vale Blake, *Arctic Experiences: Containing Capt. George E. Tyson's Wonderful Drift on the Ice-Floe* (1874), 89-90.

9. W. Gillies Ross, *Arctic Whalers, Icy Seas: Narratives of the Davis Strait Whale Fishery* (1985), 155-56. The emergence of an English-Inuktitut pidgin is noted on page 172.

10. Ibid., 173.

11. Ibid., 172.

12. Franz Boas, *The Eskimo of Baffin Land and Hudson Bay, Bulletin of the American Museum of Natural History* 15, no. 2: 377-78. Boas never visited Hudson Bay. His information came from George Comer, captain of the New England whaler *Era*, who had met Boas and agreed to send him ethnographic information on a regular basis. Everything known about Captain Comer suggests he was a reliable witness. His understanding of

Inuit demography, derived from local informants, accords with what Lyon, Rae, and HBC observers reported. Lyon, *The Private Journal*, 342; John Rae, *Narrative of an Expedition to the Shores of the Arctic Sea in 1846 and 1847* (1850), 27-34, 178-99; HBCA, PAM, Churchill District Report, 1844, D5/12:130.

13. Samuel Isaac Robinson, *The Influence of the American Whaling Industry on the Aivilingmiut, 1860-1919* (1973), 49-50.

14. Ibid., 33.

15. W. Gillies Ross, *Whaling and Eskimos: Hudson Bay 1860-1915* (1975), 49, 64-65.

16. On the re-occupation of Nuvuk, see Charles Francis Hall, *Narrative of the Second Arctic Expedition Made By Charles F. Hall: His Voyage to Repulse Bay, Sledge Journeys to the Straits of Fury and Hecla and to King William's Land, and Residence Among the Eskimos During the Years 1864-69* (1879); and Therkel Mathiassen, *Report of the Fifth Thule Expedition, 1921-24, Material Culture of the Iglulik Eskimos* (1928), 28. On the midpoint village, see Albert P. Low, *Report on the Dominion Government Expedition to Hudson Bay and the Arctic Island on Board the D.G.S. Neptune 1903-04* (1906), 32.

17. 1864-65 observations: Robinson, *The Influence of the American Whaling Industry*, 114; 1866 observations: Hall, *Narrative of the Second Arctic Expedition*, 275, 278.

18. Robinson, *The Influence of the American Whaling Industry*, 47.

19. Hall, *Narrative of the Second Arctic Expedition*, 100.

20. George Comer, in Robinson, *The Influence of the American Whaling Industry*, 111.

21. Robinson, *The Influence of the American Whaling Industry*, 47-50.

22. Ibid., 111-12.

23. Ross, *Whaling and Eskimos*, 66.

24. Ibid., 65.

25. Robinson, *The Influence of the American Whaling Industry*, 33.

26. Heinrich Klutschak, *Overland to Starvation Cove* ([1881] 1987), 22.

27. Peter Freuchen, *Arctic Adventure: My Life in the Frozen North* (1935), 385; Archie Hunter, *Northern Traders: Caribou Hair in the Stew* (1983), 17.

28. The 1861 incident was reported in Robinson, *The Influence of the American Whaling Industry*, 69. For a description of boat owners at Wager Bay in 1865, see Hall, *Narrative of the Second Arctic Expedition*, 63, 173. Marble Islanders and "faraway" Inuit arriving at Churchill in 1874 and 1875 are described in HBCA, PAM, Churchill Post Journals, B42/a/192, 128, 149d. William Ouligbuck's success as a marine entrepreneur, as well as the use of boats generally after 1878, were described by Frederick Schwatka, *The Long Arctic Search: The Narrative of Lieutenant Frederick Schwatka* (1880), 26.

William Ullebuk had accompanied John Rae on the journey to Chantrey Inlet in search of the lost Franklin expedition from 1852 to 1854. Rae considered him a good interpreter and hunter, but dishonest and unreliable. See John Rae, *John Rae's Correspondence with the Hudson's Bay Company on Arctic Exploration, 1844-1855* (1953), 239. The Pelly Bay Inuit called him Mar-ko or Mokko, possibly Makkok, meaning "two." Rumours among the Inuit that Captain Marco had come by his schooner in devious ways reached the whaling captains, and were recorded in the logbook of the whaler *Isabella*. See Ross, *Whaling and Eskimos*, 93, and Schwatka, *The Long Arctic Search*,

26. He worked for the Hudson's Bay Company from 1856 to 1861, 1872 to 1874, and 1882 to 1894. See E.E. Rich, ed., Appendix B, biographical B1 lists in Rae, *John Rae's Correspondence*, 370-74.

29. William Gilder, *Schwatka's Search* (1881), 41; Hall, *Narrative of the Second Arctic Expedition*, 62, 302, 337; Robinson, *The Influence of the American Whaling Industry*, 66-69; and HBCA, PAM, London Letter Books, A6/40.

30. Hall, *Narrative of the Second Arctic Expedition*, 302.

31. HBCA, PAM, Churchill Post Journals, B42/a/190, 23.

32. Ibid., B42/a/191, 54; London Letter Books, A6/40, 237; and Ross, *Whaling and Eskimos*, 66.

33. Robert Ferguson, *Arctic Harpooner: A Voyage on the Schooner Abbie Bradford, 1878-1879* (1879), 84.

34. Ross, *Whaling and Eskimos*, 47.

35. Log of *A.R. Tucker*: Robinson, *The Influence of the American Whaling Industry*, 55. Log of *Era*: Ross, *Whaling and Eskimos*, 69-70.

36. HBCA, PAM, Churchill Post Journals, B42/a/191, 49, 52d, 93d; Churchill Correspondence Books; B42/b/61, 57; Churchill Post Journals, B42/a/189b, 68d.

37. Ibid., Churchill Correspondence Books. In 1862: B42/b/61, 65d; in 1866, B42/b/61, 84.

38. Ibid., B42/b/61, 60, 63.

39. Ibid., 1862: B42/b/61, 65d; 1862-63 winter: B42/b/61, 67; 1863 summer: B42/b/61:68; 1869: B42/b/62, 11.

40. Ibid., B42/b/62, 3; B42/b/62, 9d-10.

41. Ibid., B42/b/62, 9d.

42. Ibid., B42/b/62, 14d-15.

43. Ibid., B42/b/62, 16; B42/b/62, 20.

44. Ibid., B42/b/62, 2; 26.

45. Ibid., Churchill Post Journals, B42/a/192, 58. Chief Factor James MacTavish did not believe Ullebuk's story. On reading Churchill's report of the incident in his Letter Book, he pencilled in the margin, "The above is one of Buck's yarns and not true." See Churchill Correspondence Books, B42/b/62, 27.

46. Ibid., Churchill Correspondence Books, B42/a/62, 58.

47. Ibid., 59.

48. Ibid., Churchill Post Journals, B42/a/191, 70.

49. Ibid., B42/a/192, 91.

50. Ibid., Churchill Correspondence Books, B42/b/62, 26-26d.

51. Ibid., Churchill Post Journals. On snowfall: B42/a/192, 114. On miserable plight and ammunition: B42/a/192, 93-94, 113.

52. Ibid. For 1871 events, see Churchill Post Journals, 1871-1906; and for 1872, B42/a/192, 142. For 1873 events, see Churchill Correspondence Books, B42/b/62, 34d, 35d.

53. Ibid., Churchill Post Journals, B42/a/192.

54. Alphonse Gasté's 1869 journal, Father Gasté meets the Inland Eskimos; and comments by Guy Mary-Rousselière, Importance of Father Gasté's voyage, *Eskimo* 57 (December 1960): 13-17.

55. HBCA, PAM, Churchill Correspondence Books, B42/b/62, 22-22d.

56. Ibid., B42/b/62, 13, 36.

57. Ibid., Census Books, B42/z/2; Cumberland House District Report, B49/e/9, 4.

58. Ibid., Churchill Correspondence Books, B42/b/62, 58d.

59. Ibid., Churchill Correspondence Books, B42/b/62, 72a, and Cumberland House District Reports, B49/b/13, 2, on the 1887 winter. Lac du Brochet District Reports, B296/e/1, 1, on the 1889-90 winter.

60. Ibid., Churchill Correspondence Books, B42/b/62, 62-63d.

61. Ernest S. Burch, Muskox and man in the central Canadian subarctic, 1689-1974, *Arctic* 30, no. 3 (September 1977): 144.

62. HBCA, PAM, Churchill Correspondence Books, B42/b/62, 72ad-72b, 98d-99; London Letter Books, A11/16, 54-54d.

63. Ibid., Churchill Post Journals, B42/a/189a, 34d, and B42/a/190-191 for count of robes brought to the post; Churchill Correspondence Books, 1810-91, B42/b/62, 11, for returns from Marble Island.

64. Ibid., Churchill Correspondence Books, B42/b/62, 63.

65. Ibid., Churchill Post Journals, B42/a/190.

66. From counts taken by or reported to members of the government expeditions, in Albert P. Low, *Report on the Dominion Government Expedition to Hudson Bay and the Arctic Islands on Board the D.G.S. Neptune 1903-04* (1906), 270; and from ships' logs in Robinson, *The Influence of the American Whaling Industry*, 117-18.

67. Kaj Birket-Smith, *Report of the Fifth Thule Expedition, 1921-1924,* vol. 5, *The Caribou Eskimos: Material and Social Life and Their Cultural Position I: Descriptive Part* (1929), 67; Knud Rasmussen, *Report of the Fifth Thule Expedition, 1921-24,* vol.7, *Iglulik and Caribou Eskimo Texts* (1930), 5; Thomas Correll, Language and location in traditional Inuit societies, in *Report: Inuit Land Use and Occupancy Project* 2 (1976), 174; Robert G. Williamson, *Eskimo Underground: Socio-Cultural Changes in the Canadian Central Arctic* (1974), 17-18.

68. Birket-Smith, *The Caribou Eskimos*, 67-68; Ernest S. Burch, The Caribou Inuit, in *Native Peoples: The Canadian Experience* (1986), 109, 127.

69. Christian Leden, *Across the Keewatin Icefields: Three Years Among the Canadian Eskimos, 1913-1916* ([1927] 1990), 145, 150, 152-53.

70. John Franklin, *Narrative of a Journey to the Shores of the Polar Sea in the Years 1819-20-21-22* (1823), 264; HBCA, PAM, Churchill Post Journals, B42/a/142; John West, *Substance of a Journal During a Residence at the Red River Colony, British North America in the Years 1820-1823* (1824), 182-83.

71. Guy Mary-Rousselière, Eskimo migrations, *Eskimo* 51 (June 1959): 13; Rasmussen, *Report of the Fifth Thule Expedition,* vol.7, 28; Thomas Simpson, *Narrative of the Discoveries on the North Coast of America; Effected by the Officers of The Hudson's Bay Company During the Years 1836-39* (1843), 70-71.

72. HBCA, PAM, Adam Snodie, in Churchill Post Journal, B42/a/142, 13d. John Rae, On the Esquimaux, *Transactions of the Ethnological Society of London*, new series, 4 (1866), 139.

73. Birket-Smith, *Report of the Fifth Thule Expedition*, vol.5, 161.

74. Robinson, *The Influence of the American Whaling Industry*, 120.

75. James W. Tyrrell, *Across the Sub-Arctics of Canada: A Journey of 3,200 Miles by Canoes and Snow-Shoe* (1898), 107-08, 111.

76. Observations at Chesterfield Inlet by Klutschak, *Overland to Starvation Cove*, 152; at Rankin Inlet by J. Lofthouse, A trip on the Tha-anne River, Hudson Bay, *Geographical Journal* 13 (1922): 107; by Pelletier, in *Royal Canadian Mounted Police Annual Report* (1910), 155.

77. Alphonse Gasté's 1869 journal, Father Gasté meets the Inland Eskimos, 10-12.

78. Klutschak, *Overland to Starvation Cove*, 200.

79. Hall, *Narrative of the Second Arctic Expedition*, 81-82. Revenge journey described by Klutschak, *Overland to Starvation Cove*, 201.

80. Roald Amundsen, *The North West Passage*, vol. 1 (1908), 292-93.

81. Ibid., vol. 1, 287-319; vol. 2 (1908), 3.

82. Amundsen, *The North West Passage*, vol. 1, 293-94.

83. Population estimate for 1920s, David Damas, The contact-traditional horizon of the central arctic: reassessment of a concept and reexamination of an era, *Arctic Anthropology* 25, no. 2 (1988): 115; for 1938, Gontian de Poncins, *Kabloona* (1941).

84. George Comer, A geographical description of Southampton Island and notes upon the Eskimo, *Bulletin of the American Geographical Society* 42, no. 1 (1910): 86, 89, 90; George Comer, Notes by G. Comer on the natives of the northwestern shores of Hudson Bay, *American Anthropologist* 23 (1921): 243.

85. H.H. Lamb, *Climate, History and the Modern World* (1982), 250.

86. Therkel Mathiassen, *Report of the Fifth Thule Expedition, 1921-24,* vol.6: 1, *Material Culture of the Iglulik Eskimos* (1928), 17-19, 81.

87. Damas, The contact-traditional horizon, 113-14.

88. Mathiassen, *Report of the Fifth Thule Expedition,* vol.6: 1, 15-20.

89. Four Hudson's Bay Company posts proved to be permanent: Chesterfield Inlet, established in 1911; Baker Lake in 1914; Repulse Bay in 1920; and Coral Harbour (Southampton Island) in 1924. Others were of shorter duration: Coats Island, from 1918 to 1928; Bury Cove at a now-unknown site on Roes Welcome, 1919-20; and Wager Bay from 1926 to 1947. Still others were operated by other companies: Monjo & Company at Fullerton Harbour, from 1913 to 1919; Henry Toke Munn at Coral Harbour from 1916 to 1918; Lamson and Hubbard at Chesterfield Inlet and Baker Lake from 1920 to 1922; and Revillon Frères at Baker Lake and Repulse Bay from 1924 to 1936. For names and dates of trading posts see Peter Usher, *Fur Trade Posts of the Northwest Territories, 1870-1970* (1971), 139-45.

90. James VanStone, Changing patterns of Indian trapping in the Canadian subarctic, *Arctic* 16 (1963): 160-61.

91. Milton M.R. Freeman, *Inuit Land Use and Occupancy Project* (1976).

92. Sydney A. Keighley, *Trader, Tripper, Trapper: The Life of a Bay Man* (1989), 100–14; Peter Usher, *Fur Trade Posts of the Northwest Territories, 1870-1970* (1971), 140–45.

93. Keighley, *Trader, Tripper, Trapper*, 110.

Chapter 8

1. Knud Rasmussen, *Report of the Fifth Thule Expedition, 1921-24,* vol. 10: 3, *The Alaskan Eskimos as Described in the Posthumous Notes of Knud Rasmussen* (1952), 180.

2. Barbara J. Price, The truth is not in accounts but in account books: on the epistemological status of history, in *Beyond the Myths of Culture: Essays in Cultural Materialism* (1980), 156–57.

3. J.L. Anderson, History and climate: some economic models, in *Climate and History: Studies in Past Climates and Their Impact on Man* (1981), 339; John O'Shea and Paul Halstead, Conclusions: bad year economics, in *Bad Year Economics: Cultural Responses to Risk and Uncertainty* (1989), 123.

4. For discussions of economic uncertainty in hunter–gatherer societies, see Charles D. Laughlin and Ivan A. Brady, eds., *Extinction and Survival in Human Populations* (1978), especially articles by Charles A. Bishop, Cultural and biological adaptations to deprivation: the Northern Ojibwa case, and John J. Cove, Survival or extinction: reflections on the problem of famine in Tsimshian and Kaguru mythology. Also E. Colson, In good years and in bad: food strategies of self-reliant societies, *Journal of Anthropological Research* 35 (1979); Paul Halstead et al., *Symposium on Cultural Responses to Risk and Uncertainty* (1984); and James G.E. Smith, Economic uncertainty in an 'original affluent society': caribou and caribou eater Chipewyan adaptive strategies, *Arctic Anthropology* 115 (1978).

5. Paul Halstead and John O'Shea, Introduction: cultural responses to risk and uncertainty, in *Bad Year Economics: Cultural Responses to Risk and Uncertainty* (1989), 4. "Appropriation" is an unfortunate word here. It means to adopt for one's own use without depriving the original owner. In the context of "negative reciprocity," "expropriation," meaning to "dispossess" or "deprive," expresses the intended meaning more aptly.

6. Robert G. Williamson, *Eskimo Underground: Socio-Cultural Change in the Canadian Central Arctic* (1974), 58.

7. Ibid., 20.

8. Thomas Correll, *Ungalaqlingmiut: A Study in Language and Society* (1972), 119.

9. George Lyon, *The Private Journal of Captain G. F. Lyon of H.M.S. Hecla During the Recent Voyage of Discovery Under Captain Parry* (1824), 342.

10. Williamson, *Eskimo Underground*, 27.

11. Lewis R. Binford, When the going gets tough, the tough get going: Nunamiut local groups, camping patterns and economic organization, in *Ethnoarchaeological Approaches to Mobile Campsites: Hunter-Gatherer and Pastoralist Case Studies* (1991), 132.

12. For description and discussion of caribou distributional cycles, see Leah Minc, Scarcity and survival: the role of oral tradition in mediating subsistence crises, *Journal of Anthropological Archaeology* 5 (1986): 71; and Christian Vibe, Arctic animals in relation to climatic fluctuations, *Meddelelser om Grønland* 170, no. 5 (1967).

13. Definition of oral testimony is from Jan Vansina, Once upon a time: oral traditions as history in Africa, *Daedalus* 100 (1971): 444. For examples and discussion of institutionalized information in Alaskan societies, see Minc, Scarcity and survival, 74–77, and Edwin S. Hall, *The Eskimo Storyteller: Folktales from Noatak, Alaska* (1975), 39, 410.

14. Yup'ik storytelling is treated by Ann Fienup-Riordan, *Eskimo Essays: Yup'ik Lives and How We See Them* (1990), 128-29, 244. Inupiat storytelling is described by N. Gubser, *The Nunamiut Eskimos: Hunters of Caribou* (1965), 28-29; Hall, *The Eskimo Storyteller*, 39; Froelich Rainey, *The Whale Hunters of Tigara* (1947), 269; and Minc, Scarcity and survival, 75, 78, 87. Discussion of Greenland stories and storytelling is in Eigil Knuth, Singajuk's family saga, *Folk* 5 (1963): 209-10; Knud Rasmussen, *Report of the Fifth Thule Expedition, 1921-24*, vol. 7: 2, *Observations on the Intellectual Culture of the Caribou Eskimos* (1930), 111; and Hinrich Rink, *Tales and Traditions of the Eskimo* (1875), 83-86.

15. Only stories collected in the field from Eskimo or Inuit informants have been used here. Published collections that meet the criterion appear in: Reports of the Fifth Thule Expedition, Reports of the Canadian Arctic Expedition, and in Franz Boas, *The Central Eskimo, Sixth Annual Report of the Bureau of Ethnology* (1888); Boas, *The Eskimo of Baffin Land and Hudson Bay* 15, no. 1 (1901), and 15, no. 2 (1907); Frank Ellanna, et al., *King Island Tales: Eskimo History and Legends from Bering Strait* (1988); Gubser, *The Nunamiut Eskimos*; Hall, *The Eskimo Storyteller*; Tom Imgalrea, et al., *Eskimo Narratives and Tales From Chevak* (1984); Leoni Kappi, *Inuit Legends* (1977); Diamond Jenness, *Eskimo Folk-Lore* (1926); Maurice Metayer and Agnes Nanogak, *Tales from the Igloo* (1972); John Murdoch, A few legendary fragments from the Point Barrow Eskimo, *American Naturalist* 20 (1886); Agnes Nanogak, *More Tales from the Igloo* (1986); Henry Y. Noholnigee, *The Stories That Chief Henry Told* (1972); Zebedee Nungak and Eugene Arima, *Inuit Stories: Povungnituk* (1988); William A. Oquilluk, *People of Kauwerak: Legends of the Northern Eskimo* (1973); Rink, *Tales and Traditions of the Eskimo*; and Knud Rasmussen, *Eskimo Songs and Stories* (1973).

   In addition to the analysis of particular stories that appears in Minc, Scarcity and survival, see Susan Rowley, *The Significance of Migration for the Understanding of Inuit Cultural Development in the Canadian Arctic* (1985).

16. Minc, Scarcity and survival, 80.

17. Gubser, *The Nunamiut Eskimos*, 33-34, 43-42; Minc, Scarcity and survival, 90-91; Rasmussen, *The Alaskan Eskimos*.

18. Inuit cosmology in: Williamson, *Eskimo Underground*, 21-28. Yup'ik metaphysics in: Fienup-Riordan, *Eskimo Essays*, 172.

19. Vilhjalmur Stefansson, *Greenland* (1942), 163.

20. Fienup-Riordan, *Eskimo Essays*, 188-89.

21. Edward Parry, *Journal of a Second Voyage for the Discovery of a North-West Passage From the Atlantic to the Pacific: Performed in the Years 1821-22-23 in His Majesty's Ships Fury and Hecla* (1824), 190.

22. Ibid., 193.

23. Pars's testimony is in Finn Gad, *The History of Greenland*, vol. 2, *1700-1782* (1973). For Boas's observations at Cumberland Sound, see Boas, *The Central Eskimo* ([1888] 1964),

173-74. Pelly Bay sharing partnership rules are in F.Van de Velde, Rules governing the sharing of seal after the 'aglus' hunt amongst the Arviligjuarmiut, *Eskimo* 41 (September 1956). Sharing practices in Ungava are described in F.F. Payne, *Eskimo of Hudson's Strait, Extract from Proceedings of the Canadian Institute,* Series 3, no. 2 (1889): 2.

24. Diamond Jenness, *The Life of the Copper Eskimos,* vol. 12, part A, *Report of the Canadian Arctic Expedition, 1913-18* (1923), 90. Alaskan Eskimo sharing is described by Lewis R. Binford, When the going gets tough, 28. Conclusions about sharing in hunter-gatherer societies outside the arctic are discussed in O'Shea and Halstead, Conclusions: bad year economics, 124.

25. Williamson, *Eskimo Underground,* 55-56. Williamson's understanding, which he first explained to me in Rankin Inlet in 1962, that in Inuit thought, "love" and "responsibilty to care for" are the same thing, enabled me to make sense of a puzzling conversation I had with a young woman in Cambridge Bay in 1966. She told me she loved her newborn daughter, but regretted her "love" because it had created a conflict with her own mother. Her mother had impressed on her that she (the young woman) could not "love" the baby and must therefore find an adoptive home for it. At the same time, my young friend insisted that her mother was right and she did not love her child. What she was telling me, *in English,* was that she did indeed love the baby (as an English-speaker would use the word "love"), while at the same time telling me, *out of an Inuktitut mental framework,* that because she did not have the resources to feed, clothe, shelter, and otherwise nurture the infant, she could not "love" the baby (as an Inuktitut speaker would use the word "love").

26. Jenness, *The Life of the Copper Eskimos,* vol. 12, part A, 94; Boas, *The Central Eskimo,* 174.

27. Geert van den Steenhoven, Caribou Eskimo legal concepts, *Proceedings of the 32nd International Congress of Americanists,* in *Eskimo of the Canadian Arctic* ([1956] 1968), 82.

28. Asen Balikci, *The Netsilik Eskimo* (1970), 185, 192; Fienup-Riordan, *Eskimo Essays,* 212; Geert van den Steenhoven, *Legal Concepts Among the Netsilik Eskimos of Pelly Bay* (1959), 60, and Caribou Eskimo legal concepts, 79-84; and Williamson, *Eskimo Underground,* 47-49.

29. Balikci, *The Netsilik Eskimo,* 129, 182; Knud Rasmussen, *Report of the Fifth Thule Expedition, 1921-24,* vol. 8, *The Netsilik Eskimos, Social Life and Spiritual Culture* (1931), 88; Geert van den Steenhoven, *Leadership and Law Among the Eskimos of the Keewatin District, Northwest Territories* (1962), 97.

30. Idjuaduk's case is described in van den Steenhoven, Caribou Eskimo legal concepts, 82. The case of Krittark is described in Rasmussen, *Report of the Fifth Thule Expedition,* vol. 8, 143-44, and in van den Steenhoven, *Legal Concepts Among the Netsilik Eskimos of Pelly Bay,* 51.

31. Kaj Birket-Smith, *The Eskimos* (1936), 156.

32. Dorothy Eber Harley, *First Impressions: Inuit Oral Accounts of Early Contact with Whites* (1986), 9.

33. Peter Pitseolak, *People From Our Side* (1975), 77.

34. John Franklin, *Narrative of a Journey to the Shores of the Polar Sea in the Years 1819-20-21-22* (1823), 263.

35. Frank Vallee, Kabloona and Eskimo in the Central Keewatin, in *Canadian Society: Sociological Perspectives* (1964), 411.

36. Franz Boas, *The Eskimo of Baffin Land and Hudson Bay*, Bulletin of the American Museum of Natural History 15, no.1 (1901): 115.

37. Ernest S. Burch, *The Eskimos* (1988), 23-24; Archibald L. Fleming, *Archibald The Arctic*, (1957); Moreau S. Maxwell, The Lake Harbour region: ecological equilibrium in sea coast adaptation, in *Thule Eskimo Culture: An Anthropological Retrospective* (1979), 84; and Clifford G. Hickey, The historic Beringian trade network: its nature and origins, in *Thule Eskimo Culture: An Anthropological Retrospective* (1979), 424.

38. Benjamin Kohlmeister and George Kmoch, *Journal of a Voyage from Okkak on the Coast of Labrador to Ungava Bay Westward of Cape Chudleigh* (1814), 4-5.

39. Harley, *First Impressions*, 9.

40. Boas, *The Eskimo of Baffin Land and Hudson Bay*, 117; F.F. Payne, A few notes upon the Eskimo of Cape Prince of Wales, Hudson's Strait, *Proceedings of the American Association for the Advancement of Science* 38 (1890), 359.

41. General discussion and other examples of Inuit attitudes to strangers are in Boas, *The Central Eskimo*; Boas, *The Eskimo of Baffin Land and Hudson Bay*, nos. 1 and 2; Diamond Jenness, *Myths and Traditions from Northern Alaska, the Mackenzie Delta, and Coronation Gulf*, Report of the Canadian Arctic Expedition 1913-18, 13(A) (1924); Minc, Scarcity and survival; Rowley, Population movements in the Canadian arctic, *Études/Inuit/ Studies* 9, no. 1 (1985): 16-17; Vilhjalmur Stefansson, *The Friendly Arctic: The Story of Five Years in Polar Regions* ([1921] 1943), 426.

42. Copper Indian attitude toward Inuit in 1821 was described by Robert Hood, *To the Arctic by Canoe, 1819-1821: The Journal and Paintings of Robert Hood, Midshipman with Franklin* (1974), 132-33. Copper Inuit attitude toward Netsilingmiut from 1813 to 1818 is described in Jenness, *The Life of the Copper Eskimos*, 49. Netsilingmiut-Aivilingmiut relations are described in William Gilder, *Schwatka's Search: Sledging in the Arctic in Quest of the Franklin Records* (1881), 66. Amulets and other religious means for warding off the danger of strangers are described in Knud Rasmussen, *Across Arctic America* (1927), 184-85.

43. Rasmussen, *Report of the Fifth Thule Expedition,* vol. 8, 202.

44. Heinrich Klutschak, *Overland to Starvation Cove: With the Inuit in Search of Franklin, 1878-1880* (1987), 200; Charles E. Whittaker, *Arctic Eskimo* (1937), 75.

45. Inuit kinship systems and relationships have been described by David Damas, *Iglulingmiut Kinship and Local Groupings: A Structural Approach* (1963); also Damas, The structure of Central Eskimo associations, in *Alliance in Eskimo Society* (1972), 41; also David Damas, Three kinship systems from the central arctic, *Arctic Anthropology* 12, no. 1 (1975); D. Lee Guemple, Kinship and alliance in Belcher Island Eskimo Society, in *Proceedings of the American Ethnological Society for 1971* (1972), 67; also D. Lee Guemple, *Inuit Adoption* (1979), 35; also D. Lee Guemple, Saunik: name sharing as a factor governing Eskimo kinship terms, *Ethnology* 4 (1965): 327; also D. Lee Guemple, *Inuit Spouse-Exchange* (1961); David Riches, *Northern Nomadic Hunter-Gatherers: A Humanistic Approach* (1982), 85; Jenness, *The Life of the Copper Eskimos*, 85-86; Bernard Saladin d'Anglure, Inuit of Quebec, in *Handbook of North American Indians,* vol. 5, *Arctic* (1984), 494.

46. Partnerships in Netsilingmiut society are described by F.Van de Velde, Rules governing the sharing of seal, *Eskimo* 41 (September 1956). Copper Inuit male partnerships are in Jenness, *The Life of the Copper Eskimos*, 923, 87. Mackenzie and Copper Inuit trade partnerships are discussed by Derek Smith, Mackenzie Delta Eskimo, in *Handbook of North American Indians,* vol. 5, *Arctic* (1984), 354. Keewatin Inuit approaches to kinship are in Eugene Y. Arima, Caribou Eskimo, in *Handbook of North American Indians*, vol. 5, *Arctic* (1984), 455. The beginnings of whaleboat partnerships on the west coast of Hudson Bay are seen in HBCA, PAM, Churchill Post Journals, B42/a/132, 20; B42/a/146, 9-10, 11d, and B42/a/148, 98.

47. George Lyon, *A Brief Narrative of an Unsuccessful Attempt to Reach Repulse Bay Through Sir Thomas Rowe's "Welcome" in His Majesty's Ship Griper in the Year MDCCCXXIV* ([1824] 1825), 55.

48. Gilder, *Schwatka's Search*, 83-84. See also eyewitness accounts of meetings in Diamond Jenness, *The People of the Twilight* (1928), 51-52, 121; Lyon, *A Brief Narrative*, 55-56; Rasmussen, *Across Arctic America*, 116; John Ross, *Narrative of a Second Voyage in Search of a North-west Passage and of a Residence in the Arctic Regions During the Years 1829-30-31-32* (1835), 27, 169-70.

49. Francis Leopold McClintock, *The Voyage of the "Fox" in the Arctic Seas: A Narrative of the Discovery of the Fate of Sir John Franklin and His Companions* (1859), 260.

50. William Gilder, *The Search for Franklin: A Narrative of the American Expedition Under Lieutenant Schwatka, 1878 to 1880* (1882), 32.

51. Ibid., 32.

52. Frank Speck, Inland Eskimo bands of Labrador, in *Essays in Anthropology in Honor of Alfred Louis Kroeber* (1936), 316.

53. Therkel Mathiassen, *Report of the Fifth Thule Expedition 1921-24,* vol. 6: 1, *Material Culture of the Igluik Eskimos (*1928), 23.

54. HBCA, PAM, Proposed Transfer of Natives to Spence Bay (Boothia Peninsula) Area from Hudson Straits. Mimeographed memo. Undated [but 1951 or 1952], and Letter from C.K. LeCapelain, to R.H. Chesshire, September 5, 1951, General Correspondence, RG7/1/1752.

55. Yvon Csonka, *Les Ahiarmiut(1920-1950) Dans La Perspective de l'Histoire des Inuit Caribous* (1991), 458.

56. Samuel Robinson, *The Influence of the American Whaling Industry* (1973), 111.

57. Peter Freuchen, *Arctic Adventure: My Life in the Frozen North* (1935), 382.

58. Williamson, *Eskimo Underground*, 19.

59. See Appendix 2 on "infanticide," "suicide," and "gerontocide," as understood and practised by Inuit.

60. Knud Rasmussen, *Report of the Fifth Thule Expedition, 1921-24,* vol.7: 1, *Intellectual Culture of the Iglulik Eskimos* (1929), 56.

61. Ibid., 54.

Appendix 1

1. Ives Goddard, Synonymy, in *Handbook of North American Indians*, vol. 5, *Arctic* (1984), 6; José Mailhot, L'étymologie de 'Esquimau': revue et corrigée, *Études/Inuit/Studies* 2, no. 2 (1978): 65.

2. Richard Hakluyt, *The Original Writings and Correspondence of the Two Richard Hakluyts*, ([1584] 1935), 269.

3. Samuel de Champlain, *The Works of Samuel de Champlain*, vol.5 ([1632] 1933), 177.

4. A consonant shift involving *s* and *h* sounds occurred at some point in the evolution of Inuktitut dialects in the region between the west coast of Hudson Bay and the Great Fish River. The People of the Potstone Place appear in the literature as Utkusiksalingmiut and also as Utkuhikhalingmiut. Similarly, the lake known to eighteenth-century Chipewyan as Yathkyed has been written and pronounced in Inuktitut as Sikolikjuaq and Hikolikjuaq, The Big Ice Place. "Sikimiut" and "Hikimiut" are renderings of the basic word, meaning People of the Ice in different dialects.

5. See dictionaries by Lucien Schneider, *Ulirnaisigutiit: An Inuktitut-English Dictionary of Northern Quebec, Labrador and Eastern Arctic Dialects (with an English Inuktitut Index)* (1985), and Arthur Thibert, *English-Eskimo Dictionary Eskimo-English* (1970).

6. Therkel Matthiassen, *Report of the Fifth Thule Expedition*, vol. 2, *Material Culture of the Iglulik Eskimos* (1928), 21.

7. Ernest S. Burch, *The Eskimos* (1988), 13.

8. Helge Klievan, Greenland Eskimo: introduction, in *Handbook of North American Indians*, vol. 5, *Arctic* (1984), 524, based on eyewitness testimony of Paul Egede in 1750 and David Cranz in 1770.

9. William Thalbitzer, A phonetical study of the Eskimo language based on observations made on a journey in North Greenland 1900-1901, *Meddelelser om Grønland* 31 (1904): 36; Dirmid Ronan F. Collis, Reviews and debates, *Études/Inuit/Studies* 12, nos. 1-2 (1988): 259.

10. On Yup'ik, see Ann Fienup-Riordan, *Eskimo Essays: Yup'ik Lives and How We See Them*, (1990), 5; on St Lawrence Island and Yupiit languages, see Terence Armstrong and Hugh Brody, The term 'Eskimo', *Polar Record* 19, no. 119 (1978): 178.

11. Goddard, Synonymy, 7.

12. Eric Alden Smith, *Inujjuamiut Foraging Strategies: Evolutionary Ecology of an Arctic Hunting Economy* (1991), xix.

13. Armstrong and Brody, The term 'Eskimo', 178.

14. Ibid.

15. Moreau S. Maxwell, Introduction, in *Eastern Arctic Prehistory: Paleoeskimo Problems* (1976), 4.

16. Robert McGhee, *Canadian Arctic Prehistory* (1978), 14.

17. David Morrison, *Arctic Hunters* (1992), 7, and David Morrison, *Thule Culture in Western Coronation Gulf, N.W.T.* (1983), 2. Also see Smith, *Inujjuamiut Foraging Strategies*, xix; and Albert C. Heinrich, Letter to the editor, *Arctic* 33, no.1 (March 1980): 205.

Appendix 2

1. Albert P. Low, *Report on the Dominion Government Expedition to Hudson Bay and the Arctic Islands on Board the D.G.S. Neptune 1903-04* (1906), 165.

2. F.F. Payne, *Eskimo of Hudson's Strait, Extract from Proceedings of the Canadian Institute*, Series 3, 6 (1889): 2.

3. HBCA, PAM, Churchill Post Journals, B42/a/179, 18-19.

4. Frederick Schwatka, *The Long Arctic Search: The Narrative of Lieutenant Frederick Schwatka, U.S.A., 1878-1880* (1880), 62; Francis Leopold McClintock, *The Voyage of the 'Fox'* (1859), 153-54.

Appendix 3

1. Harvey Nichols, The post-glacial history of vegetation and climate at Ennadai Lake, Keewatin, and Lynn Lake, Manitoba (Canada), *Euszeitalter und Gegenwart* 18 (1967); Harvey Nichols, Pollen diagrams from sub-arctic Central Canada, *Science* 155 (1967); and Harvey Nichols, Central Canadian palynology and its relevance to northwestern Europe in the late Quaternary period, *Review of Paleobotany and Palynology* 3 (1967). H.H. Lamb, *Climate: Present, Past, and Future*, vol. 2, *Climatic History and the Future* (1977), 400; Reid Bryson and Thomas J. Murray, *Climates of Hunger: Mankind and the World's Changing Weather* (1977).

2. Lamb, *Climate: Present, Past and Future*, vol. 2, 372.

3. H.H. Lamb, *Climate, History and the Modern World* (1982), 121.

4. A.A. Dekin, Climatic change and cultural change: a correlative study from eastern arctic prehistory, *Polar Notes* 12 (1972): 14.

5. Lamb, *Climate, History and the Modern World,* 121-22; H.H. Lamb, *Weather, Climate & Human Affairs* (1988), 87.

6. Dekin, Climatic change and cultural change, 15.

7. Ross Wein and David A. MacLean, eds., *The Role of Fire in Northern Circumpolar Ecosystems* (1983).

8. Ronald Nash, *The Arctic Small Tool Tradition in Manitoba* (1969).

9. Robert McGhee, Speculations on climatic change and Thule culture development, *Folk* 11-12 (1970).

10. William C. Noble, Archaeological surveys and sequences in Central District Mackenzie, N.W.T., *Arctic Anthropology* 8 (1971).

11. William E. Taylor, The Arnapik and Tyara sites: an archaeological study of Dorset culture origins, *Memoirs of the Society for American Archaeology* 22 (1968).

12. Reid Bryson and W.M. Wendland, Tentative climatic patterns for some late glacial and post-glacial episodes in central North America, in *Life, Land and Water* (1967); Lamb, *Climate: Present, Past and Future*, 373-74.

13. William Fitzhugh, *Environmental Archeology and Cultural Systems in Hamilton Inlet, Labrador: A Survey of the Central Labrador Coast from 3000 BC to the Present* (1972).

14. Dekin, Climatic change and cultural change.

15. McGhee, Speculations on climatic change.

16. Harvey Nichols, Late quaternary pollen diagrams, *Arctic and Alpine Research* 2, no.1 (1970); Lamb, *Climate: Present, Past and Future*, 438.

17. Lamb, *Climate: Present, Past and Future*, 451; and H.H. Lamb, Climate changes and food production: observations and outlook in the modern world, *Geo-Journal* (Weisbaden) 5, no. 2 (1981).

Bibliography

Unpublished Sources

Hudson's Bay Company Archives, Provincial Archives of Manitoba
London Letter Books
A1/35, 1740-43; A6/1-45, 1679-1870; A11/13, 1761; A11/15, 1774-91; A12/Ft. Misc/207, 1913

Albany
B3/a/59-62 Post Journals, 1766-1770

Fort Chimo
B38/a/1-7 Post Journals, 1832-39

B38/b/2 Correspondence Books Outward, 1834-40

B38/e/1 Annual Report, 1833

Fort Churchill
B42/a/1-196 Post Journals, Logbooks, and Meteorological Journals, 1718-1895

B198/a/97, Post Journal, 1850-51

B220a/17, Post Journal, 1850-51

B42/b/44-62 Correspondence Books, 1783-1891

B42/d/1-139 Account Books, 1717-1832

B42/e/5-8 District Reports, 1827-33

B42/z/2 Census Books, 1881

Cumberland House
B49/b/13 Correspondence Books, 1887

B49/e/9 District Report, 1885

Moose Fort
B135/b/16 Correspondence Book, 1785

Richmond Post

B182/b/1 Correspondence Book, 1754

Rupert House

B186/b/53-56 Correspondence Books, 1845-48

Severn Post

B198/a/97 Post Journal, 1850

Trout Lake Post

B220/a/17 Post Journal, 1850-51

York Factory

B239/a/2-5 Post Journals, 1716-20

B239/b/1-3 Council Books, 1719-22

Lac du Brochet Post

B296/d/1 Account Books, 1875-76

B296/e/1-4 District Reports, 1890-1902

Logbooks

C1/204-205 *Beaver*, 1791-1792

C1/617-618 *Ocean Nymph*, 1866-1867

C7/175 Letters to ships' captains, 1790

E18/2 Journal of *California* from London, Francis Smith

District Reports

D5/12 Churchill District, 1844

D25/1-3 Cumberland District, 1886

D25/17 Cumberland District, 1894

Maps

E3/4:16 Inuit map of coast from Churchill to Chesterfield Inlet, 1809

F3/2:109 Inuit map of coast, Churchill to Chesterfield Inlet, 1811

General Correspondence

RG7/1/1752 (1) Proposed Transfer of Natives to Spence Bay (Boothia Peninsula) Area from Hudson Straits. Mimeographed memo. [Undated, probably 1951 or 1952]; (2) Letter, C.K. LeCapelain, Acting Director, Department of Resources and Development, Northern Administration and Lands Branch, to R.H. Chesshire, General Manager, Fur Trade Department, September 5, 1951

Native Welfare Files

RG7/1/1753 General Correspondence, 1958. Letter from H.W. Sutherland to B.G. Sivertz, May 30, 1958

Published Sources

Abel, Kerry M.

1993 *Drum Songs: Glimpses of Dene History*. Montreal, Kingston: McGill-Queen's University Press.

Alt, B.T., et al.

1985 Arctic climate during the Franklin era, as deduced from ice cores. In *The Franklin Era in Canadian Arctic History, 1845-1859*, edited by Patricia D. Sutherland. National Museum of Man Mercury Series. Archaeological Survey of Canada Paper #131. Ottawa: National Museums of Canada.

Amsden, Charles Wynn

1979 Hard times: a case study from northern Alaska and implications for arctic prehistory. In *Thule Eskimo Culture: An Anthropological Retrospective*, edited by A. McCartney. National Museum of Man Mercury Series. Archaeological Survey of Canada Paper #88. Ottawa: National Museums of Canada.

Amundsen, Roald

1908 *The North West Passage*. 2 vols. London: Archibald Constable.

Anderson, Douglas

1968 A stone age campsite at the gateway to America. *Scientific American* 218, no. 6: 24-33.

Anderson, J.L.

1981 History and climate: some economic models. In *Climate and History: Studies in Past Climates and Their Impact On Man*, edited by T.M.L. Wigley, M.J. Ingram, and G. Farmer. Cambridge, MA: Cambridge University Press.

Anderson, James

1855 Chief Factor James Anderson's Back River Journal of 1855. *Canadian Field Naturalist* 54, no. 5 (May 1940): 63+; 55, no. 3 (March 1941): 9+.

Andrews, John T.

1967 Radiocarbon dating obtained through geographical branch field observation. *Geographical Bulletin* 9: 2.

Andrews, John T., and Gifford H. Miller

1979 Climatic change over the last 1000 years, Baffin Island, N.W.T. In *Thule Eskimo Culture: An Anthropological Retrospective*, edited by A. McCartney. National Museum of Man Mercury Series. Archaeological Survey of Canada Paper #88. Ottawa: National Museums of Canada.

Andrews, M., and John T. Andrews

1979 Bibliography of Baffin Island environment over the last 1000 years. In *Thule Eskimo Culture: An Anthropological Retrospective*, edited by A.P. McCartney. National Museum of Man Mercury Series. Archaeological Survey of Canada Paper #88. Ottawa: National Museums of Canada.

Appleby, Joyce, Lynn Hunt, and Margaret Jacoby

1994 *Telling the Truth about History*. New York: W.W. Norton & Company.

Arima, Eugene Y.

1984 Caribou Eskimo. In *Handbook of North American Indians*.Vol. 5. *Arctic*, edited by David Damas. Washington, DC: Smithsonian Institution.

Armstrong, Terence E., and Hugh Brody

1978 The term 'Eskimo'. *Polar Record* 19, no. 119: 177-80.

Arnold, Charles D., and Karen McCullough

1990 Thule pioneers in the Canadian arctic. In *Canada's Missing Dimension: Science and History in the Canadian Arctic Islands*. Proceedings of the conference on The Canadian Arctic Islands: Canada's Missing Dimension, Ottawa, November 21-24, 1987. Vol. 2, edited by C.R. Harington. Ottawa: Canadian Museum of Nature.

Asher, G.M.

1860 *Henry Hudson, the Navigator; from the Original Documents....* London: Hakluyt Society.

Auger, Réginald

1987 Probabilities for a late eighteenth century Inuit occupation of the Strait of Belle Isle. *Études/Inuit/Studies* 11, no. 1: 47-66.

Axtell, James

1978 The ethnohistory of early America: a review essay. *The William and Mary Quarterly* 35, no. 4: 110-44.

Back, George

[1822] 1994. *Arctic Artist: The Journal and Paintings of George Back, Midshipman with Franklin, 1819-1822*, edited by C. Stuart Houston. Kingston: McGill-Queen's University Press.

1836 *Narrative of the Arctic Land Expedition to the Mouth of the Great Fish River, and Along the Shores of the Arctic Ocean, in the Years 1833, 1834, and 1835*. London: J. Murray.

Bacqueville de la Potherie, Claude C. LeRoy

[1722] 1931. Letters of La Potherie. In *Documents Relating to the Early History of Hudson Bay*, edited by J.B. Tyrrell. Toronto: Champlain Society. Originally published in *Histoire de l'Amerique septentrionale*. Vol. 1. Paris: Nyon Fils.

Baker, R.R.

1978 *The Evolutionary Ecology of Animal Migration*. New York: Holmes & Meier.

Balikci, Asen

1967. Female infanticide on the arctic coast. *Man: The Journal of the Royal Anthropological Institute* 2 (new series): 615-25.

1970 *The Netsilik Eskimo*. Garden City, NY: Natural History Press.

Ball, T.F.

1988 Historical and instrumental evidence of extreme climatic conditions in central Canada, 1770–1820. *Annales Geophysicae.* Proceedings of the Annual Geophysical Society General Assembly, Bologna, March 1988. Also in *Climate Since A.D. 1500*, edited by Raymond S. Bradley and Philip D. Jones. London: Routledge.

Barry, Thomas F.

1880 Appendix No. 1: Thomas F. Barry's statement: Arctic meeting at Chickering Hall October 28th, 1880. *Journal of the American Geographical Society of New York* 12: 275–79.

Bergthorssen, P.

1969 An estimate of drift ice and temperature in Iceland in 1000 years. *Jokull: Journal of the Icelandic Glaciological Society* 19: 94–101.

Bell, Robert

1901 Legends of the Slave Indians of the Mackenzie River. *Journal of American Folklore* 14, no. 61: 26–29.

Bernard, H. Russell, and Pertti Pelto, eds.

1972 *Technology and Social Change.* New York: Macmillan.

Best, George

[1578] 1975. *Tokens of Possession: The Voyages of Martin Frobisher.* Toronto: Royal Ontario Museum. New translation edited by Walter A. Kenyon. Originally published as *A True Discourse of the Late Voyages of Discoverie, for the Finding of a Passage to Cathaia.* London: Henry Bynnyman.

1578 *A True Discourse of the Late Voyages of Discoverie, for the Finding of a Passage to Cathaia, by the Northwest, Under the Conduct of Martin Frobisher, General, Divided into Three Bookes.* London: Henry Bynnyman. Microfilm. Early English Books Before 1640, Reel 196.

Binford, Lewis R.

1978 *Nunamiut Ethnoarchaeology.* New York: Academic Press.

1991 When the going gets tough, the tough get going: Nunamiut local groups, camping patterns and economic organization. In *Ethnoarchaeological Approaches to Mobile Campsites: Hunter-Gatherer and Pastoralist Case Studies*, edited by C.S. Gamble and W.A. Boismier. Ethnoarchaeological Series I. Ann Arbor, MI: International Monographs in Prehistory.

Birket-Smith, Kaj

[1924] 1976 *Ethnography of the Egedesminde District With Aspects of the General Culture of West Greenland.* Copenhagen: Bianco Lunos. Reprint, New York: AMS Press.

1929 *Report of the Fifth Thule Expedition, 1921-24.* Vol. 5: 1. *Descriptive Part: The Caribou Eskimos: Material and Social Life and Their Cultural Position.* Copenhagen: Gyldendal.

1929 *Report of the Fifth Thule Expedition, 1921-24.* Vol. 5: 2. *Analytical Part: The Caribou Eskimos: Material and Social Life and Their Cultural Position.* Copenhagen: Gyldendal.

1930 *Report of the Fifth Thule Expedition, 1921-24.* Vol. 6: 3. *Contributions to Chipewyan Ethnology.* Copenhagen: Gyldendal.

1936 *The Eskimos.* London: Methuen and Co.

1940 *Report of the Fifth Thule Expedition, 1921-24.* Vol. 3: 2. *Anthropological Observations on the Central Eskimos.* Copenhagen: Gyldendalske Boghandel.

1945 *Ethnographical Collections from the Northwest Passage. Meddelelser om Grønland,* Bd 66. Copenhagen: Gyldendalske Boghandel.

Bishop, Charles A.

1978 Cultural and biological adaptations to deprivation: the Northern Ojibwa case. In *Extinction and Survival in Human Populations,* edited by Charles D. Laughlin and Ivan A. Brady. New York: Columbia University Press.

Black, G.F., and Northcote W. Thomas

[1901] 1967. *Examples of Printed Folk-Lore Concerning the Orkney & Shetland Islands.* County Folk-Lore Series 3, no 5. Reprint, New York: Kraus Reprint.

Blake, E. Vale

1874 *Arctic Experiences: Containing Capt. George E. Tyson's Wonderful Drift on the Ice-Floe.* New York: Harper.

Blake, Weston

1966 *End Moraines and Deglaciation Chronology in Northern Canada with Special Reference to Southern Baffin Island.* Geological Survey of Canada Paper #66-26. Ottawa: Department of Mines and Technical Surveys.

Boas, Franz

1884 A journey in Cumberland Sound and on the west shore of Davis Strait in 1883 and 1884. *American Geographical Society of New York Bulletin* 16: 241-72.

[1888] 1964. *The Central Eskimo,* with introduction by Henry B. Collins. Lincoln, NE: University of Nebraska Press. Facsimile. Originally published in the Sixth Annual Report of the Bureau of Ethnology. Washington, DC: Smithsonian Institution.

1901 *The Eskimo of Baffin Land and Hudson Bay. Bulletin of the American Museum of Natural History* 15, no 1.

1907 *The Eskimo of Baffin Land and Hudson Bay. Bulletin of the American Museum of Natural History* 15, no 2.

Boserup, Ester

1965 *The Conditions of Agricultural Growth.* Chicago: Aldine.

Brady, Ivan A., and Charles D. Laughlin

1978 Epilogue: adaptation and anthropological theory. In *Extinction and Survival in Human Populations*, edited by Charles D. Laughlin and Ivan A. Brady. New York: Columbia University Press.

Brand, John

1701 *A Brief Description of Orkney, Zetland, Pightland-Firth and Caithness*. Edinburgh.

Braudel, Fernand

1976-81 *The Mediterranean and the Mediterranean World in the Age of Philip II*. 3 vols. New York: Harper Colophon Books/Harper & Row.

Bray, J. Roger

1967 Variations in atmospheric Carbon-14 activity relative to a sunspot-auroral solar index. *Science* 156, no. 1 (May 5): 640-42.

1971 Solar-climate relationships in the post-pleistocene. *Science* 171: 1242-43.

Bryson, Reid A., and W.M. Wendland

1967 Tentative climatic patterns for some late glacial and post-glacial episodes in central North America. In *Life, Land and Water*, edited by William Mayer-Oakes. Winnipeg: University of Manitoba Press.

Bryson, Reid A., W.M. Wendland, J.D. Ives, and J.T. Andrews

1969 Radiocarbon isochrones on the disintegration of the Laurentide Ice Sheet. *Arctic and Alpine Research* 1, no.1: 1-14.

Bryson, Reid A., and Thomas J. Murray

1977 *Climates of Hunger: Mankind and the World's Changing Weather*. Madison: University of Wisconsin Press.

Burch, Ernest S.

1972 The caribou/wild reindeer as a human resource. *American Antiquity* 37: 339-68.

1974 Eskimo warfare in northwest Alaska. *Anthropological Papers of the University of Alaska* 16, no. 2: 1-14.

1977 Muskox and man in the central Canadian subarctic, 1689-1974. *Arctic* 30, no. 3 (Sept): 135-54.

1978 Caribou Eskimo origins: an old problem reconsidered. *Arctic Anthropology* 15, no. 1: 1-35.

1979 The Thule-Historic Eskimo transition on the west coast of Hudson Bay. In *Thule Eskimo Culture: An Anthropological Retrospective*, edited by Allen P. McCartney. National Museum of Man Mercury Series. Archaeological Survey Paper #88. Ottawa: National Museums of Canada.

1986 The Caribou Inuit. In *Native Peoples: The Canadian Experience*, edited by Bruce Morrison and C. Roderick Wilson. Toronto: McClelland and Stewart.

1988 War and trade. In *Crossroads of Continents: Cultures of Siberia and Alaska*, edited by William W. Fitzhugh and Aron Crowell. Washington, DC: Smithsonian Institution.

1988 *The Eskimos*. Norman: University of Oklahoma Press.

Burch, Ernest S., and Thomas C. Correll

1972 Alliance and conflict: inter-regional alliance in north Alaska. In *Alliance in Eskimo Society*, edited by Lee Guemple. Proceedings of the American Ethnological Society Supplement. Seattle: University of Washington Press.

Burke, James

1985 *The Day the Universe Changed*. Boston: Little, Brown and Company.

Cameron, Catherine M., and Steve A. Tomka, eds.

1993 *Abandonment of Settlements and Regions: Ethnoarchaeological and Archaeological Approaches*. Cambridge, MA: Cambridge University Press.

Canadian Permanent Committee on Geographical names

1971 *Gazeteer of Canada. Northwest Territories*. Provisional Edition. Ottawa: Surveys and Mapping Branch. Department of Energy, Mines and Resources.

1977 *Gazeteer of Canada. Northwest Territories*. Cumulative Supplement. Ottawa: Surveys and Mapping Branch. Department of Energy, Mines and Resources.

Catchpole, A.J.W.

1985 Evidence from Hudson Bay region of severe cold in the summer of 1816. In *Climatic Change in Canada 5: Critical Periods in the Quaternary Climatic History of Northern North America: Syllogeus 55*, edited by C.R. Harington. Ottawa: National Museums of Canada.

1992 Hudson's Bay Company ships' log-books as sources of sea ice data, 1751-1870. In *Climate Since A.D. 1500*, edited by Raymond S. Bradley and Philip D. Jones. London: Routledge.

Catchpole, A.J.W., and Marcia-Anne Faurer

1983 Summer sea ice severity in Hudson Strait, 1751-1870. *Climatic Change* 5, no. 2: 115-39.

Champlain, Samuel de

[1632] 1933 *The Works of Samuel de Champlain,* vol. 5, edited by H.P. Biggar. Toronto: The Champlain Society.

Chappell, Edward

1817 *Narrative of a Voyage to Hudson's Bay in His Majesty's Ship Rosamond: Containing Some Account of the North-eastern Coast of America and of the Tribes Inhabiting that Remote Region*. London: Printed for J. Mawman.

Cheshire, Neil, Tony Waldron, Alison Quinn, and David Quinn

1987 Frobisher's Eskimos in England. In *Indians and Europe: An Interdisciplinary Collection of Essays*, edited by Christian Feest. Aachen: Edition Herodot, Rader Verlag.

Christy, Miller., ed.

[1894] *The Voyages of Captain Luke Foxe of Hull and Captain Thomas James of Bristol in Search of Northwest Passage in 1631-32*, edited by M. Christy. 2 vols. London: Hakluyt Society.

Claiborne, Robert

1970 *Climate, Man and History*. New York: W.W. Norton.

Clark, Brenda L.

1977 *The Development of Caribou Eskimo Culture*. National Museum of Man Mercury Series. Archaeological Survey of Canada Paper #59. Ottawa: National Museums of Canada.

1979 Thule occupation of west Hudson Bay. In *Thule Eskimo Culture: An Anthropological Retrospective*, edited by Allen P. McCartney. National Museum of Man Mercury Series. Archaeological Survey of Canada Paper #88. Ottawa: National Museums of Canada.

Clarke, C.H.D.

1940 *A Biological Investigation of the Thelon Game Sanctuary*. National Museum of Canada Bulletin #96. Ottawa: Department of Mines and Resources.

Claxton, Robert H.

1985 Climate and history: the state of the field. In *Environmental History: Critical Issues in Comparative Perspective*, edited by Kendall E. Bailes. New York: University Press of America.

Clerke, Agnes M.

1894 [Auroral studies.] *Knowledge* 17: 206.

Clermont, N.

1980 Les Inuit de Labrador méridional avant Cartwright. *Études/Inuit/Studies* 4, nos. 1–2: 147–64.

Coats, W.

[1752] 1852 *The Geography of Hudson's Bay*, edited by J. Barrow. London: Hakluyt Society.

Collins, Henry Bascom

1937 The archaeology of St. Lawrence Island, Alaska. *Smithsonian Miscellaneous Collections* 96, no. 1.

1950 Excavations at Frobisher Bay, Baffin Island, Northwest Territories. *Annual Report of the National Museum of Canada for 1948-49*. Bulletin #118: 18-43. Ottawa: Department of Mines and Resources, National Museum of Canada.

1951 Excavations at Thule culture sites near Resolute Bay, Cornwallis Island, N.W.T. *Annual Report of the National Museum of Canada for 1949-50*. Bulletin #123: 49-63. Ottawa: Department of Mines and Resources, National Museum of Canada.

1952 Archaeological Excavations at Resolute, Cornwallis Island, N.W.T. *Annual Report of the National Museum of Canada for 1950-51.* Bulletin #126: 48-63. Ottawa: Department of Mines and Resources, National Museum of Canada.

1955 Excavations of Thule and Dorset culture sites at Resolute, Cornwallis Island, N.W.T. *National Museum of Canada Bulletin* 136: 22-35. Ottawa: Department of Mines and Resources, National Museum of Canada.

1956 Archaeological investigations on Southampton and Coats Islands, N.W.T. *Annual Report of the National Museum of Canada for 1954-55.* Bulletin #142: 82-113. Ottawa: Department of Mines and Resources, National Museum of Canada.

1956 The T-1 site at Native Point, Southampton Island, N.W.T. *Anthropological Papers of the University of Alaska* 4, no. 2: 63-89.

1956 Vanished mystery men of Hudson Bay. *National Geographic* 110: 669-87.

1957 Archaeological investigations on Southampton and Walrus Islands, N.W.T. *Annual Report of the National Museum of Canada.* Bulletin 147: 22-61. Ottawa: Department of Mines and Resources, National Museum of Canada.

Collis, Dirmid Ronan F.

1988 Reviews and debates. *Études/Inuit/Studies* 12, nos.1-2: 259.

Colson, E.

1979 In good years and in bad: food strategies of self-reliant societies. *Journal of Anthropological Research* 35: 18-29.

Comer, George

[1905] 1985 *An Arctic Whaling Diary: The Journal of Captain George Comer in Hudson Bay 1903-1905,* edited by W. Gillies Ross. Toronto: University of Toronto Press.

1910 A geographical description of Southampton Island and notes upon the Eskimo. *Bulletin of the American Geographical Society* 42, no.1: 84-90.

1921 Notes by G. Comer on the natives of the northwestern shores of Hudson Bay. *American Anthropologist* n.s. 23: 243-44.

Cooke, Alan

1973 The Eskimos and the Hudson's Bay Company. In *Le Peuple Esquimau Aujourd'hui et Demain/The Eskimo People To-Day and To-Morrow,* edited by Jean Malaurie. Fourth International Congress of the Fondation Francaise d'Études Nordiques. Paris: Mouton.

Cooke, Alan, and Clive Holland

1978 *The Exploration of Northern Canada, 500-1920: A Chronology.* Toronto: Arctic History Press.

Correll, Thomas

1972 *Ungalaqlingmiut: A Study in Language and Society.* Ph.D. thesis, Anthropology, University of Minnesota. Facsimile, Ann Arbor: University Microfilms.

1976 Language and location in traditional Inuit societies. In *Report: Inuit Land Use and Occupancy Project* 2: 173-78, edited by M.R. Milton Freeman. Ottawa: Department of Indian and Northern Affairs.

Cove, John J.

1978 Survival or extinction: reflections on the problem of famine in Tsimshian and Kaguru mythology. In *Extinction and Survival in Human Populations*, edited by Charles D. Laughlin and Ivan A. Brady. New York: Columbia University Press.

Crosby, Alfred

1972 *The Columbian Exchange: Biological and Cultural Consequences of 1492.* Westport, CN: Greenwood Publishing Company.

1986 *Ecological Imperialism: The Biological Expansion of Europe, 900-1900*. Cambridge, MA: Cambridge University Press.

Csonka, Yvon

1991 *Les Ahiarmiut (1920-1950) Dans La Perspective de l'Histoire des Inuit Caribous.* Ph.D. thesis. Département d'Anthropologie. Québec: Université Laval.

Damas, David

1963 *Igluligmiut Kinship and Local Groupings: A Structural Approach.* Anthropological Series 64. Bulletin 196. Ottawa: National Museums of Canada.

1968 The Eskimo. In *Science, History, and Hudson Bay*, edited by C.S. Beals. Vol. 1. Ottawa: Department of Energy, Mines and Resources.

1975 Three kinship systems from the central arctic. *Arctic Anthropology* 12, no.1: 10-30.

1988 The contact-traditional horizon of the central arctic: reassessment of a concept and reexamination of an era. *Arctic Anthropology* 25, no. 2: 101-38.

Damas, David, ed.

1984 *Handbook of North American Indians.* Vol. 5. *Arctic.* Washington, DC: Smithsonian Institution.

Damon, Paul E., Austen Long, and Donald C. Grey

1966 Fluctuation of atmospheric Carbon 14 during the last six millennia. *Journal of Geophysical Research* 71, no 4 (Feb 15): 1055-63.

Dauphiné, T.C.

1976 Biology of the Kaminuriak population of barren-ground caribou, Part 4. *Canadian Wildlife Service Report Series 38*. Ottawa: Environment Canada Wilflife Service.

Davies, K.G.

1963 Appendix A: Post histories. In *Northern Quebec and Labrador Journals and Correspondence, 1819-1835*, edited by K.G. Davies. London: Hudson's Bay Record Society.

Davies, K.G., ed.

1963 Map: Northern Quebec and Labrador Exploration and Settlement by Hudson's Bay Company to 1835. Accompanies *Northern Quebec and Labrador Journals and Correspondence 1819-35*. London: Hudson's Bay Record Society.

1965 *Letters from Hudson Bay 1703-40*. London: Hudson's Bay Record Society.

de Laguna, Frederica

1972 *Under Mount Saint Elias: The History and Culture of the Yakutat Tlingit. Contributions to Anthropology* 7. Washington DC: Smithsonian Institution.

Dekin, A.A.

1972 Climatic change and cultural change: a correlative study from eastern arctic prehistory. *Polar Notes* 12: 11-31.

1975 *Models of Pre-Dorset Culture: Towards an Explicit Methodology*. Ph.D. thesis. Anthropology. Michigan State University.

Diamond, Jared

1997 *Guns, Germs, and Steel: The Fates of Human Societies*. New York: W.W. Norton & Co.

Divale, William, and Marvin Harris

1976 Population, warfare, and the male supremacist complex. *American Anthropologist* 78: 521-38.

Dobbs, Arthur

1744 *An Account of the Countries Adjoining to Hudson's Bay in the North-West Part of America*. London: J. Robinson.

Douglass, A.E.

1919 *Climatic Cycles and Tree Growth*. Publication #289, Vol. 1: 102. Washington, DC: Carnegie Institution of Washington.

1928 *Climatic Cycles and Tree Growth*. Publication #289, Vol. 2: 125-26. Washington, DC: Carnegie Institution of Washington.

Dumond, Don E.

1977 *The Eskimos and Aleuts*. London: Thames and Hudson.

1979 Eskimo-Indian relationships: a view from prehistory. *Arctic Anthropology* 16, no. 2: 3-22.

[Eberbing, Joe] Ipervik

1880 Appendix No. 1. Joseph Eberling's statement. Arctic meeting at Chickering Hall October 28th, 1880. *Journal of the American Geographical Society of New York* 12: 279-81.

Eddy, John A.

1976 The Maunder Minimum. *Science* 192: 1189-1202.

Ellanna, Frank, et al.

1988 *King Island Tales: Eskimo History and Legends from Bering Strait*. Fairbanks, AK: Alaska Native Language Center and University of Alaska Press.

Ellis, Henry

[1748] 1967 *A Voyage to Hudson's Bay by the Dobbs Galley and California in the Years 1746 and 1747 for Discovering a North West Passage; with An Accurate Survey of the Coast, and a Short Natural History of the Country....* London: H. Whitridge. Reprint, New York: Johnson Reprint Corporation.

Eurola, S.

1971 The driftwoods of the Arctic Ocean. *Report of Kevo Subarctic Statistics* 7: 74-80.

Fagan, Brian M.

1987 *The Great Journey: The Peopling of Ancient America*. London: Thames and Hudson.

1991 *Ancient North America: The Archaeology of a Continent*. London: Thames and Hudson.

Febvre, Lucien

1932 *A Geographical Introduction to History*. London: Kegan Paul.

Fenton, Edward

[1578] 1981 The Canadian arctic journal of Captain Edward Fenton, 1578, edited by Walter A. Kenyon. *Archivaria* 11: 171-203.

Ferguson, R. Brian

1984 Introduction: studying war. In *Warfare, Culture, and Environment*, edited by R. Brian Ferguson. Orlando, FL: Academic Press.

1984 A reexamination of the causes of northwest coast warfare. In *Warfare, Culture, and Environment*, edited by R. Brian Ferguson. Orlando, FL: Academic Press.

Ferguson, R. Brian, ed.

1984 *Warfare, Culture, and Environment*. Orlando, FL: Academic Press.

Ferguson, R. Brian, and Neil L. Whitehead, eds.

1992 *War in the Tribal Zone: Expanding States and Indigenous Warfare*. Santa Fe: School of American Research Press.

Ferguson, Robert

[1879] 1938 *Arctic Harpooner: A Voyage on the Schooner Abbie Bradford, 1878-1879*, edited by Leslie D. Stair. Philadelphia: University of Pennsylvania Press.

Fienup-Riordan, Ann

1990 *Eskimo Essays: Yup'ik Lives and How We See Them*. New Brunswick: Rutgers University Press.

Fischer, David Hackett

1981 Climate and history: priorities for research. In *Climate and History: Studies in Interdisciplinary History*, edited by Robert I. Rotberg and Theodore K. Rabb. Princeton, NJ: Princeton University Press.

Fisher, Alexander

1821 *Journal of a Voyage of Discovery to the Arctic Regions in His Majesty's Ships Hecla and Griper, in the Years 1819 & 1820*. London: Longman, Hurst, Rees, Orme, and Brown.

Fitzhugh, William W.

1972 *Environmental Archeology and Cultural Systems in Hamilton Inlet, Labrador: A Survey of the Central Labrador Coast from 3000 B.C. to the Present*. Smithsonian Contributions to Anthropology no. 16. Washington, DC: Smithsonian Institution Press.

1973 Environmental approaches to the prehistory of the north. *Journal of the Washington Academy of Sciences* 63, no. 2: 39-53.

1975 A comparative approach to northern maritime adaptations. In *Prehistoric Maritime Adaptations of the Circumpolar Zone*, edited by William Fitzhugh. The Hague: Mouton.

1975 The Thule-Historic Eskimo transition on the west coast of Hudson Bay. In *Thule Eskimo Culture: An Anthropological Retrospective*, edited by William Fitzhugh. The Hague: Mouton.

1976 Environmental factors in the evolution of Dorset culture: a marginal proposal for Hudson Bay. In *Eastern Arctic Prehistory: Paleoeskimo Problems*, edited by M.S. Maxwell. Memoirs of the Society for American Archaeology 31. Washington, DC: School for American Archaeology.

1977 Indian and Eskimo/Inuit settlement history in Labrador: an archaeological view. In *Our Footprints Are Everywhere: Inuit Land Use and Occupancy in Labrador*, edited by Carol Brice-Bennett. Nain, NF: Labrador Inuit Kattekategeninga.

1984 Paleo-Eskimo cultures of Greenland. *Handbook of North American Indians*. Vol. 5. *Arctic*, edited by David Damas. Washington, DC: Smithsonian Institution.

1985 Early contacts north of Newfoundland before A.D. 1600: a review. In *Cultures in Contact: The Impact of European Contacts on Native American Cultural Institutions, A.D. 1000-1800*, edited by William W. Fitzhugh. Washington, DC: Smithsonian Institution.

1985 Introduction [and] Commentary on Part I. In *Cultures in Contact: The Impact of European Contacts on Native American Cultural Institutions, A.D. 1000-1800*, edited by William W. Fitzhugh. Washington, DC: Smithsonian Institution.

Fitzhugh, William W., and Aron Crowell, eds.

1988 *Crossroads of Continents: Cultures of Siberia and Alaska*. Washington, DC: Smithsonian Institution Press.

Fleming, Archibald L.

1957 *Archibald The Arctic*. London: Hodder & Stoughton.

Fogelson, Raymond D.

1989 The ethnohistory of events and nonevents. *Ethnohistory* 36, no.2 (Spring): 133-47.

Fornel, Jean-Louis

[1743] 1921 Relation de la découverte qu'a faite le Sieur Fornel en 1743 de la Baye des Eskimaux nommée par les sauvages Kessessakiou. In *Rapport de l'Archiviste de la Province de Québec, 1920-21.*

Foxe, Luke

[1635] 1894 North-West Fox, or Fox from the North-West Passage.... London: B. Alsop & Tho. Fawcet. In *The Voyages of Captain Luke Foxe of Hull, and Captain Thomas James of Bristol, in Search of Northwest Passage in 1631-32,* edited by Miller Christy. 2 vols. London: Hakluyt Society.

[1635] 1965 *North-West Fox, or Fox from the North-West Passage....* London: B. Alsop & Tho. Fawcet. Facsimile, New York: S.R. Publishers Ltd and Johnson Reprint Corporation.

Francis, Daniel

1979 Les relations entre Indiens et Inuit dans l'est de la baie d'Hudson. *Études/Inuit/Studies* 3, no. 2: 73-83.

Francis, Daniel, and Toby Morantz

1983 *Partners in Furs: A History of the Fur Trade in Eastern James Bay, 1600-1870.* Montreal, Kingston: McGill-Queen's University Press.

Franklin, John

1823 *Narrative of a Journey to the Shores of the Polar Sea in the Years 1819-20-21-22.* London: John Murray.

[1828] 1971 *Narrative of a Second Expedition to the Shores of the Polar Sea in the Years 1825, 1826, and 1827.* Reprint, Rutland, VT: Charles E. Tuttle & Co.

Freeman, Milton M.R.

1979 A critical view of Thule culture and ecological adaptation. In *Thule Eskimo Culture: An Anthropological Retrospective,* edited by A.P. McCartney. National Museum of Man Mercury Series. Archaeological Survey of Canada Paper #88. Ottawa: National Museums of Canada.

1984 Arctic ecosystems. In *Handbook of North American Indians.* Vol. 5. *Arctic,* edited by David Damas. Washington, DC: Smithsonian Institution Press.

Freeman, Milton M.R., ed.

1976 *Inuit Land Use and Occupancy Project.* Ottawa: Department of Indian and Northern Affairs. 3 vols. Ottawa: Department of Indian and Northern Affairs.

Freuchen, Peter

1935 *Arctic Adventure: My Life in the Frozen North.* Toronto: Farrar & Rinehart.

Fritts, H.C., and J.M. Lough

1985 An estimate of average annual temperature variations for North America, 1602 to 1961. *Climatic Change* 7, no. 2: 203-24.

Fritts, H.C., and X.M. Shao

1992 Mapping climate using tree-rings from western North America. In *Climate Since A.D. 1500*, edited by Raymond S. Bradley and Philip D. Jones. London: Routledge.

Gad, Finn

1970 *The History of Greenland.* Vol. 1. *Earliest Times to 1700*, translated by Ernest Dupont. London: C. Hurst & Company.

1973 *The History of Greenland.* Vol. 2. *1700-1782*, translated by Gordon Bowden. London: C. Hurst & Company.

1982 *The History of Greenland.* Vol. 3. *1782-1808*, translated by Charles Jones. Kingston: McGill-Queen's University Press.

1984 History of colonial Greenland. In *Handbook of North American Indians.* Vol. 5. *Arctic*, edited by David Damas. Washington, DC: Smithsonian Institution.

Gaskin, D.E.

1982 *The Ecology of Whales and Dolphins*. London: Exeter.

Gasté, Alphonse

1869 Father Gasté meets the Inland Eskimos. *Eskimo* 57 (Dec 1960): 3+.

Gates, W.L., and Y. Mintes, eds.

1975 *Understanding Climate Change.* Washington, DC: National Academy of Sciences.

Gilberg, R.

1975 Changes in the life of the Polar Eskimo resulting from a Canadian immigration to the Thule District, North Greenland. *Folk* 16-17: 159-70.

Gilder, William

1881 *Schwatka's Search: Sledging in the Arctic in Quest of the Franklin Records*. New York: C. Scribner's Sons.

1882 *The Search for Franklin: A Narrative of the American Expedition Under Lieutenant Schwatka, 1878 to 1880*. London: T. Nelson and Sons. [Abridged version of Colonel Gilder's serialized account in the *New York Herald*, September and October 1880.]

Glover, Richard

1965 Introduction. In *Letters From Hudson Bay, 1703-40*, edited by K.G. Davies. London: Hudson's Bay Record Society.

1969 Introduction. In *Andrew Graham's Observations on Hudson's Bay 1767-1791*, edited by Glyndwr Williams. London: Hudson's Bay Record Society.

Goddard, Ives

1984 Synonymy. In *Handbook of North American Indians.* Vol. 5. *Arctic,* edited by David Damas. Washington, DC: Smithsonian Institution.

Goldring, Philip

1986 Inuit economic responses to Euro-American contacts: southeast Baffin Island, 1824–1940. In *Historical Papers: A Selection from the Papers Presented at the Annual Meeting Held at Winnipeg 1986.*

Gordon, Bryan

1972 *Archaeological Investigations in the Thelon Game Sanctuary, Central Barrenlands.* Manuscript #726. On file with the Archaeological Survey of Canada. Ottawa: National Museums of Canada.

1974 Thule culture investigations at Baker Lake, N.W.T. *Canadian Archaeological Association Bulletin* 6: 218-24.

1975 *Of Men and Herds in Barrenland Prehistory.* National Museum of Man Mercury Series. Archaeological Survey of Canada Paper #28. Ottawa: National Museums of Canada.

Gordon, Kate

1981 *The Vikings and Their Predecessors.* Ottawa: National Museums of Canada.

Gosch, C.C.A.

1897 *Danish Arctic Expeditions, 1605 to 1620.* London: Hakluyt Society.

Gossman, Lionel

1989 *Towards a Rational Historiography. Transactions of the American Philosophical Society.* Vol. 79, part 3. Philadelphia.

Graburn, Nelson H.H., and R. Stephen Strong

1973 *Circumpolar Peoples: An Anthropological Perspective.* Pacific Palisades: Goodyear Publishing Company.

Graham, Andrew

[1775] 1949 Indians. In *James Isham's Observations on Hudson's Bay, 1743, and Notes and Observations on a Book Entitled A Voyage to Hudsons Bay in the Dobbs Galley, 1759,* edited by E.E. Rich. London: Hudson's Bay Record Society.

[1791] *Observations on Hudson's Bay, 1767-91,* edited by Glyndwr Williams. London: Hudson's Bay Record Society.

Grove, Jean M.

1988 *The Little Ice Age.* London: Methuen.

Gubser, N.

1965 *The Nunamiut Eskimos: Hunters of Caribou.* New Haven: Yale University Press.

Guemple, D. Lee

1961 *Inuit Spouse-Exchange*. Chicago: Dept. of Anthropology, University of Chicago.

1965 Saunik: name sharing as a factor governing Eskimo kinship terms. *Ethnology* 4: 323–35.

1972 Kinship and alliance in Belcher Island Eskimo Society. In *Proceedings of the American Ethnological Society for 1971*, edited by L. Guemple. Seattle: University of Washington Press.

1979 *Inuit Adoption*. National Museum of Man Mercury series. Canadian Ethnology Service Paper #47. Ottawa: National Museums of Canada.

Hakluyt, Richard

[1584] 1935 *The Original Writings and Correspondence of the Two Richard Hakluyts*, 1584. Hakluyt Society 2nd Series, Nos. 76–77, 2 vols.

Hall, Charles Francis

[1862] 1970 *Life with the Esquimaux: A Narrative of Arctic Experience in Search of Survivors of Sir John Franklin's Expedition*. Reprint, Edmonton: Hurtig. [Originally published as *Arctic Researches and Life Among the Esquimaux: Being the Narrative of an Expedition in Search of Sir John Franklin, in the Years 1860, 1861, and 1862*. New York: Harper, 1864–66.]

1879 *Narrative of the Second Arctic Expedition Made By Charles F. Hall: His Voyage to Repulse Bay, Sledge Journeys to the Straits of Fury and Hecla and to King William's Land, and Residence Among the Eskimos During the Years 1864-69*, edited by J.E. Nourse. Washington, DC: US Government Printing Office.

Hall, Edwin Spurr

1975 *The Eskimo Storyteller: Folktales from Noatak, Alaska*. Knoxville: University of Tennessee Press.

Halstead, Paul, and John O'Shea

1989 Introduction: cultural responses to risk and uncertainty. In *Bad Year Economics: Cultural Responses to Risk and Uncertainty*, edited by Paul Halstead and John O'Shea. Cambridge: Cambridge University Press.

Halstead, Paul, J. O'Shea, and T. Whitelow

1984 *Symposium on Cultural Responses to Risk and Uncertainty*. Cambridge: Theoretical Archaeology Group.

Hanbury, David

1900 A journey from Chesterfield Inlet to Great Slave Lake, 1898-9. *Geographical Journal* 16: 63–77.

1903 Through the barren ground of northwestern Canada to the arctic coast. *Geographical Journal* 22: 178–91.

1904 *Sport and Travel in the Northland of Canada*. New York: Macmillan.

Hardesty, Donald L.

1980 Ecological explanation in archaeology. In *Advances in Archaeological Method and Theory*. Vol. 3, edited by M.B. Schiffer.

Hargrave, Letitia

[1852] 1947 *The Letters of Letitia Hargrave*, edited by Margaret Arnett MacLeod.Toronto:The Champlain Society.

Harley, Dorothy Eber

1986 *First Impressions: Inuit Oral Accounts of Early Contact with Whites*. Paper presented at the 1986 Canadian Historical Association.

Harp, Elmer, Jr.

1958 Prehistory in the Dismal Lake Area, N.W.T., Canada. *Arctic* 11, no. 4: 219-49.

1959 The Moffatt archaeological collection from the Dubawnt country, Canada. *American Antiquity* 24, no. 4: 412-22.

1961 *The Archaeology of the Lower and Middle Thelon, Northwest Territories.* Technical Paper #8. Montreal: Arctic Institute of North America.

1962 The culture history of the Central Barren Grounds. In *Prehistoric Cultural Relations Between the Arctic and Temperate Zones of North America*, edited by John M. Campbell. Technical Paper #11. Montreal: Arctic Institute of North America.

1963 Archaeological evidence bearing on the origin of the Caribou Eskimo. *Proceedings of the International Congress of Anthropological and Ethnological Science* 2, no. 1: 409-13.

1964 *The Cultural Affinities of the Newfoundland Dorset Eskimo.* Bulletin #200, Anthropological Series #67. Ottawa: National Museums of Canada.

1974 A late Dorset copper amulet from southeastern Hudson Bay. *Folk* 16: 33-44.

Harris, Marvin

1984 A cultural materialist theory of band and village warfare: the Yanomamo test. In *Warfare, Culture, and Environment*, edited by R. Brian Ferguson. New York: Academic Press.

1991 *Cannibals and Kings: The Origins of Cultures.* New York: Vintage.

Harris, R. Cole, ed.

1987 *Historical Atlas of Canada.* Vol. 1. *From the Beginning to 1800.* Toronto: University of Toronto Press.

Hearne, Samuel

[1795] 1958 *A Journey from Prince of Wales's Fort in Hudson's Bay to the Northern Ocean: Undertaken by Order of the Hudson's Bay Company, for the Discovery of Copper Mines, a North West Passage, &c. in the Years 1769, 1770, 1771 & 1772*, edited by Richard Glover. London: A. Strahan & T. Cadell; Toronto: Macmillan Company of Canada.

Heinrich, Albert C.

1980 Letter to the editor. *Arctic* 33, no. 1(March): 204-05.

Helm, June, ed.

1968 *Essays on the Problem of Tribe: Proceedings of the 1967 Annual Spring Meeting of the American Ethnological Society.* Seattle: AES.

Hickey, Clifford G.

1979 Archaeological and ethnohistorical research on Banks Island. *Études/Inuit/Studies* 3, no. 2: 132-33.

1979 The historic Beringian trade network: its nature and origins. In *Thule Eskimo Culture: An Anthropological Retrospective*, edited by A. McCartney. National Museum of Man Mercury Series. Archaeological Survey of Canada Paper #88. Ottawa: National Museums of Canada.

1984 An examination of processes of cultural change among nineteenth century Copper Inuit. *Études/Inuit/Studies* 8: 13-35.

Hiller, J.K.

1971 The Moravians in Labrador, 1771-1805. *The Polar Record* 15, no. 99: 839-54.

Hodder, Ian

1986 *Reading the Past: Current Approaches to Interpretation in Archaeology.* Cambridge: Cambridge University Press.

Hoebel, E. Adamson

1961 *The Law of Primitive Man: A Study in Comparative Legal Dynamics.* Cambridge, MA: Harvard University Press.

Hoffman, David

1976 Inuit land use on the barren grounds: supplementary notes and analysis. *Report: Inuit Land Use and Occupancy Project.* Vol. 2: 69-84. Ottawa: Department of Indian and Northern Affairs.

Holm, Gustav

[1888] 1914 Ethnological Sketch of the Angmagsalik Eskimo. Part I. *Meddelelser om Grønland* 39, no. 1, edited by William Thalbitzer. Copenhagen.

Holtved, Erik

1944 Archaeological Investigations in the Thule District. Parts I and II. *Meddelelser om Grønland* 146, no. 3.

Hood, Robert

[1821] 1974 *To the Arctic by Canoe, 1819-1821: The Journal and Paintings of Robert Hood, Midshipman with Franklin*, edited by C. Stuart Houston. Montreal: Arctic Institute of North America.

Hunter, Archie

1983 *Northern Traders: Caribou Hair in the Stew.* Victoria: Sono Nis.

Idiens, Dale

1987 Eskimos in Scotland: c. 1682-1924. In *Indians and Europe: An Interdisciplinary Collection of Essays*, edited by Christian Feest. Aachen: Edition Herodot, Rader Verlag.

Imgalrea, Tom, Leo Moses, and Anthony C. Woodbury

1984 *Eskimo Narratives and Tales From Chevak*. Fairbanks: Alaska Native Language Center, University of Alaska.

Irving, W.N.

1968 Prehistory of Hudson Bay: the barren grounds. In *Science, History and Hudson Bay*, edited by C.S. Beals. Vol. 1. Ottawa: Department of Energy, Mines, and Resources.

1970 The Arctic Small Tool tradition. *VIIIth International Congress of Anthropological and Ethnological Sciences* 3: 340-42.

Isham, James

[1743] 1949 Observations on Hudsons Bay, 1743. In *James Isham's Observations on Hudsons Bay, 1743*, edited by E.E. Rich. London: Hudson's Bay Record Society.

[1749] 1949 Notes and Observations on a book entitled A Voyage to Hudsons Bay in the *Dobbs Galley*, 1749. In *James Isham's Observations on Hudsons Bay, 1743*, edited by E.E. Rich. London: Hudson's Bay Record Society.

Ives, J.D.

1962 Indications of recent extensive glacierization in north-central Baffin Island, N.W.T. *Journal of Glaciology* 4: 197-205.

Jacobs, John D., and George Sabo

1978 Environments and adaptations of the Thule culture on the Davis Strait coast of Baffin Island. *Arctic and Alpine Research* 10, no. 3: 595-615.

Jacoby, Gordon C., and Rosanne D'Arrigo

1989 Reconstructed northern hemisphere annual temperatures since 1671 based on high-latitude tree-ring data from North America. *Climatic Change* 14, no. 1: 39-59.

Janes, John

[1589] 1635, 1965 The first voyage of Captain John Davis of Sandruge in Devonshire 1585 to the North-West. In *North-West Fox, or Fox from the North-West Passage...*, edited by Luke Foxe. London: B. Alsop & Tho. Fawcet. [Facsimile, 1965, New York: S.R. Publishers Ltd and Johnson Reprint Corporation. Originally published by Richard Hakluyt.]

Jansen, Henrik M.

1972 A critical account of the written and archaeological sources' evidence concerning the Norse settlements in Greenland. *Meddelelser om Grønland* 182, no. 4.

Jenness, Diamond

[1916] 1991 *Arctic Odyssey: The Diary of Diamond Jenness, Ethnologist with the Canadian Arctic Expedition in Northern Alaska and Canada, 1913-1916*, edited by Stuart E. Jenness. Hull: Canadian Museum of Civilization.

1923 *Report of the Canadian Arctic Expedition, 1913-18.* Vol. 12, part A. *The Life of the Copper Eskimos.* Ottawa: Department of Mines and Resources.

1924 *Report of the Canadian Arctic Expedition 1913-18.* Vol. 13, part A. *Myths and Traditions from Northern Alaska, the Mackenzie Delta, and Coronation Gulf.* Ottawa: Department of Mines and Resources.

1926 *Report of the Canadian Arctic Expedition, 1913-18.* Vol. 13. *Eskimo Folk-Lore.* Ottawa: F.A. Acland.

1928 *The People of the Twilight.* Chicago: University of Chicago Press.

1940 Comments on James Anderson's Back River Journal of 1855. *Canadian Field Naturalist* 54, no. 5 (May).

1941 Comments on James Anderson's Back River Journal of 1855. *Canadian Field Naturalist* 55, no. 3 (March).

Jenness, Stuart E.

1991 Preface and prologue. In *Arctic Odyssey: The Diary of Diamond Jenness, Ethnologist with the Canadian Arctic Expedition in Northern Alaska and Canada, 1913-1916*, edited by Stuart E. Jenness. Hull: Canadian Museum of Civilization.

Jérémie de la Montagne, Nicolas

[1720] 1926 *Twenty Years of York Factory 1694-1714.* Trans. from the French edition of 1720, and edited by R. Douglas and J.N. Wallace. Ottawa: Thorburn & Abbott.

Jones, Gwyn

1964 *The Norse Atlantic Saga: Being the Norse Voyages of Discovery and Settlement to Iceland, Greenland, America.* London: Oxford University Press.

Jones, R. Fossett

1989 *The Keewatin Inuit and Interband Trade and Communication, 1717-1900.* M.A. thesis. Department of History. University of Winnipeg.

Jordan, Richard H.

1977 Inuit occupation of the central Labrador coast since 1600 AD. In *Our Footprints Are Everywhere: Inuit Land Use and Occupancy in Labrador*, edited by Carol Brice-Bennett. Nain, NF: Labrador Inuit Kattekategeninga.

1978 Archaeological investigations of the Hamilton Inlet Labrador Eskimo: social and economic response to European contact. *Arctic Anthropology* 15, no. 2: 175-85.

Jordan, Richard H., and Susan Kaplan

1980 An archaeological view of the Inuit/European contact period in Central Labrador. *Études/Inuit/Studies* 4, nos. 1-2: 35-45.

Kanda, Sigeru

1933 [Comprehensive list of sunspot sighting from ancient records of Japan, Korea, and China, 28 B.C. through A.D. 43.] *Proceedings of the Imperial Academy (Tokyo)* 9: 293.

Kaplan, Susan A.

1984 Eskimo-European contact archaeology in Labrador. In *Comparative Studies in the Archaeology of Colonialism*, edited by S. Dyson. Oxford: British Archaeological Reports.

1985 European goods and socio-economic change in early Labrador Inuit society. In *Cultures in Contact: The Impact of European Contacts on Native American Cultural Institutions, A.D. 1000-1800*, edited by William W. Fitzhugh. Washington, DC: Smithsonian Institution.

Kappi, Leoni, ed.

1977 *Inuit Legends.* Yellowknife: Department of Education.

Keeley, Lawrence H.

1996 *War Before Civilization.* London: Oxford University Press.

Keene, A.S.

1981 Optimal foraging in a nonmarginal environment: a model of prehistoric subsistence strategies in Michigan. In *Hunter-Gatherer Foraging Strategies*, edited by B. Winterhalder and E.A. Smith. Chicago: University of Chicago Press.

Keighley, Sydney A.

1989 *Trader, Tripper, Trapper: The Life of a Bay Man.* Winnipeg: Watson & Dwyer.

Kelly, P.M., J.H.W. Karas, and L.D. Williams

1984 Arctic climate: past, present and future. *Arctic Whaling.* Proceedings of the International Symposium Arctic Whaling, February 1983. University of Groningen.

Kelsall, D.R.

1968 *The Migratory Barren-Ground Caribou of Canada.* Ottawa: Canadian Wildlife Service.

Kelsey, Henry

[1689] 1929 A Journal of a Voyage and Journey Undertaken by Henry Kelsey.... June the 17th, 1689. In *The Kelsey Papers*, with an introduction by A.G. Doughty and C. Martin. Ottawa: Public Archives of Canada and Public Record Office of Northern Ireland.

Kenney, J.F., ed.

[1717] 1932 *The Founding of Churchill: being the journal of Captain James Knight, Governor in Chief in Hudson Bay, from the 14th of July to the 13th of September, 1717...*, with an historical introduction and notes by James F. Kenney. Toronto: J.M. Dent.

Kenyon, Walter Andrew

1981 Introduction. The Canadian arctic journal of Captain Edward Fenton, 1578. *Archivaria* 11: 171-203.

Klutschak, Heinrich

[1881] 1987 *Overland to Starvation Cove: With the Inuit in Search of Franklin, 1878-1880,* translated and edited by William Barr. Toronto: University of Toronto Press.

Knight, James

[1717] 1932 Journal kept at Churchill River, 14 July to 13 September, 1717. In *The Founding of Churchill...,* edited by James F. Kenney. Toronto: J.M. Dent.

Knight, John, and Oliver Brownel

[1606] 1877 *Journal of the Voyage of John Knight to Seek the North-West Passage 1606,* edited by Clement R. Markham. Hakluyt Society #56. London: Hakluyt Society.

Knuth, Eigil

1963 Singajuk's family saga. *Folk* 5: 209-18.

1967 *Archaeology of the Musk-Ox Way.* Paris: Ecole Pratique des Hautes Études, Sorbonne.

Kohlmeister, Benjamin, and George Kmoch

1814 *Journal of a Voyage from Okkak, on the Coast of Labrador, to Ungava Bay, Westward of Cape Chudleigh.* London: Brethren's Society for the Furtherance of the Gospel Among the Heathen.

Kupp, Jan, and Simon Hart

1976 The Dutch in the Strait of Davis and Labrador during the 17th and 18th centuries. *Man in the Northeast* 11: 3-20.

Lamb, H.H.

1966 *The Changing Climate.* London: Methuen.

1972 Atmospheric circulation and climate in the arctic since the last ice age. In *Climatic Changes in Arctic Areas During the Last Ten-thousand Years.* Proceedings of a symposium held at Oulanka and Keo, 4-10 October 1971, edited by Y. Vasari, H. Hyvarinen, and Sheila Hicks. *Acta Universitatisu Ouluensis. Series A, Scientiae Rerum Naturalium, #3, Geologica #1.* Oulu, Finland: University of Oulu.

1977 *Climate: Present, Past and Future.* Vol. 2. *Climatic History and the Future.* London: Methuen.

1979 Climatic variations and changes in the wind and ocean circulation: the Little Ice Age in the northeast Atlantic. *Quaternary Research* 11:1-20.

1981 Climate changes and food production: observations and outlook in the modern world. *Geo-Journal* [Weisbaden] 5, 2: 101-12.

1982 *Climate, History and the Modern World.* London: Methuen.

1988 *Weather, Climate & Human Affairs: A Book of Essays and Other Papers.* London: Routledge.

Laughlin, Charles D., and Ivan A. Brady

1978 Introduction: diaphasis and change in human populations. In *Extinction and Survival in Human Populations*, edited by Charles D. Laughlin and Ivan A. Brady. New York: Columbia University Press.

Laughlin, Charles D., and Ivan A. Brady, eds.

1978 *Extinction and Survival in Human Populations*. New York: Columbia University Press.

Leacock, Eleanor

1961 Comments on symposium. *Ethnohistory* 8: 256-61.

Leden, Christian

[1927] 1990 *Across the Keewatin Icefields:Three Years Among the Canadian Eskimos, 1913-1916*, translated from the German by Leslie Neatby, edited by Shirlee Anne Smith. Winnipeg:Watson and Dwyer.

Leroy Ladurie, E.L.

1972 *Times of Feast, Times of Famine: A History of Climate since the Year 1000*, translated by Barbara Bray. New York: Doubleday.

Linnamae, Urve

1975 *The Dorset Culture:A Comparative Study in Newfoundland and the Arctic*. Technical Papers of the Newfoundland Museum, #1. St John's, NF: Newfoundland Museum.

Linnamae, Urve, and Brenda L. Clark

1976 Archaeology of Rankin Inlet, N.W.T. *Musk Ox* 19: 37-73.

Lofthouse, J.

1899 A trip on the Tha-anne River, Hudson Bay. *Geographical Journal* 13: 274-77.

Lough, J.M., and H.C. Fritts

1987 An assessment of the possible effects of volcanic eruptions on North American climate using tree-ring data, 1602 to 1900 A.D. *Climatic Change* 10, no. 3: 219-40.

Low, Albert P.

1903 *Report on an Exploration of the East Coast of Hudson Bay from Cape Wolstenholme to the South End of James Bay*. Geological Survey of Canada Annual Report 1900 N.S.Vol. 13. Ottawa: Geological Survey of Canada.

1906 *Report on the Dominion Government Expedition to Hudson Bay and the Arctic Islands on Board the D.G.S. Neptune 1903-04*. Ottawa: Government Printing Office.

Lyon, George Francis

1824 *The Private Journal of Captain G.F. Lyon of H.M.S. Hecla During the Recent Voyage of Discovery Under Captain Parry*. London: John Murray.

1825 *A Brief Narrative of an Unsuccessful Attempt to Reach Repulse Bay, Through Sir Thomas Rowe's "Welcome," in His Majesty's Ship Griper in the Year MDCCCXXIV.* London: John Murray.

Lytwyn, Victor P.
1993 *The Hudson Bay Lowland Cree in the Fur Trade to 1821: A Study in Historical Geography.* Ph.D. thesis. Geography. University of Manitoba.

McCartney, Allen P.
1977 *Thule Eskimo Prehistory Along Northwestern Hudson Bay.* National Museum of Man Mercury Series. Archaeological Survey of Canada Paper #70. Ottawa: National Museums of Canada.

1978 *Study of Whale Bones for the Reconstruction of Canadian Arctic Bowhead Whale Stocks and Whale Use by Prehistoric Inuit.* Northern Environmental Branch, Final Report. Ottawa: Department of Indian and Northern Affairs.

1979 Whale bone assessment. In *Archaeological Whale Bone: A Northern Resource,* edited by Allen McCartney. Anthropological Papers of the University of Arkansas 1.

1980 The nature of Thule Eskimo whale use. *Arctic* 33: 517-41.

1984 History of native whaling in the arctic and subarctic. *Arctic Whaling.* Proceedings of the International Symposium Arctic Whaling, February 1983. University of Groningen.

McCartney, Allen P., and D.J. Mack
1973 Iron utilization by Thule Eskimos of central Canada. *American Antiquity* 38, no.3: 328-38.

McCartney, Allen P., and James M. Savelle
1985 Thule Eskimo whaling in the central Canadian arctic. *Arctic Anthropology* 22: 37-58.

McClintock, Francis Leopold
1859 *The Voyage of the "Fox" in the Arctic Seas: A Narrative of the Discovery of the Fate of Sir John Franklin and His Companions.* London: John Murray.

1859 *In the Arctic Seas: A Narrative of the Discovery of the Fate of Sir John Franklin and His Companions.* Philadelphia: Porter & Coates.

1857 Reminiscences of Arctic ice travel in search of Sir John Franklin and his companions. *Journal of the Royal Dublin Society* 1: 183-238.

McCullough, Karen M.
1986 *The Ruin Islanders: Thule Culture Pioneers in the Eastern High Arctic.* Mercury Series. Archaeological Survey of Canada Paper #141. Ottawa: Canadian Museum of Civilization.

McDonald, Alexander
1841 *A Narrative of Some Passages in the History of Eenoolooapik.* Edinburgh: Fraser & Co.

McGhee, Robert
1970 Excavations at Bloody Falls, N.W.T., Canada. *Arctic Anthropology* 6, no. 2: 53-73.

1970 Speculations on climatic change and Thule culture development. *Folk* 11/12: 173-84.

1972 *Copper Eskimo Prehistory*. Publications in Archaeology #2. Ottawa: National Museums of Canada.

1972 Climatic change and the development of Canadian arctic cultural traditions. In *Climatic Changes in Arctic Areas During the Last Ten-Thousand Years*. Proceedings of a symposium held at Oulanka and Kevo, 4-10 October 1971, edited by Y.Vasari, H. Hyvarinen, and Sheila Hicks. *Acta Universitatisu Ouluensis. Series A, Scientiae Rerum Naturalium, #3, Geologica #1*. Oulu, Finland: University of Oulu.

1974 A current interpretation of central Canadian arctic prehistory. *Inter-Nord* 13-14 (December): 171-80.

1976 Paleoeskimo occupations of central and high arctic Canada. In *Eastern Arctic Prehistory: Paleoeskimo Problems*, edited by Maxwell S. Moreau. The Joint Project of the National Museums of Canada and the School of American Research. Memoirs of the Society for American Archaeology #31. Washington, DC: Society for American Archaeology.

1978 *Canadian Arctic Prehistory*. Toronto: Van Nostrand Reinhold.

1981 The Norse in North America. In *The Vikings and Their Predecessors*, edited by Kate Gordon. Ottawa: National Museums of Canada.

1984 Thule prehistory in Canada. In *Handbook of North American Indians*. Vol. 5. *Arctic*, edited by David Damas. Washington, DC: Smithsonian Institution.

1984 Contact between native North Americans and the medieval Norse: a review of the evidence. *American Antiquity* 49, no. 1:4-26.

1990 The peopling of the arctic islands. In *Canada's Missing Dimension: Science and History in the Canadian Arctic Islands*. Vol. 2. Proceedings of the conference on The Canadian Arctic Islands: Canada's Missing Dimension, Ottawa, November 21-24, 1987, edited by C.R. Harington. Ottawa: Canadian Museum of Nature.

McNeill, William H.

1998 *Plagues and Peoples*. New York: Anchor/Doubleday.

MacRitchie, David

1912 Kayaks of the North Sea. *Scottish Geographical Magazine* 28: 126-33.

Mailhot, José

1978 L'étymologie de 'Esquimau': revue et corrigée. *Études/Inuit/Studies* 2, no. 2: 59-69.

Manley, Gordon

1961 *Annals of the New York Academy of Science* 95: 162.

Manning, Thomas H.

1943 Notes on the coastal district of the eastern barren grounds and Melville from Igloolik to Cape Fullerton. *Canadian Geographical Journal* 26: 84-105.

1960 *The Relationship of the Peary and Barren-Ground Caribou*. Technical Paper #4. Montreal: Arctic Institute of North America.

Martijn, C.A.

1980 The 'Esquimaux' in the 17th and 18th century cartography of the Gulf of St. Lawrence: a preliminary discussion. *Études/Inuit/Studies* 4, nos. 1-2: 77-104.

1980 The Inuit of southern Quebec-Labrador: a rejoinder to J. Garth Taylor. *Études/Inuit/Studies* 4, nos. 1-2: 194-98.

1980 La présence inuit sur la Cote Nord du golfe St-Laurent à l'époque historique. *Études/Inuit/Studies* 4, nos. 1-2: 105-26.

Marwick, Ernest W.

1975 *The Folklore of Orkney and Shetland.* Totowa, NJ: Rowman and Littlefield.

Mary-Rousselière, Guy

1959 Eskimo migrations. *Eskimo* 51 (June): 8-9, 12-15.

1960 The grave of Kukigak. *Eskimo* 57 (December): 18-22.

1960 Importance of Father Gasté's voyage. *Eskimo* 57 (December): 16-17.

1961 *Beyond the High Hills: A Book of Eskimo Poems.* Cleveland: The World Publishing Company.

1976 The Paleoeskimo in northern Baffinland. In *Eastern Arctic Prehistory: Paleoeskimo Problems,* edited by Moreau S. Maxwell. Washington, DC: Memoirs of the Society for American Archaeology 31.

1979 The Thule culture of north Baffin island: early Thule characteristics and the survival of Thule tradition. In *Thule Eskimo Culture: An Anthropological Retrospective,* edited by A. McCartney. National Museum of Man Mercury Series. Archaeological Survey of Canada Paper #88. Ottawa: National Museums of Canada.

1983 Gone leaving no forwarding address, the Tununirusirmiut. *Eskimo,* NS 24 (Fall-Winter): 3-15.

1985 Factors affecting human occupation of the land in the Pond Inlet region from prehistoric to contemporary times. *Eskimo* NS 28 (Fall-Winter): 8-24.

1991 *Qitdlarssuaq: The Story of a Polar Migration.* Winnipeg: Wuerz.

Maslow, Abraham

1973 *Dominance, Self-Esteem, Self-Actualization: Germinal Papers of A.H. Maslow,* edited by Richard J. Lowry. Monterey, CA: Brooks/Cole Publishing Company.

Mathiassen, Therkel

1927 *Report of the Fifth Thule Expedition, 1921-24.* Vol. 4. *Archaeology of the Central Eskimos I: Descriptive Part.* Copenhagen: Gyldendal.

1927 *Report of the Fifth Thule Expedition, 1921-24.* Vol. 4. *Archaeology of the Central Eskimos II: Analytical Part.* Copenhagen: Gyldendal.

1928 *Report of the Fifth Thule Expedition, 1921-24. Material Culture of the Central Eskimos.* Copenhagen: Gyldendal.

1928 *Report of the Fifth Thule Expedition, 1921-24.* Vol. 6: 1. *Material Culture of the Iglulik Eskimos.* Copenhagen: Gyldendal.

1930 *Report of the Fifth Thule Expedition, 1921-24.*Vol. 10: 1. *Archaeological Collections from the Western Eskimos.* Copenhagen: Gyldendal.

1931 *Ancient Eskimo Settlements on the Kanagmiut Area.* Copenhagen: C.A. Reitzel.

1931 *Report of the Fifth Thule Expedition, 1921-24.*Vol. 1: 2. *Contributions to the Physiography of Southampton Island.* Copenhagen: Gyldendal.

1933 *Report of the Fifth Thule Expedition, 1921-24.*Vol. 1: 3. *Contributions to the Geography of Baffin Land and Melville Peninsula.* Copenhagen: Gyldendal.

1935 Archaeology in Greenland. *Antiquity* 9, no. 34 (June): 195-203.

1945 *Report of the Fifth Thule Expedition, 1921-24.*Vol. 1: 1. *Report on the Expedition.* Copenhagen: Gyldendal.

Maunder, Edward Walter

1890 [Summary of Spörer's sunspot studies.] *Notes to the Royal Astronomical Society* 50: 251.

1894 A prolonged sunspot minimum. *Knowledge* 17: 173.

1922 A prolonged sunspot minimum. *Journal of the British Astronomical Association* 32: 140.

Maxwell, Moreau S.

1960 *An Archaeological Analysis of Eastern Grant Land, Ellesmere Island, Northwest Territories.* National Museum of Man Bulletin #170. Ottawa: National Museums of Canada.

1976 Introduction. In *Eastern Arctic Prehistory: Paleoeskimo Problems,* edited by Moreau S. Maxwell. Memoirs of the Society for American Archaeology 31.Washington, DC: Society for American Archaeology.

1979 The Lake Harbour region: ecological equilibrium in sea coast adaptation. In *Thule Eskimo Culture: An Anthropological Retrospective,* edited by A. McCartney. National Museum of Man Mercury Series. Archaeological Survey of Canada Paper #88. Ottawa: National Museums of Canada.

1984 Pre-Dorset and Dorset Prehistory of Canada. In *Handbook of American Indians.*Vol. 5. *Arctic,* edited by David Damas.Washington, DC: Smithsonian Institution.

1985 *Prehistory of the Eastern Arctic.* New World Archaeological Series. Orlando, FL: Academic Press.

Maxwell, Moreau S., ed.

1976 *Eastern Arctic Prehistory: Paleoeskimo Problems: A Monograph Resulting from a Joint Project Sponsored by the National Museums of Canada and the School of American Research.* Memoirs of the Society for American Archaeology, #31.Washington, DC: Society for American Archaeology.

Mead, Margaret

1964 Warfare is only an invention. In *War: Studies from Psychology, Sociology, Anthropology,* edited by Leon Bramson and George W. Goethals. New York: Basic Books.

1968 Alternatives to war. In *War: The Anthropology of Armed Conflict and Aggression,* edited by M. Fried, M. Harris, and R. Murphy. Garden City, NY: Natural History Press.

Meldgaard, Jorgen

1960 Origin and evolution of Eskimo cultures in the eastern arctic. *Canadian Geographic Journal* 60, no. 2: 64-75.

1962 On the formative period of the Dorset culture. In *Prehistoric Cultural Relations Between the Arctic and Temperate Zones of North America*, edited by J. Campbell. Arctic Institute of North America Technical Paper #11. Montreal: Arctic Institute of North America.

Meltzer, David, and J.I. Mead, eds.

1985 *Environments and Extinctions: Man in Late Glacial North America.* Orono, ME: Center for the Study of Early Man.

Metayer, Maurice, and Agnes Nanogak

1972 *Tales From the Igloo.* Edmonton: Hurtig Publishers.

Middleton, Christopher

[1741-42] 1852 Extracts from the log [of H.M.S. *Furnace*]. In William Coats, *The Geography of Hudson's Bay...; with an Appendix containing extracts from the Log of Capt Middleton on his Voyage for the Discovery of the North-west Passage in H.M.S. Furnace in 1741-42.* London: Hakluyt Society.

Mikkelsen, E.

1954 Kajakmandan fra Aberdeen. *Grønland* 53-58.

Minc, Leah

1986 Scarcity and survival: the role of oral tradition in mediating subsistence crises. *Journal of Anthropological Archaeology* 5: 39-113.

Miracle, Preston T., Lynn E. Fisher, and Jody Brown, eds.

1991 *Foragers in Context: Long-Term, Regional and Historical Perspectives in Hunter-Gatherer Studies.* Michigan Discussions in Anthropology. Vol. 10. Ann Arbor: Department of Anthropology. University of Michigan.

Morrison, David

1983 *Thule Culture in Western Coronation Gulf, N.W.T.* National Museum of Man Mercury Series. Archaeological Survey of Canada Paper #116. Ottawa: National Museums of Canada.

1988 *The Kugaluk Site and the Nuvorugmiut.* National Museum of Man Mercury Series. Archaeological Survey of Canada Paper #137. Ottawa: National Museums of Canada.

1990 *Iglulualumiut Prehistory: The Lost Inuit of Franklin Bay.* National Museum of Man Mercury Series. Archaeological Survey of Canada Paper #142. Ottawa: National Museums of Canada.

1992 *Arctic Hunters: The Inuit and Diamond Jenness.* Ottawa: Canadian Museum of Civilization.

Munk, Jens

[1624] 1980 *The Journal of Jens Munk, 1619-1620*, edited by Walter A. Kenyon. Toronto: Royal Ontario Museum. [Originally published in *Danish Arctic Expeditions, 1605 to 1620*, edited by C.C.A. Gosch. London: Hakluyt Society, 1897.]

Munn, Henry Toke

1922 The economic life of the Baffin Island Eskimo. *Geographical Journal* 59, no. 4 (June).

Murdoch, John

1886 A few legendary fragments from the point Barrow Eskimo. *American Naturalist* 20: 593-99.

Nanogak, Agnes

1986 *More Tales From the Igloo*. Edmonton: Hurtig.

Nash, Ronald J.

1969 *The Arctic Small Tool Tradition in Manitoba*. Department of Anthropology Occasional Paper 2. Winnipeg: University of Manitoba.

1972 Dorset culture in northeastern Manitoba, Canada. *Arctic Anthropology* 9, no. 1: 10-16.

1976 Cultural systems and culture change in the central arctic. In *Eastern Arctic Prehistory: Paleoeskimo Problems*, edited by Moreau S. Maxwell. Memoirs of the Society for American Archaeology, 31. Washington, DC: Society for American Archaeology.

Nelson, Edward W.

[1899] 1983 The Eskimo about Bering Strait. In *Eighteenth Annual Report of the Bureau of American Ethnology for the Years 1896-97*. Vol. 18, no. 1. Reprint, Washington, DC: Smithsonian Institution.

Nichols, Harvey

1967 The post-glacial history of vegetation and climate at Ennadai Lake, Keewatin, and Lynn Lake, Manitoba (Canada). *Euszeitalter und Gegenwart* 18: 176-97.

1967 Pollen diagrams from sub-arctic Central Canada. *Science* 155: 1665-68.

1967 Central Canadian palynology and its relevance to northwestern Europe in the Late Quaternary period. *Review of Paleobotany and Palynology* 3: 231-43.

1968 Pollen analysis, paleotemperatures, and the summer position of the arctic front in the postglacial history of Keewatin, Canada. *Bulletin of the American Meteorological Society* 49, no. 4: 387-88.

1970 Late quaternary pollen diagrams from the Canadian arctic barren grounds at Pelly Lake, northern Keewatin, N.W.T. *Arctic and Alpine Research* 2, no. 1: 43-61.

1972 Summary of the palynological evidence for late-quaternary vegetational and climatic change in the central and eastern Canadian arctic. In *Climatic Changes in Arctic Areas During the Last Ten-Thousand Years*. Proceedings of a symposium held at Oulanka and Kevo, 4-10 October 1971, edited by Y. Vasari, H. Hyvarinen, and Sheila Hicks. *Acta Universitatisu Ouluensis. Series A, Scientiae Rerum Naturalium, #3, Geologica #1*. Oulu, Finland: University of Oulu.

1975 Palynological and paleoclimatic study of Holocene displacement of the forest limit in MacKenzie and Keewatin, N.W.T., Canada. *Arctic and Alpine Research.* Occasional Paper 15.

1975 *Palynological and Paleoclimatic Study of the Late Quaternary Displacement of the Boreal Forest-Tundra Ecotone in Keewatin and Mackenzie, N.W.T., Canada.* Institute of Arctic and Alpine Research Occasional Paper 15.

Nichols, Harvey, P.M. Kelley, and J.T. Andrews

1978 Holocene palaeo-wind evidence from palynology in Baffin Island. *Nature* 273: 140-42.

Noble, William C.

1971 Archaeological surveys and sequences in Central District Mackenzie, N.W.T. *Arctic Anthropology* 8, no. 1: 102-35.

Noholnigee, Henry Yugh

1982 *The Stories That Chief Henry Told,* edited by Eliza Jones. Fairbanks: Alaska Native Language Center, University of Alaska.

Nooter, G.

1971 Old Kayaks in the Netherlands. *Mededlingen van het Rijksmuseum voor Volkenkunde,* Leiden No. 17. Leiden.

Nudds, Thomas D.

1988 Effects of technology and economics on the foraging behaviour of modern hunter-gatherer societies. In *Knowing the North: Reflections on Tradition, Technology and Science,* edited by William Wonders. Edmonton: Boreal Institute for Northern Studies.

Nungak, Zebedee, and Eugene Arima

1988 *Inuit Stories: Povungnituk.* Canadian Museum of Civilization, National Museums of Canada.

Ogilvie, Astrid E.J.

1984 The past climate and sea-ice record from Iceland, part 1: data to A.D. 1780. *Climatic Change* 6: 131-52.

1992 Documentary evidence for changes in the climate of Iceland, A.D. 1500 to 1800. In *Climate Since A.D. 1500,* edited by Raymond S. Bradley and Philip D. Jones. London: Routledge.

Ohokto

1948 [Inuit account of meeting between Netsilik and John Ross, 1830.] In L.A. Learmonth, Ross meets the Netchiliks. *The Beaver* (September 1948): 10.

Oldmixon, John

[1708] 1931 The history of Hudson's Bay. In *Documents Relating to the Early History of Hudson Bay,* edited by J.B. Tyrrell. Toronto: Champlain Society. [Originally published as a chapter in John Oldmixon, *The British Empire in America.* Vol. 1. London, 1708.]

Olson, I.U., ed.

1970 *Radiocarbon Variations and Absolute Chronology*. Stockholm: Almqvist & Wiksell.

Oquilluk, William A.

1973 *People of Kauwerak: Legends of the Northern Eskimo*. Anchorage: AMU Press.

O'Shea, John, and Paul Halstead

1989 Conclusions: bad year economics. In *Bad Year Economics: Cultural Responses to Risk and Uncertainty*, edited by Paul Halstead and John O'Shea. Cambridge: Cambridge University Press.

Oswalt, Wendell H.

1979 *Eskimos and Explorers*. Novato, CA: Chandler and Sharp.

Parker, E.N.

1973 Chapter 1. In *Solar Terrestrial Relations,* edited by D. Venkatesan. Calgary: University of Calgary Press.

1975 The sun. *Scientific American* 233 (September): 42.

Parker, G.R.

1972 Biology of the Kaminuriak population of barren-ground caribou, Part 1. *Canadian Wildlife Service Report* Series 20.

Parry, William Edward

1821 *Journal of a Voyage for the Discovery of a North-West Passage from the Atlantic to the Pacific; Performed in the Years 1819-20 in His Majesty's Ships Hecla and Griper*. London: John Murray.

1824 *Journal of a Second Voyage for the Discovery of a North-West Passage From the Atlantic to the Pacific: Performed in the Years 1821-22-23 in His Majesty's Ships Fury and Hecla....* London: John Murray.

1828 *Journal of a Third Voyage for the Discovery of a North-West Passage From the Atlantic to the Pacific: Performed in the Years 1824-27 in His Majesty's Ships Fury and Hecla....* London: John Murray.

1828 *Narrative of an Attempt to Reach the North Pole in Boats Fitted for the Purpose, and Attached to His Majesty's Ship Hecla in the Year MDCCCXXVII....* London: John Murray.

Payne, F.F.

1889 *Eskimo of Hudson's Strait. Extract from Proceedings of the Canadian Institute*. Series 3, no. 6: 213-30.

1890 A few notes upon the Eskimo of Cape Prince of Wales, Hudson's Strait. *Proceedings of the American Association for the Advancement of Science* 38: 358-60.

Petulla, Joseph M.

1985 Environmental values: the problem of method in environmental history. In *Environmental History: Critical Issues in Comparative Perspective*, edited by Kendall E. Bailes. New York: University Press of America.

Pitseolak, Peter, with Dorothy Eber Harley

1975 *People From Our Side.* Edmonton: Hurtig.

Plumet, Patrick

1979 Thuléens et Dorsetiens dans l'Ungava (Nouveau-Quebec). In *Thule Eskimo Culture: An Anthropological Retrospective,* edited by A. McCartney. National Museum of Man Mercury Series. Archaeological Survey of Canada Paper #88. Ottawa: National Museums of Canada.

Poncins, Gontran de

1941 *Kabloona.* New York: Reynal & Hitchcock.

Price, Barbara J.

1977 Shifts of production and organization: a cluster-interaction model. *Current Anthropology* 18: 209-33.

1980 The truth is not in accounts but in account books: on the epistemological status of history. In *Beyond the Myths of Culture: Essays in Cultural Materialism,* edited by Eric B. Ross. New York: Academic Press.

1984 Competition, productive intensification, and ranked society: speculations from evolutionary theory. In *Warfare, Culture, and Environment,* edited by Brian Ferguson. New York: Academic Press.

Prickett, Abacuck

[1635] 1965 A large discourse of the said Voyage, and the success thereof, written by Abacuk Pricket, who lived to come home. In Luke Foxe, *North-West Fox, or Fox from the North-West Passage....* London: B. Alsop & Tho Fawcet. [Facsimile, New York: S.R. Publishers Ltd. and Johnson Reprint Corporation.]

Quimby, G.I.

1940 The Manitunik culture of east Hudson Bay. *American Antiquity* 6, no. 2: 148-65.

Rae, John

1850 *Narrative of an Expedition to the Shores of the Arctic Sea in 1846 and 1847.* London: Boone.

1855 *John Rae's Correspondence with the Hudson's Bay Company on Arctic Exploration, 1844-55,* edited by E.E. Rich. London: Hudson's Bay Record Society, 1953.

1855 Arctic exploration with information respecting Sir John Franklin's missing party. *Royal Geographical Society Journal* 25: 246-56.

1866 On the Eskimaux. *Transactions of the Ethnological Society of London* N.S. 4: 138-53.

1878 Eskimo migrations. *The Journal of the Anthropological Institute of Great Britain and Ireland* VII: 125-31.

1882 On the conditions and characteristics of some of the Indian tribes of the Hudson's Bay Company's Territories. *Address to the Royal Society of Arts, London.* [Reprint, Rae and the Eskimos. *The Beaver* (March 1954): 38-41.]

Rainey, Froelich

1947 *The Whale Hunters of Tigara.* Anthropological Papers of the American Museum of Natural History. Vol. 41, part 2. New York.

Rasmussen, Knud

1921 *Greenland by the Polar Sea: The Story of the Thule Expedition from Melville Bay to Cape Morris Jesup.* London: W. Heinemann.

1927 *Across Arctic America.* New York, London: G.P. Putnam's Sons.

1929 *Report of the Fifth Thule Expedition, 1921-24.* Vol. 7: 1. *Intellectual Culture of the Iglulik Eskimos.* Copenhagen: Gyldendal.

1930 *Report of the Fifth Thule Expedition, 1921-24.* Vol. 7: 3. *Iglulik and Caribou Eskimo Texts.* Copenhagen: Gyldendal.

1930 *Report of the Fifth Thule Expedition, 1921-24.* Vol. 7: 2. *Observations on the Intellectual Culture of the Caribou Eskimos.* Copenhagen: Gyldendal.

1931 *Report of the Fifth Thule Expedition, 1921-24.* Vol. 8: 1-2. *The Netsilik Eskimos, Social Life and Spiritual Culture.* Copenhagen: Gyldendal.

1932 *Report of the Fifth Thule Expedition, 1921-24.* Vol. 9. *Intellectual Culture of the Copper Eskimos.* Copenhagen: Gyldendal.

1938 *Report of the Fifth Thule Expedition, 1921-24. Igluglik and Caribou Eskimo Texts.* Copenhagen: Gyldendal.

1939 *Posthumous Notes on East Greenland Legends and Myths. Meddelelser om Grønland.* Vol. 109, no. 3. Edited by Hother Ostermann. [Notes from the 6th and 7th Thule Expeditions, 1831-33.]

1952 *Report of the Fifth Thule Expedition, 1921-24.* Vol. 10: 3. *The Alaskan Eskimos as Described in the Posthumous Notes of Knud Rasmussen.* Copenhagen: Gyldendal.

1973 *Eskimo Poems from Canada and Greenland,* translated by Tom Lowenstein from material originally collected by Knud Rasmussen. Pittsburgh: University of Pittsburgh Press.

1973 *Eskimo Songs and Stories.* Collected by Knud Rasmussen on the Fifth Thule Expedition, selected and translated by Edward Field. New York: Delacorte Press.

Ray, Dorothy Jean

1967 Land tenure and polity of the Bering Strait Eskimos. *Journal of the West* 7: 371-94.

Rich, Edwin E.

1953 Appendix B, Biographical. In *John Rae's Correspondence with the Hudson's Bay Company on Arctic Exploration, 1844-1855,* edited by E.E. Rich. London: Hudson's Bay Record Society.

Richardson, John

1822 *Arctic Ordeal: The Journal of John Richardson, Surgeon-Naturalist with Franklin, 1820-1822,* edited by C. Stuart Houston. Kingston: McGill-Queen's University Press, 1984.

1851 *Arctic Searching Expedition: A Journal of a Boat-Voyage Through Rupert's Land and the Arctic Sea, In Search of the Discovery Ships Under Command of Sir John Franklin: With an*

Appendix on the Physical Geography of North America. 2 vols. London: Longman, Brown, Green, and Longman.

Riches, David

1982 *Northern Nomadic Hunter-Gatherers: A Humanistic Approach.* London: Academic Press.

Rink, Hinrich

1875 *Tales and Traditions of the Eskimo.* Edinburgh, London: W. Blackwood.

1887-1891 *The Eskimo Tribes: Their Distribution and Characteristics, Especially in Regard to Language, with Comparative Vocabulary and Sketch Map.* 2 vols. *Meddelelser om Grønland* 11.

Robinson, Samuel Isaac

1973 *The Influence of the American Whaling Industry on the Aivilingmiut, 1860-1919.* M.A. thesis. Anthropology. McMaster University.

Robson, Joseph

1752 *An Account of Six Years Residence in Hudson's Bay, from 1733 to 1736 and 1744 to 1747.* London.

Roesdahl, Else

1987 *The Vikings,* translated by Susan M. Margeson and Kirsten Williams. London: Penguin Press.

Ross, James Clark

1850 Narrative of the proceedings of Captain Sir James C. Ross in command of the expedition through Lancaster Sound and Barrow Strait. *Great Britain, Parliament, House of Commons, Sessional Papers, Accounts and Papers* 35, no. 107: 58-64.

Ross, John

1835 *Narrative of a Second Voyage in Search of a North-west Passage, and of a Residence in the Arctic Regions, During the Years 1829-30-31-32-33.* London: A. W. Webster.

1835 *Appendix to the Narrative of a Second Voyage in Search of a North-West Passage.* London: A. W. Webster.

1855 *Rear Admiral Sir John Franklin: A Narrative of the Circumstances and Causes which Led to the Failure of the Searching Expeditions Sent by Government and Others for the Rescue of Sir John Franklin.* 2nd ed., London: Longmans, Green, Brown, & Longmans.

Ross, W. Gillies

1975 *Whaling and Eskimos: Hudson Bay 1860-1915.* Publication in Ethnology 10. Ottawa: National Museum of Man.

1985 *Arctic Whalers, Icy Seas: Narratives of the Davis Strait Whale Fishery.* Toronto: Irwin Publishing.

Rouse, Irving

1986 *Migrations in Prehistory: Inferring Population Movement From Cultural Remains.* New Haven: Yale University Press.

Rowley, Susan

1985 Population movements in the Canadian arctic. *Études/Inuit/Studies* 9, no.1: 3-22.

1985 *The Significance of Migration for the Understanding of Inuit Cultural Development in the Canadian Arctic.* Ph.D. thesis. Anthropology. University of Cambridge.

Rowley-Conwy, Peter, and Marek Zvelebil

1989 Saving it for later: storage by prehistoric hunter-gatherers in Europe. In *Bad Year Economics: Cultural Responses to Risk and Uncertainty*, edited by Paul Halstead and John O'Shea. Cambridge: Cambridge University Press.

Saladin d'Anglure, Bernard

1967 L'Organisation sociale traditionelle des Esquimaux de Kangirsujuaak (Nouveau-Québec). *Centre d'Études Nordiques Travaux* 17. Québec: Université Laval.

1984 Inuit of Quebec. In *Handbook of North American Indians.* Vol. 5. *The Arctic,* edited by David Damas. Washington, DC: Smithsonian Institution.

Savelle, J.M.

1981 The nature of nineteenth century Inuit occupations of the High Arctic Islands of Canada. *Études/Inuit/Studies* 5: 109-23.

1985 Effect of nineteenth century European exploration on the development of the Netsilik Inuit culture. In *The Franklin Era in Canadian Arctic History*, edited by Patricia D. Sutherland. Archaeological Survey of Canada Paper 131. Ottawa: National Museum of Man.

Savelle, James M., and Allen P. McCartney

1988 Geographical and temporal variation in Thule Eskimo subsistence and economies: a model. *Research in Economic Anthropology* 10: 21-72.

1990 Prehistoric Thule Eskimo whaling in the Canadian arctic islands: current knowledge and future research directions. In *Canada's Missing Dimension: Science and History in the Canadian Arctic Islands*. Proceedings of the conference on The Canadian Arctic Islands: Canada's Missing Dimension, Ottawa, November 21-24, 1987. Vol II, edited by C.R. Harington. Ottawa: Canadian Museum of Nature.

Schledermann, Peter

1975 *Thule Eskimo Prehistory of Cumberland Sound, Baffin Island, Canada.* National Museum of Man Mercury Series. Archaeological Survey of Canada #38. Ottawa: National Museums of Canada.

1976 The effect of climatic/ecological changes on the style of Thule culture winter dwellings. *Arctic and Alpine Research* 8, no.1: 37-47.

Schneider, Lucien

1985 *Ulirnaisigutiit: An Inuktitut-English Dictionary of Northern Quebec, Labrador and Eastern Arctic Dialects (with an English Inuktitut Index).* Québec: Les Presses de l'Université Laval.

Schneider, Stephen H., and Clifford Maas

1975 Volcanic dust, sunspots and temperature trends. *Science* 190, no. 4216 (Nov 21): 741-46.

Schwatka, Frederick

1880 *The Long Arctic Search: The Narrative of Lieutenant Frederick Schwatka, U.S.A., 1878-1880, Seeking the Records of the Lost Franklin Expedition*, edited by E.A. Stackpole. Mystic, Connecticut: Marine Historical Association Inc., 1965.

Silvy, Antoine

[1684] 1931 Journal of Father Silvy from Belle Isle to Port Nelson. In *Documents Relating to the Early History of Hudson Bay*, edited by J.B. Tyrrell. Toronto: The Champlain Society.

Simpson, Thomas

1843 *Narrative of the Discoveries on the North Coast of America; Effected by the Officers of The Hudson's Bay Company During the Years 1836-39.* 2nd ed., London: Richard Bentley.

Smith, Derek

1984 Mackenzie Delta Eskimo. In *Handbook of North American Indians.* Vol. 5. *Arctic*, edited by David Damas. Washington, DC: Smithsonian Institution.

Smith, Eric Alden

1991 *Inujjuamiut Foraging Strategies: Evolutionary Ecology of an Arctic Hunting Economy.* New York: Aldine De Gruyter.

Smith, James G.E.

1978 Economic uncertainty in an "original affluent society": caribou and caribou eater Chipewyan adaptive strategies. *Arctic Anthropology* 15: 68-88.

1981 Chipewyan, Cree and Inuit relations west of Hudson Bay, 1714-1955. *Ethnohistory* 28, no.2 (Spring): 133-56.

Smith, James G.E., and E.S. Burch

1979 Chipewyan and Inuit in the central Canadian subarctic, 1613-1977. *Arctic Anthropology* XVI, no. 2: 76-101.

Souter, William Clark

1935 *The Story of Our Kayak and Some Others.* Presidential Address to the Aberdeen Medico-Chirurgical Society, 1933. Aberdeen.

Speck, Frank G.

1936 Inland Eskimo bands of Labrador. In *Essays in Anthropology in Honor of Alfred Louis Kroeber.* Berkeley: University of California Press.

Spiess, Arthur E.

1979 *Reindeer and Caribou Hunters: An Archaeological Study.* New York: Academic Press.

Staunton, Richard

1738 Letter 70. In *Letters From Hudson Bay*, edited by K.G. Davies. London: Hudson's Bay Record Society, 1965.

Steenhoven, Geert van den

1956 Caribou Eskimo legal concepts. In *Eskimo of the Canadian Arctic*, edited by Victor Valentine and Frank Vallee. Toronto: McClelland & Stewart, 1968. [Originally published in *Proceedings of the 32nd International Congress of Americanists*, Copenhagen, 1956.]

1959 *Legal Concepts Among the Netsilik Eskimos of Pelly Bay.* Ottawa: Department of Northern Affairs and National Resources.

1962 A 'Good Old Days' Eskimo story at the Netsilike. *Eskimo* 61 (March–June): 10–13.

1962 *Leadership and Law Among the Eskimos of the Keewatin District, Northwest Territories.* Rijswijk: Uitgeverij Excelsior.

Stefansson, Vilhjalmur

1922 *Hunters of the Great North.* New York: Harcourt, Brace.

1921 *The Friendly Arctic: The Story of Five Years in Polar Regions.* Reprint, New York: The Macmillan Co., 1943.

1942 *Greenland.* Garden City: Doubleday.

Stefansson, Vilhjalmur, ed.

1938 *The Three Voyages of Martin Frobisher in Search of a Passage to Cathay and India by the North-West, A.D. 1576-8. From the Original 1578 text of George Best, Together with Numerous Other Versions, Additions, etc.* 2 vols. Edited by Vilhjalmur Stefansson. London: Argonaut Press.

1991 Caribou population dynamics and Thule culture adaptations on southern Baffin Island, N.W.T. *Arctic Anthropology* 28, no. 2: 15–43.

Stevenson, Marc

1997 *Inuit Whalers and Cultural Persistence: Structure in Cumberland Sound and Central Inuit Social Organization.* London: Oxford University Press.

Steward, J.H.

1955 *Theory of Culture Change: The Methodology of Multilinear Evolution.* Urbana: University of Illinois Press.

Stuiver, Minze

1961 Variations in radiocarbon concentration and sunspot activity. *Journal of Geophysical Research* 66, no. 1 (Jan): 273–76.

1965 Carbon-14 content of 18th- and 19th-century wood: variations correlated with sunspot activity. *Science* 149 (July 30): 533-37.

Stupart, R.F.

1886 The Eskimo of Stupart Bay. *Proceedings of the Canadian Institute.* Series 3, Vol. 4: 95-114.

Sturtevant, William C.

1980 The first Inuit depiction by Europeans. *Études/Inuit/Studies* 4, nos. 1-2: 47-49.

Sturtevant, William C., and David Beers Quinn

1987 This new prey: Eskimos in Europe in 1567, 1576, and 1577. In *Indians and Europe: An Interdisciplinary Collection of Essays*, edited by Christian Feest. Aachen: Edition Herodot, Rader Verlag.

Sumner, William Graham

1964 War. In *War: Studies from Psychology, Sociology, Anthropology*, edited by Leon Bramson and George W. Goethals. New York: Basic Books.

Suess, Hans E.

1965 Secular variations of the cosmic-ray-produced Carbon 14 in the atmosphere and their interpretations. *Journal of Geophysical Research* 70, no. 23 (Dec 1): 5937-52.

1968 Climatic changes, solar activity and the cosmic-ray production rate of natural radiocarbon. *Meteorological Monographs* 8: 146-50.

Swaine, Theodore [Clerk of the *California*]

1749 *An Account of a Voyage for the Discovery of a North-West Passage by Hudson's Streights, to the Western and Southern Ocean of America: Performed in the Year 1746 and 1747, in the Ship California, Capt. Francis Smith, Commander.* Vol. 1. London.

1749 *An Account of a Voyage for the Discovery of a North-West Passage by Hudson's Streights, to the Western and Southern Ocean of America: Performed in the Year 1746 and 1747, in the Ship California, Capt. Francis Smith, Commander.* Vol. 2. London.

Szathmary, Emöke J.E.

1979 Blood groups of Siberians, Eskimos, and subarctic and northwest coast Indians: the problem of origins and genetic relations. In *The First Americans: Origins, Affinities and Adaptations*, edited by William S. Laughlin and Albert B. Harper. New York: Gustav Fischer.

1981 Genetic markers in Siberian and northern North American populations. *Yearbook of Physical Anthropology* 24: 37-73.

1984 Human biology of the arctic. In *Handbook of North American Indians.* Vol. 5. *Arctic*, edited by David Damas. Washington, DC: Smithsonian Institution.

1985 Peopling of North America: clues from genetic studies. In *Out of Asia: Peopling the Americas and the Pacific*, edited by Robert Kirk and Emöke Szathmary. Canberra: The Journal of Pacific History.

Taylor, Bea

1985 1550-1620: a period of summer accumulation in the Queen Elizabeth Islands. In *Climatic Change in Canada 5: Critical Periods in the Quaternary Climatic History of Northern North America.* Syllogeus 55. Edited by C.R. Harington. Ottawa: National Museums of Canada.

Taylor, J. Garth

1972 Eskimo answers to an eighteenth century questionnaire. *Ethnohistory* 19, no. 2 (Spring): 135-45.

1974 *Labrador Eskimo Settlements of the Early Contact Period.* Publications in Ethnology 9. Ottawa: National Museum of Man.

1975 Demography and adaptations of eighteenth-century Eskimo groups in northern Labrador and Ungava. In *Prehistoric Maritime Adaptations of the Circumpolar Zone*, edited by William Fitzhugh. The Hague: Mouton Publishers.

1979 Indian-Inuit relations in eastern Labrador, 1600-1675. *Arctic Anthropology* 16, nos. 1-2: 49-58.

1984 Historical ethnography of the Labrador coast. In *Handbook of North American Indians.* Vol. 5. *Arctic*, edited by David Damas. Washington, DC: Smithsonian Institution.

Taylor, William Ewart

1962 Pre-Dorset occupations at Ivugivik in northwestern Ungava. In *Prehistoric Cultural Relations Between the Arctic and Temperature Zones of North America*, edited by John M. Campbell. Arctic Institute of North America Technical Paper 11. Montreal.

1963 Hypotheses on the origin of Canadian Thule culture. *American Antiquity* 28, no. 4: 456-64.

1964 The prehistory of the Quebec-Labrador Peninsula. In *Le Nouveau-Québec, Contribution a l'Etude de l'Occupation Humaine.* Ecole Pratique des Hautes Études. Paris: Mouton & Co.

1966 An archaeological perspective on Eskimo economy. *Antiquity* 40: 114-20.

1967 Summary of archaeological field work on Banks and Victoria Islands, Arctic Canada, 1965. *Arctic Anthropology* 4, no. 1: 221-43.

1968 The Arnapik and Tyara sites: an archaeological study of Dorset culture origins. *Memoirs of the Society for American Archaeology* #22.

1972 *An Archaeological Survey Between Cape Parry and Cambridge Bay, N.W.T., Canada in 1963.* National Museum of Man Mercury Series. Archaeological Survey of Canada Paper #1. Ottawa: National Museums of Canada.

Taylor, William E., and Robert McGhee

1979 *Archaeological Material from Creswell Bay, N.W.T., Canada.* National Museum of Man Mercury Series. Archaeological Survey of Canada Paper #85. Ottawa: National Museums of Canada.

1981 *Deblicquy, A Thule Culture Site on Bathurst Island, N.W.T., Canada.* National Museum of Man Mercury Series. Archaeological Survey of Canada Paper # 102. Ottawa: National Museums of Canada.

Thalbitzer, William

1904 A phonetical study of the Eskimo language based on observations made on a journey in North Greenland 1900-1901. *Meddelelser om Grønland* 31.

1912 Ethnographical collections from East Greenland (Angmagsalik and Nualik) made by G. Holm, G. Amdrup, J. Peterson, and described by W. Thalbitzer. *Meddelelser om Grønland* 39: 7. Copenhagen.

Thibert, Arthur

1970 *English-Eskimo Dictionary Eskimo-English*. Ottawa: Canadian Research Centre for Anthropology, Saint Paul University.

Tomka, Steve A., and Marc G. Stevenson

1993 Understanding abandonment processes: summary and remaining concerns. In *Abandonment of Settlements and Regions: Ethnoarchaeological and Archaeological Approaches*, edited by Catherine M. Cameron and Steve A. Tomka. Cambridge: Cambridge University Press.

Trigger, Bruce

1969 *The Huron: Farmers of the North*. New York: Holt, Rinehart & Winston.

1976 *The Children of Aataentsic: A History of the Huron People to 1660*. Kingston: McGill-Queen's.

Trudel, François

1978 The Inuit of southern Labrador and the development of French sedentary fisheries (1700-1760). In *Papers from the Fourth Annual Congress, Canadian Ethnology Society, 1977*, edited by Richard J. Preston. Canadian Ethnology Service Paper #40. Ottawa: National Museum of Man.

1978 Les inuit de Labrador méridional face à l'exploitation canadienne et française des pecheries (1700-1760). *Revue d'histoire de l'Amérique française* 31: 481-500.

1978 Les inuit face à l'expansion commerciale européene dans la région du Détroit de Belle-Isle au XVIe et XVIIe siècles. *Recherches amérindiennes au Québec* 9, nos. 1-2: 141-50.

1980 Les relations entre les Francais et les Inuit au Labrador méridional, 1660-1760. *Études / Inuit / Studies* 4, nos. 1-2: 135-45.

1981 *Inuit, Amerindians and Europeans: A Study of Interethnic Economic Relations on the Canadian South-Eastern Seaboard (1500-1800)*. Ph.D. thesis. Anthropology. University of Connecticut.

Trudel, Marcel

1960 *L'Esclavage au Canada francais*. Québec: Les Presses de l'Université Laval.

Turner, Lucien M.

1887 On the Indians and Eskimos of the Ungava District, Labrador. *Transactions of the Royal Society of Canada* 2: 99-119.

Tyrrell, James W.

1898 *Across the Sub-Arctics of Canada: A Journey of 3,200 Miles by Canoe and Snow-Shoe.* London.

Usher, Peter

1971 *Fur Trade Posts of the Northwest Territories, 1870-1970.* Northern Science Research Group 71-4.

Vallee, Frank

1964 Kabloona and Eskimo in the Central Keewatin. In *Canadian Society: Sociological Perspectives,* edited by Bernard R. Blishen et al. Toronto: Macmillan of Canada.

Van de Velde, F.

1954 Infanticide among the Eskimo. *Eskimo* 34: 6-8.

1956 Rules governing the sharing of seal after the 'aglus' hunt amongst the Arviligjuarmiut. *Eskimo* 41(September).

Vansina, Jan

1971 Once upon a time: oral traditions as history in Africa. *Daedalus* 100: 442-68.

VanStone, James

1962 An archaeological collection from Somerset Island and Boothia Peninsula, N.W.T. In *Occasional Paper 4,* 1-63. Ontario: Art and Archaeology Division, Royal Ontario Museum.

1963 Changing patterns of Indian trapping in the Canadian subarctic. *Arctic* 16: 159-74.

Vasari, Y., Hannu Hyvarinen, and Sheila Hicks, eds.

1972 *Climatic Changes in Arctic Areas During the Last Ten-Thousand Years.* Proceedings of a symposium held at Oulanka and Kevo, 4-10 October, 1971. *Acta Universitatisu Ouluensis. Series A, Scientiae Rerum Naturalium, #3, Geologica #1.* Oulu, Finland: University of Oulu.

Vaughan, Richard

1984 Historical survey of the European whaling industry. In *Arctic Whaling.* Proceedings of the International Symposium Arctic Whaling, February 1983. University of Groningen.

Vibe, Christian

1967 Arctic animals in relation to climatic fluctuations. *Meddelelser om Grønland* 170, no. 5.

Wallace, Reverend James

1693 *Descriptions of the Isles of Orkney.* Edinburgh.

Wallace, Doctor James

1700 *An Account of the Islands of Orkney.* London.

Warkentin, John, and Richard Ruggles

1970 *Manitoba Historical Atlas: A Selection of Facsimile Maps, Plans, and Sketches from 1612 to 1959.* Winnipeg: Historical and Scientific Society of Manitoba.

Wein, Ross W., and David A. MacLean, eds.

1983 *The Role of Fire in Northern Circumpolar Ecosystems.* The Scientific Committee on Problems of the Environment of the International Council of Scientific Unions. New York: Wiley.

West, John

1824 *The Substance of a Journal During a Residence at the Red River Colony, British North America in the Years 1820-1823.* London: L.B. Seeley & Son.

Weyer, E.

1962 *The Eskimos: Their Environment and Folkways.* Hamden, CT: Archon Books.

Whitaker, Ian

1954 The Scottish kayaks and the 'Finn-men.' *Antiquity* XXVIII, no. 110 (June): 99–104.

1977 The Scottish kayaks reconsidered. *Antiquity* LI, no. 201(March): 41-45.

Whittaker, Charles E.

1937 *Arctic Eskimo.* London: Seeley, Service and Co.

Williams, Glyndwr

1963 Introduction. In *Northern Quebec and Labrador Journals and Correspondence, 1819-1835,* edited by K.G. Davies. London: Hudson's Bay Record Society.

1975 Introduction. In *Hudson Bay Miscellany,* edited by Glyndwr Williams. London: Hudson's Bay Record Society.

Williams, L.D.

1979 An energy balance model of potential glacierization of northern Canada. *Arctic and Alpine Research* 11: 443-56.

Williamson, Robert G.

1974 *Eskimo Underground: Socio-Cultural Change in the Canadian Central Arctic.* Occasional Papers II. University of Uppsala.

Winterhalder, Bruce, and Eric A. Smith, eds.

1981 *Hunter-Gatherer Foraging Strategies: Ethnographic and Archaeological Analyses.* Chicago: University of Chicago Press.

Woodman, David C.

1991 *Unravelling the Franklin Mystery: Inuit Testimony.* Kingston: McGill-Queen's University Press.

Wright, J.V.

1972 *The Aberdeen Site, Keewatin District, N.W.T.* National Museum of Man Mercury Series. Archaeological Survey of Canada Paper #2. Ottawa: National Museums of Canada.

1976 *The Grant Lake Site, Keewatin District.* National Museum of Man Mercury Series. Archaeological Survey of Canada Paper #47. Ottawa: National Museums of Man.

1977 *Thule Eskimo Prehistory Along Northwestern Hudson Bay.* National Museum of Man Mercury Series. Archaeological Survey of Canada Paper #70. Ottawa: National Museums of Canada.

Wright, John Kirtland

1966 *Human Nature in Geography: Fourteen Papers, 1925-1965.* Cambridge, Harvard University Press.

Yorga, Brian

1979 Migration and adaptation: a Thule culture perspective. In *Thule Eskimo Culture: An Anthropological Retrospective,* edited by Allen P. McCartney. National Museum of Man Mercury Series. Archaeological Survey of Canada Paper #88. Ottawa: National Museums of Canada.

1980 *Washout: A Western Thule Site on Herschel Island, Yukon Territory.* National Museum of Man Mercury Series. Archaeological Survey of Canada Paper #98. Ottawa: National Museums of Canada.

Index